Limits of Freedom of Public Authorities with Respect to Obtaining Evidence at the Stage of Investigation

Ius Comparatum

VOLUME 3

The titles published in this series are listed at *brill.com/iacl*

Limits of Freedom of Public Authorities with Respect to Obtaining Evidence at the Stage of Investigation

A Comparative Legal Study

Edited by

Maria Rogacka-Rzewnicka

BRILL | NIJHOFF

LEIDEN | BOSTON

Library of Congress Cataloging-in-Publication Data

Names: Rogacka-Rzewnicka, Maria, editor.
Title: Limits of freedom of public authorities with respect to obtaining evidence at the stage of investigation : a comparative legal study / Maria Rogacka-Rzewnicka.
Description: Leiden ; Boston : Brill, 2024. | Series: Ius comparatum, 22146881 ; vol 3 | Includes bibliographical references and index.
Identifiers: LCCN 2024031494 (print) | LCCN 2024031495 (ebook) | ISBN 9789004710313 (hardback) | ISBN 9789004710320 (ebook)
Subjects: LCSH: Evidence, Criminal. | Admissible evidence. | Criminal investigation. | Criminal procedure.
Classification: LCC K5465 .L56 2024 (print) | LCC K5465 (ebook) | DDC 345/.06–dc23/eng/20240716
LC record available at https://lccn.loc.gov/2024031494
LC ebook record available at https://lccn.loc.gov/2024031495

Typeface for the Latin, Greek, and Cyrillic scripts: "Brill". See and download: brill.com/brill-typeface.

ISSN 2214-6881
ISBN 978-90-04-71031-3 (hardback)
ISBN 978-90-04-71032-0 (e-book)
DOI 10.1163/9789004710320

Contents

Introduction

Maria Rogacka-Rzewnicka

This publication entitled "*Limits of freedom of public authorities with respect to obtaining evidence at the stage of investigation. A comparative legal study*" has been jointly authored by a number of representatives of different legal systems and cultures. It consists of a general report and national reports drawn up for the XXIth Congress of International Academy of Comparative Law in Asunción, Paraguay, held from 23 to 28 October 2022. I had the honour and pleasure to be the general reporter for the criminal procedure section. The general report constitutes a synthesis of the content of national reports prepared based on a questionnaire I devised earlier. The questionnaire contained a number of detailed questions falling into the general topical categories: (1) A presentation of the main and most distinctive features of evidence system in the light of the applicable model of criminal procedure and major procedural principles of examining and evaluating evidence; (2) Public authorities are entitled to acquire evidence in a criminal action at the stage of investigation; (3) Principles of acquiring evidence at the stage of investigation; (4) Identifications of risks of violating freedom in the acquisition of evidence by law enforcement authorities; (5) Inviolable boundaries in the acquisition of evidence by law enforcement authorities and (6) Conclusion. The national reports were contributed from the following countries: Germany, Turkey, Hungary, Estonia, Taiwan, Poland, Canada, Japan, and Italy. I wish to cordially thank all the authors for their intensive and valuable work, and very interesting and inspiring texts, with which I familiarized myself being much intrigued and thrilled. With just as great satisfaction I take note of the fact that our joint work took the shape of a Brill publication. I trust it will become a valuable source of knowledge about the *Limits of freedom of public authorities with respect to obtaining evidence at the stage of investigation*.

The aspects embraced under the report title are of major significance not only from the perspective of criminal procedure, but also in view of the contemporarily fundamental civilizational categories, such as: legalism, the rule of law, human rights, the fairness of trial, loyalty, or justice. Pre-trial investigation, being a stage at which crucial decisions are made about committed crimes, is especially threatened by the abuse of power due to the various criss-crossing antagonistic objectives and interests. One of the major threats is the arbitrariness of authorities' actions that may give rise to the infringement of individuals' rights and fair trial principles. At the investigation stage,

 | DOI:10.1163/9789004710320_002

legal restrictions imposed on public authorities apply first and foremost to decisions about: instituting and carrying on criminal procedure, acquiring evidence, and using procedural coercive measures. From among the indicated decision-making areas, considerable risk that the stated objectives will be pursued too extensively applies to the evidence acquisition stage. Anti-legalistic practices of law-enforcement authorities may be of different sources and origins. One of the factors is the general political and institutional environment in which those authorities function. Non-law-abiding reality may pose a serious threat to the adherence to the standards of the law of evidence. Conformist conduct and submissiveness to political authorities may take on the form of different actions or omissions which, being driven by self-interested complaisance, correspond to the ruling authorities' expectations and entail submission to the principles accepted by the authorities and their social supporters. Such attitudes bear concrete social and individual consequences. Significantly, investigative bodies operate in most of the countries within hierarchical and centralized structures that are undermined by the danger of the investigators being submissive to the superiors' endeavours, or being inclined to demonstrate to them high qualifications and operability. Another factor that may affect the investigators' conduct may be social pressure for efficient actions, which leads to the overemphasis on the arguments of efficiency and operability – especially in difficult or alarming criminal cases – at the expense of other values. And finally, an objective cause of danger are new technologies and the associated temptation to extensively use them in the drive to reach the objective, at times to the detriment of individual rights and guarantees.

In addition to the aforesaid systemic perspective that relies on constitutional and international-law solutions, the national reports discuss diversified and detailed issues from the realm of evidentiary aspects. In all, they make up very interesting cognitive and comparative material. Not only are the reports an important source of knowledge about solutions applicable in particular countries, but in sum they demonstrate interesting regularities in restrictions imposed on public law enforcement authorities during the acquisition of evidence at the stage of pre-trial investigation across numerous juridical systems and vast areas of our globe. The general report also highlights differences in the accepted legal models and concrete legal solutions. Ultimately, the collected material shows an uplifting picture of the reality how evidence is acquired at the investigation stage, especially at the level of legal regulations and developed standards. In general, we did not examine within our project empirical aspects of the applicable normative restrictions imposed on investigators in the acquisition of criminal evidence, however even without references being made to the practice, the received national reports fashion material that is rich in compelling and important content.

In conclusion, I wish to express hope on my own and all the authors' behalf that our joint research project, which materialized into this publication, will catch interest and will enjoy a friendly reception; while I personally hope to stay in scientific contact with all the reporters.

CHAPTER 1

Limits of Freedom of Public Authorities with Respect to Obtaining Evidence at the Stage of Investigation/Les limites au principe de la liberté des preuves dans la phase des enquêtes

General Report/Rapport Général

*Maria Rogacka-Rzewnicka**

1 Introduction[1]

The question of limits of freedom of law enforcement authorities to obtain evidence at the stage of investigation is just an aspect of a broader fundamental problem, being the limits of action of public authorities. One of the universal contexts of this limitation is the principle of legalism which requires the authorities to act lawfully, within the limits set in the applicable duly enacted regulations. Thus an authority should be deemed to be prohibited from taking a certain action unless legally authorised to do so. The requirement to act under the law is intrinsically linked to the requirement to act within the limits of the law. The inherent connection between these two prerequisites needs to

* Head of Criminal Procedure Department, Faculty of Law and Administration, University of Warsaw, Poland.

1 This general report is based on the country reports we received from nine countries: Germany (Dr Anne Schneider, University of Düsseldorf), Turkey (Dr Haluk Toroslu, Assistant Professor, i.D. Bilkent University Faculty of Law, Uğur Orhan L.L.M. Research Assistant, i.D. Bilkent University Faculty of Law, Bedirhan Erdem LL.M. student, German and European Law and Legal Practice, Humboldt University of Berlin Faculty of Law); Hungary (dr. HERKE Csongor, dr. SZABÓ Barbara, University of Pécs), Estonia (Anneli Soo, PhD, Associate Professor in Criminal Law the University of Tartu); Taiwan (Kai-Ping Su, Associate Professor, National Taiwan University, College of Law); Poland (Karolina Kremens, LL.M., Ph.D. University of Wrocław, Faculty of Law, Administration and Economics); Canada (Alexandre Stylios Professor, Faculty of Law, Université Laval, Gustave Warby LL.B candidate); Japan (Tatsuhiko Inatani, Kyoto University); Italy (Thomas Di Candia, PhD student at Department of Law, Economics and Cultures – University of Insubria). I am grateful to all the authors and thank them for taking their efforts to draw up their country reports. I would also like to thank all my colleagues from Criminal Procedure Department for their help. I especially thank Prof. Katarzyna Girdwoyń, Dr Anna Grochowska-Wasilewska and Dr Kacper Oleksy.

 | DOI:10.1163/9789004710320_003

be emphasised as it manifests itself in the law, which gives authorisation to the public authorities to take certain actions and, at the same time, binds them to act within the limits established. Going beyond these limits is tantamount to acting without a legal basis and as such is deemed illegitimate.

The source of the authority's legitimacy is its acting within the limits of duly and specifically defined powers. Power conferring norms are always subject to strict interpretation. No powers are to be presumed to exist unless they have been expressly and clearly stipulated in a relevant legal regulation, even if such presumption might seem expedient, e.g. to follow considerations of general public interest. With the principle of legalism of public authorities' actions in place, power conferring norms cannot be interpreted to the extent that the legislator is deemed to have an intention other than the one expressed in the legislation. At the same time, it is presupposed that a state authority cannot evade taking a decision if it is legally required to take the same. The above-mentioned abstract rules that form the canon of the rule of law must be transposed into the relevant institutional guarantees for citizens, which virtually shape the obligation of public authorities to act under and within the limits of the law. This concerns the institutions and means of enforcing subjective rights in the event of a breach of competence by public authorities. This is an issue of general legal importance, but there are areas, and criminal procedure is one of them, where the above principles of the rule of law are of absolutely fundamental significance. They are an element of legal security, which is one of the most common and concurrently most elementary individual and collective need associated with the operation of law. J. Carbonnier described it as almost an "animal" need.[2] One of the main threats to legal security of individuals and the society is that the authorities act arbitrarily, which results in the rights of individuals and fair trial principles being violated. Restrictions set for public authorities affect many aspects of criminal proceedings, one of the most important being the process of obtaining evidence, specifically, at the stage of investigation. It lies in the very nature of this stage of the criminal trial that the suspect is not provided with similar safeguards as in court proceedings. Law enforcement authorities are not independent in the sense assumed for a court of law. The investigation stage primarily serves to establish the grounds for bringing charges against a specific person. There is always the risk of this objective being pursued too extensively, which results in investigators going beyond the permissible limits of action, while the possibilities of controlling these actions are quite limited. In legal systems where this stage of

2 J. Carbonnier, *Flexible de droit*, Paris 1998, p. 194.

the process is traditionally of vital importance (Germany, Poland, Italy, Turkey, Estonia, Hungary, Taiwan),[3] there is a risk of errors possibly committed by the investigators being carried over to the trial stage and perpetuated by the court. The pre-trial investigation stage serves important purposes, but it might also become a "burdensome load". This does not apply to adversarial systems (such as the one in Canada), where the starting point from which the battle for a judgment begins is the judicial stage which, consequently, makes them free of this risk. It is characteristic of Japanese criminal procedure, which is subordinated to the principle of adversarial trial, that an indictment being sent to the court is not accompanied by any evidence in order to prevent any influence on the court (Article 256 of the Japanese Criminal Procedure Law). In Italy, on 24 October 1984 the mixed model of criminal procedure deriving from Napoleonic tradition was replaced by adversarial model. Evidentiary activities carried out at investigation stage serve first of all the purpose of determining the grounds for bringing an indictment to court, but in specific situations, e.g. while using the institution of *incidente probatorio*, they have the value of direct evidence in the court action.[4]

At the end of the 19th century, the eminent Polish criminalist E. Krzymuski wrote: "no criminal procedure can do without certain pre-trial investigations. For the prosecutor always needs to find out whether there are at least some grounds to demand from the court to launch criminal proceedings against an individual The pre-trial investigation is conducted in the suspect's interests, so as not to expose him to the shame of sitting on the dock."[5] Even if the above described motivation for conducting the pre-trial investigation sounds somewhat archaic today, it still expresses the truth that the investigating authorities need to be aware of their responsibility for decisions taken. Dishonour for an individual as a result of having been unjustifiably accused of a crime was an argument for investigators to act prudently and with restraint towards the suspect. The idea behind the self-restraint mechanism was to appeal to the investigators' ethics and their fairness to the individual. It was not derived from legal norms at that time. In the common law system, a similar selective purpose is served by the preliminary (pre-trial) examination of evidence presented by the

3 When analysing the specific case of Taiwan, it must be taken into account that, until the 1999 reform, Taiwan's criminal procedure had an inquisitorial structure, which immanently brings the investigation stage to prominence. With the "reformed adversarial system" having been introduced in 1999 in Taiwan, some inquisitorial elements have been diminished, though not completely eliminated.

4 Cf. Thomas Di Candia, *Italian Evidence Law System: Limits to the Investigative Power*, p. 155.

5 E. Krzymuski, *Wykład procesu karnego austryackiego* [*Lecture on Austrian criminal procedure*], Kraków 1910, p. 24.

prosecution and the defence. As the Canadian report points out, in Part XVIII of the Canadian Criminal Code, the role of discovery at the stage of the preliminary inquiry is to determine whether, in light of the *prima facie* reliability of the evidence, a jury duly instructed could return a verdict of guilty. In jurisdictions with an examining magistrate, it is he or she who decides whether to bring charges before the court. This control is intended, among other things, to prevent unfounded accusations.

A factor that can influence the behaviour of investigators is the pressure to act effectively and to succeed. Such expectations can lead to an abuse of power or overstepping its limits. With investigative bodies operating within hierarchical structures, there is a risk of investigators striving to meet their superiors' expectations or to demonstrate high qualifications and effectiveness to them. Public pressure and expectations, especially in difficult and shocking criminal cases, can also be a source of psychological pressure for investigators. As we believe, there are cases in every country when the public demands a quick and harsh response and the trial authorities succumb to this pressure, at the expense of the truth and fairness of the proceedings. One of the most recent infamous cases of the Polish justice system concerns Tomasz Komenda, sentenced to 25 years imprisonment for brutal rape and murder, who, having spent 18 years in prison, was eventually found to be innocent. First the investigators had been at fault, and then the court was, which based its verdict on false evidence gathered during the pre-trial investigation. All this combined resulted in many years of undeserved suffering for the man. It would be probably hard to count how many people suffer the same fate worldwide. Hence, the question of limits of freedom of law enforcement authorities in obtaining evidence in a criminal procedure is not yet another theoretical legal issue, but touches upon the very essence of state responsibility, the rule of law and humanism. For these reasons, it is unacceptable that officers of a democratic state could gather evidence in contravention of the applicable law, while citizens would, pursuant to the law, bear criminal liability on the basis of this very evidence. Every state is responsible for the unlawful activities of its officials, and this responsibility cannot be excluded by invoking the public interest in combating crime.

It also needs to be emphasised that the law is not only about the wording of a rule, but also the meaning that is given to it by interpretation. The essence of the law consists of rules for understanding its meaning and operation, as well as its place in the overall legal system. Only within such a broad context, the meaning of a legal norm can be properly read. Finally, the law is not only the wording of a provision, but also the correct practice of its application. J. Zajadło put it as follows "the law as a decision of the legislator is merely a quantity of paper on which a formalised conventional text is written, its true face is revealed only in the process of its application and interpretation. Judges often encounter so-called hard cases where morality, economics, politics, and religion meet in addition to the law."[6] The above truths are widely applicable in criminal proceedings. Their expression is, *inter alia*, the distinction between illegal evidence, i.e. evidence contrary to the legal norm, and evidence obtained unethically, i.e. as a result of a violation of moral norms, i.e. reprehensible behaviour, e.g. by deception. This distinction originates from the common law tradition, but it is a universal feature of legal systems based on the rule of law. The two categories, which are distinguished only in terms of how specifically the norms of the law of evidence have been violated, are complementary when assessing the correctness of the evidence examination. The most important criteria for this assessment are the principle of fair trial and the principle of loyalty of the trial authority towards the parties to the proceedings. With the investigation stage being largely kept secret from the public and the parties themselves and a number of procedural acts carried out at that time being not subject to verification, its fairness can be ensured mainly by the correct practice of law enforcement agencies. Codes of Criminal Procedure regulate more or less precisely how individual evidentiary activities are to be carried out, which always implies a certain margin of discretion on the investigators' part. Thus the pre-trial investigation is the phase of the criminal procedure in which the importance of general legal and systemic directives as well as legally unspecified rules of procedural fairness comes to the forefront. In this case, the ordinary fairness of the proceedings on the part of the authorities is often the main criterion for the legality of the activities carried out. In the assessment of the standards of proper conduct of the investigating authorities, emphasis should be placed on procedural behaviours which are not legally regulated but which evidently affect the fairness of the criminal procedure to the same extent as the codified rules. In highlighting this aspect, we have in mind the ethical context of the law, which depends on the individual attitudes and behaviour of specific people. It is often not enough to refer to the axiology expressed in positive law. This is because, in democratic legal systems, it is usually comprehensively reflected in the spirit of the fair trial standard. The dissemination of this standard should also consist in the observance of good procedural practices, including the culture of conduct. The sphere of behaviour that is not regulated by any codes contributes to the image of criminal proceedings and is subject to an assessment of fairness, in accordance with

6 J. Zajadło, Sumienie sędziego [*Judge's conscience*], Ruch Prawny Ekonomiczny i Socjologiczny [*Economic and Sociological Legal Movement*], Year LXXIX-issue 4–2017.

the legal and moral rules embodied in the principle of fair trial.[7] This category proves to be of vital importance at the stage of the evidentiary procedure. The objectives of criminal proceedings can only be achieved with the observance of the rules of the law of evidence, and this also involves behaviour that is not regulated by the law but might be of relevance when assessing the fairness of the proceedings of the trial authorities.

The issue of limits of freedom of public authorities has a long history and many references in various sciences, such as philosophy, history, sociology or law. The motive of protecting the public from abuses of power is constantly present in the history of civilisation. Different methods of limiting power have been tested in different eras and states. The liberal concept, which involves the rulers' power being equated with the people's power, as adapted in many states, did not eliminate the question of the limits of power, but merely changed the way this problem is viewed. These interesting general themes need to be analysed in the narrower context of the criminal procedure.

The most important contemporary point of focus in the analysis of the limits of action of public authorities in the context of criminal procedure are human rights. Human rights are not only the basic justification for the existence, organisation, and operation of the modern state but also constitute the limits of public power in all areas in which it is manifested. The civilisational motto that defines the relationship between the state and the citizen is as follows: while the citizen may do anything that the law does not prohibit, the state organs may only do what they have a basis for in the applicable law.[8] This truth, which can be deemed as *communis opinio,* is of special importance within the context of criminal proceedings where the realm of justice exercised by the state over citizens and the social objectives of this activity encounter the individual rights and guarantees vested in persons subject to criminal liability. In other words, the above encounter entails, on one hand, that the repression of offenders is indispensable and, on the other hand, that individual procedural guarantees need to be provided to the parties to the proceedings. This relationship is symbolically expressed by the popular 19th century phrase according to

---

7 M. Rogacka-Rzewnicka, *Znaczenie niepisanych reguł postępowania dla tworzenia podstaw rzetelnego procesu karnego* [*Significance of unwritten rules of procedure for the creation of the foundations of a fair criminal trial*] (in:) *Rzetelny Proces Karny. Księga Jubileuszowa Profesor Zofii Świdy* [*The Fair Criminal Procedure. Jubilee Book of Professor Zofia Świda*], scient. ed. J. Skorupka, Warsaw 2009, p. 92 et seq.

8 M. Wyrzykowski, *Państwo a obywatel. Granice władzy,* [*State and citizen. Limits of power*] Państwo. Academia. Panorama. Magazyn Polskiej Akademii Nauk [Magazine of the Polish Academy of Sciences], 2/66/2021, p. 10.

which substantive criminal law is the law of criminals, whereas the criminal procedure is the law of honest people.

Even if the aspect of procedural rights and guarantees is one of the better institutionalised contemporary trends in the criminal procedure, it is still not a separate target in itself and thus is constantly subject to the pressure of endeavours seeking to make the justice system more economical and ensure its efficiency and praxeological rationality. The contemporary objectives of criminal proceedings are multi-faceted and this has its costs and risks. They are brought into focus in two major areas: efficient operation of procedural bodies plus the lowest economic calculus, and respect for the rights and guarantees of individuals in criminal proceedings. When juxtaposed, these two areas illustrate how these objectives prove to be antagonistic in some respects and often impossible to be proportionally achieved in practical terms. Contemporary reality oscillates around opposing visions and concepts of law. The postulate of due process versus simplified justice is in fact an affirmation of an antinomy, even if the European Union, the European Court of Human Rights, and individual states strive to overcome this contradiction by arguing that the philosophy of the guaranteed procedural rights in criminal proceedings can be reconciled with the requirement of its pragmatism and economic efficiency. When thinking about contemporary extremes, one must bear in mind how subtle the boundaries are between the reasonable speediness of criminal proceedings and excessive haste, or between the act of trying and the prospective outcome of the case, or between the pursuit of justice and the formal administration of the procedure, etc. The classical principled approach to how the criminal procedure model, the roles of different actors in the proceedings, and specific solutions are defined has nowadays been replaced by flexible forms oriented towards pragmatism and effective and rapid results. Even if they do not result in the procedure being dematerialised or the principles of criminal procedure and the guarantees of individuals being negated, they are sometimes an example of a dangerously flexible approach of legislators and law enforcers to issues that unequivocally deserve fundamental treatment.[9] This situation is well illustrated by most of the country reports concluding that the law does not clearly define the consequences of violations committed at the stage of evidence examination in criminal proceedings and that the judicature and doctrine fail to present a uniform view on how to assess such violations and their consequences. Indeed, the question of the balance between the

9 M. Rogacka-Rzewnicka, *Proces karny w perspektywie ewolucji naukowej i współczesnych trendów rozwojowych* [*Criminal trial in the perspective of scientific evolution and contemporary trends of development*], Warsaw 2021, p. 344 et seq.

requirement for effective repression of committed crimes including the corresponding powers of the trial authorities on one hand and the safeguarding of the fundamental rights and freedoms of individuals against unauthorised interference by these authorities on the other is not easy to resolve. This problem is acute in countries that have not adopted the American concept of the fruit of a poisonous tree in their legal systems.

One of the perspectives from which the problem of limits of public authorities' actions can be viewed is the postmodern concept of law the assumptions of which are much reflected in the solutions applied in the contemporary criminal trial. Unlike the modernist principled vision of law, which is based on reason, justice, and progress, the postmodern concept assumes, among other things, that law is a product of political power which adopts the perspective not of values but rather of a legal text that serves to define the conditions of validity and enforceability of the law. According to J. Chevallier, this task is the administration of efforts on the part of the legislator within the realm of discretion and freedom to shape specific situations.[10] Such perspective bears the risk of some objectives prevailing over others and legal changes being justified with political reasons, by invoking higher social needs and rationales. An extreme example of such approach is the introduction of the provision of Article 168a in the Polish Code of Procedure, in the wording in force since 15 April 2016, which – as a rule – stipulates that evidence obtained in violation of the rules of procedure or by means of a prohibited act might be admitted in the course of a criminal trial following the rule that the ends justify the means.

The dilemmas, as described in the country reports submitted, which arise in the process of resolving contradictions that exist between the imperative for an effective response of the state to crimes committed, and the constraints that are universally derived from civilisational standards for obtaining evidence in criminal proceedings, taking into account human rights and the requirement to ensure a fair trial, essentially not only outline the strictly legal context of the issue under analysis, but also its dialectical and ontological significance. This complexity is probably the reason why there are no ideal (model) solutions. Most of the country reports refer to regulatory shortcomings, in particular the lack of clear legal solutions, the inconsistent approach of the bodies applying the law to the issue of how to treat evidence obtained in an unlawful manner and the divergent views on the subject held by legal academics. The dilemmas described in the country reports emerge in the absence of easy and satisfactory solutions. The main difficulty arises from the fact that there is no good

10 J. Chevallier, *Vers un droit post-moderne? Les transformations de la régulation juridique*, "Revue du droit public et de la science politique" 1998/3, p. 7.

alternative to the concept of the fruit of a poisonous tree, which would match it in terms of sticking to ethical principles. The doctrine of the fruit of a poisonous tree is, however, not ideal from the perspective of the practice of law and the realisation of justice. Consequently, the subject raises numerous legal dilemmas. These are clearly illustrated in the reports, which proves that we are still searching for the right solutions, despite the numerous positive examples from the legislation and practice of individual states.

2 A Presentation of the Main and Most Distinctive Features of Evidence System in the Light of the Applicable Model of Criminal Procedure and Major Procedural Principles of Examining and Evaluating Evidence[11]

Modern models of criminal procedure have their roots in the ancient procedure types, i.e. the complaint (accusatorial) and inquisitorial procedures. Even if they are most frequently characterised only by an appropriate share of properties characteristic of those models, in sum they prove to show the dominance of one of them. Although modern mixed procedural forms reflect the unequal presence of inquisitorial and complaint procedural assumptions, it is generally accepted that the essential delimitation is between the common law and the codified law systems. While common law system states follow a homogeneous complaint model, a mixed (adversarial-inquisitorial) system prevails in continental European and many non-European states. One of the decisive criteria for this categorisation is different rules of initiating and examining evidence. Even though the inquisitorial structure of criminal trials has been significantly reduced in recent years in many countries and the adversarial approach is becoming prevalent in the procedures, this did not bring about a fundamental change in the role of the court in the evidentiary proceedings in those countries. In many states, this authority still has a pivotal role in initiating evidence at the trial stage.

11 Sources used: M. Rogacka-Rzewnicka, *Nowa kultura poszukiwania prawdy w procesie karnym w świetle nowelizacji kodeksu postępowania karnego na podstawie ustawy z dnia 27 września 2013 roku. Perspektywa systemowa* [*A new culture of truth-seeking in criminal procedure in light of the amendments to the Code of Criminal Procedure of 27 September 2013. Systemic perspective*](in:) *Polski proces karny i materialne prawo karne w świetle nowelizacji z 2013 roku.* [*Polish criminal procedure and substantive criminal law in light of the 2013 amendments.*] *Księga jubileuszowa dedykowana Profesorowi Januszowi Tylmanowi w z okazji Jego 90. Urodzin*[*Jubilee book dedicated to Professor Janusz Tylman on the occasion of his 90th Birthday*], ed. Tomasz Grzegorczyk, Warsaw 2014, pp. 107–124.

The issue of limits of authorities' actions in obtaining evidence in the criminal trial has a rich historical[12] context and shows how far it has gone to reach contemporary standards. This is one of the most striking examples illustrating how the culture of particular historical eras shaped the procedures for adjudication of criminal cases, and at the same time one of the most important measures of the evolution of our civilisation. From today's perspective, all methods of obtaining evidence used up to the end of the 18th century would have to be generally considered inadmissible. During the Middle Ages, they were based on superstitions, sacred, symbolic, metaphysical and supernatural aspects, which corresponded to the culture of that era, but at the same time signified the irrationality of the justice thus conceived. Most of the procedural institutions of that period even arouse horror today, such as the trials by ordeal ("judgments of God"), based on the belief that God, as the creator of man, is best placed to decide his guilt or innocence, and therefore – by performing a miracle – will prevent harm to the innocent. They consisted of cruel, refined and completely irrational practices to force confessions. Although trials by ordeal were forbidden by Pope Innocent II at the Lateran Council in 1215, not all states immediately complied with the decision. In some Italian cities, trials by ordeal were continued to be used until the end of the 14th century, and in many countries even longer.

The next model of criminal procedure has to do with the development of the Holy Inquisition, a movement in the church against heretics. It first gave rise to the ecclesiastical and then to the secular judiciary. A fundamental institution of this model was the legal theory of evidence, granting strictly defined probative force to individual pieces of evidence. A suspect's confession was crown evidence in this hierarchy. Persistent denial of the charges by the suspect gave rise to either detention or torture. The latter were intended to help the suspect confess. For the courts, they were a convenient measure due to the then exaggerated importance of the suspect's confession. The main punishment for hardened heretics was death by burning alive at the stake. If such a suspect managed to convert, burning at the stake was preceded by strangulation, meaning that the execution was in fact for a person already dead. In either case, the exhumation of the condemned person from consecrated ground was mandatory.

In the secular judiciary, a fundamental act for the development of the inquisitorial process was the German *Constitutio Criminalis Carolina* (*Kaiser Karls des funfften und des heyligen römanischen Reichs peinlich gerichtsordnung*) of

12 T. Maciejewski, *Narzędzia tortur, sądów bożych i prób czarownic* [*Instruments of torture, judgments of God and witch trials*], Koszalin 1997.

1532.[13] The work of Emperor Charles v Habsburg resembled rules of criminal procedure. It was applied throughout Europe until the end of the 18th century. According to the legal theory of evidence applicable to the inquisition process, the "queen of evidence" was the suspect's confession. To this end, the law permitted the use of torture. This was regulated in as many as 40 articles of *Carolina* (Articles 21–61). The regulation is quite intimidating even with regard to the solutions limiting the use of torture by specifying the maximum duration of torture, the successive stages and the order in which various measures were to be applied in order to coerce specific type confessions. In judicial practice, legal exemptions or limitations on the use of torture were often not followed. The justice system of that time consisted of inflicting physical and mental suffering on suspects. The cruel ingenuity of the designers of the instruments of torture and their strange names is noteworthy: the Nuremberg virgin, the witches' chair, the bed of justice, the Judas cradle, the Alsatian shoes, or the Spanish spider. The inquisition process was secret. The judge concentrated in his hands all the procedural roles of the court, accuser, and defender. He was the only one to decide about the suspect's fate. A cruel variant of the inquisitorial process were witchcraft trials. Beginning with the issuing of a bull by Pope Innocent VIII in 1484, this type of heresy was prosecuted *ex officio* and was punishable by death. The evidentiary methods used in these cases referred to the medieval trials by ordeal. The most well-known evidentiary methods were the test of water, the test of fire, the test of weight, and the test of tears. This absurd type of prosecution led to the death of many innocent victims, who were almost exclusively women.

An epochal breakthrough came at the end of the 18th century. From the criticism of unjust, cruel and irrational inquisitorial proceedings, a so-called mixed trial was born, based on the Enlightenment ideology of humanitarianism. The entire system of legal evidentiary theory, first and foremost with the principle of *confessio est regina probationum*, was then challenged and the concept of assessing the credibility of witnesses based on their social status and with cruel evidence-obtaining methods were rejected. Instead, the suspect was recognised as the subject and the criminal trial was based on new principles which, as shaped in the late 18th and early 19th centuries, form the basis of

13 E. Schmidt, *Einführung in die Geschichte der deutschen Stafrechtspflege*, Göttingen 1995, p. 131 ff.; A. Eser, *A Century of Penal Legislation in Germany. Development and trends* (in:) A. Eser, J. Thormundsson, *Old Ways and New Needs in Criminal Legislation. Documentation of a German-Icelandic Colloquium on the Development of Penal Law in General and Economic Crime in Particular*, https://freidok.uni-freiburg.de/fedora/objects/freidok:3756/datastreams/FILE1/content, s. 1.

the modern criminal procedural order in most parts of the world. Those foundations of the modern criminal procedure based on top-quality civilisational theories need to be relatively confronted with the political and social conditions prevailing at the time. The modernist vision of the criminal procedure, in spite of many progressive legal and mental changes, did not quite correspond with the punishment system of the time, which was still cruel, with commonly ordered death penalty and mutilation. Human rights, symbolised by freedom, equality, property, and other similar values associated with the turn of the 18th and 19th centuries, are in fact a category from recent human history, which came into existence when those rights were given a universal character and became a tangible reality.

This brief retrospection, referring to well-known facts from the history of the criminal trial, is meant to show how important it is to consider the historical context when evaluating contemporary legal solutions in order to gain a broader, more accurate and proper view of the surrounding reality. At the same time, the historical perspective shows to what extent the criminal procedure has been transformed. Most initiatives aimed at guaranteeing certain judicial procedures were taken in the period after the Second World War. This tragic experience of humanity gave rise to the need to arrange many matters anew, in the spirit of the philosophy of human rights.

What was fundamental to the law of evidence were the post-war acts prohibiting torture and other cruel inhuman or degrading treatment or punishment (Article 5 of the Universal Declaration of Human Rights of 10 December 1948; Article 3 of the Convention for the Protection of Human Rights and Fundamental Freedoms; Article 7 of the International Covenant on Civil and Political Rights of 16 December 1966; Declaration on the Protection of All Persons from Torture and Other Cruel, Inhuman or Degrading Treatment or Punishment, adopted by the General Assembly on 9 December 1975; European Convention for the Prevention of Torture and Inhuman or Degrading Treatment or Punishment, drawn up in Strasbourg on 26 November 1987; Article 4 of the Charter of Fundamental Rights of the European Union). The prohibition of torture and other cruel inhuman or degrading treatment or punishment expressed in these instruments is not limited to a mere declaration, but is based on enforcement mechanisms that turn it into a tangible reality in individual legal systems and at the supranational level. The European Court of Human Rights declares inadmissible all personal evidence obtained in violation of the prohibitions set under Article 3 of the Convention. Once admitted into the trial, it automatically renders it unfair (see Chahal v. the United Kingdom, 15 November 1996, § 79; Ramirez Sanchez v France [GC], 4 July 2006, § 116; Gäfgen v. Germany, 30 June 2008, § 63). A similar standard applies to material evidence obtained in breach of the prohibition of torture. With regard to evidence obtained in violation of the prohibition of inhuman or degrading treatment, the Court has held that unless this is decisive for the course of the proceedings, it may be introduced into the proceedings, which for that reason do not lose the attribute of fairness. From the point of view of the wording of Article 3 of the Convention, this latter position may be questionable. This shows that the Court's views are not strict and categorical, which corresponds to a similarly variable approach followed by legislators in many states as to how to treat violations of the law of evidence, with the violations varying in their gravity and not always being a reason for a criminal trial to be declared unfair. Despite the casuistic approach of the European Court to the issue of evidence bans in criminal proceedings, there are some general rules that can be identified. The first rule assumes that a violation of an absolute evidence ban, which is not subject to revocation under any circumstances, results in the trial being automatically recognised as unfair. The second rule provides for a violation of other evidence bans to be assessed individually and in terms of relevance of such evidence and the impact of the violation on the fairness of the trial in general. In addition to the perspective of Article 3 of the Convention, three other areas of violations of the law of evidence can be distinguished in light of the ECHR case law, which are: the use of evidence obtained by exceeding the limits of permissible police provocation, the use of the suspect's evidentiary statements made in the absence of a defence attorney, and the use of evidence derived from unauthorised evidentiary activities (e.g. illegal wiretapping or violations of Article 3 or Article 8 of the Convention).

The main guarantee mechanism of the evidentiary procedure is related to the validity of the "fair trial" principle, which plays a significant role not only in the states that are parties to the European Convention for the Protection of Human Rights and Fundamental Freedoms, but throughout the civilised world. This category is a universal general clause, an expression of the validity of natural law in the sphere of human rights and "a formula close to the classical expression of law."[14] It is applicable across jurisprudential cultures, in many geographical spaces, in international and domestic law, in the fields of public and private law and within specific branches of law. By migrating into different systems and normative areas, the "fair trial" serves as some kind of a procedural meta-clause ensuring that internal systems correlate with each other within the limits of its application and that major legal solutions underlain

14 Ch. Girard, *Procès équitable et enchevêtrement des espaces normative* (*Réflexions sur la problématique générale*) [in:] *Travaux de l'atelier de droit international de l'UMR de droit comparé de Paris*, ed. H. Ruiz Fabri, Société de Législation Comparée 2003, pp. 21–52.

by its content share common standards. None of the current general clauses in judicial law has reached a similar scope of applicability or a similar level of internationalisation.[15] It includes within its scope, *inter alia*, the right to a fair hearing.[16]

Even if the Convention does not specify the rules of admissibility of evidence and leaves it to the legislation of individual states, the ECHR case law clearly shows that the use of evidence obtained illegally is assessed from the perspective of Article 6 of the Convention. This provision also serves as a legal basis for unlawfully obtained evidence to be declared inadmissible. It follows from Article 6 of the Convention that each case must be decided on the basis of such evidence as, within the framework of a particular procedural system, is provided for by law or is not incompatible with it, and as such is deemed lawful. It is in the sphere of evidence that the guarantees of the individual's rights in the criminal procedure are anchored, and it is only by respecting these guarantees that the decision of a criminal court can be considered correct. In the context of Article 6 of the Convention, the European Court analysed the use of particular evidence, both at the pre-trial stage of operational activities and in the course of pending criminal proceedings, indicating the boundary conditions required to recognise a particular evidentiary activity as lawful and, as such, capable of serving as the basis for a judgment.

Another Convention-based perspective on violations of the law of evidence is Article 8 of the European Convention on Human Rights, which provides for the individual's right to respect privacy. According to the ECHR, a violation of this provision does not always amount to the trial being unfair. When assessing the impact of evidence obtained in breach of the right to privacy on the fairness of the trial, the Court finds it necessary to examine whether, during the proceedings, the party had an opportunity to challenge the lawfulness of the evidence acquisition process and whether there was other credible evidence pointing to the defendant's guilt. As regards Article 8 of the Convention, the European Court has analysed both cases in which the pertinent evidence (e.g. from a wiretap) was obtained in breach of the conditions laid down by national law, such as the absence of an adequate request, the failure to obtain the consent of the competent authority or the use of evidence not envisaged for a specific type of offence, and those in which, although the evidence

15 M. Rogacka-Rzewnicka, *Proces karny w perspektywie ewolucji naukowej … [Criminal procedure in the perspective of scientific evolution …]*, p. 379.

16 (ed. A. Lach), *Rzetelne postępowanie dowodowe w sprawach karnych w świetle orzecznictwa strasburskiego [Fairness of evidence in criminal matters in light of Strasbourg case law]*, Warsaw 2018.

was obtained lawfully, the law was not characterised by an adequate level of guarantees. Such situation is the absence of judicial control or the failure to indicate in the law a catalogue of cases allowing the use of the evidence in question, being an interference in an individual's right to privacy (e.g. Dumitru Popescu v. Romania, 26 April 2007, §§ 39–46).

The gathering of evidence is subject to the principle of the presumption of innocence, which means that the accused is exempt from the obligation to provide evidence. The onus is on the law enforcement authorities to prove the guilt of the accused, and any doubts are to be resolved in his or her favour. The principle of the presumption of innocence also prohibits the trial authorities from being guided by a prejudice that the accused has committed an offence. The presumption of innocence is one of the most important universal procedural guarantees, defining the status of the suspect and the legal framework for the evidentiary procedure.

As it has been said "the criminal trial is a struggle for evidence. To obtain, preserve, and present it before the one who will decide the fate of the accused."[17] The struggle for evidence is a struggle for the truth, which is of utmost importance in a criminal trial of any type, despite various mechanisms used to establish the truth in different legal systems. As A. Garapon and J. Papadopulos stated, there are different cultures of truth-seeking.[18] When analysing this phenomenon in the context of criminal trial, these authors consider the persons performing this task and the forms in which it takes place to be the most important criterion of systemic differentiation. While in common law systems the obligation to establish the truth rests with the parties to the proceedings, in continental Europe and in many non-European countries these are procedural authorities, especially the court. In German and Polish criminal procedures, truth is a procedural principle, according to which it is incumbent on the authorities in charge of the criminal procedure to ensure that all judgments rendered, especially those that concern the question of the perpetrator's criminal liability, are based on findings of fact which are consistent with the actual state of affairs, i.e. on true findings supported by reliable evidence. The inquisitorial approach is sometimes even equated with the principle of truth,[19] by assuming that in order to attain the truth, the judicial bodies must apply the inquisitorial approach. Guided by this principle, the court investigates the facts on its own without being bound by the conclusions or statements of the

---

17 S. Waltoś, *Owoce zatrutego drzewa* [*The fruit of a poisonous tree*], Warsaw 2010, p. 321.

18 A. Garapon, J. Papadopulos, *Juger en Amerique et en France*, Odile Jacob, Paris 2003, p. 123.

19 H. Kühne, *Strafprozessrecht: eine systematische Darstellung des deutschen und europäischen Strafverfahrensrechts*, C.F. Müller, Heidelberg 2010, p. 195.

participants in the proceedings. The said principle is expressed in § 155(2) of the German StPO. According to this provision, the courts are at the same time entitled and obliged to act independently within the limits set by the prosecutor's accusation; specifically, they are not bound by any motions of other parties when applying the norms under the criminal statutes. This regulation is supplemented by § 244(2) StPO, stating that, in order to discover the truth, the court must, *ex officio*, extend the evidentiary activities to all circumstances and means of evidence which are of relevance to determine the case ("Das Gericht hat zur Erforschung der Wahrheit die Beweisaufnahme von Amts wegen auf alle Tatsachen und Beweismittel zu erstrecken, die für die Entscheidung von Bedeutung sind"). In the Polish criminal procedure, the principle of truth is expressed in Article 2(2) of the Code of Criminal Procedure (CCP), according to which: "All decisions should be based on true findings of facts." Pursuant to Article 81(1) of the French Code of Criminal Procedure (*Code de procédure pénale*), the investigating judge participates, as specified in the statute, in all investigative acts that they consider appropriate for the discovery of the truth ("le juge d'instruction procède, conformément à la loi à tous les actes d'information qu'il juge utiles à la manifestation de la vérité"). The mixed model of criminal procedure implies the ultimate responsibility of the court for the outcome of the trial, hence the right of the court to actively participate in the evidentiary activities at the trial stage. This is mirrored in Taiwan's Code of Procedure, even though, since the 1999 reform, the country's criminal procedural system shows many characteristics of the adversarial model. The importance of the principle of truth in the Turkish criminal procedure is reflected in the provisions of Article 163 of the Code of Criminal Procedure, which stipulates that "If the public prosecutor cannot be reached in case of flagrante delicto and in case of peril in delay, or if the scope of the case exceeds the work force of the public prosecutor, the judge (magister) can also carry out all procedures at the phase of investigation." In the other countries (Turkey, Estonia, Hungary, Canada and Japan), the pursuit of the truth about a crime is embedded in the objectives and essence of criminal proceedings, even if this principle is not as explicitly expressed as in the said countries. In Italy, the pursuit of the truth is underlain by the principle of adversarial examination of evidence in criminal procedure, which principle has constitutional significance (Article 111 of the Constitution).

From the historical and comparative perspectives, four theories of evidence should be distinguished: a positive one characterised by the law exhaustively defining evidence and its probative value, a negative one assuming the need for evidence in a quantity and quality prescribed by the law being necessary to convict the accused, a third one based on the formula of "intimate conviction", and a fourth one known as "justified conviction". Today, the last two theories of evidence are the most widely represented. The theory of "intimate conviction" as to the content of the adjudication exposes the judge's personal involvement in the decision, in the form of their certainty and their personal conviction. The concept that the decision is based on a reasonable conviction established beyond reasonable doubt refers to external circumstances determined without the involvement of the judge's personal beliefs. An interesting description of the presented evidentiary models is provided in the Hungarian report, together with the information that the evidentiary system of Hungarian criminal procedural law is shaped according to the fourth model.[20] This model is generally characteristic of the common law states. The judge, being bound by the verdict of the jury, is obliged to passively endure their role at the stage of deciding the key issue of the guilt or innocence of the accused. In other cases, some form of active participation by the judge in the proceedings is allowed at the trial stage, such as the judge refusing to take evidence or declaring it inadmissible. The judge may also ask questions of witnesses and interrupt their statements if they go too far from the facts to be established in their testimony or are otherwise unhelpful.

Differences between the systems indicated are also apparent at the evidence administration stage. In the countries with the so-called mixed model, truth is the result of an investigation, whereas in common law states it is the "fruit of a struggle". As A. Garapon argues, in the inquisitorial system the truth is the result of structured sources, such as interrogation records, analyses, expert reports, which are obtained with the participation of authorities, progressively and according to the judge's concept and conviction. The procedure in this model is linear, has a systematic composition and is characterised by an appropriate timing. Everything is regularly recorded in the file and eventually the judge determines the truth. It is the judge who is the final and most important link in the process, whereas in the Anglo-American adversarial system, "the truth is deduced from the spectacle of a carefully prepared battle".[21] The role of the judge is not to interfere directly in the fact-finding process which is designed to determine the winner, who is eventually declared in the final judgment. In the "battle" model, the evidence is not accumulated and stored as a set but rather provided by the parties in a dynamic discourse. In this case, credibility is achieved not only by the truth but also by the form, including the rhetoric.

20 Csongor Herke, Barbara Szabó, *Limits of freedom of public authorities with respect to obtaining evidence at the stage of investigation.* HUNGARY, p. 130.

21 A. Garapon, *Preuve et vérité dans les procès français et américain* (in:) http://academielegislation.fr/IMG/pdf/garaponpreuverite.pdf, p. 2.

The systemic differences indicated are not equally categorical at the stage of initial acquisition of evidence within the competence of the investigating authorities. Some characteristic similarities can be observed in the states that provided their country reports. These result from the prosecution and trial functions being separated, which is one of the most important systemic features of criminal proceedings in those countries, even if it originates from different legal cultures. What also seems to be largely in common is the principle that it is up to the court to use some of the more serious means of evidence at the pre-trial investigation stage, such as searches or telephone tapping. In Canada, under the common-law ancillary power doctrine, the police may use measures that infringe a citizen's individual liberty, provided that the infringement is ancillary to the fulfilment of recognised police duties and is considered reasonably necessary for the police to fulfil their duties ("The basis of the doctrine is that police actions that interfere with individual liberty are permitted at common law if they are ancillary to the fulfilment of recognized police duties. Intrusions on liberty are accepted if they are reasonably necessary – in accordance with the test set out below – in order for the police to fulfil their duties" (Fleming v Ontario, 2019 SCC 45).[22]

By contrast, the court is not involved in the examination of evidence at the pre-trial investigation stage. All the country reports emphasise that at this stage it is the duty of investigating authorities, mainly the police, to investigate evidence. In the German report, it is accentuated that the court first fully assesses the evidence in the intermediate phase (after the case has been referred to the court) as the court has to decide whether there are sufficient grounds to suspect that the indicted suspect has committed an offence (Article 203 StPO).[23] A similar solution is in force in the Polish Code of Criminal Procedure (Article 339(3)(1) and (2) thereof). In Turkey, according to Article 170(2) of the Code of Criminal Procedure, the task of collecting and presenting evidence before the criminal court to substantiate a criminal charge lies with the public prosecutor and serves a different purpose than the evidentiary activities carried out by the court at the trial stage.[24] The Estonian Report states that the responsibility for the course of evidentiary proceedings at the investigation stage rests with the

22 Alexandre Stylios, Gustave Warby, *Limits of freedom of public authorities with respect to obtaining evidence at the stage of investigation. Canadian report*, p. 212.

23 Anne Schneider, *Limits of freedom of public authorities with respect to obtaining evidence at the stage of investigation*, p. 72.

24 Haluk Toroslu, Uğur Orhan, Bedirhan Erdem, *On Limits of Freedom of Public Authorities with Respect to Obtaining Evidence at the Stage of Investigation under Turkish Criminal Procedure and Evidence*, p. 106.

prosecution.[25] In the case of Hungary, during the preparatory procedure and the first (cleaning up) part of pre-trial investigation, this power is exercised by the competent investigative authorities, while at the second stage of pre-trial proceedings, pending against a specific person, the responsibility lies with the prosecutor (Article 31(2) of the Code of Criminal Procedure).[26] The Italian report stresses that there are several subjects that may have to deal with the collection of evidence during the investigative stage: public authorities (public prosecutor and police), lawyer (both of the defendant and the victim) and the judge for pre-trial investigations (or judge of freedom, in Italian «*giudice per le indagini preliminari*»).[27] In Japan, the prosecutor monopolizes investigative powers (Article 247 of the JCPL). He has broad competences by tradition. At this stage of the proceedings, the court may not – in principle – use evidentiary procedure due to the applicability of the adversarial conduct principle. However, in accordance with Article 226 of the JCPL, at the prosecutor's request the court hears witnesses who have the knowledge needed to prove a crime, if they refuse to testify before the prosecutor or the police.[28] According to Article 161(1) of Taiwan's Code of Criminal Procedure "(t)he public prosecutor shall bear the burden of proof as to the facts of the crime charged against an accused, and shall indicate the method of proof".[29] Considering the broader comparative context, it should be noted that in the few countries where the institution of the examining magistrate has been preserved, this entity has the power to take evidence. In Canada, the majority of investigations are undertaken by traditional law enforcement agencies at the provincial and local level, but some administrative bodies also have investigative powers (e.g. Competition Act, RSC, 1985, *c.* C-34).[30]

One of the vital aspects related to the limits of public authorities in the acquisition of evidence in a criminal trial is the aspect of legality of evidence and the procedural consequences of violations of law in the evidence acquisition and examination process. This issue has an important axiological context. It involves the need to resolve a difficult legal and ethical dilemma, by defining

25 Anneli Soo, *Limits of freedom of public authorities with respect to obtaining evidence at the stage of investigation in Estonia*, p. 249.

26 Csongor Herke, Barbara Szabó, *Limits of freedom of public authorities with respect to obtaining evidence at the stage of investigation. HUNGARY*, p. 132.

27 Thomas Di Candia, *Italian Evidence Law System: Limits to the Investigative Power*, p. 148.

28 Tatsuhiko Inatani, *National Report of Japan*, pp. 264–265.

29 Kai-Ping Su, *Limits of freedom of public authorities with respect to obtaining evidence at the stage of investigation*, p. 229.

30 Alexandre Stylios, Gustave Warby, *Limits of freedom of public authorities with respect to obtaining evidence at the stage of investigation. Canadian report*, p. 212.

the permissible limits of using the means of evidence and methods of proof in the criminal process in order to enforce criminal liability. This dilemma essentially boils down to the confrontational nature of the two objectives, which are: on the one hand the need to respond to the crime committed under the applicable criminal procedure, which is an imperative of the rule of law, and on the other hand the need to consider and ensure the procedural guarantees on which modern criminal proceedings are based. They are the reason why criminal procedure is nowadays the law with many different boundaries. The main dividing line in the approach to the issue of the legality of evidence runs between countries belonging to the common law system and countries representing the civil law model, though it is not categorical. Of the countries from which we received country reports, Canada is the most representative example of the adversarial criminal trial (but for the Québec province where the civil law system prevails) with the adversarial-inquisitorial model prevailing in the other states. In the other states, criminal procedure functions in the adversarial-inquisitorial formula with a diverse distribution of features characteristic of both criminal action models. Solutions appropriate for the adversarial system clearly dominate in Japanese criminal procedure. In Italy, the adversarial principle has constitutional force.

2.1 *Illegal Evidence in Criminal Proceedings from a Comparative Perspective*

The pursuit of the truth about a crime clashes with the constraints of modern civilisation standards (e.g. the prohibition of torture), the characteristics of individual criminal procedural models, and the solutions adopted in national legal systems. In the last case, these are not only regulations contained in criminal procedure codes, but also those anchored in the national constitutions, which are the source of fundamental rights of parties. One of these is human dignity from which stems the prohibition of any external interference in the personal spheres of a person's life. Evidence obtained as a result of such interference cannot enjoy the attribute of legality. The reliance on constitutional rights and freedoms is caused by the absence of any sufficient or exhaustive statutory regulations of evidence bans, yet it is about priorities and values subject to the highest degree of legal protection. These are the dignity of the human being, integrity of their body and property, important interests of the state, protection of important secrets, family relations, and other rights of parties. The accumulation of these values also naturally leads to the evidentiary proceedings becoming more and more international. The multiplicity and diversity of contemporary normative and extra-normative sources which have an impact on how the boundaries of legality of actions of participants in criminal proceedings, including investigative bodies, are defined, certainly does not facilitate a synthetic study of this issue. Our conclusions focus on the different approach to the issue of illegal evidence in the common law and civil law systems, with the proviso that nowadays the dividing line running between the two systems is not that rigid. More and more legal solutions are gaining the supranational quality, which also applies to the issue of evidence obtained in breach of the law being used in a criminal trial.

Let us begin, however, by noting that only general or isolated standards of evidence have been developed at the international level. In the first case, these are deemed to be mainly embodied by the right to a fair trial. They are expressed in Article 14(3)(e) and (g) of the 1966 International Covenant on Civil and Political Rights which provides that in the determination of any criminal charge against him, everyone shall be entitled to examine, or have examined, the witnesses against him and to obtain the attendance and examination of witnesses on his behalf under the same conditions as witnesses against him and shall not be compelled to testify against himself or to confess guilt. A similar wording is contained in Article 6(3)(d) of the European Convention on Human Rights (Everyone charged with a criminal offence has at least the right: (...) to examine or have examined witnesses against him and to obtain the attendance and examination of witnesses on his behalf under the same conditions as witnesses against him). As noted earlier, the "fair trial" category is not ethnically assigned to European legal culture. It is referred to in all country reports in the context of obtaining evidence. The US Supreme Court has held that the fruit of a poisonous tree doctrine is an essential element of due process of law.[31]

The second group of international law instruments dealing with illegally obtained evidence are treaties prohibiting torture and other cruel, inhuman or degrading treatment. Article 15 of the Convention against Torture and Other Cruel, Inhuman or Degrading Treatment or Punishment adopted on 10 December 1984 states that "(e)ach State Party shall ensure that any statement which is established to have been made as a result of torture shall not be invoked as evidence in any proceedings, except against a person accused of torture as evidence that the statement was made." This prohibition is more broadly-worded in Article 12 of the Declaration on the Protection of All Persons from Being Subjected to Torture and Other Cruel, Inhuman or Degrading Treatment or Punishment of 9 December 1975 which stipulates that all forms of action indicated in its title (not only torture) exclude the use of evidence obtained as a result of

31 In the US Supreme Court's ruling in *Mapp. v. Ohio*, it was accepted that the ban on the use of indirectly illegal evidence applies not only in federal courts but also in state courts.

such action ("Any statement which is established to have been made as a result of torture or other cruel, inhuman or degrading treatment or punishment may not be invoked as evidence against the person concerned or against any other person in any proceedings"). The prohibition of torture is an *ius cogens* norm that has legal effects *erga omnes*, meaning that it is absolutely imperative and cannot be abrogated by any other non-*ius cogens* norm of international law (whether contractual or customary).

The prohibition of torture and other cruel, inhuman or degrading treatment and the principle of fair trial currently have the most universal impact on shaping the limits of the legitimacy of evidence in criminal proceedings of any type. Other limitations on the acquisition of evidence derive from the characteristics of the two most important legal systems: common law and civil law, although, as highlighted above, they are not today the source of rigid divisions in how illegal evidence is treated. In general, neither of them focused on the concept of illegal evidence *per se*, but rather on whether it is admissible to use illegally obtained evidence in a criminal trial. In analysing this issue, the distinction between directly and indirectly obtained illegal evidence is crucial. Major legal and ethical dilemmas concern the latter case. Indirectly illegal evidence is considered to be evidence that is acquired as a result of another piece of evidence that has itself the quality of being illegal (e.g. a law enforcement agency got to know the place where the murder weapon had been hidden from information acquired from the accused in the course of an illegally conducted interrogation, e.g. through torture). Against this background, there is a difference between the principled approach of the states representing the common law system and the more liberal attitude of the states with the civil law model. This statement is based on a certain generalisation, with the caveat that not all states with the common law tradition take the ban on the use of indirectly illegal evidence in a criminal trial to extremes (e.g. England, Wales). The Canadian report shows that the exclusionary rule is not automatically applied in Canada.[32] The case law of the Supreme Court of Canada emphasises the need to strike a balance between the overly categorical evidence acquisition boundaries and those that were insufficiently defined by law, and the rationale to approach the issue in a pragmatic and context-sensitive manner. In contrast, not all states representing the inquisitorial-contradictory model have rejected the "fruit of the poisonous tree" doctrine (e.g. Austria). In these states, the ethical aspect of the concept denying the admissibility of indirectly illegal

32 Alexandre Stylios, Gustave Warby, *Limits of freedom of public authorities with respect to obtaining evidence at the stage of investigation. Canadian report*, pp. 216–217.

evidence, even at the expense of the principle of the truth, is increasingly appreciated.

As a general rule, the inadmissibility of using both directly illegal evidence and that obtained through prohibited evidence is recognised in the common law states, even if this approach is not extreme in any of them. In countries with the civil law system in place, the prohibition covers directly illegal evidence (which is prohibited by law), while it does not generally apply to indirectly illegal evidence, i.e. from an originally illegal source. The issue of indirectly illegal evidence is at the heart of the US doctrine of the fruit of a poisonous tree, which is based on the Fourth Amendment to the US Constitution. Under this doctrine "indirectly illegal evidence" is one obtained as a result of an illegal act, when proving facts was inadmissible at all due to the evidence originating from an illegal source or having been illegally obtained or taken. The said doctrine restricts state officials in their power and prescribes that they refrain from actions that go beyond the scope of their competence. Its parallel purpose is to protect citizens, their homes and property from unjustified and unlawful interference by the authorities, and to protect individuals from arbitrary violations of civil liberties by representatives of public authorities. The ethical context of the fruit of a poisonous tree doctrine is expressed in lawbreaking practices by officials being disapproved, and judgments based on the results of such unlawful behaviour not being recognised. This doctrine contains an unambiguous axiological message, which proves to be its strength and its weakness at the same time. When thinking of its positives, we are primarily concerned with the fact that it protects the individual from arbitrary law enforcement actions. However, the result of anti-practical intransigence of the concept of the fruit of a poisonous tree may be the impunity of the actual crime perpetrators and the associated negative social consequences, as well as the position of the victim of crime being marginalised. This realised weakness of the analysed doctrine became the basis for the search for compromise solutions in the USA. The rigour of the exclusionary rule is mitigated there by, among other things: the "inevitability discovery" rule, the "extraneous ground" concept, the "good faith exception" or the "independent source" rule.

The consequent dilemmas arising in the states with the civil law system in place have a similar background, but are resolved by way of different reasoning. What is prevalent in this case is generally the motive of truth and justice, the fear of the crime perpetrator escaping criminal liability and the state's duty to combat crime and provide an accurate criminal response. The above values and objectives are the source of a more tolerant attitude of legislators and law enforcement authorities towards the evidence obtained from proof that was taken unlawfully. Such approach exposes suspects to the risks of law enforcement knowingly breaking the law in order to obtain incriminating evidence or of law enforcement acting in the forms meant to cover up a breach of the law, which in both cases will undermine the principle of fair trial. With the "fruit of a poisonous tree" doctrine not being generally applied in the civil law states, evidence obtained from an originally prohibited source is fully used in a criminal trial and can form the basis of a conviction under the principle of free evaluation of evidence. In those countries, the concept of autonomous legality of evidentiary activities applies, which implies that the legality of a particular piece of evidence is independent of the legality of other evidentiary activities. It is generally recognised that violations of the law committed in the evidence gathering process are gradable and that not every violation of the law makes such evidence inadmissible at trial. Such approach is characterised by a rational pragmatism which may, however, lead to a conflict between the principle of truth and the pertinent criminal response on one side, and individual guarantees that have been compromised as a result of illegally obtained evidence being admitted in a criminal trial on the other. The supremacy of state policy over civil liberties in criminal justice enforcement process is not widely accepted today, which is why in many countries – despite the concept of the "fruit of a poisonous tree" having been generally rejected – the values that make up its content are promoted in order to achieve a balance between the public and the individual goals of criminal proceedings. This argument clearly permeates the reports sent, even if they do sometimes highlight certain obstacles in achieving this goal. Let us move on to the third level of the issue of using illegal evidence in the criminal trial, which will involve references to solutions used in particular countries.

All the country reports received cast intense light on the issue of evidence directly prohibited by law, by specifying the types of such evidence as well as legal grounds, mechanisms of its elimination, and consequences of violations of evidence bans. In the case of indirectly illegal evidence, it is apparent that a general rule on how to treat such evidence in criminal proceedings can hardly be formulated in those countries' legal regulations. In the absence of specific legal solutions in this respect, as underlined in almost all reports, guidance is provided by the case law and legal scholars and commentators, also with the applicable international standards in mind. Each report emphasises the strong influence of courts, especially the hierarchically superior court, in shaping the rules of evidence. While in the common law countries such a solution is essentially included in the system, the far-reaching influence of judicial decisions in the civil law countries may be perceived as a substitution of the legislator, which is a fairly common pattern today. Thus, it can be concluded that in both legal orders, legal standards of evidentiary matters are nowadays formulated from the perspective of individual cases (*ad casum*). This example demonstrates how the traditional rule on which the civil law system is based, according to which state law is the source for deciding individual cases and shaping procedural practice (from general to specific) as opposed to the common law system where this direction is reversed (from specific to general), has devalued. In addition, it should be pointed out that in the latter case the state law consistently gains on importance.

The country reports emphasise that the deficit of legal regulations on evidentiary matters is compensated by case law. Given that it is not a source of universally binding law in the civil law system and is not generally applicable, there is a certain risk of litigants not following the interpretation provided by the highest judicial authority or making interpretations that do not correspond in content to the top-down case law indications. With no mechanisms for judicial control of investigators' actions in the evidence-taking process, as highlighted in the country reports, this risk is greater at the investigation stage. The court's involvement is limited only to the application of evidentiary measures that most interfere with the suspects' personal rights. However, bearing in mind the existing objective limitations which prevent all violations of the law of evidence and their legal consequences from being comprehensively and exhaustively regulated, an individual approach to this issue seems to be the right solution and a reasonable alternative. Once added, the individual perspectives ultimately offer a comprehensive view of the general rules of evidence applicable in criminal proceedings in particular states. We are aware that this approach complicates the issue of defining the limits of actions of investigative bodies acquiring evidence. The term "limits of actions" conventionally implies the acme of action and the maximum limitation of the powers of investigative bodies. A top-down and rigid definition of these limits in legislation is difficult, as shown in each report. At the same time, nowadays there are many scattered sources (normative and extra-normative) that define the limits of actions of criminal investigation bodies in the process of obtaining evidence. The main problem lies in their proper application and the provision of means to control the correctness of evidentiary activities. The country reports underline that there are no such mechanisms at the pre-trial investigation stage and that it is hardly possible to immediately eliminate evidence unlawfully obtained by investigators. These prerequisites do not facilitate a constructive discussion on the limits of law enforcement's freedom to obtain evidence. Given that in many countries the pre-trial investigation phase is traditionally important and has more and more autonomous procedural functions in relation to judicial proceedings, it would be advisable that further discussion include the question of how to properly ensure the accuracy of evidence acquisition by investigators.

Referring to the German report, it should be pointed out that it was in Germany that the earliest theoretical concepts concerning evidence bans in criminal proceedings were developed. In 1903, E. Beling's work entitled *Die Beweisverbote als Grenzen der Wahrheitserforschung im Strafprozess* [*Evidence bans as limits to the search for truth in a criminal trial*] was published in Wrocław. Legal scholars and commentators in Germany commonly distinguish between evidence bans (proof of specific circumstances, use of means of proof, bans on specific methods of proof) and bans on the use of specific evidence. The German report emphasises the absence of general legal principles regarding the legality of evidence and its use in the criminal trial. Restrictions on the use of certain evidence do not always have a statutory basis. In such a case, courts decide on a case-by-case basis whether evidence obtained in breach of law can be admitted. Non-statutory bans, resulting from the interpretation of constitutional norms, play a major role in this assessment. In this respect, the German Federal Constitutional Court, which has defined the limits of the freedom of public authorities in obtaining and admitting evidence in its case law, plays an important role. According to the general principles developed: evidence is to be excluded only if the violation of the procedure affected the legal position of the defendant substantially (*Rechtskreistheorie*); the exclusion must serve the purpose of the procedural guarantee (*Schutzzwecktheorie*). It should be borne in mind that the principles cited do not have any normative value, which diminishes their binding force; specifically, they are subject to interpretation in the law application process. The German report also emphasises that when giving judgments courts are mindful of balancing the public interest in prosecuting crimes with the defendant's interest in protecting their personal rights (*Abwägungslehre*). In the German criminal trial, the admissibility of evidence obtained in breach of the law of evidence is often determined by the seriousness of the offence under investigation.[33]

In Turkey, Article 38(6) of the Constitution provides that "findings obtained illegally cannot be accepted as evidence." Despite the categorical wording of this prohibition, the Turkish Court of Cassation allows its restrictive interpretation on the grounds of an important legal interest, e.g. relating to the violation of human rights as a result of such evidence being used. The argument about the need to weigh legal interests is also accepted by legal scholars and commentators who mostly recognise that an absolute prohibition on the

33 Anne Schneider, *Limits of freedom of public authorities with respect to obtaining evidence at the stage of investigation*, p. 72.

illegal acquisition of evidence could lead to extremely serious consequences for criminal justice. The Turkish Code of Criminal Procedure does not contain specific provisions on the effectiveness and legality of evidence. The prevailing view in Turkey is that the use of illegal evidence in criminal proceedings is inadmissible. It was underlined that the Turkish Court of Cassation does recognise the "fruit of a poisonous tree" doctrine. At the same time, some Turkish legal scholars and commentators consider this position too strict and advocate that the legal interest in assessing the admissibility of illegally obtained evidence based on a comparison between the individual rights violated by it and the benefit of such disclosure of facts should be weighed. Other legal scholars and commentators and the Turkish Constitutional Court recognise the right of the court to decide on the use of illegally obtained evidence in terms of its impact on the fair trial.[34]

The Hungarian report points out that Hungarian law basically defines the limits of admissibility of the collection of evidence. They are neither narrowed nor broadened by jurisprudence in general. The importance of fair proof procedure was emphasised, even if the Hungarian Criminal Prosecution Act does not use this term. Hungary has an institution of evidence excluded by law. According to it, a fact derived from a means of proof obtained by a court, a public prosecutor or an investigating authority by criminal offence, by other prohibited means or by substantially restricting the procedural rights of participants cannot be regarded as evidence.[35]

The Estonian report states that the Code of Criminal Procedure does not provide for a mechanism to automatically exclude illegal evidence. The law sets these boundaries but does not clearly define the consequences of their transgression. The most imperative are evidentiary activities that require a court approval (surveillance activities). Other violations are subject to the assessment by the court, which should be guided by the criteria for evaluating evidence developed by the Supreme Court of Estonia. These are: what provision of the law was breached, i.e. the defensive purpose of the provision; how extensive the breach was; whether the breach was intentional; what crime was being investigated; how extensive is the public interest or the interest of the victims in investigating the crime; would it have been possible to acquire the same evidence without the breach by using a different method; what is

34 Haluk Toroslu, Uğur Orhan, Bedirhan Erdem, *On Limits of Freedom of Public Authorities with Respect to Obtaining Evidence at the Stage of Investigation under Turkish Criminal Procedure and Evidence Law*, p. 120 et seq.

35 Csongor Herke, Barbara Szabó, *Limits of freedom of public authorities with respect to obtaining evidence at the stage of investigation. HUNGARY*, p. 138 et seq.

the relevance of the evidence in the case; whether the right to defence of the accused is being considered when admitting the evidence (Ruling of the Supreme Court 1–16–6179, 18 June 2021, p. 59). It is emphasised in the Estonian report that there are no special consequences in the Code of Criminal Procedure for violations committed by investigators in the course of evidence activities. Instead, their disciplinary responsibility may come into play.[36]

The Italian report stresses the existence in the Code of Criminal Procedure of several provisions which directly regulate inadmissibility of evidence obtained in violation of the law and which apply to the protection of certain fundamental interests, such as personal freedom, the inviolability of the home or communication privacy. Under Article 188 of the Italian CCP, evidence taken (whether during the investigation or at a trial) by methods or techniques likely to affect the freedom of self-determination or alter the ability to remember and evaluate facts is invalid, or rather not usable. As to atypical sources of evidence not regulated by the Code, the condition of their admissibility in criminal procedure is their adequacy for the determination of the facts and respect for personal freedom (Article 189 of the CCP). In addition, evidence that, although abstractly admissible, was in practice acquired in violation of prohibitions established by law (Article 191 of the Code of Criminal Procedure) cannot be used. Irrespective of the aforesaid detailed prohibitions, the inadmissibility of certain evidence or evidentiary methods arises from general norms, including those laid down in the Constitution.[37]

The Taiwanese report emphasises that the Taiwan's Code of Criminal Procedure provides the main principles for evidence collection, whereas other regulations are made to regulate specific evidentiary activities in certain situations. In addition to the Code of Criminal Procedure, the Communication Security and Surveillance Act, which sets out the procedure and conditions for obtaining evidence, plays an important role. Much relevance is also placed upon Article 154 of the Taiwan's Code of Criminal Procedure, which stipulates that "(t)he admissibility of the evidence, obtained in violation of the procedure prescribed by the law by an official in execution of criminal procedure, shall be determined by balancing the protection of human rights and the preservation of public interests, unless otherwise provided by law." The admissibility of evidence is determined by the court; such assessment is not made for evidence obtained against the law (e.g. by violence, threat, fraud, exhausting interrogation, unlawful detention or other improper means), as it cannot constitute

36 Anneli Soo, *Limits of freedom of public authorities with respect to obtaining evidence at the stage of investigation in Estonia*, p. 256.

37 Thomas Di Candia, *Italian Evidence Law System: Limits to the Investigative Power*, pp. 161–162.

evidence. A limiting factor for investigators in the taking of evidence is the well-established practice of courts not accepting certain types of evidence, such as the polygraph. The Taiwanese Judicial Yuan plays a significant role in setting standards for the legality of evidence.[38]

The Japanese report states that evidence obtained from a search or a seizure of an object without a judicial warrant (in violation of Article 218 of the JCPL) should be excluded from trial.[39] However, evidence acquired from the independent activities of illegal investigation is not necessarily excluded from trial.[40] Moreover, obtaining a judicial warrant does not guarantee the legality of the evidentiary action. An example is evidence deriving from digital data carriers. Once the court's consent is obtained to seize them, investigators retrieve and use information from such carriers without the court's supervision.[41] Currently the Legislation Committee is working on the digital transformation of criminal procedural law.[42] Furthermore, there is no law in Japan that would allow challenging the admissibility of evidence at the stage of investigation, as the JCPL does not guarantee the right to access evidence acquired by public authorities at the investigative stage, due to its adversarial character. This is possible only before the court (Articles 316–14 and Articles 316–27 of the JCPL). The basic measures to control the legality of evidence at the investigation stage are: the judicial warrant required for evidentiary activities that most strongly interfere with civil rights and freedoms, and Article 31 of the JCPL that enables the exclusion of evidence violating the Constitution due to the fair trial principle, subject to other the exclusions provided for in the JCPL. A failure by officials to adhere to the principles above deprives their actions of evidentiary value, which causes such evidence to be excluded from the procedure, or the indictment to be dismissed.[43]

In Polish criminal procedural law, until 1 July 2015, there was no regulation explicitly referring to the admissibility of indirectly illegal evidence. However, even if the "fruit of a poisonous tree" concept was not applied, it did not imply

---

38 See Kai-Ping Su, *Limits of freedom of public authorities with respect to obtaining evidence at the stage of investigation*, pp. 161–162.

39 *See* Judgement of Japanese Supreme Court 1978.9.7. *Keishuu* 32–6-1327, Judgement of Japanese Supreme Court 2003.2.14. *Keishuu* 57–2-121, Decision of Japanese Supreme Court 2009.9.28 *Keishuu* 63–7-868. (Tatsuhiko Inatani, National Report of Japan, p. 265).

40 *See* Decision of Japanese Supreme Court 1988.9.16 *Keishuu* 42–7-1051 (Tatsuhiko Inatani, National Report of Japan, p. 265).

41 *See* Tatsuhiko Inatani, PRIVACY PROTECTION IN CRIMINAL PROCEDURE-TOWARD DUE PROCESS ON DELIBERATIVE DEMOCRACY (『刑事手続におけるプライバシー保護–熟議による適正手続の実現を目指して』) (Kohbundo 2017), pp. 339–341.

42 See Tatsuhiko Inatani, *National Report of Japan*, p. 271.

43 See Tatsuhiko Inatani, *National Report of Japan*, p. 269.

that the standards of evidence based on the principle of fair trial were not respected. The Polish Supreme Court developed rigorous standards for the legality of evidentiary activities in criminal proceedings and in the course of operational intelligence activities, which were mainly based on police statutes. With a view to perpetuating them, a new provision (Article 168a) was introduced into the Polish Code of Criminal Procedure by the Act of 27 September 2013, which stipulates that "(i)t is inadmissible to conduct and use evidence obtained for the purposes of criminal proceedings by means of a criminal act referred to in Article 1(1) of the Criminal Code." A complete change in the law occurred under the Act of 11 March 2016. The provision of Article 168a of the Code of Criminal Procedure, valid from 15 April 2016 onwards, stipulates that evidence cannot be declared inadmissible solely on the grounds that it was obtained in breach of the rules of procedure or by means of a prohibited act referred to in Article 1(1) of the Criminal Code, unless the evidence was obtained in connection with the performance of official duties by a public officer, as a result of: murder, intentional infliction of bodily harm or deprivation of liberty. This controversial regulation, which directly allows the use of illegal evidence in a criminal trial, is contested by Polish legal scholars and commentators and courts that attempt to reinterpret the provision of Article 168a of the Code of Criminal Procedure in the spirit of the principle of legalism, as expressed in Article 7 of the 1992 Polish Constitution and the Convention principle of a fair trial (*inter alia*, judgment of the Appellate Court in Wrocław of 27 April 2017, II AKa 213/16). The solution currently applied shows that the Polish legislature has recognised the predominance of the public interest over the interest of individuals and is unacceptable in this form.[44]

In Canada, there are diverse sources of law governing evidence in criminal proceedings. Common law is predominant. Due to the specific nature of criminal proceedings in this country, evidence obtained at the investigative stage is assessed by the court once presented by the prosecution. A criterion for this assessment is the legality of the evidence, but most of all it is assessed in terms of how relevant and useful it is for the case. In both aspects, it is the court that decides upon its discretion whether evidence is to be excluded. The court cannot, however, declare evidence admissible if it is subject to exclusion, e.g. in order to ensure a fair trial. In *R v Wray*,[45] the SCC held that where the prejudicial nature of otherwise admissible evidence greatly outweighs its probative

44 See Karolina Kremens, *Power to Search and Its Limits in Polish Criminal Investigations*, p. 201.

45 R v Wray, [1971] 1 SCR 272 (see Alexandre Stylios, Gustave Warby, *Limits of freedom of public authorities with respect to obtaining evidence at the stage of investigation. Canadian report*, p. 218.).

value, the presiding judge may declare it inadmissible as a means of ensuring procedural fairness. In this case, the exclusionary principle, known as the principle of proportionality, was applied.

When summarising this part of the General Report considerations, it should be emphasised that the limits of the public authority's freedom to obtain evidence at the investigative stage are determined in a given country by weighing many factors, primarily such as contemporary standards of civilisation, adherence to a particular juridical system, the specific nature of a given criminal procedural order and the general level of the rule of law. Those elements are not the source of significant discrepancies between the countries that sent in their country reports. They emphasise the importance of the principle of fair evidentiary procedure, even if it is not directly expressed in the legislation of any of these countries. Instead, it constitutes one of the criteria of fair criminal proceedings. The reports state that when assessing the admissibility of evidence that is not absolutely prohibited, a moderate approach aimed at weighing the legal interest prevails. Its most important perspective is the balance between public and private interests. There is a widespread appreciation of the need to get to the truth about a crime and respond appropriately to it, but only with due consideration being given to the rights and guarantees of individuals in criminal proceedings. Even if the public interest is prioritised by allowing the use of illegal evidence in a criminal trial (Poland), courts try to correct this direction in order to ensure a procedural balance between both types of interests. The influence of court case law in shaping the standards of evidentiary procedure is characteristic. Apart from Hungary, all other countries point to the significant role of courts and tribunals in defining the boundaries of evidence acquisition. A rational pragmatism can be observed in the approach of the courts, with the said balance between the public interest in performing the function of criminal prosecution and the private interest that may be harmed by violations of fair evidence standards being set as a reference point. With minimalist regulations on the limits of the legality of evidence and the consequences of their violation or due to their high level of generality, as highlighted in most reports, courts play a significant role in defining these standards. Consequently, it is up to the courts to decide in individual cases whether to admit or exclude evidence. The criterion for these decisions is the degree and nature of the infringement of the suspect's interest. The means of verifying whether the evidentiary procedure is correct, listed in the reports, mainly concern the stage of court proceedings. The country reports emphasise that at the investigation stage, the evidentiary activities are to be taken mostly by the investigators, and the court's participation is limited to agreeing to a particular action (e.g. a search or wiretapping) when it is subject to the court's decision under the applicable law. This applies to evidentiary activities that most deeply interfere with civil rights and freedoms. With regard to other evidentiary activities carried out during the investigation, there are generally no mechanisms for them to be verified for correctness by external entities and for the unlawful evidence to be eliminated. It is only when a criminal charge is brought before a court that the evidence on which such charge is based can be examined. Consequently, the investigators' ethics and integrity are of vital importance at the investigation stage. The country reports show that regulations on evidence in criminal proceedings in individual states have a different level of detail; with most authors stating that the regulations seem to be inadequate as they do not define the consequences of pertinent violations. This deficiency does affect the legibility and accuracy of the limits of law enforcement action. It may, however, be justified by the objectives of these actions. Investigators around the world are expected to effectively combat crime that leads to disruption of the legal and social order. A reasonable compromise is required to reconcile these opposing objectives. This final conclusion is supported by the content of each of the country reports submitted. Given how many various failings can be committed, it is objectively impossible to precisely determine the consequences of violations of the law of evidence. There is a consensus that not every one of them should have comparable legal consequences, which is an argument for the courts' right to assess violations of the law of evidence and their legal consequences on a case-by-case basis.

3 Public Authorities Are Entitled to Acquire Evidence in a Criminal Action at the Stage of Investigation

The idea of the rule of law implies that state authorities should act only if there is an explicit legal basis to do so.

The country reports submitted confirmed that the primary sources of the law governing the conduct of criminal proceedings in the civil law countries, including the powers of the relevant authorities to conduct the pre-trial investigation, are either national codes of criminal procedure or equivalent statutory acts (the Criminal Code in Canada). In addition to laws dedicated strictly to the criminal procedure, the authorities' evidentiary powers may also, to some extent, be derived from specific laws regulating a particular area of activity (e.g. the Communication Security and Surveillance Act in Taiwan) or the operations of specific authorities (e.g. the Hunting Act of 13 October 1995 in Poland). In the common law countries, including Canada, customary law is also crucial in determining the powers of specific authorities acting at the pre-trial investigation stage in addition to codified law. Regardless of the type of legal system in force in a given country, the framework for the operation of statutory provisions and customary law is determined by the constitutions of individual countries. For more information on the sources of the law of evidence, see Section 4 of this report.

Particular country reports showed that pre-trial investigations are generally conducted by the police, regardless of the system. Even if prosecutors in the civil law countries presented are vested with the broadest powers during pre-trial investigations, in practical terms, this stage of criminal proceedings is usually handled by the police under the prosecutor's supervision.[46] In these countries, however, the law still treats the prosecutor as the host of the pre-trial investigation responsible for its conduct. Given this position of the prosecutor in the pre-trial investigation, all results of police actions go to his or her account. This is, however, not the case in the Canadian system. The authors of the report pointed out that in Canada most investigations are conducted by traditional law enforcement agencies, notably the Royal Canadian Mounted Police, as well as provincial and local police forces.[47]

In individual countries, pre-trial investigations may also be conducted by other specialised bodies authorised to operate at this stage of the proceedings, to the extent expressly stipulated by specific laws. In Germany, the tax investigation service (*Steuerfahndung*) is considered the most important of these authorities.[48] In Hungary, in addition to the public prosecutor and the police, the authorities entitled to conduct the pre-trial investigation are: the Hungarian National Tax and Customs Office, the captain of a vessel (aircraft) and the military commander.[49]

In Taiwan, the public prosecutor may be assisted by bodies that are part of the judicial police, which include the police of the railway, forestry, fisheries, mining or other professional police agencies, patrol team police of customs or salterns.[50] In Estonia, the powers to undertake investigation activities are vested in, among others, the Border Guard, Internal Security Service, Tax and

---

46 With the caveat that in the case of Hungary, the police have the authority to conduct the *in rem* phase of the investigation themselves.

47 Alexandre Stylios, Gustave Warby, *Limits of freedom of public authorities with respect to obtaining evidence at the stage of investigation. Canadian report*, p. 212.

48 Anne Schneider, *Limits of freedom of public authorities with respect to obtaining evidence at the stage of investigation*, pp. 74–75.

49 Csongor Herke, Barbara Szabó, *Limits of freedom of public authorities with respect to obtaining evidence at the stage of investigation. HUNGARY*, p. 132.

50 Kai-Ping Su, *Limits of freedom of public authorities with respect to obtaining evidence at the stage of investigation*, pp. 230–231.

Customs Board, Environment Board.[51] In Poland, authorities competent to run pre-trial investigations are, *inter alia*, the Border Guard, Internal Security Agency, National Revenue Administration, Central Anticorruption Bureau, Trade Inspection Authority, State Sanitary Inspection Authority, President of the Office of Electronic Communications, Forest Guard, and National Hunting Guard. These authorities can only conduct proceedings to the extent limited by law.[52] In Japan, such specialized authorities that function as part of the Police are departments dealing with e.g. cybercrime and economic crimes, including white collar crimes and corruption. Drug-related crimes are investigated by drug enforcement officers.[53] The Italian structures of the prosecutor and the police involve specialized units to combat mafia, terrorist, economic, computer, and scientific crimes, including: the Anti-Mafia District Prosecutors (*Procure Distrettuali Antimafia*), *Direzioni Distrettuali Antimafia*), National Anti-Mafia and Counter-Terrorism Central Prosecutor. The Anti-Mafia Investigation Directorate, Guardia di Finanza, Postal Police.[54] In Canada, certain administrative agencies possessing delegated powers may also initiate investigations. For example, the Commissioner of Competition possesses broad investigative powers pursuant to Part II of the *Competition Act*. These powers include *ex parte* applications for warrants and the ability to compel witnesses.[55]

Despite the diversity of the authorities having the right to conduct pre-trial investigations in different countries, the country reports conclude that the police have a dominant role in carrying out the investigative activities. Unlike in the civil law countries, in Canada extensive investigative powers have been accorded to administrative bodies, such as the Commissioner of Competition. As indicated, a review by an administrative body may be considered a criminal investigation if the main purpose of the proceedings is to determine criminal liability. When making such evaluation "courts must assess the totality of the circumstances, and make a determination as to whether the inquiry or question in issue engages the adversarial relationship between the state and the individual."[56] What is lacking in Canada, and what is characteristic of countries with the civil law system, is a statutory definition of the authorities vested with

51 Anneli Soo, *Limits of freedom of public authorities with respect to obtaining evidence at the stage of investigation in Estonia*, pp. 251–252.

52 Karolina Kremens, *Power to Search and Its Limits in Polish Criminal Investigations*, pp. 194–195.

53 Tatsuhiko Inatani, *National Report of Japan*, p. 264.

54 Thomas Di Candia, *Italian Evidence Law System: Limits to the Investigative Power*, p. 150 et seq.

55 Alexandre Stylios, Gustave Warby, *Limits of freedom of public authorities with respect to obtaining evidence at the stage of investigation. Canadian report*, p. 212.

56 R v Jarvis, [2002] 3 SCR 757.

the right of investigation, which bears the risk of an uncontrolled extension of investigative powers to administrative authorities.

Each report submitted shows that state authorities are the only entities entitled to conduct criminal investigations. Consequently, none of the discussed legal systems allows private investigations conducted by victims, suspects or their agents for litigation, such as investigations conducted by the defence lawyer in the Italian system (*investigazioni difensive*).[57] The Code of Criminal Procedure regulates the activities that the lawyer can carry out in investigations. In particular, the lawyer may take information from witnesses at the investigation stage, may request access to documents available to the public administration, may make «technical findings». The lawyer may also enter private or closed places with the prior authorization of the judge.

Nor are private investigations permitted in cases where it is the victim who brings the charge before the court. In the civil law countries in question, two possible modes of prosecution by the victim can be distinguished. The first one consists in filing a private indictment in the case of minor offences, where the victims are entitled to initiate court proceedings without a public prosecutor. In the Polish criminal procedure, the offences falling into the category of private prosecution offences are very infrequent, namely: causing slight bodily injury or slight damage to health, defamation, insult, and violation of physical integrity. Additionally, German law allows private prosecution for minor offences such as trespass or (simple) bodily harm (Article 374(1) StPO). In both Polish and German systems, the rule is that there is no investigation in private prosecution proceedings.[58] The public prosecutor is, however, entitled to take over private prosecution proceedings. In Germany, pre-trial investigations can also be launched under private prosecution if the court refers such case to the public prosecutor for pre-trial investigation to be run under general rules.[59] In Poland, cases brought by private prosecution are practically of negligible

57 The provision of Article 327-bis of the Italian Code of Criminal Procedure grants the defence lawyer the power to conduct investigations (*investigazioni*) in order to seek evidence in favour of the client (see Thomas Di Candia, *Italian Evidence Law System: Limits to the Investigative Power*, p. 175).

58 In Poland, Article 488 of the Code of Criminal Procedure stipulates that the police must secure evidence, if necessary, in a situation where the victim has decided to initiate private prosecution by filing a complaint with the police, which is subsequently forwarded to the court. All other evidentiary measures are taken by the police upon the court's request, if the court deems it necessary. Yet these are still isolated evidentiary activities which are not carried out as part of the pre-trial investigations.

59 Anne Schneider, *Limits of freedom of public authorities with respect to obtaining evidence at the stage of investigation*, pp. 75–76.

significance, which means that public authorities enjoy here almost an exclusive right to take criminal enforcement actions.[60] The institution of private prosecution does exist in Taiwan under its Code of Criminal Procedure (Article 319).[61] In Japan, the prosecutor monopolizes investigation (Article 247 of the JCPL). This system does not recognize private prosecution.[62] Similarly in Turkey (Article 160 of the CCP et seq.)[63] and in Estonia.[64] In Hungary, in essence, private prosecutions are almost never investigated. The private prosecutor (or his legal representative) does not have investigative powers, nor is there any common practice of private investigation in Hungary. There are only two exceptions under the law to this principle.[65]

A second possible way for a victim to prosecute in countries with the civil law system is to bring a charge instead of the prosecutor, in the case of an act prosecuted by public indictment – if the prosecutor or other prosecuting authorities are unwilling to prosecute such an offence. In systems where victims have been granted the power to bring such charges (Poland, Taiwan), the law does not provide for the possibility of a private investigation being launched to gather evidence justifying the prosecution.

Even if private individuals are broadly entitled to bring private prosecutions in Canada, law enforcement agencies in this country have a monopoly on criminal investigations. Numerous restrictions, which primarily involve the judicial review of private prosecutions and possible interference by the Attorney General or the Crown, are the reason why the citizens rarely decide to exercise their right.[66]

All the country reports submitted emphasised that the court is not an authority with the power to conduct pre-trial investigations. None of the jurisdictions in question has the institution of an investigating magistrate, acting as a pre-trial investigation authority with the power to conduct the same, as it is the case in France. .This does not, however, mean that the courts in the relevant

60 Karolina Kremens, *Power to Search and Its Limits in Polish Criminal Investigations*, pp. 185–186.

61 Kai-Ping Su, *Limits of freedom of public authorities with respect to obtaining evidence at the stage of investigation*, p. 231.

62 Tatsuhiko Inatani, *National Report of Japan*, p. 264.

63 Haluk Toroslu, Uğur Orhan, Bedirhan Erdem, *On Limits of Freedom of Public Authorities with Respect to Obtaining Evidence at the Stage of Investigation under Turkish Criminal Procedure and Evidence Law*, p. 108.

64 Anneli Soo, *Limits of freedom of public authorities with respect to obtaining evidence at the stage of investigation in Estonia*, pp. 252–253.

65 Csongor Herke, Barbara Szabó, *Limits of freedom of public authorities with respect to obtaining evidence at the stage of investigation. HUNGARY*, p. 133.

66 Alexandre Stylios, Gustave Warby, *Limits of freedom of public authorities with respect to obtaining evidence at the stage of investigation. Canadian report*, p. 213.

jurisdictions have no influence on the pre-trial investigations. In countries without the institution of an investigating magistrate, the court's involvement in the evidentiary procedure at the pre-trial investigation stage is reduced to carrying out specific evidentiary activities with a view to securing evidence for future court proceedings or deciding on the use of the so-called sensitive evidentiary measures (e.g. telephone tapping, searches), i.e. those that most interfere with the individual's personal rights and freedoms. In Germany, the pre-trial investigating magistrate (*Ermittlungsrichter*) is responsible for carrying out pre-trial judicial acts. This authority also occurs in Italian criminal procedure. Other countries (Poland, Taiwan, Estonia, Japan, Turkey, Hungary and Canada) have not adopted this model.

Within the legal systems analysed, the court is entitled, to a statutorily limited extent, to participate in the recording of evidence at the investigation stage – in Poland, Germany, and Turkey. In Poland, the court has the power to examine a witness if there is a risk that it will be impossible for the witness to be examined in the course of the trial, e.g. due to his or her likely death (Article 316 CCP). In addition, the court is the authority to carry out questioning at the investigation stage in situations where it would be undesirable or impossible to carry out this activity again (Articles 185a–185c CCP). This applies to interrogations of minor victims and witnesses in cases of violent crimes, unlawful threats or crimes against sexual freedom, as well as adult victims of selected crimes against sexual freedom. In Germany, the court may launch investigative measures when requested to do so by the public prosecutor's office. In practice, this is often the case when victims of domestic violence are questioned because, as the case law stands, only a hearing conducted by a judge can be used in a trial if the witness refuses to testify at a later stage.[67] Furthermore, according to Article 165 StPO, the court may only take evidence *ex officio* if there is a risk of evidence being lost due to delay and the prosecutor is unavailable (*Gefahr im Verzug*). In Turkey, the courts are authorised to take evidentiary activities if the prosecutor is unable to do so. According to Article 163 of the Turkish Code of Criminal Procedure, "(i)f the public prosecutor cannot be reached in case of flagrante delicto and in case of peril in delay, or if the scope of the case exceeds the work force of the public prosecutor, the judge (magister) can also carry out all procedures at the phase of investigation."

By contrast, in each[68] of the jurisdictions in question, the court has the power to make certain decisions on the use of specific means of proof that

67 BGHSt 61, 221, 221 ff. margin no. 25 ff.

68 Although the authors of the Hungarian report pointed out that at the investigation stage the court has no power to control evidentiary activities taken by law enforcement

most interfere with the individual's personal rights and freedoms. The court's decision may take the form of a mandatory pre-authorisation of evidentiary measures or a post-factum review of the decision, in a situation where the prosecutor or the police have taken steps as immediate action was needed. As indicated above, with respect to other evidentiary measures carried out at the pre-trial investigation stage, there are generally no mechanisms for judicial review. However, in the German and Polish systems, as stated in the relevant reports, the parties concerned that have a legal interest may challenge certain investigative actions on an ongoing basis. The general rule, however, is that evidence obtained in violation of the applicable rules can only be challenged at the court stage.

4 Principles of Acquiring Evidence at the Stage of Investigation

Obtaining evidence at the pre-trial stage is primarily subject to the applicable legal regulations, which obviously refers to the states with the civil law system in place, but also broadly applies to those representing the common law system. What most of the legal systems analysed have in common is that the major rules of evidentiary procedure, the prerequisites authorising interference by law enforcement authorities, and the guarantees owed to persons subjected to evidentiary measures have been regulated in legal acts that are differently ranked in the hierarchy of the sources of law. In some systems, i.e. the Federal Republic of Germany, Italy Poland, Turkey, Japan or Canada, regulations relating to the acquisition of evidence by law enforcement authorities have been given constitutional status (at least to some extent). In this respect, especially Italy is the most prominent example. Article 111 of the Constitution provides that every trial must be held in the adversarial proceedings between the parties, on equal terms, before a third-party and impartial judge (paragraph 2). The evidence must be formed in the cross-examination between the parties (paragraph 4), unless otherwise agreed with the accused or due to objective impossibility (paragraph 5).[69]

As highlighted in the German report, with the need to protect the fundamental rights of citizens being anchored in the Basic Law, trial authorities are obliged to demonstrate the grounds and legal justification for any action that violates fundamental rights. Furthermore, the interference with constitutionally

agencies, the report goes on to list among the examples of illegal evidence certain specific evidence obtained against the court's consent.

69 Thomas Di Candia, *Italian Evidence Law System: Limits to the Investigative Power*, p. 157.

protected freedoms must be "suitable for reaching its purpose, necessary and appropriate. [...] This shows that criminal procedure law is, indeed, «constitutional law in practice» (angewandtes Verfassungsrecht)".[70] Apart from this, an important role of the basic laws is to provide interpretative directions for the criminal procedural laws governing the evidence gathering process.

Detailed evidence collection regulations are laid down in the Turkish Constitution, especially Articles 36–38.[71]

On the contrary, in Taiwan the Code of Criminal Procedure provides the main principles of the law of evidence.[72]

In Canada, it was accepted that: as the *Constitution Act, 1982* is the supreme law of the land, all rules governing the conditions of obtaining and adducing of evidence must conform with those rights that are constitutionally entrenched, notably but not exclusively: s. 7 (Life, liberty and security of persons); s. 8 (protection against illegal search and seizure); s. 9 (protection against unlawful detention and arrest) and s. 10b) (right to instruct counsel).[73]

In all the systems analysed, issues related to obtaining evidence are regulated in the Code of Criminal Procedure or its equivalent acts. These are indicated as the main or, as in the case of the reports from two countries, even the only sources of law in this area. In addition to the Criminal Procedure Act, evidence collection is also regulated by other laws. In Taiwan, it is the previously mentioned Communication Security and Surveillance Act and provisions regulating specific evidentiary activities; in Poland the Police Act and the Prosecution Act, Crown Witness Act, in Turkey Polis Vazife ve Salahiyet Kanunu, Adlî ve Önleme Aramaları Yönetmeliği; Yakalama, Gözaltına Alma ve İfade Alma Yönetmeliği. The inclusion of rules of evidence in sub-statutory acts is also a feature common to the above systems.

In Canada, due to historical circumstances and legal tradition, most of the regulations on the acquisition of evidence at the pre-trial stage still stem from the common law, but for the 1982 Constitution Act and the Canadian Charter of Rights and Freedoms, and despite the enactment of the Evidence Act and other laws enacted at both the federal and provincial levels. According to the

70 As cited in: Anne Schneider, *Limits of freedom of public authorities with respect to obtaining evidence at the stage of investigation*, p. 86.

71 Haluk Toroslu, Uğur Orhan, Bedirhan Erdem, *On Limits of Freedom of Public Authorities with Respect to Obtaining Evidence at the Stage of Investigation under Turkish Criminal Procedure and Evidence Law*, pp. 110–111.

72 Kai-Ping Su, *Limits of freedom of public authorities with respect to obtaining evidence at the stage of investigation*, pp. 239–240.

73 Alexandre Stylios, Gustave Warby, *Limits of freedom of public authorities with respect to obtaining evidence at the stage of investigation. Canadian report*, pp. 210–211.

authors of the report, regulations relating to the law of evidence have not yet been fully laid down in positive law. Hence, judicial case law plays an important role. The multiplicity of rules of procedure and guidelines governing the conduct of Crown prosecutors and the police is also characteristic of common law states.[74]

Only the authors of the Estonian[75] and Hungarian[76] reports point to normative homogeneity with regard to the issue of evidence (although the Polish report also indicates that, despite the multiplicity of legal sources relating to evidence, the system is generally based on the rules set out by the Code of Criminal Procedure, which in its author's opinion makes it "relatively homogeneous)."[77] As the Taiwanese report explicitly emphasised with regard to the regulations related to the collection of evidence, there is a duplication of norms.[78]

The statement about different levels of protection of individual's personal rights and freedoms is not limited only to where the pertinent act is placed in the hierarchy of the sources of law, but also refers to how detailed the regulations that express values of significant importance for the activities of procedural authorities in obtaining evidence really are. In most countries, legal acts of constitutional rank set out general principles. There are, however, some examples of specific regulations, like those in the German Basic Law, which describe the competences of the authorities, the prerequisites and the procedure protecting against a broadly defined interference with the inviolability of the home, whereas the provisions on human dignity remain "rather vague".[79] The law in force in Germany does not leave law enforcement authorities much freedom when taking measures, including evidentiary measures, as evidenced by the existence of a detailed legal regulation that defines the rules and course of evidentiary activities and the procedural requirements. At the same time, the legal consequences of infringements are hardly regulated in that system,

---

74 Alexandre Stylios, Gustave Warby, *Limits of freedom of public authorities with respect to obtaining evidence at the stage of investigation. Canadian report*, p. 210.

75 Anneli Soo, *Limits of freedom of public authorities with respect to obtaining evidence at the stage of investigation in Estonia*, p. 256.

76 Csongor Herke, Barbara Szabó, *Limits of freedom of public authorities with respect to obtaining evidence at the stage of investigation. HUNGARY*, p. 135.

77 Karolina Kremens, *Power to Search and Its Limits in Polish Criminal Investigations* p. 184.

78 Kai-Ping Su, *Limits of freedom of public authorities with respect to obtaining evidence at the stage of investigation*, pp. 233–234.

79 Anne Schneider, *Limits of freedom of public authorities with respect to obtaining evidence at the stage of investigation*, p. 82.

which means that a great deal of discretion is left to the courts when ruling on the admissibility of evidence.[80]

In other countries, the legal limits set relate only to certain evidentiary activities. As pointed out in the Hungarian report, there are no strict regulations in Hungary that would bind the law enforcement authorities in the evidence acquisition process. The legality of investigators' actions is controlled through prosecutor office's internal supervisory measures. In the investigation stage, the court does not have any control measures in relation to investigators' actions. In the court stage, the court has the right to a discretionary assessment of the evidence gathered and to collide the evidence at oral and adversary hearings. The grounds for the court's assessment are established by both general evidentiary principles and the rules applicable under law to particular pieces of evidence.[81] In the Italian system there is not a criterion of the legality of evidence. The Code of Criminal Procedure expressly provides for the possibility of recourse to atypical evidence, where «atypical» means «not described by the law». In addition, the case law of the *Corte di Cassazione* plays an important role creating the principle of «atypicality» of the investigation acts in the pre-trial investigation. The public prosecutor and the Police have a certain freedom to carry out investigative activities and to collect evidence in the investigation. This power, however, is not absolute and arbitrary: the system provides for a series of prescriptions and prohibitions, general or specific, whose violation leads to sanctions (e.g. Articles 188, 189 and 191 Paragraph 2 bis of the CCP). The violation of the norms leads both to the liability of officials acting in contravention of the law and to the exclusion of the evidence obtained in contravention of the law.[82] In Poland, it is the gravity of violations that determines whether an action taken at the pre-trial investigation stage can be used for evidentiary purposes or not. While confessions obtained by means of coercion or unlawful threat cannot constitute evidence, a breach of the search regulations in the context of a violation of the principle of proportionality does not have such effect any more.[83] The rules in force in Estonia also grant investigative authorities considerable discretion in the conduct of their activities, with exceptions being the so-called surveillance activities (i.e. covertly watching a person, thing or area, covertly taking comparative samples

80 Anne Schneider, *Limits of freedom of public authorities with respect to obtaining evidence at the stage of investigation*, p. 85.

81 Csongor Herke, Barbara Szabó, *Limits of freedom of public authorities with respect to obtaining evidence at the stage of investigation. HUNGARY*, p. 132 and p. 133 et seq.

82 Thomas Di Candia, *Italian Evidence Law System: Limits to the Investigative Power*, p. 161 et seq.

83 Karolina Kremens, *Power to Search and Its Limits in Polish Criminal Investigations* pp. 200–201.

and performing initial examinations, covertly examining a thing and covertly replacing it). According to the Estonian report, it is not only the failure to seek the relevant permission from the court that would render the evidence so obtained automatically inadmissible. The same effect, as stated by the Supreme Court of Estonia, will arise if the evidence was obtained following the relevant court decision, which, however, was groundless or otherwise defective.[84] In Japan, evidence examined without obtaining the mandatory consent of the court envisaged for each type of means that contains an element of compulsion is excluded, save for the exceptions admitted by the Supreme Court's case law.[85]

The country reports also show that, irrespective of how formalised the rules binding the investigating authorities are, in all the countries the courts are given discretion to declare specific evidence inadmissible. As a general rule, if a particular piece of evidence is not covered by an evidence ban, it is up to the court to decide whether to admit such evidence taken at the pre-trial investigation stage. The law in Taiwan generally indicates the rationale to be followed by the courts in deciding whether to admit or exclude evidence obtained in violation of the legally prescribed procedure. According to the wording of Article 154 of the Criminal Procedure Code, the trial authority is to balance the protection of human rights and the preservation of public interests.[86] As already mentioned, in the case of Estonian law – apart from actions subject to the court's prior consent – the general principle set by the Supreme Court's case law is to declare evidence inadmissible only if there has been a material breach of the law when obtaining it. In addition to the type of offence under investigation, the type of evidence obtained, and the extent of the social interest or individual harm, the main criteria to be followed by courts in this respect are: the nature of the provision violated (whether it was a guarantee); to what extent it was violated and whether it was an intentional act of the officers, and whether there was any possible alternative way or method of obtaining the same evidence that would not necessitate a violation of law. Finally, an important factor for courts to consider when deciding whether to

84 Anneli Soo, *Limits of freedom of public authorities with respect to obtaining evidence at the stage of investigation in Estonia*, pp. 254–255.

85 *See* Judgement of Japanese Supreme Court 1978.9.7. *Keishuu* 32-6-1327, Judgement of Japanese Supreme Court 2003.2.14. *Keishuu* 57-2-121, Decision of Japanese Supreme Court 2009.9.28 *Keishuu* 63-7-868; Decision of Japanese Supreme Court 1988.9.16 *Keishuu* 42-7-1051 (Tatsuhiko Inatani, *National Report of Japan*, p. 265).

86 Kai-Ping Su, *Limits of freedom of public authorities with respect to obtaining evidence at the stage of investigation*, p. 234.

admit evidence is how the relevant decision will impact the accused's right to defence.[87] In the case of Canada, as the country report shows, the duality of sources of law also relates to the grounds to be taken into account by the court in deciding whether to admit or exclude evidence. The grounds that should guide courts in making the relevant decision, as set out in Article 24(2) of the Charter are: the effect of the admission of the evidence on the fairness of the trial, the nature of the violations in obtaining the evidence, and the impact of the exclusion of evidence on the public perception of the administration of justice. As highlighted in *Hill v Church of Scientology of Toronto*, [1995] 2 SCR 1130, when setting standards or clarifying regulations, courts must ensure that the application of the law is consistent with the values listed in the Charter. With the most of legal regulations on evidence being derived from the common law, this is where the case law comes into play. When analysing the case law presented in the report, two trends regarding the extent of judicial discretion can be identified. As in civil law states – the judge cannot admit evidence that is legally inadmissible, however, in certain situations he or she may take a discretionary decision to exclude admissible or even relevant evidence. The criteria to guide the judge are the possible negative impact of the evidence on the fairness of the trial and its probative value. As pointed out in R v. Seaboyer: "In fact, the use of judicial discretion allows the judge not to admit relevant and admissible evidence if he considers that its probative value is too low in relation to the prejudice it causes to the accused."[88] The basic criterion for evidence to be deemed admissible is its relevance from a logical or legal point of view, with "logical relevance" to be understood as the connection between the fact proved and the fact to be proved.

In all the countries analysed (but for Turkey), consensual procedures which allow limitations or even waiving evidence during the trial were confirmed to exist. The Japanese report indicates limited application of alternative procedures.[89] While some of the reports note the existence of risks that they may pose due to abandoning the judicial review of the legitimacy of evidence taken by law enforcement agencies, one gets the impression that in most of the countries, the focus is rather on the benefits that these mechanisms bring in terms of the speediness and efficiency of the adjudication process. The Taiwanese report points to the convenience in terms of reduced time to adjudicate cases

87 As cited in: Anneli Soo, *Limits of freedom of public authorities with respect to obtaining evidence at the stage of investigation in Estonia*, p. 255.

88 As cited in: Alexandre Stylios, Gustave Warby, *Limits of freedom of public authorities with respect to obtaining evidence at the stage of investigation*, Canadian report, p. 216.

89 Tatsuhiko Inatani, *National Report of Japan*, p. 268.

and a more favourable court verdict in the event of a guilty plea, but also to the dissenting voices raised in legal circles or among ordinary citizens over the forms of consensual resolution of criminal cases.[90] Some of the country reports highlighted potential risks of the court abandoning to directly take evidence in an adversarial trial for those facing criminal charges. The Polish document highlights that consensual termination of criminal proceedings is subject to criticism mainly due to the standards of evidence being lowered without the defendant being awarded any additional guarantees: "Worse, there is no mechanism that forces the court in each case to verify whether the guilty plea has been delivered by the accused knowingly and willingly".[91] The Estonian approach is, however, quite different in this respect. The author of the report emphasised that the conclusion of an agreement by the parties to the proceedings (which she compared to plea bargaining) does not relieve the court of its duty to determine whether the defendant understood the consequences of its conclusion and agreed to it knowingly and willingly. Furthermore, the court is neither bound by the legal classification provided by the prosecution nor by the proposed type or extent of punishment. Another institution allows the case to be decided on the basis of the pre-trial investigation file and offers the accused the advantage of a one-third reduction in his or her sentence. Even if his or her consent to the proceedings being terminated in this manner allows the direct taking of evidence at trial to be dispensed with, the court is not relieved of its duty to assess the admissibility and legality of the evidence presented by law enforcement authorities.[92] Likewise, in Germany, where simplified modes have gained importance in the administration of criminal justice in recent years, attention has been drawn to how the suspect's interests may be jeopardised as a result of dispensing with the full evidentiary procedure. Firstly, this is a consequence of the defendant not being granted legal remedies at the pre-trial stage to effectively force the law enforcement authorities to collect evidence favourable to him or her and to provide the defence with access to the pre-trial investigation file. If a criminal warrant is issued (e.g. if the defendant fails to appear at trial), the defendant's right to be heard is violated as well. According to the German report, a requirement to obtain the court's consent to the proceedings being discontinued by the law enforcement authorities, and certain penalties or other conditions

90 Kai-Ping Su, *Limits of freedom of public authorities with respect to obtaining evidence at the stage of investigation*, pp. 240–241.

91 Karolina Kremens, *Power to Search and Its Limits in Polish Criminal Investigations* p. 187.

92 Anneli Soo, *Limits of freedom of public authorities with respect to obtaining evidence at the stage of investigation in Estonia*, p. 259.

being imposed on the defendant (Article 153a StPO), or the possibility for the defendant to object to a criminal warrant issued without his/her participation (Article 407(1) StPO) have made a sufficient system of checks and balances. Doubts are also raised in German literature on the subject about the institution of a negotiated agreement (*Verständigungsverfahren* – § 257c StPO), introduced in 2009 by the Amendment Act of 26 July 2009 on the Regulation of Agreements in the Criminal Process (BGBI. I 2009, 2353).[93] It consists in the court being relieved from the obligation to conduct an evidentiary procedure and assess the evidence in terms of criminal legal consequences to be suffered by the defendant. However, even if such agreement has been concluded by the parties, this does not imply that the evidentiary procedure before the court is completely abandoned, as the court needs to make findings of fact and the defendant's guilt. At the same time, it is recognised in the German literature on the subject that it would be pointless to keep the same standard of proof in cases where an agreement has been concluded as in traditionally tried cases.

5 Identifications of Risks of Violating Freedom in the Acquisition of Evidence by Law Enforcement Authorities

In most of the reports, in the section dealing with extensive law enforcement activities aimed at acquiring evidence of the defendant's guilt, particular attention was paid to the issue of interrogations, which may indicate that ensuring adequate procedural safeguards during the conduct of this activity is an important challenge.

In Turkey, as already mentioned, the prohibition to compel statements incriminating a given person or a member of his or her immediate family or to provide evidence of this nature has been anchored in the Constitution (Article 38(5)). Additionally, this issue is regulated in great detail in both the Criminal Procedure Act and the substantive law. According to the wording of Article 148 of the Code of Criminal Procedure, evidentiary statements by the suspect or accused person must be made voluntarily. The use of torture, ill-treatment of the interrogated person, administration of drugs, deception, induced fatigue, use of force, threats and certain objects are considered inadmissible. The prohibition of inadmissible interrogation methods that tamper with free will is

---

93 A. Sinn, *Porozumienie w niemieckim procesie karnym* [*Agreement in the German criminal trial*] (*§ 257 c STPO*). in: *Nowe tendencje w prawie karnym procesowym: Niemcy, Polska, Ukraina*. [*New tendencies in law of criminal procedure: Germany, Poland, Ukraine*] ed. F-Ch Schroeder, T. De Vries, Bialystok 2016, p. 208.

linked to a ban on using statements for evidentiary purposes, even if they have been made with consent (Article 148(3) of the Code of Criminal Procedure). In addition to physical or moral interference, promises of unlawful benefit are also considered to be circumstances that prevent statements made from being deemed as voluntary. It has been demonstrated by analogy which interventions in the law are physical or moral interventions that affect free will. The Turkish Constitutional Court in the case of Cezmi Demir and others[94] clarified what is meant by the term "misbehaviour", indicating that it is: "beating, making startling or loud noises, spitting, reflecting bright light, throwing something dirty on one's body, dragging, gagging, negligent acts such as not allowing medical treatment, or not giving food." At the same time, the Turkish legislature has defined the term "torture", which is considered to be acts that cause physical or mental suffering to a person, incompatible with human dignity, affecting perception or willpower, and humiliation (Article 94 of the Turkish Criminal Code "*Türk Ceza Kanunu*"). Any statement or evidence obtained by these methods are against the law.

According to the authors of the Hungarian report, in addition to the exclusion of evidence obtained by the procedural authorities as a result of a criminal offence, the use of prohibited means or a substantial violation of the rights of the participants in the proceedings, it is also a criminal offence for public officials to extort statements to be used in the course of the proceedings.[95] The Hungarian Code of Criminal Procedure provides for a number of evidentiary prohibitions applicable to the interrogation activities and methods, the violation of formal requirements envisaged for that purpose, and detailed conditions attached to particular means of evidence (Article 169 Section 3; Article 177 Section 3; Article 185 Section 3; Article 196 Section 3; Article 223 Section 3; Article 229 Section 5, Article 238 Section 5; Article 254 Section 1; Article 255 Section 7; Article 262 Section 3; Article 303 Section 3; Article 314 Section 2; Article 314 Section 2; Article 346 Section 2; Article 406 Section 2; Article 409 Section 4; and Article 414 Section 3). In each of the aforesaid cases the appropriate evidence must not be used, and it is not possible to legally validate the defective action. In addition pursuant to Article 303 of the Hungarian Criminal Code, an attempt to compel another person to provide information, to make a statement or to conceal information by actual or threatened use of force or other similar means is subject to penalty. Irrespective of this, in general, a fact derived from a means of the proof obtained by the authority through a

---

94 Complaint no. 2013/293, (17.07.2014), section 84.

95 Csongor Herke, Barbara Szabó, *Limits of freedom of public authorities with respect to obtaining evidence at the stage of investigation.* HUNGARY, p. 140.

criminal offence, by other prohibited means or by a material violation of the criminal rights of participants cannot be assessed as evidence (§ 167 (5)).[96]

Likewise, Article 156 of the Criminal Procedure Code of Taiwan stipulates that a confession that has not been extracted by violence, threat, inducement, fraud, exhausting interrogation, unlawful detention or other improper means and is consistent with facts may be admitted as evidence. According to the author of the report, the essential mechanism for complying with the requirements set by this regulation, as amended in 2003, is the construction of the burden of proof: "If the accused claims that his confession was extracted by improper means, his confession shall be investigated prior to investigating other evidence; if the said confession is presented by the public prosecutor, the court shall order the public prosecutor to prove the method used to obtain the confession".[97]

As noted in the Canadian report, the means of countering violations of regulations on evidence acquisition by law enforcement agencies is primarily to exclude evidence so obtained. However, pursuant to Article 24(2) of the Charter, this may also lead to the proceedings being discontinued, as well as compensation being awarded to such person if, in the court's view, the prosecutor acted in bad faith or with malicious intent (cf. Henry v British Columbia (Attorney General).[98]

In Estonia, measures to counteract such situations are that participants in the proceedings and other persons are given an opportunity to complain to the public prosecutor's office about a procedural act or decision made in breach of procedural rules, where they resulted in individual rights being violated. Additionally, the suspect is granted the possibility to apply to the Chancellor of Justice (cf. Sections 228 and 34 of the Estonian Code of Criminal Procedure, respectively).[99]

In Germany, Article 136a of StPO is of key importance for interrogation activities.[100] It forbids ill-treatment, induced fatigue, physical intervention on the body, the administration of drugs, torture, deception or hypnosis. Threats and compulsion must be based on the measures provided for in criminal

96 Csongor Herke, Barbara Szabó, *Limits of freedom of public authorities with respect to obtaining evidence at the stage of investigation. HUNGARY*, p. 141 et seq.

97 Kai-Ping Su, *Limits of freedom of public authorities with respect to obtaining evidence at the stage of investigation*, pp. 241–242.

98 Henry v British Columbia (Attorney General).

99 Anneli Soo, *Limits of freedom of public authorities with respect to obtaining evidence at the stage of investigation in Estonia*, pp. 259–260.

100 Anne Schneider, *Limits of freedom of public authorities with respect to obtaining evidence at the stage of investigation*, p. 100.

procedure law. Measures which impair the suspect's memory or his capacity to understand the wrongfulness of an act are also forbidden, § 136a StPO also applies to the interrogation of witnesses (§ 69(3) StPO). The evidence is excluded by law (§ 136a(3)2 StPO). Furthermore, the report stresses that German law allows the use of oppressive investigative measures, violation of human dignity within certain limits or use of measures forcing citizens to comply with evidentiary obligations only if they do not unreasonably undermine the rights and freedoms guaranteed by the Constitution. As a rule, such actions are to be counteracted by imposing an obligation upon the public prosecution office to ascertain both incriminating and exonerating circumstances (Article 160(2) StPO). In addition to the possibility to complain about the actions of the law enforcement authorities and to object to their use of evidence in the proceedings, according to Article 93(1)(4a) of the Basic Law, if one of the fundamental rights is deemed to have been infringed by the public authority, a citizen may also lodge a constitutional complaint following an unsuccessful judicial review (*Verfassungsbeschwerde*). With several judgments having been issued by the European Court of Human Rights in German cases,[101] a debate has been sparked on the extent to which individuals can be provoked to provide incriminating evidence against themselves. Even though Article 136a StPO states that it is not permitted to mislead a suspect: the line between legal undercover missions and forbidden deceptions is small.[102] According to the author of the report, the current discussion concerns the consequences of using provocation against the defendant, e.g. in the form of a reduced sentence or even discontinuation of proceedings.

Polish law does not contain any rules that would comprehensively address the legality of evidence. There are, however, a few regulations that tackle the issue. The criteria of the legality of evidence can be divided into positive and negative conditions. The interrogation conditions are laid down in Article 171 of the CCP. In Poland, the use of prohibited or oppressive methods or methods violating human dignity by law enforcement authorities is documented in the annual reports of the National Mechanism for Prevention of Torture, operating in the Ombudsman Office. The need for proper implementation of the six EU Directives issued in the aftermath of the Stockholm Programme, which focus on the rights of suspected and accused persons in criminal proceedings, such as ensuring access to a lawyer at an early stage of the proceedings, is identified

101 *Furcht v. Germany* App no 54648/09 (ECtHR, 23 October 2014); *Akbay v. Germany* App no 40495/15 (ECtHR, 15 October 2020).

102 Anne Schneider, *Limits of freedom of public authorities with respect to obtaining evidence at the stage of investigation*, pp. 87–88.

as measures to counter such practices. Other desirable measures called for by the Helsinki Foundation for Human Rights are: the mandatory recording of interrogations and other procedural actions concerning the suspect, as well as the use of body-worn cameras by officers to record police actions at the scene.[103]

As the author of the Italian report states, interrogation is subject to strict regulations due to the risk of abuse by public authorities, such as the use of threats and other methods violating human dignity. The use of methods or techniques which are likely to affect the freedom of self-determination or to alter the capacity to remember and evaluate facts, which are detrimental to human dignity, is prohibited. Particular manifestations of abuse by public officials are subject to penalization and disciplinary liability.[104]

The Japanese report stresses the existence of threats that may arise during interrogation activities. Article 36 of the JC is of fundamental importance as it prohibits torture. The term "torture" is interpreted broadly, also covering actions that affect a person's consciousness.[105]

It is also evident from the content of the submitted reports that in none of the described systems particular evidentiary value is attributed to specific sources or means of evidence (including scientific evidence). In Estonia, the fact that the principle of free assessment of evidence applies has been repeatedly emphasised by the Supreme Court.[106] This principle is also expressed in Article 217 of the Turkish Code of Criminal Procedure. The court, when passing judgments, is to be guided primarily by whether the fact in question is established with full conviction and full faith: The "conscientious evidence system", which emerged as the opposite of the legal evidence system and accepted in Turkish law, expresses both the freedom of evidence and the freedom to evaluate evidence".[107]

The reports highlighted that when analysing the practice, one may get an impression of some evidence being given special weight.

In Taiwan, special importance is given to the confession of the accused, even if the principle that it cannot be the only basis for conviction has been introduced in the Taiwanese legal system if the accused claims that his

103 Karolina Kremens, *Power to Search and Its Limits in Polish Criminal Investigations*, p. 192.

104 Thomas Di Candia, *Italian Evidence Law System: Limits to the Investigative Power*, pp. 168–169.

105 Tatsuhiko Inatani, *National Report of Japan*, p. 270.

106 Anneli Soo, *Limits of freedom of public authorities with respect to obtaining evidence at the stage of investigation in Estonia*, p. 260.

107 Haluk Toroslu, Uğur Orhan, Bedirhan Erdem, *On Limits of Freedom of Public Authorities with Respect to Obtaining Evidence at the Stage of Investigation under Turkish Criminal Procedure and Evidence Law*, p. 114.

confession was extracted by violence, threat, inducement, fraud, exhausting interrogation, unlawful detention or other improper means; in such a case, the trial authorities are obliged to seek other evidence in order to establish the probative value of the confession (Article 156 of the Code of Criminal Procedure).[108] The German report also points out that, despite the principle of free evaluation of evidence having been adopted in the German system, some evidence is attributed greater credibility than the other (e.g. it is assumed that the defendant's relatives are granted the right to refuse to testify due to their testimony being considered unreliable).[109] In Poland, there is an increase in importance of expert evidence and the insufficiently critical approach of the courts to the assessment of that means of proof. This is particularly true of medical experts in cases where it is necessary to establish the nature of injuries. This observation does not, however, apply to all experts. While DNA testing is seen as trustworthy, evidence from osmological testing is considered less reliable. By contrast, in Hungary, the over-reliance on DNA evidence is the subject of criticism due to the increased costs of proceedings. It has been found that the prosecutor's office orders it in all anti-life and anti-health cases (where comparative material exists), even if the defendant has pleaded guilty and despite the existence of other evidence.[110] In this respect, the Italian report says that the current system does not provide for a hierarchy of evidence, yet it is evident that in practice scientific evidence plays an increasingly important role. Therefore, in order to protect the accused person and guarantee an adversarial process even in the taking of scienific evidence, the Code of Criminal Procedure generally provides that the accused person may be assised by a technical advisor during the oerations at both the investigation and trial stages.[111] As pointed out in the Canadian report, a tendency to hierarchize evidence in favour of scientific evidence and at the expense of other pieces of evidence can pose a risk. In this system, courts are, however, bound by the standards set by the Supreme Court when making their assessment. In R. v. Mohan, it was emphasised that evidence, apart from meeting the general criteria for being admitted, such as logical relevance and necessity for the facts to be established, cannot be excluded. In addition, the expert must be sufficiently qualified, while the court is obliged to assess, based on a cost-benefit analysis, whether that evidence is

108 Kai-Ping Su, *Limits of freedom of public authorities with respect to obtaining evidence at the stage of investigation*, pp. 241–242.

109 Anne Schneider, *Limits of freedom of public authorities with respect to obtaining evidence at the stage of investigation*, pp. 98–99.

110 Csongor Herke, Barbara Szabó, *Limits of freedom of public authorities with respect to obtaining evidence at the stage of investigation. HUNGARY*, pp. 140–141.

111 Thomas Di Candia, *Italian Evidence Law System: Limits to the Investigative Power*, p. 167.

admissible in terms of its credibility: "*the judge not to be obsequious and uncritical when scrutinising the scientific evidence that is adduced, the judge must not abdicate their role as the ultimate arbiter when evaluating the admissibility of evidence and – in the absence of a jury – its probative value.*" Furthermore, the text of the cited judgment emphasises that the logical connection between the fact proved and the fact to be proved must be significant if the expert uses a new theory or research method. In that case, the idea of a decisive expertise is evoked, which means that the judge needs to be more vigilant to check how far the evidence is logically related to the fact that it is to establish. To do so, the judge should answer four questions. First: What is the nature of the matter to which the evidence refers (an important or incidental/crucial matter or accessory)? Is the deduction drawn from the new scientific theory really related to a fact important in the case? Another issue that the judge should determine is the degree of adequacy of the conclusions drawn (minor or significant) and to what extent they are subjective in methodological terms. The final issue for the judge to decide is the matter of substantive applicability and whether the scientific theory supports the facts established in the case.[112]

An important part of the issue under analysis is the attitude of legislators and law enforcement bodies to new technologies being used in criminal proceedings. In this respect, the standards are all but uniform. The author of the Polish report notices that Polish law responds very slowly to the new challenges emerging from the developments of new technologies,[113] which results in a large number of undetected acts of cybercrime or failure to identify their perpetrators. The last changes in this area were introduced between 2003 and 2004 and concerned the seizure of electronic correspondence. With no adequate and effective legislative steps being taken, the exchange of information via various social media platforms is not covered by an adequate standard of protection of the right to privacy, as no court order is required here: while the lower standard of protection triggered by prosecutorial warrants is designed to intercept "static" content, such as packages or letters, including those sent by email, the tapping of conversations is regulated by a higher standard demanding judicial warrant, which is justified by the "dynamic" nature of the telephone or live conversations Significant practical problems also arise with the question of law enforcers' right to search mobile phones of arrested persons and to gain access to the information contained therein not being sufficiently regulated.

112 R. v Mohan ([1994] 2 SCR 9 – as cited in: Alexandre Stylios, Gustave Warby, *Limits of freedom of public authorities with respect to obtaining evidence at the stage of investigation. Canadian report*, p. 222.

113 Karolina Kremens, *Power to Search and Its Limits in Polish Criminal Investigations*, p. 202.

The German national report takes a more approving tone of the legislator's actions and acknowledges its attempts to keep up with technological changes, as well as biological innovations, by introducing appropriate regulations on how they might possibly be used for evidentiary purposes. This is a consequence of the enforcement authorities being already subject to the existing restrictive legal regulations, as mentioned above. As an example of this trend, the report cites the regulations on covert, remote searches of information and communications technology systems (*Online-Durchsuchung*). In the debate preceding the introduction of the provision of Article 100b StPO in 2017, it was pointed out that it was permissible under pre-existing legislation. That interpretation was negated by the Federal Court of Justice in 2007,[114] which confirmed the need for appropriate regulations to be enacted. The general rules allowing investigative measures (Articles 161(1) and 163(1) StPO) apply to actions by trial authorities that slightly impair the fundamental rights and do not involve any highly intrusive measures. Hence, according to the author of the report, similar changes apply to the issue of biological evidence.

With respect to new technologies being used in criminal procedure, the Italian report states that case-law tolerates the use by the public authorities of non-regulated investigative activities, applying only the general principles of unsuitability to affect a person's freedom of self-determination and the moral freedom of the person when assessing the usability of evidence collected in investigations. In this way, the recourse to atypical activities based on the use of advanced technologies, such as GPS tracking and the use of the Trojan malware for purposes other than acoustic surveillance (such as acquiring the content of a mobile device or to remotely activate the camera or, again, to record the screen or, finally, to steal passwords), may result in serious violations of fundamental rights, in particular the right to privacy (Article 8 of the ECHR), due to the lack of a legal basis.[115]

In Japan, scientific evidence is not privileged in the fact-finding process in the case where a suspicious scientific evidence leads to the conviction of the innocent. Evidently, a reliable scientific evidence is introduced to trial, including DNA testing; however, Japanese judges are generally very cautious in reviewing its admissibility which requires the competence of an examiner, scientific accuracy and reliability of the method, and an appropriate procedure for scientific examination.[116]

114 BGHSt 51, 211 – as cited in: Anne Schneider, *Limits of freedom of public authorities with respect to obtaining evidence at the stage of investigation*, pp. 99–100.

115 Thomas Di Candia, *Italian Evidence Law System: Limits to the Investigative Power*, p. 172 et seq.

116 Tatsuhiko Inatani, *National Report of Japan*, p. 269.

In contrast, Estonia's rules on the use of new technological means in law enforcement work are significantly influenced by the case law of the Court of Justice of the European Union (C-746/18). In a preliminary ruling, the Court assumed that the use of a person's movement or location data by public authorities is generally not allowed as evidence. An exception to this rule may be justified by action to combat serious crime or to prevent a serious threat to public security. Consequently, the national legislation allowing the prosecution to access such data was declared invalid.[117] The Estonian Supreme Court has ruled that it is inadmissible to store mobile phone location data for the purposes of criminal proceedings.[118]

In Taiwan, as a general rule, the regulations on obtaining evidence apply to all proceedings, regardless of the crime type. There are, however, some cases where the seriousness of the act may affect the scope of powers vested in the investigating authorities. Section 11 of the Communication Security and Surveillance Act stipulates that the prosecutor may access the content of recorded conversations and information about communicating persons, under a court order in the case of offences punishable by imprisonment of at least three years. Two exceptions to this rule have been introduced. Firstly, in the case of offences punishable by a sentence of up to 3 years' imprisonment, access to such data should be prohibited. Secondly, if the offence under investigation is punishable by a minimum imprisonment of ten years or falls under a specific crime category (such as robbery, human trafficking or drug offences), the prosecutor may access the relevant data *ex officio*, without the court's consent. The use of new technologies to obtain evidence (e.g. drones or surveillance cameras) is subject to general rules, and the key question to be considered in this context is whether their use involves a violation of human rights. As the author of the report states: "My general impression is that Taiwan's law enforcement is not keen to apply new technology to investigate crimes and collect evidence, perhaps because they know using new technology may be controversial and may result in the suppression of evidence".[119]

117 ECJ 02.03.2021, C-746/18, or a preliminary ruling under Article 267 TFEU from the Riigikohus (Supreme Court, Estonia), made by decision of 12 November 2018, received at the Court on 29 November 2018, in criminal proceedings against H. K., other party: Prokuratuur.

118 Ruling of the Supreme Court 1-16-6179, 18.06.2021 – as cited in: – as cited in: Anneli Soo, Limits of freedom of public authorities with respect to obtaining evidence at the stage of investigation in Estonia, p. 261.

119 Kai-Ping Su, *Limits of freedom of public authorities with respect to obtaining evidence at the stage of investigation*, p. 244.

As pointed out in the Hungarian report, no specific standards for digital or biological evidence have been introduced in the Hungarian law, and in the opinion of its authors "it is not typical that the use of modern methods would lead to the withering of traditional law enforcement techniques."[120]

6 Inviolable Boundaries in the Acquisition of Evidence by Law Enforcement Authorities

It seems to be a general rule that the more a certain measure of evidence interferes in the sphere of personal rights and freedoms, the higher is the legal rank and the level of detail and restrictiveness of the provision that regulates it. The above applies, for instance, to the conditions for a flat to be searched or subject to a wiretap, as set out in Article 13 of the German Basic Law (*Grundgesetz*). Article 35 of the Japanese Constitution of 1946 guarantees the citizens the right to the inviolability of home, documents and property thus preventing incursion, search, and seizure, unless a warrant was issued for a reasonable cause, which specifies in detail the place subject to search and the objects subject to seizure, or if circumstances set out in Article 33 occur. The Turkish report emphasises the constitutional nature of the principle that prohibits forcing anyone to give incriminating statements against himself or herself or against persons close to him or her or to give evidence under these conditions (Article 38(5) of the Constitution). A similar solution is anchored in Article 22(3) of the Estonian Constitution. In Poland, some general grounds concerning rules of evidence are provided in the Constitution, for example in Article 40 on the prohibition of the use of torture, Article 42(3) on the presumption of evidence, Article 49 on the freedom of communication and Article 50 on the inviolability of home and searches. The Canadian report points out that the 1982 Constitution Act sets out the conditions of obtaining and adducing evidence to the extent that they conform to the constitutionally entrenched rights, such as: s. 7 (life, liberty, and security of persons); s. 8 (protection against illegal search and seizure); s. 9 (protection against unlawful detention and arrest) and s. 10b) (right to instruct counsel). The Canadian *Charter of Rights and Freedoms* provides for remedy in the event that these rights are violated, notably at ss. 24(1) (just and appropriate remedy) and 24(2) (exclusion of evidence obtained via a violation of one's constitutional rights). The importance of the Canadian Constitution Act is also illustrated by the fact that any law or regulation can be found to be

120 Csongor Herke, Barbara Szabó, *Limits of freedom of public authorities with respect to obtaining evidence at the stage of investigation.* HUNGARY, p. 141.

in contradiction with the Constitution (Article 52). In Hungary, the main rules of evidentiary procedure are primarily reflected in the Code of Criminal Procedure. The Hungarian Constitution enshrines values that significantly – even though rather generally – contribute to the formation of appropriate evidentiary procedure standards, such as the prohibition of torture and other cruel, inhuman or degrading treatment (Article 54(2)), the principle of respect and protection of human rights (Article 8(1)), or human dignity (Article 54(1)). In Italy, in addition to the systemic principles of legal order expressed in the Constitution and significant for defining the rules of evidentiary activities in criminal procedure, also norms directly regulating this sphere exist (Article 111 of the Constitution). In Japan, the most important principles of the law of evidence are grounded in the Constitution (Chapter III).

Even if the extent to which the law of evidence is entrenched in the Constitution from one state to another, it can be assumed that its vital provisions have constitutional force. This is most true for the values that are fundamental to our civilisation and of vital – even though rather general – importance for criminal proceedings. One of them is human dignity, which has been given the highest normative rank in many states, being considered the basis of the political system and social order, and an inviolable value to be observed and protected by public authority. Similar importance is attached to the prohibition of torture and other cruel, inhuman or degrading treatment or punishment, which is universally present in the states' Constitutions. At the level of rules set in the law of evidence, which enjoy the highest legal protection, there is no room for freedom of public authorities. Any manifestation of such freedom must be considered unlawful, and such violation must result in the evidence being automatically deemed inadmissible and subject to immediate exclusion. The point is that this effect is not always defined strictly and clearly enough by the relevant legal provisions. It is quite common, that they do not specify a procedure for such defective evidence to be eliminated, either. Consequently, the inviolable limits in the acquisition of evidence in criminal proceedings cannot be consistently and comprehensively defined, as illustrated by the examples from the legal systems of the countries whose reports we analysed. This is only possible at a high level of generality. Despite the general recognition of common values, there is no uniform system for them to be reflected in the law. Thus, differences in how inviolable limits in the acquisition of evidence by law enforcement authorities need to be illustrated with specific examples.

In the German report, it was stated that the most important provision concerning the method of acquiring evidence is § 136a StPO. It forbids ill-treatment, induced fatigue, physical intervention on the body, the administration of drugs, torture, deception or hypnosis. Threats and compulsion must be based on the measures provided for in criminal procedure law. Measures which impair the suspect's memory or his capacity to understand the wrongfulness of an act are also forbidden. The evidence is excluded by law (§ 136a(3)2 StPO). Same as the one from the polygraph test, which is deemed to lack probative value. An absolute evidence ban also applies to evidence from interrogation of persons who have not been informed of the right to refuse to remain silent in the cases provided for by law, and to evidence from interrogation obtained before the person interrogated exercises that right. Another category of inviolable bans is related to the special status of a person entitled to refuse to testify. This is the case of a defence counsel, a lawyer, a person providing legal services, a clergyman and other specified persons (Article 160a(1) StPO). Another important provision is Article 100d(1) StPO, which sets a general rule that any evidence that leads to findings in the core areas of private conduct of life is excluded from trial. There is a consensus to recognise evidence obtained in violation of the prohibition on seizure as inadmissible (Article 97 StPO). An absolute evidence ban applies to the course of the judges' deliberations on the verdict and to a previous conviction in the same case. In addition to general evidence bans, there are also casuistic cases (e.g. Article 108(2) StPO).[121]

The Polish regulation of evidence bans shows a number of similarities with the solutions adopted in Germany, still Polish doctrine has developed its own concepts. There is a generally accepted division of evidence bans in the Polish literature on the subject into three categories: the ban on using certain evidence acquisition methods,[122] the ban on proving by certain means of evidence,[123]

121 For example, if a medical doctor's practice is searched and objects are seized that point at an illegal abortion by a patient, § 108(2) StPO states that these objects cannot be used as evidence against the patient. Other rules limiting the use of or excluding evidence that has been found by chance are §§ 161(3), 479(2), 100e(6) no 1 and 81a(3) StPO.

122 This category consists of: prohibition of the use of force or illicit threats during interrogation or hypnosis, chemical substances or technical means in order to influence physical processes in the body of the testifying person or to allow monitor of the unconscious reactions of the body; prohibition of obtaining testimonial evidence from the suspect/accused and witnesses as well as other statements in conditions precluding freedom of expression; prohibition of supplementing testimonial evidence by documents and notes (Article 171 CCP).

123 This category consists of: prohibition of interrogating a priest as to facts of which he learned during confession; prohibition of interrogating a defence counsel or a lawyer providing arrestee with legal advice on issues covered by lawyer–client privilege; prohibition of interrogating a mediator as to facts that he learned about from the accused or the victim during mediation; prohibition of obtaining an opinion from an expert witness who is incompetent to deliver such an opinion in that case due to his or her relation to the case or its participants; prohibition of the use of a statement of the accused made to a medical expert witness or to a physician providing medical assistance concerning the act that he is accused of; prohibition of a physical examination of a victim who has refused to testify executing her or his privilege.

and the ban on proving certain facts.[124] In this group, the bans not subject to revocation under any circumstances are the following: the prohibition to prove again a criminal offence once validly adjudicated; the prohibition to prove a right or legal relation against the constitutive findings of another court; the prohibition to prove the course of judges' deliberations and voting method; the prohibition to prove the content of the testimony of a witness who exercised his or her right to remain silent; and the prohibition to use previously given testimony if the witness subsequently refused to testify. The classification of evidence excluded by law is a compromise between different interests. It reflects the respect for the principle of truth in Polish criminal proceedings, but also for values such as human dignity, family and other close relationships, religious beliefs, and others. With these numerous evidence bans applied in Polish criminal proceedings being so strictly formulated, one might expect that the consequences of their violation would be defined in a similarly rigorous manner – this is, however, not the case. Article 171(7) CCP stipulates that testimony of interrogated persons obtained in breach of the prohibition to use force or illicit threats during interrogation or hypnosis, chemical substances or technical means in order to influence physical processes in the testifying person's body or to allow the monitoring of the unconscious reactions of the body cannot be deemed as evidence. Violation of these prohibitions at the investigation stage can only be established when the case is examined by the court, which compromises the meaning of their categorical and inviolable nature.[125]

In Italy, legal provisions protecting the basic civil rights and freedoms are of key importance. Among them, there is Article 188 of the CCP that excludes evidence obtained with certain methods and techniques that may affect the freedom of self-determination and the evaluation of the facts. Article 189 thereof has a similar function, according to which evidence not regulated by the law is admissible, providing it is suitable for the determination of the facts and does not compromise the person's freedom. And finally, evidence is prohibited that violates prohibitions laid down in law (Article 191 of the CCP).[126]

---

124 This group includes: prohibition of proving the committing of a crime for which the reoffending defendant has been already convicted; prohibition of proving a right contrary to a constitutive decision of another court; prohibition of proving the conduct of judges deliberations and voting; prohibition of proving the content of testimony given by a witness who has exercised his or her right to refuse to testify; prohibition of proving facts and circumstances concerning the crown witness.

125 Karolina Kremens, *Power to Search and Its Limits in Polish Criminal Investigations*, p. 200.

126 Thomas Di Candia, *Italian Evidence Law System: Limits to the Investigative Power*, pp. 171–172.

In Turkey, with the Act of 3 October 2001 (Act No. 4709), the provision stipulating that "findings obtained illegally cannot be accepted as evidence" was introduced into the Constitution (Article 38(6) of the Constitution). From this regulation, legal scholars and commentators derive an absolute ban on using directly illegal evidence in a criminal trial; opinions diverge, however, as to whether the constitutional ban also covers indirectly illegal evidence. There are some Turkish legal scholars and commentators who share this view, the majority tends, however, to consider the ban on decisions based on illegal evidence as absolute. The categorical wording of Article 38(6) of the Constitution actually excludes the freedom of trial authorities to obtain evidence. Another provision of the Turkish Constitution prohibits anyone from being compelled to make a statement that would incriminate themselves, their legal next of kin, or from presenting such incriminating evidence (Article 38(5) of the Constitution). There is a consensus that the suspect cannot be convicted based on his or her testimony obtained through unlawful interrogation methods, e.g. physical or mental violence, torture, ill-treatment, induced fatigue, deception, threats, even with his or her consent. Nor does the defendant's consent waive the illegality of other evidentiary activities. Established evidence bans cover various individual situations.[127] The limits for certain evidence to be used in criminal proceedings (e.g. evidence from a wiretap or recording of correspondence) are defined by indicting specific types of offences for which a certain measure, which is otherwise deemed illegal, can be used. The Turkish criminal procedure law was reported to be mostly homogeneous in its approach towards illegal evidence. A collective evaluation of the above mentioned provisions of the Constitution and the CPC demonstrate very clearly that a verdict cannot be made based on evidence obtained illegally.[128]

The Japanese Constitution regulates a number of aspects of the law of evidence. In addition to Article 35 thereof mentioned above (the right to privacy),

---

127 E.g. pursuant to CPC Article 253/20, it is not possible to use the statements made during the mediation negotiations as evidence in any investigation, prosecution, or lawsuit; pursuant to CPC Article 250/10 it is not possible to use suspect's acceptance of the accelerated procedure, and accompanying documentation for application to accelerated procedure, as evidence in subsequent investigation and prosecutions; in accordance with Article 210/2, the testimony obtained in the investigation phase of a witness who has exercised his right to withdraw at the hearing cannot be used as evidence; in accordance with Article 140, it is not possible to use the findings obtained as a result of monitoring the suspect or the accused's residence with technical means as evidence.

128 Haluk Toroslu, Uğur Orhan, Bedirhan Erdem, *On Limits of Freedom of Public Authorities with Respect to Obtaining Evidence at the Stage of Investigation under Turkish Criminal Procedure and Evidence Law*, p. 116 et seq.

the defendant is guaranteed under Article 37 to have unrestricted opportunity to have all the witnesses interrogated, together with the right to compulsorily bring defence witnesses for interrogation at the expense of the state. Article 38 of the Japanese Constitution expresses the prohibition to force anyone to testify against himself and provides that confession made under compulsion, torture or threat, or after a prolonged arrest or detention must not be admitted as evidence, and in addition – it excludes convicting or punishing the defendant if the only evidence against him is his own confession.[129]

In Hungary, the general principle of absolute inadmissibility of evidence in a criminal trial is expressed in Article 167(5) of the Code of Criminal Procedure, which stipulates that a fact derived from a means of the proof obtained by the authority through a criminal offence, by other prohibited means or by a material violation of the criminal rights of participants cannot be assessed as evidence. Specific prohibitions concern particular procedural situations.[130]

129 Tatsuhiko Inatani, *National Report of Japan*, p. 265 and p. 270.

130 The testimony of a witness questioned in breach of the provisions on impediments to giving evidence cannot be taken into account as a means of proof (Section 169 (3)); in the event of failure to record a witness warning or a response to a warning, the witness's testimony shall not be taken into account as a means of proof, unless the witness maintains his or her previous communication after the witness warning (§ 177 (3)); in the event of failure to record the defendant's (Miranda) warning and the response to the warning, the defendant's testimony shall not be taken into account as a means of proof, unless the defendant has already received a warning previously charged during the proceedings and his defence counsel was present during his continued questioning, or he maintains his previous communication after the defendant's warning (§ 185 (3)); the communication of the accused, witness and victim to the expert concerning the subject matter of the investigation, the investigation procedures and instruments, or the changes in the subject matter of the investigation or the act on which the proceedings are based shall not be used as evidence (196 (3)); if the court or the public prosecutor's office rejects the motion for retrospective authorisation of the disguised device, the result of the use of the disguised instrument subject to authorisation shall not be used as evidence and the data thus obtained shall be deleted without delay (§ 223 (3)); § 229 (5); § 238 (5); the result of the use of a disguised instrument subject to judicial authorisation shall not be used as evidence if the person concerned is a person acting as a defender or a relative or a person subject to a witness barrier against whom a disguised instrument subject to judicial authority would not have been applicable (§ 254 (1)); the result of the use of the undercover investigator cannot be used as evidence if the public prosecutor's office does not intend to use the result of the use of the undercover investigator as evidence, and becoming known for the fact of employing an undercover detective would directly endanger the life, physical integrity and personal freedom of the undercover detective (§ 255 (7)); if the request for data subject to authorisation is not authorised by the public prosecutor's office, the data thus obtained cannot be used as evidence and must be deleted immediately (§ 262 (3)); if the research is to be ordered by a court (research to be carried out in a notarial or law firm) and is not ordered by the court, the result thereof

In the Hungarian report, it was underlined that in the event of a breach of the bans on proof expressly or implicitly formulated in the Hungarian Criminal Prosecution Act, or in the case of obtaining evidence in violation of the Constitution or of the Hungarian Criminal Code, the evidence will be completely excluded, and that there is no possible remedial to rectify this (e.g. in the event of failure to warn the witness or the accused). At the same time, it is pointed out that, after the regime change in 1990, coercing confessions through violence or threats is rare in Hungary.[131]

In the Taiwanese Code of Criminal Procedure, the prohibition of certain methods of obtaining evidence and of using evidence form one common category. This is because evidence obtained in violation of the conditions for its acquisition set out in the Code is excluded. This applies when the provisions of Article 100–1 of the Code of Criminal Procedure are violated (if there is an inconsistency between the content of the written record and that of the audio or video recording regarding the statements made by the accused, the said portion of the statement will not be used as evidence). Evidence obtained from the confession by or any other unfavourable statement from the defendant in breach of Article 93–1(2) or Article 100–3(1) will also be excluded.[132] The preceding provision does not apply to a situation where it is proved that the said violation was not in bad faith and the confession or statement concerned was made voluntarily out of free will. Furthermore, pursuant to Article 158–3 CCP if a witness or expert witness fails to sign an affidavit that his statement is truthful, as required by the law, his testimony or expert opinion will not be admitted as evidence. In addition to the regulations explicitly prohibiting the

---

cannot be used as evidence (§ 303 (3)); if the public prosecutor's office or the court does not order the seizure of the sealed document, the document may not be used as a means of proof in the ongoing case or in other criminal proceedings (§ 314 (2)); in the event of termination of the preparatory proceedings, the data obtained in the course thereof may not be used as evidence in criminal proceedings (§ 346 (2)); if the suspect accepts and fulfils the measure or decision envisaged by the public prosecutor's office and its conditions, or if the prospect of action or decision of the public prosecutor's office was unlawful, his testimony to that effect cannot be taken into account as evidence (§ 406 (2)); if the public prosecutor's office and the defendant have not reached an agreement, the initiative and the related case-file may not be used as evidence or as a means of proof (§ 409 (4)); the statement made by the suspect and the victim during the mediation procedure cannot be used as evidence in the case (§ 414 (3)).

131 Csongor Herke, Barbara Szabó, *Limits of freedom of public authorities with respect to obtaining evidence at the stage of investigation.* *HUNGARY*, p. 144.

132 The violations cited in the report relate to the conditions for holding interrogations, which are broadly and casuistically formulated in the Taiwanese Code of Criminal Procedure.

use of certain evidence and thus setting impassable limits on the acquisition of evidence, there are some subjective restrictions. They originate from Article 158(4) of the Code of Criminal Procedure which stipulates that "(t)he admissibility of the evidence, obtained in violation of the procedure prescribed by the law by an official in execution of criminal procedure, shall be determined by balancing the protection of human rights with the preservation of public interests, unless otherwise provided by law".[133]

There is a provision in the Estonian Code of Criminal Procedure which stipulates that "(e)vidence shall be taken in a manner which is not prejudicial to the honour and dignity of the persons participating in the taking of the evidence, does not endanger their life or health or cause unjustified proprietary damage. Evidence shall not be taken by torturing a person or using violence against him or her in any other manner or by means affecting a person's memory capacity or degrading his or her human dignity" (CCP, § 64 (1)). The most restrictive conditions apply to surveillance evidence, which interferes the most with the sphere of individual's rights and freedoms. These are: covertly watching a person, thing or area, covertly taking comparative samples and performing initial examinations, covertly examining a thing and covertly replacing it. These measures can only be decided by the court. The Court's permit is also required for conducting searches of a notary's office or an attorney's law office or those of persons processing information for journalistic purposes, if there is reason to believe that the suspect used or uses the site or vehicle to be searched at the time of commission of a criminal act or during the pre-court proceedings, and the person is suspected of committing a more serious crime specified in the Code of Criminal Procedure. The Estonian Supreme Court has ruled that an evidentiary activity carried out by an investigative body without the court's permission is automatically inadmissible. Furthermore, even if the permit has been issued by the Court, but without sufficient grounds or incorrectly in some other way, the evidence collected via surveillance activities is still automatically inadmissible.[134]

133 The criteria for this assessment are as follows: the scenario where legal proceedings were violated in obtaining evidence; the intention of the people who violated legal process to obtain evidence; the kinds and degrees of rights and interests of the suspects and defendants that were infringed; the risks or harms of the investigated criminal offenses; the deterrence effect, towards future illegal evidence collection, if the evidence is suppressed; the availability of legal means to obtain evidence; the degree of damage to defendant's defence caused by the illegally obtained evidence.

134 Anneli Soo, *Limits of freedom of public authorities with respect to obtaining evidence at the stage of investigation in Estonia*, p. 262.

As stated in the Canadian report, it is difficult to speak of truly "inviolable" boundaries in Canadian criminal law. Indeed, s. 1 of the Charter provides that rights may be subject to "such reasonable limits prescribed by law as can be demonstrably justified in a free and democratic society".[135] With that in mind, it is acknowledged that certain methods of proving facts in a criminal trial are prohibited, e.g. the unlawful obtaining of evidence from a bodily examination, harming personal integrity and the right to privacy (Article 8 of the Charter), or about a person's sexual activity (Article 276 of the CC). The prohibition also covers evidence illustrating the defendant's character. When assessing the inadmissibility of evidence, the interests of the legal system as a whole are also taken into account. The Charter provides for the exclusion of evidence where the use of the said evidence is likely to bring the administration of justice into disrepute, s. 24(2). There was an interesting discussion of Canadian Supreme Court rulings being interpretations of the Charter, providing protection for the accused from being compelled to testify and from self-incrimination pursuant to ss. 11c) and 13, except in the case of perjury or the giving of contradictory testimony. The authors of the report analyse the case law of the Supreme Court for developments in the protection of the relevant Charter provisions.[136] Using the example of the Mister Big operation, a new police technique used mainly in cases of serious and unsolved crimes, the controversies surrounding the admissibility of a suspect's testimony obtained in this manner are presented. The Supreme Court in R. v. Hart[137] acknowledged that while unreliable confessions "provide compelling evidence of guilt and present a clear and straightforward path to conviction," they "have been responsible for wrongful convictions – a fact we cannot ignore. The solution proposed by the Court has two parts. First, there is a presumption that a confession is inadmissible in the context of the Mr Big operation, but this can be rebutted if it is proved on the balance of probabilities that the probative value of the confession outweighs its harmful effect. Then irregularities in police conduct are examined in terms of possible abuse of the law. The cases described demonstrate a specific systemic approach in Canadian law to the issue of inadmissible evidence in criminal proceedings. For the most part, these issues are addressed by common law.

135 The s. 1 test was first articulated by the SCC in *R v Oakes*, [1986] 1 SCR 103.

136 In the judgment issued on 13 March 2010, Moldaver, J., the Supreme Court stated that "to invoke the protection afforded by s. 13, one must prove not only that they were compelled in the earlier proceedings but also, and most importantly, that the nature of the testimony is itself incriminating.

137 R v Hart, 2014 SCC 52.

7 Conclusion

Every democratic legal system recognises that the pursuit of the truth about a crime must have impassable limits and that it cannot be achieved at any cost. Defining these limits is a continuous process, as illustrated by the evolution of the evidentiary methods used in criminal proceedings in different historical periods, but also by the current reality, with its challenging need to reconcile different antagonistic situations and objectives. The criminal trial has been largely influenced by scientific and technological developments that offer ever better tools to find the truth about important facts. These are on the one hand a welcome response to the increasingly perfected methods of committing crimes, however – on the other hand – modern information and telecommunication technologies, when used in criminal proceedings, may increase the risk of fundamental human rights being violated as they offer possibilities to interfere with these rights. In general, it can be stated that the legislators have not adequately responded to the challenges posed by the development of new technologies. This sphere is developing slowly and reluctantly, which does not facilitate the process of defining the limits for trial authorities to use modern evidentiary methods. Measures such as searches, seizure of objects, wiretapping of the flat, telephone tapping, remote searches of IT systems or control of correspondence clash with the rights and guarantees, such as freedom, inviolability of the home or the right to privacy. Additionally, these measures sometimes also extend to third parties who have no connection with the investigative activities being carried out. Control over these measures is most often limited to the court's general consent of such measures being applied. Added to this is the pressure exerted on investigators by their superiors and public opinion, which can lead to the efficiency and operability argument being exaggerated in their work at the expense of other values. Another problematic aspect is the narrow focus of investigators on obtaining incriminating evidence, despite their general commitment to remain objective and impartial. These endeavours are sometimes associated with the risk of breaching the permissible boundaries of action. There is a fine line between legitimate evidentiary activities and those prohibited by law. An example is the use by investigators of techniques that provoke persons to provide evidence against themselves.

These circumstances are of prime relevance when defining the limits of the investigating authorities' freedom of action in obtaining evidence. Some country reports also refer to the existence of implied evidence bans, in addition to those that are explicitly set out in the legislation. Normative sources are, therefore, not the only criteria determining the limits of the freedom of trial authorities to obtain evidence. It is also important for investigators to properly understand these limits and to adhere to them in practice. The risk of an overly extensive use of the means of evidence which most interfere with human rights is much higher at the investigation stage than in court proceedings. This is because the investigation phase generally lacks appropriate mechanisms to counteract that risk. Reports have highlighted the weaker procedural position of the suspect at this stage who generally has no influence on the course of the evidentiary procedure and the evidence gathered. Under civil law, the prosecutor traditionally has a strong position and the pre-trial investigation phase is of much significance. Even in common law countries, private investigations are becoming less and less common as they generate high costs and it is hardly possible to create a counterbalance to the professional prosecution. With no legal or practical possibilities to control the actions of investigators, the imperative order for them to respect the limitations on the acquisition of evidence is much impaired. Another characteristic problem in many states is the lack of an adequate procedure to eliminate violations of the law of evidence committed by investigators. In most countries, the first review is not carried out until a charge has been brought to court, which may be considered a late response. In Canada, Article 24(1) of the Charter of Rights and Freedoms provides as follows: "Anyone whose rights or freedoms, as guaranteed by this Charter, have been infringed or denied may apply to a court of competent jurisdiction to obtain such remedy as the court considers appropriate and just in the circumstances."

The Codes of Criminal Procedure sometimes use the formula that the investigating authorities are entitled to undertake all investigative activities or sometimes it is implied. This formula does not, however, imply discretionary action, but freedom within the boundaries of the law. The limits of these activities have not been expressed in the form of an integral regulation in any country. It seems that sources of the law of evidence are widely dispersed and diversified in civil law countries. In the case of Canada, the law of evidence is partly codified (*Canada Evidence Act*) and to some extent based on common law. This differentiation is due to the unequal weight of various evidence bans. Many of them have constitutional value. The Constitution either expressly formulates a particular evidence ban (e.g. torture) or directly defines the conditions for the application of a particular measure (e.g. a search of a flat) or does so indirectly by reference to general values that are of significance while assessing the admissibility of the evidence in question, such as human dignity, the right to privacy, the inviolability of the home, etc. In Canada, all rules governing the conditions of obtaining and adducing evidence must conform to those rights that are entrenched constitutionally.

The principal source of the law governing evidence in the criminal proceedings are the Codes of Criminal Procedure, with the exception of Canada, which is the sole representative of the common law system. The civil law countries' regulations on inadmissible means of obtaining evidence, and on the prohibition to use certain evidence or to establish certain facts generally sound imperative in terms of how the evidence ban is expressed, but much less emphatic in the part defining the legal consequences of their violation. This is due to the varying impact of possible violations of the law of evidence. The country reports highlight this differentiation. On this basis, it is possible to identify a hierarchy of violations of the law defining the rules of gathering and taking evidence in criminal proceedings. In principle, the less serious breaches do not lead to the evidence being excluded in any of the countries from which we received country reports, even if a uniform list of such breaches can hardly be identified. The fruit of a poisonous tree doctrine in its pure form does not apply in any of the countries (but for some isolated manifestations of it). The second level consists of violations of the law of evidence, where an evaluation of legal interests is allowed. The basic criteria in assessing the admission or exclusion of evidence are the public interest and the individual interest. In the states where criminal proceedings are based on the inquisitorial-contradictory model, the category of "public interest" is of momentous importance, though it is confronted with the interests of the parties, especially the suspect. The perspective of individual interests is persistently gaining importance in a mixed-type criminal trial. The basis for excluding evidence, as provided for in the Canadian Charter, may be that – once admitted – it would jeopardise the reputation of the administration of justice.[138] Finally, the third level is formed by violations of absolute standards, which render such evidentiary activity totally ineffective. At this level, the most far-reaching similarities between the different legal systems, based on the foundation of the system of values shared by the civilised part of the world, come into view. The reports emphasise the inviolability of such evidence ban and the fact that evidence obtained in breach of it is automatically rejected. The hierarchy of evidence bans presented

138 Section 24(2) : "Where, in proceedings under subsection (1), a court concludes that evidence was obtained in a manner that infringed or denied any rights or freedoms guaranteed by this Charter, the evidence shall be excluded if it is established that, having regard to all the circumstances, the admission of it in the proceedings would bring the administration of justice into disrepute.

corresponds to an appropriate degree of restriction on the freedom of the authorities involved in the criminal proceedings to obtain evidence.

Generally, it can be stated that the most far-reaching restrictions were placed on the evidence that most interferes with the sphere of universally protected rights and freedoms. For the trial authorities, this means that they are the most limited in obtaining such evidence. In the case of evidence that might be admitted in a criminal trial depending on how various interests to be considered in the circumstances of a particular case are assessed, the theoretical margin of discretion is limited by the developed position of the judicature and legal scholars and commentators on fundamental matters. The country reports emphasise the important role of judicial case law and its impact on how the standards of evidence are shaped. International courts also play an important role in this process. While in Canada courts have traditionally held a law-making function, in other countries there is a general increase in the importance of this source. The body of evidence is intrinsically linked to the sphere of the facts of a particular case. This interdependence reinforces the need for the trial authorities to adopt a case-by-case approach, while respecting the overall standards for gathering and taking evidence in criminal proceedings. A case-by-case perspective should prevail in the procedural decisions taken, which entails a high degree of responsibility on the part of the authorities applying the law.

It needs to be emphasised that the widespread use of consensual ways of settling criminal cases in recent years is on the one hand the necessity and on the other hand a threat to the exercise of procedural rights and guarantees, due to natural limitations that result from the use of such agreements. The essence of the consensual approach, being that the judgment is based on the evidence taken at the pre-trial investigation stage, is a major undertaking for investigators. Much depends on their work and integrity in a situation where the mechanisms for controlling the accuracy and legality of evidence guaranteed by the traditional adversarial trial are significantly weakened.

Despite legal solutions applied being imperfect as emphasised in the country reports, in our opinion, the overall balance of the analysed legal systems comes out positively. Consequently, we can conclude that in each of them, in principle, the most important limits of the law enforcement authorities' freedom to obtain evidence at the investigation stage is defined in a manner corresponding to modern standards. The term "in principle" is used here to cover a few examples of solutions that did not meet this requirement.

Another important aspect that needs to be considered is the practical implementation of the law of evidence applicable in each country. Even if it was not indicated in the questionnaire, it definitely bears significance in this context and as such calls for a separate study. For regardless of the boundaries set by the law, the most important boundaries are those that are grounded in the individual axiology of those who observe them, based on the power of legitimate objectives and the imperative of fair dealing. Ultimately, everything always depends on the people.

CHAPTER 2

Limits of Freedom of Public Authorities with Respect to Obtaining Evidence at the Stage of Investigation

German Report

Anne Schneider

1 A Presentation of the Main and Most Distinctive Features of Evidence System in the Light of the Applicable Model of Criminal Procedure and Major Procedural Principles of Examining and Evaluating Evidence

German criminal procedure is based on the inquisitorial system. Criminal proceedings can be divided into three phases.[1] The first phase is the investigation phase (*Ermittlungsverfahren*) which starts when the prosecuting authorities obtain knowledge of a suspected offence (§ 160(1) Code of Criminal Procedure (*Strafprozessordnung* – StPO).[2] If the public prosecution office decides to indict the suspect (§ 170(1) StPO), there is an intermediate phase (*Zwischenverfahren*) in which the court decides, on the basis of the evidence submitted, whether or not to open main proceedings. The main proceedings (*Hauptverfahren*) are the phase in which witnesses are subpoenaed for trial and the trial takes place.

The public prosecution office (*Staatsanwaltschaft*) is solely responsible for leading criminal investigations and gathering both incriminating and exonerating evidence (§ 160(1, 2) StPO). During the investigative phase, it is the public prosecution office's task to examine evidence gathered and to decide which further investigative measures to take. It is also the public prosecution

1 See also T. Weigend, *The Potential to Secure a Fair Trial Through Evidence Exclusion: A German Perspective. Do exclusionary rules ensure a fair trial? A comparative analysis of evidentiary rules*, S. Gleß and T. Richter (eds), Springer 2019, pp. 61, 67 ff.

2 An English translation of the StPO can be found on a webpage operated by the Ministry of Justice and Consumer Protection at https://www.gesetze-im-internet.de/englisch_stpo/englisch_stpo.html#p1432 (last access on 03.02.2023). Unless otherwise indicated, all references to the code are taken from this official translation.

 | DOI:10.1163/9789004710320_004

office that decides whether to indict the suspect or to terminate proceedings (§ 170 StPO).

Although the court may become involved in the investigation to some extent (infra 3 b), it typically fully assesses the evidence for the first time at the intermediate phase. In the intermediate phase of criminal proceedings, the court has to decide whether there are sufficient grounds to suspect that the indicted suspect (*Angeschuldigter*)[3] has committed an offence (§ 203 StPO). This rule serves to protect the suspect from arbitrary indictments.[4] The court sends the bill of indictment to the suspect and asks them whether they want to raise objections to the indictment or apply for new evidence to be taken (§ 201(1) StPO). The court may also take evidence itself (§ 202 StPO). In practice, the overwhelming majority of indictments is accepted by the court and new evidence is very rarely taken.[5] Subsequently, it has been argued that the control function of the intermediate phase has derogated.[6]

In the following main proceedings, the same court decides on whether or not the defendant is guilty. In order to do so, the court decides which evidence is brought into trial and assesses it (§ 244 StPO). The main proceedings are governed by the principle of immediacy which means that the court has to hear all the evidence itself and cannot rely on hearsay or on the public prosecutor's file.[7] Therefore, witness statements are always heard directly in trial. The court is free to evaluate the evidence (§ 261 StPO). The fact that the court that has decided on opening main proceedings is the same one that decides

3 German law distinguishes between persons who are suspected of an offence (*Beschuldigte*), persons suspected of an offence that have been indicted (*Angeschuldigte*) and indicted persons against which main proceedings have been opened (*Angeklagte*), see § 157 StPO. The official translation translates "*Beschuldigter*" with "accused person", "*Angeschuldigter*" with "indicted accused" and "*Angeklagter*" with "defendant". However, in my opinion, this translation is misleading because EU law uses the term "accused" for indicted suspects. Therefore, this report will use the term "suspect" for the person that is the focus of criminal investigations in the pre-trial phase.

4 M. Vormbaum, 'Effektive Kontrolle oder überflüssige Schreibarbeit? Kritik des strafprozessualen Zwischenverfahrens und Möglichkeiten seiner Reform' [2015] *Zeitschrift für Internationale Strafrechtsdogmatik* 328, 328 f. with further references.

5 Ibid. 329 f.; T. Weigend, *The Potential to Secure a Fair Trial Through Evidence Exclusion: A German Perspective. Do exclusionary rules ensure a fair trial? A comparative analysis of evidentiary rules*, S. Gleß and T. Richter (eds), Springer 2019, pp. 61, 67.

6 M. Vormbaum 'Effektive Kontrolle oder überflüssige Schreibarbeit? Kritik des strafprozessualen Zwischenverfahrens und Möglichkeiten seiner Reform' [2015] *Zeitschrift für Internationale Strafrechtsdogmatik* 328, 329.

7 See A. Eser et al., *Alternativ-Entwurf Beweisaufnahme*, Goltdammer's Archiv 2014, p. 1.

on a possible conviction is criticized in German law.[8] This criticism is based on psychological effects that show that people prefer evidence agreeing with their hypothesis to evidence disagreeing with it (confirmation bias).[9] Accordingly, judges who have already found that there is sufficient evidence for opening proceedings might be more likely to convict than neutral judges. However, others point out that the assessment in the intermediate phase is very superficial and does not construct such a bias.[10]

It should also be noted that German criminal courts have large discretion in admitting or excluding evidence, even if it was illegally gathered. German law distinguishes between independent exclusionary rules (*selbständige Beweisverwertungsverbote*) and dependent exclusionary rules (*unselbständige Beweisverwertungsverbote*).[11] The former concern evidence that was acquired legally. In this case, the exclusion of the evidence is still possible. The latter concern evidence that was acquired illegally. Such evidence can be excluded but this is by no means an automatic result of a violation of the law.

2 Public Authorities Are Entitled to Acquire Evidence in a Criminal Action at the Stage of Investigation

2.1 *Notion: Public Authorities Are Entitled to Carry Out Investigations*

a) *Please indicate legal grounds or other sources giving rise to the competence of appropriate authorities to carry out investigations, within which to examine evidence. In addition to the traditional law enforcement authorities of*

8 M. Vormbaum, 'Effektive Kontrolle oder überflüssige Schreibarbeit? Kritik des strafprozessualen Zwischenverfahrens und Möglichkeiten seiner Reform' [2015] *Zeitschrift für Internationale Strafrechtsdogmatik* 328, 329; B. Schünemann, 'Der Richter im Strafverfahren als manipulierter Dritter? Zur empirischen Bestätigung von Perseveranz- und Schulterschlußeffekt' [2000] *Strafverteidiger* 159, 159 ff.

9 B. Schünemann 'Der Richter im Strafverfahren als manipulierter Dritter? Zur empirischen Bestätigung von Perseveranz- und Schulterschlußeffekt' [2000] *Strafverteidiger* 159, 160 ff.

10 On this argument (disagreeing) M. Vormbaum 'Effektive Kontrolle oder überflüssige Schreibarbeit? Kritik des strafprozessualen Zwischenverfahrens und Möglichkeiten seiner Reform' [2015] *Zeitschrift für Internationale Strafrechtsdogmatik* 328, 329; see also M. Wenske, '§ 199 StPO', margin no. 36 ff., in C. Knauer, H. Kudlich, H. Schneider (eds), *Münchener Kommentar zur Strafprozessordnung,* vol. 2, C.H.Beck 2016.

11 S. Gleß, *Germany: Balancing the truth against protected constitutional interests. Exclusionary rules in Comparative Law,* S. Thaman (ed.), Springer 2013, pp. 113, 116 f; see also the overview in M. Jahn, *Beweiserhebungs- und Beweisverwertungsverbote im Spannungsfeld zwischen den Garantien des Rechtsstaates und der effektiven Bekämpfung von Kriminalität und Terrorismus, Gutachten C für den 67. Deutschen Juristentag 2008,* C.H.Beck 2008, C 51–65.

the prosecutor and the police, are any other entities admissible, such as special forces or specialized administrative authorities? What is the scope of their procedural competence and how can their procedural position be defined vis-à-vis the traditional enforcement authorities? Can a growing significance be found in the participation in criminal investigations of specialized law enforcement authorities, other than the traditional group of investigation bodies? Can the phenomenon of normative disintegration be observed, paving the way for numerous public authorities to conduct investigations in criminal cases?

The competent authority for carrying out investigations is the public prosecution office. When it obtains knowledge of a suspected offence, the prosecution office is "obliged to take action in relation to all prosecutable criminal offences, provided there are sufficient factual indications" (§ 152(1) StPO, see also § 160(1) StPO). This means it must be possible, according to experience, that a crime has been committed.[12] The factual indications can come from the report of an offence or by other means (§ 160a(1) StPO). The public prosecution office is entitled to request information from any authority and to make investigations of any kind. This general principle is laid down in § 160(1) StPO, but there are numerous provisions with detailed requirements for certain investigative measures (e.g. surveillance, search and seizure etc.). The police has the same right, but needs to report its findings to the public prosecution office because only the public prosecution office can decide whether or not to indict a person (§ 160a(1, 2) StPO). In practice, investigations are mainly led by the police because the police is primarily competent for measures that cannot be deferred.

Apart from the traditional criminal law enforcement authorities (police and public prosecution office), there are other administrative authorities that have the competence to lead criminal investigations. The most important is the tax investigation service (*Steuerfahndung*), an investigative body for tax crime (§ 386(1) Fiscal Code [*Abgabenordnung* – AO]). However, the public prosecution office can decide to take over investigations for tax crime.[13] It should also be noted that punitive administrative proceedings follow the rules of criminal

12 S. Peters, '§ 152 StPO', margin no. 35, in C. Knauer, H. Kudlich, H. Schneider (eds), *Münchener Kommentar zur Strafprozessordnung*, vol. 2, C.H.Beck 2016.

13 See Große Strafrechtskommission des Deutschen Richterbunds, *Das Verhältnis von Gericht, Staatsanwaltschaft und Polizei im Ermittlungsverfahren, strafprozessuale Regeln und faktische (Fehl?) Entwicklungen*, 2008, pp. 126, http://www.bmjv.de/SharedDocs/Downloads/DE/Fachinformationen/Das_Verhaeltnis_von_Gericht_Staatsanwaltschaft_und_Polizei_im_Ermittlungsverfahren.pdf?__blob=publicationFile (last access on 28.03.2023).

proceedings (§ 46(1) Act on Regulatory Offences [*Ordnungswidrigkeitengesetz – OWiG*]). This means that, for instance, the rules of criminal procedure apply to investigations by the Federal Cartel Office or the Commission in competition law cases, although the investigating authorities are not criminal, but administrative bodies.

Overall, the public prosecution office and the police remain by far the most important criminal law enforcement authorities in German law. Although there are other competent bodies, especially in the area of financial crime, their authority is limited in scope. They also apply the same rules as the public prosecution office. This means that the criminal courts would be asked to grant prior judicial authorization and, later on, decide on the admissibility of evidence, regardless of which body investigated. Accordingly, there is no evidence of normative disintegration.

b) *Do public law enforcement authorities enjoy a monopoly (exclusivity) of investigation rights in criminal cases, or do they share this competence with private entities (e.g. as part of private investigations or in the case of less serious actions being brought by private prosecution)? Where a given legal system envisages separate proceedings in actions brought by private prosecution, can public law enforcement authorities participate in them and if yes, what is the extent of that participation? Does it cover the right to examine evidence?*

In principle, only the public prosecutor's office and the police are authorized to conduct investigations as part of the pre-trial proceedings (§§ 160(1), 163 StPO). The Code of Criminal Procedure does not allow the outsourcing of criminal investigations to private persons. Neither are there provisions on so-called internal investigations. These are investigations led by a company into violations of the law that occurred within the company itself. Many countries grant lower sentences in exchange for receiving the final report of internal investigations, which might be considered as a privatisation of criminal investigations. However, there are no such rules in Germany, which means that such a report is treated as any other document (see §§ 94 ff. StPO).[14]

German law also allows private prosecution for minor offences such as trespass or (simple) bodily harm (§ 374(1) StPO).[15] If private prosecution is

14 See on the applicable law on seizures in these cases, A. Schneider 'Search and Seizure of Documents generated in Internal Investigations – Lessons to learn from European Law' 89 [2018] *Revue Internationale de Droit Pénal*, 311, 313 ff.

15 § 374 StPO – Admissibility; persons entitled to bring private prosecution
(1) An aggrieved person may bring a private prosecution in respect of the following offences without first needing to have recourse to the public prosecution office:
1. trespass (section 123 of the Criminal Code),

admitted, the victim can bypass the public prosecution office completely. In this respect, the rules on private prosecution are an exception to the legality principle set out in § 152(1) StPO that requires the public prosecution office to start investigations. Indeed, the indictment of the suspect for one of the offences listed in § 374(1) StPO is only allowed if this is in the public interest (§ 376 StPO).

As long as the prosecution is private, the public prosecution office is not involved in proceedings.[16] However, it may take over prosecution at any time (§ 377(1) StPO). Also, the court can transfer the file to the prosecution service when it feels that the prosecution service should take proceedings over (§ 377(2) StPO). If the public prosecution office takes over private proceedings, the general rules on criminal investigations apply.

---

2. insult (sections 185 to 189 of the Criminal Code), unless it is directed against one of the political bodies specified in section 194 (4) of the Criminal Code,
2a. violation of intimate privacy by taking photographs or other images (section 201a (1) and (2) of the Criminal Code),
3. violation of the privacy of correspondence (section 202 of the Criminal Code),
4. bodily harm (sections 223 and 229 of the Criminal Code),
5. coercion (section 240 (1) to (3) of the Criminal Code) or threatening commission of a serious criminal offence (section 241 of the Criminal Code),
5a. taking or giving of a bribe in commercial practice (section 299 of the Criminal Code),
6. criminal damage (section 303 of the Criminal Code),
6a. an offence under section 323a of the Criminal Code if the offence, having been committed in a state of intoxication, is a less serious criminal offence as referred to in nos. 1 to 6,
7. an offence pursuant to section 16 of the Act against Unfair Competition (*Gesetz gegen den unlauteren Wettbewerb*) and section 23 of the Act on the Protection of Trade Secrets (*Gesetz zum Schutz von Geschäftsgeheimnissen*),
8. an offence under section 142 (1) of the Patent Act (*Patentgesetz*), section 25 (1) of the Utility Models Act (*Gebrauchsmustergesetz*), section 10 (1) of the Semi-Conductor Protection Act (*Halbleiterschutzgesetz*), section 39 (1) of the Plant Variety Protection Act (*Sortenschutzgesetz*), section 143 (1), section 143a (1) and section 144 (1) and (2) of the Trade Mark Act (*Markengesetz*), section 51 (1) and section 65 (1) of the Design Act (*Designgesetz*), sections 106 to 108 and section 108b (1) and (2) of the Copyright Act (*Urheberrechtsgesetz*) and section 33 of the Act on the Copyright of Works of Fine Art and Photography (*Gesetz betreffend das Urheberrecht an Werken der bildenden Künste und der Photographie*).

16 A. Allgayer, '§ 377 StPO', margin no. 1 f., in R. Hannich (ed), *Karlsruher Kommentar zur Straßprozessordnung*, 9th ed., 2023.

2.2 *Court's Right to Acquire Evidence at the Investigation Stage or Its Controlling Activities in Relation to Evidence Examined by Other Entities*

a) *Is the court entitled to examine evidence at the stage of investigation and if yes, can it admit evidence ex officio or only at the parties' request, or are both those solutions possible simultaneously? Does the format of court investigation apply?*

Pre-trial investigations are the exclusive competence of the public prosecution office and its auxiliary authorities (mainly the police). The courts do not lead investigations. However, this does not mean that courts do not have any influence in the investigative phase. Some investigative measures require prior judicial authorisation (see infra b). As a form of ex ante judicial review, it is one of the core competences of the court. Furthermore, individual evidence can be challenged independently before the court in the pre-trial phase (infra c).

Apart from that, German law allows the court to undertake investigative measures, but only if the public prosecution office asks for support by the court (§ 162(1) StPO). This happens often regarding the examination of victims of domestic violence. The reason for this is that, according to well-established case-law, only the examination led by a judge may be used in trial if the witness later refuses to testify.[17] According to § 165 StPO, the judge may undertake the necessary investigatory acts if a public prosecutor is not available in exigent circumstances (*Gefahr im Verzug*). Nonetheless, the courts do not have the original competence to undertake investigations but are only a stand-in for the public prosecution office. Altogether, the role of the courts in the investigative phase is rather small.[18]

b) *At the investigation stage, does the court or another body hold the controlling rights in relation to evidentiary activities taken by law enforcement authorities and if yes, what controlling measures are afforded (e.g. does the examination of a specific piece of evidence require the court to give its prior consent)? What are the consequences of a failure to satisfy the condition of the court's or another entity's consent and other conditions from the perspective of the validity and effectiveness of the evidence examined? Can the*

---

17 BGHSt 61, 221, 221 ff., margin no. 25 ff.

18 Große Strafrechtskommission des Deutschen Richterbunds, *Das Verhältnis von Gericht, Staatsanwaltschaft und Polizei im Ermittlungsverfahren, strafprozessuale Regeln und faktische (Fehl?) Entwicklungen*, 2008, p. 130, http://www.bmjv.de/SharedDocs/Downloads/DE/Fachinformationen/Das_Verhaeltnis_von_Gericht_Staatsanwaltschaft_und_Polizei_im_Ermittlungsverfahren.pdf?__blob=publicationFile (last access on 28.03.2023).

specification of such pieces of evidence and the conditions of their admissibility established by the law be viewed as sufficient?

Many investigative measures require prior judicial authorisation. This means that the public prosecution office must apply for judicial authorization before executing the investigative measure in question. The requirement of prior judicial authorization is set down in the law. Such rules are found for the following investigative measures: physical examination of the suspect (§ 81a(2) StPO) or other persons (§ 81c(5) StPO), molecular and genetic analysis (§ 81f(1) StPO), DNA profiling (§ 81g(3) StPO), serial DNA screening (§ 81h(2) StPO), seizure (§ 98(1) StPO) and seizure of postal items (§ 100(1) StPO), dragnet investigation (§ 98b(1) StPO), telecommunications surveillance, covert remote search of information technology systems and acoustic surveillance of private premises (all § 100e(1) StPO), acoustic surveillance outside of private premises (§ 100f(4) StPO), technical investigation measures in respect of mobile terminals (§ 100i(3) StPO), and searches (§ 105(1) StPO). This overview shows that these are either the more intrusive measures (e.g. physical examination) or those undertaken by stealth because ex post judicial review is less effective in these cases (e.g. surveillance). Most of the provisions also allow the public prosecution office or the police to undertake the investigative measure themselves in exigent circumstances (*Gefahr im Verzug*).

If the investigating authorities have failed to comply with the requirement of prior judicial authorisation (either by not applying or by wrongly interpreting "exigent circumstances"), the question arises of what happens to the evidence that was gathered in breach of this requirement. The general rule in German criminal procedure law is that a violation of the law in collecting evidence does not necessarily lead to its exclusion as evidence in trial.[19] The court must assess the admissibility of evidence according to the circumstances of the individual case, in particular according to the nature of the prohibition and the weight of the violation, weighing up the conflicting interests.[20] The same is true vice versa for legally gathered evidence, which still might be excluded for a violation of fundamental rights.[21] Written provisions on the consequences of a violation of procedural law are mostly missing. Accordingly, the consequences of a failure to receive judicial authorization are decided on a case by case basis.

19 T. Weigend, *The Potential to Secure a Fair Trial Through Evidence Exclusion: A German Perspective. Do exclusionary rules ensure a fair trial? A comparative analysis of evidentiary rules*, S. Gleß and T. Richter (eds), Springer 2019, pp. 61, 73 f.

20 BVerfG *Deutsches Autorecht* 2008, 196 margin no. 10.

21 T. Weigend, *The Potential to Secure a Fair Trial Through Evidence Exclusion: A German Perspective. Do exclusionary rules ensure a fair trial? A comparative analysis of evidentiary rules*, S. Gleß and T. Richter (eds), Springer 2019, pp. 61, 73 f.

In cases of physical examination, searches and seizure, the evidence is only excluded in case of serious, deliberate or arbitrary procedural violations in which the fundamental rights safeguards were disregarded in a planned or systematic manner.[22] This would require an intentional disregard of the requirement of judicial authorisation or a blatant violation of its prerequisites.[23] German courts have also accepted the argument that the prosecuting authorities would have received judicial authorization if they had asked for it (*hypothetischer Ersatzeingriff*) and, therefore, that the evidence should be admitted.[24]

To sum up one can say that the law clearly sets out in which cases prior judicial authorisation is required and that the list of investigative measures that require such an authorization is mostly convincing. However, the results of a violation of this requirement are not clear in German law. This is because the way in which the courts deal with evidence that was illegally obtained is, in general, unpredictable.

c) *Is there a procedure at the investigation stage that enables the parties and their counsels to challenge the evidence examined in violation of the applicable principles? If yes, please present it briefly, taking into account the procedural consequences of its usage (the application of the principle of automatic exclusion of evidence; the recognition of invalidity of evidence; the judge's right to assess the consequences of a method adopted to acquire evidence and evidence content) as well as the legal consequences for those who violated the law; please indicate the level of imperativeness of responses to a violation concerning the acquisition and examination of evidence, based on the applicable law and standpoints of doctrine and judicature.*

The question of the admissibility of evidence is usually discussed in the trial phase and decided upon by the court. The defendant and their lawyer can object to the usage of evidence during the trial. If the judgment is based on evidence that one of the parties considers to be inadmissible, they can appeal the court's judgment on grounds of law (*Revision*, §§ 333 ff. StPO). It should be noted that, according to the well-established case law of the Federal Court of Justice, the defence counsel must object to the taking of inadmissible evidence

---

22 BVerfG *Neue Juristische Wochenschrift* 2009, 3225, 3225.

23 BGH *Neue Zeitschrift für Strafrecht – Rechtsprechungsreport* 2019, 94, 95.

24 M. Jahn and J. Dallmeyer 'Zum heutigen Stand der beweisrechtlichen Berücksichtigung hypothetischer Ermittlungsverläufe im deutschen Strafverfahrensrecht' [2005] *Neue Zeitschrift für Strafrecht* 297, 297; see S. Gleß, *Germany: Balancing the truth against protected constitutional interests. Exclusionary rules in Comparative Law*, S. Thaman (ed.), Springer 2013, pp. 113, 122 f.

at trial in order to make an appeal on these grounds possible (*Rügepräklusion, Widerspruchslösung*).[25]

In the investigative phase, there are procedures for challenging specific investigative measures, seizure (§ 98(2)2 StPO) and surveillance measures (§ 101(7)2 StPO).[26] Any person concerned with a legitimate interest can apply for judicial review. This includes, e.g. third parties who have talked by phone to a suspect under telecommunication surveillance. Because a general provision on judicial review in the investigative phase is lacking, the procedure laid down in § 98(2)2 StPO is applied not only to seizure, but to any other non-judicial investigative measure.[27] Judicial investigative measures such as judicial authorization or judicial interrogation can be appealed against by a complaint (§ 304 StPO).

If, e.g. the court holds that a seizure was unlawful, the seized objects must be returned.[28] Corresponding data must be deleted (§ 489(2) StPO). Nonetheless, the unlawfulness of an investigative measure does not necessarily mean that the evidence gathered is not admissible in trial.[29] This result would depend on the court's assessment when balancing the defendant's interest with the public interest in prosecution. However, it has been suggested that the decision that a certain investigative measure was illegal can be of benefit for the defendant even if the evidence is not included because it puts psychological pressure on the prosecutor.[30]

In principle, the police officers or prosecutors executing illegal investigative measures can be criminally liable. Most investigative measures would constitute criminal offences if they were not justified by the Code of Criminal Procedure.[31] Accordingly, the courts have held that police officers should be given

25 BGHSt 38, 214, 225; BGH, *Neue Juristische Wochenschrift* 1997, 2893; see also M. Böse and A. Schneider 'Germany', Admissibility of OLAF Final Reports as Evidence in Criminal Proceedings, F. Giuffrida and K. Ligeti (eds) (2019), 132, 136, available at https://orbilu.uni.lu/bitstream/10993/40141/1/ADCRIM_final_report.pdf (last access on 03.02.2023).

26 See T. Singelnstein, 'Rechtsschutz gegen heimliche Ermittlungsmaßnahmen nach Einführung des § 101 Absatz VII 2–4 StPO' (2009) *Neue Zeitschrift für Strafrecht* 481 ff.

27 For an overview, see A. Laser 'Das Rechtsschutzsystem gegen strafprozessuale Zwangsmaßnahmen' (2001) *Neue Zeitschrift für Strafrecht*, 120 ff.

28 BVerfGE 44, 353, 384; E. Menges, '§ 98 StPO' in J. Becker and others (eds), *Löwe-Rosenberg, Die Strafprozessordnung und das Gerichtsverfassungsgesetz, Band 3(§§ 94–111a)*, 27th ed., de Gruyter 2019, para 63.

29 R. Schlothauer '§ 3 Ermittlungsverfahren', margin no. 121 in E. Müller and R. Schlothauer (eds), *Münchener Anwaltshandbuch Strafverteidigung*, 3rd ed. 2022.

30 Ibid.

31 A. Schneider, *Strafprozessuale Ermittlungsmaßnahmen und Zeugnisverweigerungsrechte*, Mohr Siebeck 2021, p. 70 f.

more leeway in order to avoid individual criminal liability for persons trying to do what is right.[32] This question is still under debate.[33] In practice, individual liability of police officers is of minor importance.

Overall, the incitement to strictly follow the law and prevent the illegal gathering of evidence does not seem to be big. Faults in acquiring evidence do not necessarily make the evidence inadmissible. Neither is the fruit of a poisonous tree doctrine applicable.[34] Even if evidence is excluded in trial (*Beweisverwertungsverbot*), the exclusion is usually restricted to its use as evidence. Prohibitions to use evidence also for other investigative purposes (*Beweisverwendungsverbot*) are rare. Individual criminal liability has a marginal role and does not seem to serve as a deterrent.

3 Principles of Acquiring Evidence at the Stage of Investigation

a) *Normative grounds for evidentiary activities in a criminal action (the Constitution, procedural criminal law, police law, administrative law, regulations, instructions, guidelines, common law, others). Can a multitude of sources of regulations in this area be referred to or is there normative homogeneity in place?*

The most important legal source for evidentiary activities in criminal law is the Code of Criminal Procedure (*Strafprozessordnung*). It contains information on the whole criminal procedure including the competences of the judicial authorities, the rules on gathering evidence and assessing evidence. It also includes the police's competences in criminal investigations, whereas the police laws of the *Länder*[35] deal with preventing danger for individuals and society, i.e. administrative proceedings. Additional information on criminal investigations can be found in the Guidelines on criminal proceedings and fine proceedings (*Richtlinien für das Strafverfahren und Bußgeldverfahren – RiStBV*). These guidelines are adopted by the Federal Ministry of Justice and aid the

32 BGH *Neue Zeitschrift für Strafrecht* 2015, 574 margin no. 25 ff.

33 See A. Engländer 'Commentary' [2015] *Neue Zeitschrift für Strafrecht*, 577; T. Rönnau and K. Hohn, '§ 32 StPO' margin no. 116 ff. in G. Cirener et al. (eds) *Leipziger Kommentar zum StGB*, vol. 3, 13th ed., De Gruyter 2019.

34 See, S. Gleß, *Germany: Balancing the truth against protected constitutional interests. Exclusionary rules in Comparative Law*, S. Thaman (ed.), Springer 2013, pp. 113, 128 ff.

35 The Federal Republic of Germany consists of 16 provinces which are called "*Länder*". The Federal state has competences in some legal areas, the *Länder* in others. Criminal law and criminal procedure law are federal competences and, therefore, the same in all *Länder*.

prosecuting authorities in interpreting the law. As administrative guidelines, they rank lower than the Code of Criminal Procedure.

The Code of Criminal Procedure is a formal law that was adopted by the German Parliament. As such, it must comply with higher-ranking law. This is, first, the Basic Law (*Grundgesetz* – GG), the German Constitution. The Basic Law plays a huge part in the German legal system and has to be taken into account when interpreting the law. This is especially true for criminal investigations. Although some guarantees in the Basic Law are rather vague (human dignity, Article 1(1) GG), others are quite specific (inviolability of the home, Article 13 GG).[36] Many investigative measures foreseen in the Code of

36 See *Article 13 [Inviolability of the home]*
(1) The home is inviolable.
(2) Searches may be authorised only by a judge or, when time is of the essence, by other authorities designated by the laws and may be carried out only in the manner therein prescribed.
(3) If particular facts justify the suspicion that any person has committed an especially serious crime specifically defined by a law, technical means of acoustical surveillance of any home in which the suspect is supposedly staying may be employed pursuant to judicial order for the purpose of prosecuting the offence, provided that alternative methods of investigating the matter would be disproportionately difficult or unproductive. The authorisation shall be for a limited time. The order shall be issued by a panel composed of three judges. When time is of the essence, it may also be issued by a single judge.
(4) To avert acute dangers to public safety, especially dangers to life or to the public, technical means of surveillance of the home may be employed only pursuant to judicial order. When time is of the essence, such measures may also be ordered by other authorities designated by a law; a judicial decision shall subsequently be obtained without delay.
(5) If technical means are contemplated solely for the protection of persons officially deployed in a home, the measure may be ordered by an authority designated by a law. The information thereby obtained may be otherwise used only for purposes of criminal prosecution or to avert danger and only if the legality of the measure has been previously determined by a judge; when time is of the essence, a judicial decision shall subsequently be obtained without delay.
(6) The Federal Government shall report to the Bundestag annually as to the employment of technical means pursuant to paragraph (3) and, within the jurisdiction of the Federation, pursuant to paragraph (4) and, insofar as judicial approval is required, pursuant to paragraph (5) of this Article. A panel elected by the Bundestag shall exercise parliamentary oversight on the basis of this report. A comparable parliamentary oversight shall be afforded by the Länder.
(7) Interferences and restrictions shall otherwise only be permissible to avert a danger to the public or to the life of an individual or, pursuant to a law, to confront an acute danger to public safety and order, in particular to relieve an accommodation shortage, to combat the danger of an epidemic or to protect young persons at risk.

Criminal Procedure have been challenged before the German Federal Constitutional Court (*Bundesverfassungsgericht*) by constitutional complaint (*Verfassungsbeschwerde*).[37]

The competences set out in the Code of Criminal Procedure are also influenced by the European Convention on Human Rights and EU law. The European Convention on Human Rights has been transposed by formal law and does, accordingly, not rank higher than the Code of Criminal Procedure. However, it is universally acknowledged that the Convention must be taken into account when interpreting national law as well as possible.[38] The most important guarantees for criminal proceedings are Articles 6, 8 and 10 ECHR. EU law has become particularly important since the EU has adopted six directives on defendant's rights in criminal proceedings in order to further harmonization and, thereby, mutual recognition.[39] These directives have, insofar as they relate to criminal investigation, been implemented in the Code of Criminal Procedure. When criminal proceedings are implementations of EU law,[40] the guarantees in the Charter of Fundamental Rights also apply. Despite these influences, the main legal framework for criminal investigation is the Code of Criminal Procedure.

---

37 E.g. BVerfGE 32, 373, BVerfGE 113, 29 (§ 97 StPO); BVerfGE 109, 279 (§ 100c StPO); BVerfGE 129, 208 (§§ 100a, 160a StPO).

38 J. Meyer-Ladewig and M. Nettesheim, 'Einleitung', margin no. 19, in J. Meyer-Ladewig, M. Nettesheim and S. von Raumer (eds), *Europäische Menschenrechtskonvention*, 4th ed. C.H. Beck 2017.

39 Directive 2010/64/EU of the European Parliament and of the Council of 20 October 2010 on the right to interpretation and translation in criminal proceedings, OJ L 280/1; Directive 2012/13/EU of the European Parliament and of the Council of 22 May 2012 on the right to information in criminal proceedings, OJ L 142/1; Directive 2013/48/EU of the European Parliament and of the Council of 22 October 2013 on the right of access to a lawyer in criminal proceedings and in European arrest warrant proceedings, and on the right to have a third party informed upon deprivation of liberty and to communicate with third persons and with consular authorities while deprived of liberty, OJ L 294/1; Directive (EU) 2016/343 of the European Parliament and of the Council of 9 March 2016 on the strengthening of certain aspects of the presumption of innocence and of the right to be present at the trial in criminal proceedings, OJ L 65/1; Directive (EU) 2016/800 of the European Parliament and of the Council of 11 May 2016 on procedural safeguards for children who are suspects or accused persons in criminal proceedings, OJ L 132/1; Directive (EU) 2016/1919 of the European Parliament and of the Council of 26 October 2016 on legal aid for suspects and accused persons in criminal proceedings and for requested persons in European arrest warrant proceedings, OJ L 297/1.

40 See A. Schneider *Strafprozessuale Ermittlungsmaßnahmen und Zeugnisverweigerungsrechte*, Mohr Siebeck 2021, pp. 408 ff.

b) *Does the applicable law regulate the principles of evidentiary activities taken by law enforcement authorities restrictively (on a tight-rein basis) and, similarly – determine the consequences of violations committed by the investigators, or does it leave to them a broad discretion in the search for evidence followed by the court's right to discretionarily assess the collected evidentiary material and by the confrontation of evidence during a verbal and contradictory trial at court?*

German law has specific provisions on most major investigative measures, providing rules on applicability, procedure and procedural safeguards. Although the prosecuting authorities are allowed to use any means to investigate criminal offences (§§ 161, 163 StPO), they are bound by these special provisions when applicable. This means that there is not much discretion in executing, e.g. acoustic surveillance (§ 100c StPO).

In contrast, the consequences of violations are hardly regulated. Here, the courts have broad discretion in deciding on the admissibility of evidence and in assessing its evidentiary value. In this context, the fundamental rights set out in the Basic Law and the human rights from the European Convention on Human Rights are often used as arguments for excluding evidence that was gathered in violation of the law. The case-law is not in all parts clear. However, the underlying rationale is that the more the defendant's rights are impaired, the more likely is it that evidence will be excluded. For example, courts have refused to exclude a witness testimony in cases in which the witness had – contrary to the law (§ 55(2) StPO) – not been informed of their right to refuse to answer any questions the reply to which would subject them or one of their relatives to the risk of being prosecuted (§ 55 StPO) because this right only impaired the witness's rights, not the defendant's.[41]

c) *Are there any criteria of the legality of evidence and criteria that disqualify the same established by the law? What role does the judicature play in establishing such criteria?*

German law gives mostly detailed information on how certain evidence should be gathered. Violations of these rules make the acquiring of the evidence illegal. Moreover, general principals and fundamental rights can render the gathering of evidence illegal even if it is done by the rules set out in the Code of Criminal Procedure. Criteria for disqualifying evidence are also established by the law, but only on a piece-by-piece basis. There are no general rules on the legality of evidence and its use in trial. Therefore, it is often up to the courts

41 BGHSt 11, 213, 218.

to decide on whether a piece of evidence, gathered illegally or legally, can be admitted as evidence.

Due to the lack of regulated overarching principles, the jurisprudence by the criminal courts and the Federal Constitutional Court plays a crucial role in determining the limits to the freedom of the public authorities. Although the courts are foremost responsible for deciding a single case, there have been attempts to develop general principles on the admissibility of evidence:[42] Evidence is to be excluded only if the violation of procedural affected the legal position of the defendant substantially (*Rechtskreistheorie*).[43] The exclusion must serve the purpose of the procedural guarantee (*Schutzzwecktheorie*).[44] The courts also balance the public interest in prosecution with the defendant's interest in protecting their individual rights (*Abwägungslehre*).[45] The problem with these principles is that they are open to interpretation and do not make the law much more predictable. Accordingly, case-law is of utmost importance in this respect. This is unusual for the German legal system which places more emphasis on written statutes than case-law and does, in principle, not recognize binding precedents.

It should also be noted that the courts have developed an important restriction on the possibility to appeal against the admission of evidence. A defendant who has a lawyer must object to the use of evidence in trial (*Widerspruchslösung*, supra 2 c). A failure to do so makes this point irrelevant for the appellate court.

d) *Does the principle of freedom, meaning that any evidentiary measure and any evidentiary method are admissible (except those that a limine are unacceptable in civilized world), apply to the acquisition of evidence at the investigation stage? Or is it restricted by the applicability of general principles of the law, e.g. legalism, reliability, proportionality, necessity, and values such as human dignity, bodily inviolability, or the right to privacy? Where references are explicite missing in the law to the aforesaid standards, on what basis are those standards applied? How do doctrine and case law under-*

42 See also S. Gleß, *Germany: Balancing the truth against protected constitutional interests. Exclusionary rules in Comparative Law*, S. Thaman (ed.), Springer 2013, pp. 113, 119 ff.

43 C. Knauer and H. Kudlich '§ 337 StPO', margin no. 27 f. in C. Knauer, H. Kudlich, H. Schneider (eds) *Münchener Kommentar zur Strafprozessordnung*, vol.3, C.H.Beck 2019; see also BGHSt 11, 213; T. Paul 'Unselbständige Beweisverwertungsverbote in der Rechtsprechung' [2013] *Neue Zeitschrift für Strafrecht* 489, 490 f.

44 BGHSt 24, 125.

45 T. Paul 'Unselbständige Beweisverwertungsverbote in der Rechtsprechung' [2013] *Neue Zeitschrift für Strafrecht* 489, 490 f.; see also BGHSt 51, 285.

stand the notion of "fair evidentiary procedure"? Is this notion autonomous or does it constitute a part of the notion of "fair trial"?

German constitutional law strongly protects the citizens' fundamental rights. These rights include more specific rights like the privacy of correspondence, post and telecommunication (Article 10 GG), but also personal freedoms (Article 2 GG). Article 2 GG reads as follows:

Article 2 [Personal freedoms]

(1) Every person shall have the right to free development of his personality insofar as he does not violate the rights of others or offend against the constitutional order or the moral law.

(2) Every person shall have the right to life and physical integrity. Freedom of the person shall be inviolable. These rights may be interfered with only pursuant to a law.

Article 2 GG contains several rights that might be important in criminal investigations, i.e. the right to physical integrity and the right to freedom. The "right to free development of [their] personality" is understood to include the right to personal privacy and the general freedom of action (*allgemeine Handlungsfreiheit*). At least the latter right is impaired upon by any investigative measure; often, more specific rights which take precedence are impaired, too.

If there is an impairment of fundamental rights with any investigative measure, these measures need to be justified by law. Such a justification requires a legal rule (often a law) that in itself must be proportionate. The principle of proportionality requires the law impairing fundamental rights to be suitable for reaching its purpose, necessary and appropriate.[46] The same is true for individual measures. This shows that criminal procedure law is, indeed, "constitutional law in practice" (*angewandtes Verfassungsrecht*).[47]

Accordingly, criminal investigations are to a large extent influenced by fundamental rights such as human dignity (Article 1 GG) and the right to privacy (Art. 2(1) and 1(1) GG) and the principle of proportionality. This balancing between different interests is understood to be a part of the fair trial principle. There is no separate meaning of "fair evidentiary procedure".

---

46 On this principle A. Voßkuhle 'Grundwissen – Öffentliches Recht: Der Grundsatz der Verhältnismäßigkeit' [2007] *Juristische Schulung* 429, 429; M. Klatt and M. Meister 'Der Grundsatz der Verhältnismäßigkeit. Ein Strukturelement des globalen Konstitutionalismus' [2014] *Juristische Schulung* 193, 193.

47 M. Jahn 'Strafprozessrecht als geronnenes Verfassungsrecht – Hauptprobleme und Streitfragen des § 136a StPO' [2005] *Juristische Schulung* 1057, 1057.

e) *Is the acquisition of evidence at the investigation stage restricted by concrete prohibitions, e.g. the prohibition to use specific sources of evidence or evidentiary methods (please indicate the level of subordination of evidentiary activities to strict law; or maybe this situation depends on the nature of evidence, e.g. its interference in human rights and freedoms, or on the type of crime)? Please indicate examples of evidentiary activities that are subject to the strictest legal restrictions.*

There are three different ways in which the acquisition of evidence can be restricted.[48] First, there are facts that cannot be the object of an evidentiary method (*Beweisthemaverbot*). These are facts that have to be kept secret (e.g. discussions by the panel of judges, § 43 German Judge Law [*Deutsches Richtergesetz* – *DRiG*) or have already been bindingly established before.[49]

Secondly, there are forbidden evidentiary methods. The most important provision in this context is § 136a StPO:

Section 136a Prohibited examination methods; prohibited evidence

(1) The accused's freedom to make up his mind and to manifest his will must not be impaired by ill-treatment, induced fatigue, physical intervention on the body, the administration of drugs, torture, by means of deception or hypnosis. Compulsion may be used only insofar as this is permitted by criminal procedure law. Threatening the accused with measures not permitted under the provisions of criminal procedure law and holding out the prospect of an advantage not envisaged by statute shall be prohibited.

(2) Measures which impair the accused's memory or his capacity to understand the wrongfulness of an act shall not be permitted.

(3) The prohibitions under subsections (1) and (2) shall apply irrespective of the accused's consent. Statements which were obtained in breach of this prohibition shall not be used, even if the accused consents to their use.

§ 136a StPO refers to the examination of the suspect and protects them from a variety of methods of interrogation that violate their human rights.[50] It even

48 See U. Eisenberg *Beweisrecht der* StPO, 10th ed. C.H.Beck 2017, margin no. 338 ff.

49 It is rare that judgments are binding on other courts in Germany. However, if the defendant only appeals against the sentence in a judgment, not the conviction, the facts that form the basis of the conviction become binding.

50 For an overview, see M. Jahn 'Strafprozessrecht als geronnenes Verfassungsrecht – Hauptprobleme und Streitfragen des § 136a StPO' [2005] *Juristische Schulung* 1057.

provides an explicit and absolute exclusionary clause (§ 136a(3)2 StPO). While most forbidden methods listed in § 136a StPO are clear, it is often problematic to determine what constitutes a forbidden deception and what is only cunning.[51]

It is also possible to exclude evidentiary methods that cannot guarantee reliable evidence. For example, evidence by a polygraph has been considered to be without evidentiary value and thus excluded.[52]

Thirdly, there are sources of evidence that are off-limits. The most important example is witness privilege (§§ 52, 53 StPO). Relatives of the defendant and persons who had contact with the defendant in their professional capacity and are sworn to professional secrecy (e.g. lawyers, doctors, clergymen) can refuse to testify.[53] Interrogations are then forbidden. Nor is it allowed to read

---

51 See H. Diemer '§ 136a StPO' margin no. 19 ff., in R. Hannich (ed.) *Karlsruher Kommentar zur Strafprozessordnung*, 9th ed., C.H.Beck 2023; M. Jahn 'Strafprozessrecht als geronnenes Verfassungsrecht – Hauptprobleme und Streitfragen des § 136a StPO' [2005] *Juristische Schulung* 1057, 1059 f.

52 BGHSt 44, 308, 319; BGH NStZ 2011, 474, 475; see also W. Kargl and S. Kirsch, 'Zur Zulässigkeit eines untauglichen Beweismittels im Strafverfahren – BGHSt 44, 308' [2000] *Juristische Schulung* 537, 537.

53 In the sense of § 52 StPO, relatives are: 1. the accused's fiancé or fiancée; 2. the accused's spouse, even if the marriage no longer exists; 2a. the accused's life partner, even if the life partnership no longer exists; 3. a person who is or was lineally related or related by marriage, collaterally related to the third degree or related by marriage to the second degree to the accused.

The professional witnesses named in § 53 StPO are:

1. clergy, concerning that information which was confided to them or which became known to them in their capacity as spiritual advisers;
2. defence counsel of the accused, concerning that information which was confided to them or which became known to them in this capacity;
3. lawyers and non-lawyer providers of legal services who have been admitted to a bar association, patent attorneys, notaries, certified public accountants, sworn auditors, tax consultants (Steuerberater) and tax representatives (Steuerbevollmächtigte), doctors, dentists, psychological psychotherapists, psychotherapists specialising in the treatment of children and juveniles, pharmacists and midwives, concerning that information which was confided to them or which became known to them in this capacity; subject to section 53a, the same shall not apply to in-house lawyers (section 46 (2) of the Federal Code for Lawyers) and in-house patent attorneys (section 41a (2) of the Federal Code for Patent Attorneys (Patentanwaltsordnung)) in respect of that which was confided to them or became known to them in this capacity;

3a. members or representatives of a recognised counselling agency under sections 3 and 8 of the Act on Pregnancies in Conflict Situations (Schwangerschaftskonfliktgesetz), concerning that information which was confided to them or which became known to them in this capacity;

3b. drug dependency counsellors in a counselling agency recognised or set up by an authority, a body, an institution or a foundation under public law, concerning that information which was confided to them or which became known to them in this capacity;

out a former witness statement in court or ask the interviewing person to give evidence from hearsay (§ 252 StPO).[54]

Several other provisions refer to witness privileges in order to limit the investigating possibilities of the prosecuting authorities. § 97 StPO prohibits the seizure of written communication, notes and other objects which are covered by the right to refuse to testify under certain circumstances and for certain witnesses.[55] § 100d(5) StPO has a similar rule for professional witnesses only with regard to acoustic and telecommunication surveillance and covert remote searches of information technology systems. Provisions on witness privileges are also found in § 82c(3) (physical examination), 95(2)2 (obligation to surrender) and § 100g(4) StPO (traffic data capture). While these rules only apply to certain specific investigative measures, there is a provision in § 160a StPO that can limit any investigative measure:

§ 160a Measures directed at persons entitled to refuse testimony on professional grounds

(1) An investigation measure directed at a person designated in section 53 (1) sentence 1 no. 1, 2 or 4, a lawyer or a non-lawyer provider of legal services who has been admitted to a bar association shall be inadmissible if it is expected to produce information in respect

4. Members of the Bundestag, of the Federal Convention, of the European Parliament from the Federal Republic of Germany or of a Land parliament, concerning persons who have confided certain facts to them in their capacity as members of these bodies or to whom they have confided facts in this particular capacity, as well as concerning the facts themselves;
5. individuals who are or have been professionally involved in the preparation, production or dissemination of printed matter, broadcasts, film documentaries or in the information and communication services involved in instruction or in the formation of opinion.

The persons designated in sentence 1 no. 5 may refuse to testify concerning the author or contributor of comments and documentation or concerning any other informant or the information communicated to them in their professional capacity, including its content, as well as concerning the content of materials which they have produced themselves and matters which have received their professional attention. This shall only apply insofar as this concerns contributions, documentation, information and materials for the editorial element of their activity or information and communication services which have been editorially reviewed.

54 BGH *Neue Zeitschrift für Strafrecht* 2015, 710, 711; H. Diemer '§ 252 StPO', margin no. 1, in R. Hannich (ed.) *Karlsruher Kommentar zur Strafprozessordnung*, 9th ed., C.H.Beck 2023; H. Farthofer and C. Rückert 'Die höchstrichterliche Rechtsprechung zu § 252 StPO im Lichte eines grund- und menschenrechtskonformen Strafverfahrens' [2017] *Onlinezeitschrift für höchstrichterliche Rechtsprechung im Strafrecht* 123, 123.

55 Many details on this paragraph are unclear. For an overview, see A. Schneider *Strafprozessuale Ermittlungsmaßnahmen und Zeugnisverweigerungsrechte*, Mohr Siebeck 2021, pp. 33 ff.

of which such person would have the right to refuse to testify. Any information which is obtained nonetheless may not be used. Any recording of such information is to be deleted without delay. The fact that the information was obtained and deleted shall be included in the records. If information about a person referred to in sentence 1 is obtained through an investigation measure which is not aimed at such person and in respect of which such person may refuse to testify, sentences 2 to 4 shall apply accordingly.

(2) Insofar as a person designated in section 53 (1) sentence 1 nos. 3 to 3b or no. 5 might be affected by an investigation measure and it is to be expected that information would thereby be obtained in respect of which the person would have the right to refuse to testify, this shall be given particular consideration in the context of examining proportionality; if the proceedings do not concern an offence of substantial significance, then, in principle, no overriding interest in prosecuting the offence is to be presumed. Insofar as is expedient, the measure should be dispensed with or, to the extent possible for this type of measure, restricted. Sentence 1 shall apply accordingly to the use of information for evidential purposes. Sentences 1 to 3 shall not apply to lawyers and non-lawyer providers of legal services who have been admitted to a bar association.

(3) Subsections (1) and (2) shall apply accordingly insofar as the persons designated in section 53a would have the right to refuse to testify.

(4) Subsections (1) to (3) shall not apply if certain facts give rise to the suspicion that the person who is entitled to refuse to testify participated in the offence or in handling stolen data, aiding after the fact, obstruction of prosecution or punishment, or handling stolen goods. If the offence may be prosecuted only upon request or only upon authorisation, sentence 1 shall apply in the cases under section 53 (1) sentence 1 no. 5 as soon as and insofar as the request to prosecute has been filed or the authorisation granted.

(5) Section 97, section 100d (5) and section 100g (4) shall remain unaffected.

This long and complicated provision is fairly new but has already given rise to many questions.[56] For example, it is unclear why it only applies to professional witnesses and not to other witnesses who have a right to refuse to testify.[57]

56 For an overview, see ibid., pp. 56 ff.

57 P. Hauck, *Heimliche Strafverfolgung und Schutz der Privatheit*, Mohr Siebeck 2014, p. 444; R. Kölbel '§ 160a StPO', margin no. 6, in C. Knauer, H. Kudlich, H. Schneider (eds)

Moreover, the relationship to the other rules on witness privilege is unclear. Although some rules are to remain unaffected (§ 160a(5) StPO), others are not named in the provision and it is not clear whether § 160a StPO remains applicable in addition to other more specific rules on witness privilege.[58]

Overall, the limits to investigative activity depend on the addressee of the measure. If it is a member of a parliament or a defence lawyer, investigative measures are the most limited (see, e.g. §§ 160a(1), 97(4) StPO). The protection becomes noticeably less pronounced for other professional witnesses and journalists (see § 160a(2), 97(5) StPO) and is at its lowest for relatives of the defendant, who are not protected by § 160a StPO. Some investigative measures have extra rules on witness protection. These include investigative measures that are considered to be the most intrusive (§§ 100b, 100c StPO) but also standard measures such as seizure and surrender (§§ 97, 95 StPO).

The law also offers a special protection of privacy rights, especially of the core area of private conduct of life. This has been accepted case-law of the Federal Constitutional Court for a long time.[59] Following this approach, mutterings of a person to oneself in the hospital room are not admitted as evidence.[60] Diaries have been admitted in a controversial decision.[61] Whether this judgment still holds today remains to be seen. In order to provide better transparency, the legislator has adopted a provision on surveillance measures that is based on the constitutional law on the protection of privacy:

Section 100d Core area of private conduct of life; persons authorised to refuse to give evidence

(1) If there are factual indications to assume that a measure under sections 100a to 100c will only lead to findings in the core area of the private conduct of life, the measure shall be inadmissible.

Münchener Kommentar zur Strafprozessordnung, vol. 2, C.H.Beck 2016; J. Kretschmer '§ 160a – gelungene oder misslungene Gesetzgebung?' [2010] *Online Zeitschrift für Höchstrichterliche Rechtsprechung zum* Strafrecht 551, 556; J. Wolter, 'Alternativen zum Regierungs-Entwurf 2007 zur Neuregelung der Ermittlungsmaßnahmen – Heike Jung zum 65. Geburtstag' [2007] Goltdammer's Archiv für Strafrecht, p. 189; M. Zöller 'Heimliche und verdeckte Ermittlungsmaßnahmen im Strafverfahren' 124 (2012) *Zeitschrift für die gesamte Strafrechtswissenschaft* 411, 433.

58 On the discussion A. Schneider *Strafprozessuale Ermittlungsmaßnahmen und Zeugnisverweigerungsrechte,* Mohr Siebeck 2021, pp. 64 ff., 707 ff. with further references.

59 BVerfGE 33, 367; BVerfGE 80, 367, 379; BVerfGE 109, 279; BVerfGE 125, 260.

60 BGHSt 57, 71; BGHSt 50, 206.

61 BVerfGE 80, 367, 376 ff.

(2) Findings in the core area of the private conduct of life which are made on the basis of a measure under sections 100a to 100c may not be used. Recordings of such findings must be deleted without delay. The fact that such findings were made and their deletion shall be documented.

(3) Where possible in the case of measures under section 100b, technical means shall be employed to ensure that data concerning the core area of the private conduct of life are not captured. Findings made on the basis of measures under section 100b which concern the core area of the private conduct of life shall be deleted without delay or submitted to the court ordering the measure by the public prosecution office for a decision as to their usability and deletion. The court's decision concerning the usability of the data shall be binding in respect of the further proceedings.

(4) Measures pursuant to section 100c may be ordered only if on the basis of factual indications it may be assumed that statements concerning the core area of the private conduct of life will not be covered by the surveillance. The interception and recording is to be interrupted without delay if during the surveillance indications arise that statements concerning the core area of the private conduct of life are being recorded. Where a measure has been interrupted, it may be recommenced subject to the conditions of sentence 1. In cases of doubt, the public prosecution office shall seek a decision from the court without delay concerning the interruption or continuation of the measure; section 100e (5) shall apply accordingly. If it is considered a possibility that the use of findings already made pursuant to subsection (2) will be prohibited, the public prosecution office must also apply to the court for a decision without delay. Subsection (3) sentence 3 shall apply accordingly.

(5) In the cases under section 53, measures under sections 100b and 100c shall be inadmissible; if during or after implementation of the measure it becomes apparent that a case under section 53 exists, then subsection (2) shall apply accordingly. In the cases under sections 52 and 53a, information acquired through measures under sections 100b and 100c may be used only if, taking into consideration the significance of the underlying relationship of trust, this is not disproportionate to the interest in establishing the facts or determining the whereabouts of an accused person. Section 160a (4) shall apply accordingly.

This provision provides many details on the consequences of a violation of the core area of private conduct of life. According to the Federal Constitutional

Court, "[t]he development of personality in the core area of private conduct of life includes the possibility of expressing inner processes such as feelings and emotions as well as considerations, views and experiences of a highly personal nature [...]. In particular, non-public communication with persons of the highest personal trust, which is conducted in the justified assumption that it will not be monitored, as is the case in particular with conversations in the area of the home, is protected."[62] By this, German law protects conversation between lovers in private surroundings. Whether this protection extends to a confession of a crime is disputed in German law.[63] Nonetheless, the protection of privacy rights is very high.

German law also recognizes the privilege against self-incrimination, although there is no explicit rule on the principle. This means that the defendant has the right to remain silent and must be informed accordingly (§ 136(1)2 StPO). It is understood to apply to active participation in criminal law only.[64] Therefore, it prohibits forcing the defendant to surrender objects but not a seizure. Similarly, the defendant cannot be coerced to use a breathalyser in order to determine the alcohol level, although it is possible to get a blood sample (§ 81a StPO).

f) *Does the applicable law sufficiently define the boundaries of evidence acquisition admissibility, or maybe too categorically? What is the potential extent of the non-normative sphere in shaping such boundaries (general rules, pragmatism, habits)? Are the proportions between the two spheres (normative and non-normative) appropriate?*

The overview on the most important provisions and guarantees limiting investigation above (supra e) has shown that, while the investigative measures are mostly laid out in detail in the law, the limits are often not clearly regulated. Witnesses are strongly protected in Germany, but the reason for this is unclear and the law is chaotic.[65] The privilege against self-incrimination is hardly

62 BVerfGE 141, 220, 276 margin no. 121. Translation by the author.

63 BVerfGE 141, 220, 277 margin no. 122; C. Rottmeier *Kernbereich privater Lebensgestaltung und strafprozessuale Lauschangriffe*, Mohr Siebeck 2017, pp. 42 ff.

64 BGH NStZ-RR 2018, 319, 319; K. Amelung, 'Beschlagnahme, Notarielle Unterlagen' [1984] *Deutsche Notarzeitschrift* 195, 218; J. Dallmeyer, 'Verletzt der zwangsweise Brechmitteleinsatz gegen Beschuldigte deren Persönlichkeitsrechte?' [1997] *Strafverteidiger* 606, 608; K. Eckstein *Ermittlungen zu Lasten Dritter*, Mohr Siebeck 2013, pp. 423 ff.; P. Kasiske, 'Die Selbstbelastungsfreiheit im Strafprozess' [2014] *Juristische Schulung* 15, 16; J. Schuhr 'vor §§ 133 ff', no. 91 f., in C. Knauer, H. Kudlich and H. Schneider (eds) *Münchener Kommentar zur Strafprozessordnung*, vol. 2, C.H.Beck 2023; B. Weißer, 'Zeugnisverweigerungsrechte und Menschenwürde als Schutzschild gegen heimliche strafprozessuale Zugriffe auf Kommunikationsinhalte?' [2006] Goltdammer's Archiv für Strafrecht, p. 155.

65 In detail A. Schneider *Strafprozessuale Ermittlungsmaßnahmen und Zeugnisverweigerungsrechte*, Mohr Siebeck 2021, passim.

regulated but undisputedly recognized in German criminal law. The same is true for the protection of the core area of private conduct of life. In this respect, German law relies too much on general rules instead of a normative approach. On the other hand, the normative approach taken with witness protection is not convincing and might limit the investigation activities too severely, e.g. by allowing victims of domestic abuse to refuse to testify.[66] In my opinion, German criminal law has not yet found the perfect balance between procedural safeguards and the necessities of investigation.

g) *As regards the acquisition of evidence during investigation, how at this stage is the deficit of the inapplicability of principles of equality of parties, equality of arms, and the contradictory principle compensated for, also taking into account the fact of general primacy of law enforcement authorities, in order to ensure a fair evidentiary procedure? Can the suspect and other entities share in this?*

The public prosecution office is obliged to search for both incriminating and exonerating evidence (§ 160(2) StPO). The suspect must be interrogated before an indictment is filed (§ 163a(1) StPO) and can apply for evidence to be taken in their defence (§ 163a(2) StPO). However, the suspect has no legal way to force the public prosecution office to do so.[67] Accordingly, it has been argued that the suspect is at a disadvantage in the investigative phase.[68] Only at the trial phase does an appealable right to apply for evidence exist (§ 244(3) StPO). Moreover, the defendant has the right to object to the use of evidence that is inadmissible.

h) *Is there a balance between the freedom of law enforcement authorities' actions, on which the crime combating efficiency depends, and limitations of that freedom arising from the need to ensure appropriate standards of evidentiary procedure? Does a comparison of those antagonistic to some extent perspectives show that the purpose of repression dominates at the expense of the procedural guarantees and the rights of individuals, or rather the purpose of the reliability of evidence at the expense of its effectiveness in the detection of the truth?*

The German legal approach is based on the idea of balancing the need for effective criminal proceedings with the protection of individual rights. Each

66 Ibid., pp. 481 f.; M. Kremer *Strafprozessuale Angehörigenprivilegien im Rechtsvergleich*, Mohr Siebeck 2018, p. 76.

67 R. Schlothauer '§ 3 Ermittlungsverfahren', margin no. 121, in E. Müller and R. Schlothauer (eds) *Münchener Anwaltshandbuch Strafverteidigung*, 3rd ed., C.H.Beck 2022.

68 B. Schünemann 'Der Richter im Strafverfahren als manipulierter Dritter? Zur empirischen Bestätigung von Perseveranz- und Schulterschlußeffekt' [2000] *Strafverteidiger* 159, 163.

provision on criminal procedure restricts the suspects constitutionally guaranteed freedoms and must justify this restriction. On the whole, the German legal system does this fairly well. More intrusive investigative measures such as acoustic surveillance of private premises (§ 100c StPO) or covert remote search of information technology systems (§ 100b StPO) go hand in hand with stronger procedural safeguards (§ 100d StPO). Although some parts of German criminal procedural law do not seem to be well-balanced (e.g. massive protection of the suspect's relatives,[69] fragmentary protection of legal professional privilege)[70] and it is sometimes difficult to predict the outcome of the prevailing balancing approach for the admissibility of evidence, the result is a system that is neither too repressive nor too lenient.

i) *How can the fairness of evidentiary procedure be ensured in view of the conditions imposed by the commonly used consensual procedures, methods directed towards accelerating or shortening criminal proceedings, and the usage of alternative methods for criminal prosecution? Those measures not only fail to eliminate the issue of the boundaries of legal acquisition of evidence, but bring this issue into focus in connection with the conclusiveness of evidence being examined at the investigation stage. In these circumstances, are procedural guarantees ensured during the evidentiary procedure, together with due control over its legality at the investigation stage, bearing in mind the pressure for attaining the goal and swiftly end the proceedings?*

The German legal system places a huge emphasis on the main proceedings. All evidence must be renewed in the trial phase, i.e. all witnesses and experts must be interviewed again, all other evidence must be presented and so on.[71] This takes a lot of time and effort. Therefore, faster ways to terminate criminal proceedings have become an important part of criminal proceedings. The public prosecution office can make use of its competences under §§ 153 ff. StPO to terminate proceedings when there is a likelihood of conviction but the prerequisites of these rules are met. Non-prosecution is possible for, e.g. petty offences (§ 153 StPO), active remorse (§ 153e StPO) or offences committed abroad (§ 153c StPO). Proceedings can also be terminated subject to the imposition of conditions, e.g. the payment of a sum of money to a charity (§ 153a StPO).

---

69 See A. Schneider *Strafprozessuale Ermittlungsmaßnahmen und Zeugnisverweigerungsrechte*, Mohr Siebeck 2021, pp. 263 ff.

70 A. Schneider 'Search and Seizure of Documents generated in Internal Investigations – Lessons to learn from European Law' [2018] 89 *Revue Internationale de Droit Pénal* 311, 312 ff.

71 A. Eser et al., 'Alternativ-Entwurf Beweisaufnahme' (2014) Goltdammer's Archiv pp. 1 ff.

In this case, the suspect's consent is required. Another commonly used way to terminate proceedings is the summary penalty order (*Strafbefehl*, §§ 407 ff. StPO). A summary penalty order imposes a sanction (a fine or, if the indicted suspect has a defence lawyer, up to one year of imprisonment suspended on probation) on written application by the public prosecution office (§ 407(1) StPO). There is no main hearing and no consent required. Nonetheless, the indicted suspect can lodge an objection against the order that will lead to a trial with main hearing (§ 410(1) StPO).

All these procedures have in common that there is no main hearing at which the evidence is presented again and evaluated by the court. This might disadvantage the suspect for several reasons: First, they have no possibility to force the public prosecution office to gather exonerating evidence. Only at the main hearing does the defendant have a right to apply for taking evidence which must be rejected by court order, thus allowing judicial review (§ 244(6) StPO). Secondly, the defence counsel's right to inspect the file can be limited in the investigative phase. Only when proceedings have been concluded is full access to the file guaranteed (§ 147(2) StPO).

The proceedings explained above take this into consideration by ensuring a system of checks and balances. Whenever a sanction or another condition is imposed upon the suspect, the court must agree (e.g. §§ 153a(1), 407(1) StPO). When criminal proceedings are dispensed with (§§ 153 ff. StPO), the suspect's consent is often required. This is not true for the summary penalty order which is in practice often used when the defendant has not appeared to the main proceedings. However, the law provides a special form of judicial review, the objection, in order to allow the suspect to get a hearing in main proceedings. Nonetheless, summary penalty orders are written proceedings in which the suspect's right to be heard might be impaired.

There are also two non-standard procedures which should not have a negative effect on the evaluation of evidence. In accelerated proceedings (*Beschleunigtes Verfahren* – §§ 417 ff. StPO), the time limit for summoning is dispensed with, which means that the main hearing can start immediately (§ 418(1) StPO). Because the main hearing gives the defendant rights to participate and to dispute all evidence, their situation is not worse from an evidentiary point of view in these proceedings. The second proceeding is the proceeding on a negotiated agreement (*Verständigungsverfahren* – § 257c StPO). A negotiated agreement is a deal on the outcome of the case and the legal consequences for the defendant (see § 257c(1, 2) StPO). It is part of the main proceedings, not the investigative phase.[72] According to § 257c(1)2 StPO, the crucial provision

72 U. Kindhäuser and K. Schumann *Strafprozessrecht*, 5th ed., Nomos 2019, § 19 margin no. 12.

on the court's obligation to take evidence and examine the facts, § 244(2) StPO, remains unaffected. This means that the court still has to take evidence on the question of guilt, regardless of the negotiated agreement.[73] § 257c(1)2 StPO has been criticized severely. Scholars have pointed out that the whole purpose of a deal is to (partly) free the judicial authorities from the lengthy process of evidence taking and evaluating and that a law requiring the same evidentiary standard as without such an agreement defeats its purpose.[74] Which standards actually apply is still under debate in German law.

4 Identifications of Risks of Violating Freedom in the Acquisition of Evidence by Law Enforcement Authorities

a) *Narrow focus of enforcement authorities to acquire evidence of being guilty; oppressive investigative methods; violation of human dignity; use of measures compelling individuals to meet certain evidentiary obligations, or use of a passive tactic consisting in provoking the suspect or other entities into providing evidence. What measures are taken to counteract such practices?*

Criminal investigations are strongly regulated in German law. Due to the close connection between criminal procedure law and constitutional law, all investigative measures are subject to scrutiny and could, in the end, be subject of a constitutional complaint (*Verfassungsbeschwerde*).[75] Oppressive investigative measures, violations of human dignity and the use of measures compelling individuals to meet evidentiary obligations are therefore only admissible unless they unjustifiably violate constitutional rights. These considerations are not the prerogative of the Federal Constitutional Court but need to be undertaken by any court deciding on the matter, including the court of first instance. As has been explained above, it is possible to file a complaint against individual investigative measures and also to object to their use as evidence in trial.

The narrow focus of enforcement authorities on incriminating evidence can be problematic. The public prosecution office is obliged to ascertain both incriminating and exonerating circumstances by law (§ 160(2) StPO). Accordingly, in theory, there should be no such focus. The suspect can apply for

73 See BVerfGE 133, 168, 207 ff.

74 See e.g. M. Jahn and H. Kudlich '§ 257c' margin no. 39 f., in C. Knauer, H. Kudlich, H. Schneider (eds) *Münchener Kommentar zur Strafprozessordnung*, vol. 2, C.H.Beck 2016; C. Knauer and A. Lickleder 'Die obergerichtliche Rechtsprechung zu Verfahrensabsprachen nach der gesetzlichen Regelung – ein kritischer Überblick' [2012] *Neue Zeitschrift für Strafrecht* 366, 367.

75 Anyone can lodge a complaint alleging that one of their basic rights has been infringed by public authority after judicial review was without success, Article 93(1) no 4a GG.

evidence to be taken in their defence, but only if it is of importance (§ 163a(2) StPO). It is unclear whether this provision is merely a clarification of § 160(2) StPO or whether it grants a right to have evidence taken.[76] In any case, there is no legal way to force the public prosecution office to take evidence.[77]

The question of to what extent subjects may be provoked into providing incriminating evidence is much debated in German law, due to several convictions by the European Court of Human Rights.[78] § 136a StPO prohibits the deception of the suspect. The line between legal undercover missions and forbidden deceptions is small.[79] So far, the discussion focusses on the consequences of the provocation for the defendant during main proceedings – either a reduction of the sentence or the termination of proceedings.[80] However, the constitutional background laid out above also applies to illegal provocation.

b) *A tendency to hierarchize evidence in favour of scientific evidence and at the expense of other pieces of evidence. Can an a priori privileged treatment of such evidence be seen as a threat to the legality and fairness of evidentiary procedure in connection with unsatisfactory motivation of enforcement authorities to verify and critically evaluate the same, and with the limited opportunities for private parties to challenge the same?*

There is no rule giving higher probatory value to scientific evidence in German law. All methods of evidence available for the question of guilt (*Strengbeweisverfahren*) – witnesses, expert witnesses, documents and inspection – are of equal value. To my knowledge, there is no debate about giving precedence to scientific evidence.

However, it is true that some evidence is regarded as more reliable than others. For example, it has been claimed that witnesses that are related to the suspect have been given the right to refuse to testify because their testimony

76 W. Krekeler 'Der Beweiserhebungsanspruch des Beschuldigten im Ermittlungsverfahren' [1991] *Neue Zeitschrift für Strafrecht* 367, 367.

77 R. Schlothauer '§ 3 Ermittlungsverfahren', margin no. 121, in E. Müller and R. Schlothauer (eds) *Münchener Anwaltshandbuch Strafverteidigung*, 3rd ed. C.H.Beck 2022.

78 *Furcht v. Germany* App no. 54648/09, ECtHR, 23 October 2014; *Akbay v. Germany* App no. 40495/15, ECtHR, 15 October 2020).

79 See e.g. OLG Jena Beck-Rechtsprechung 2019, 24214, in which the undercover police officers offered to find a third person with cancer to take the fall for the suspect in a murder case.

80 See e.g. BGH NStZ 2018, 355; BGH NStZ 2016, 52; A. Sinn and S. Maly 'Zu den strafprozessualen Folgen einer rechtsstaatswidrigen Tatprovokation – Zugleich Besprechung von EGMR, Urt. v. 23.10.2014 – 54648/09 (Furcht v. Germany)' [2015] *Neue Zeitschrift für Strafrecht* 379, 379.

was unreliable.[81] Even if this were true, it does not explain why professional witnesses can refuse to testify, too. Nor does it explain why the seizure of documents and surveillance measures are also limited, although these measures are much more reliable.[82] Accordingly, the reliability of evidence does not seem to be a dominant factor in German criminal procedure law. It should also be noted that the evidence is assessed by legal professionals because there are no jury trials in Germany, so a "CSI effect"[83] is less likely. Therefore, the risk of such a priorization is rather low.

c) *Different boundaries for the freedom of law enforcement authorities to acquire evidence depending on the crime type; a failure by legal regulations to keep up with new technologies to be used in cases for most serious crimes gives rise to a threat of abuse and potentially easier excuse of such practices. How can the present legal regulation be assessed from this perspective (e.g. as to cyber or biological evidence) in the context of threats to the fairness of evidentiary procedure? Are other regulatory standards in place or are any such standards tolerated, being different from those as in the case of traditional evidence?*

The strict corset of rules in which German criminal law enforcement authorities operate make it difficult to abuse gaps in the legislation. If it is unclear whether or not a certain technological invention is covered by a specific provision and if the investigative authorities use it nonetheless, the matter will almost certainly be subject to judicial review. Generally, the German legislator takes action when biological or technological innovations make new law necessary.

A good example for this is the covert remote search of information technology systems (*Online-Durchsuchung*). Before the adoption of § 100b StPO, there was a debate about the admissibility of a remote computer search. Some were arguing that the existing provisions could apply to a remote computer

---

81 H. Baier, *Strafprozessuale Zeugnisverweigerungsrechte außerhalb der Strafprozessordnung als Ergänzung der §§ 53 ff.* StPO, Peter Lang 1996, pp. 64 ff.; K. Jansen, *Das Zeugnisverweigerungsrecht aus § 52* StPO *für besondere persönliche Nähe- und Vertrauensverhältnisse,* Duncker & Humblot 2004, pp. 153 ff.; R. Rengier *Die Zeugnisverweigerungsrechte im geltenden und künftigen Strafverfahrensrecht*, Ferdinand Schöningh 1980, pp. 56 ff.; E. Schmidt 'Die Verletzung der Belehrungspflicht gemäß § 55 II StPO als Revisionsgrund' [1958] *Juristenzeitung* 596, 599 ff.

82 A. Schneider *Strafprozessuale Ermittlungsmaßnahmen und Zeugnisverweigerungsrechte,* Mohr Siebeck 2020, pp. 338 ff.

83 See J. Chin and L. Workewych 'The CSI effect' [2016] *Oxford Handbooks Online,* available at https://academic.oup.com/edited-volume/41331/chapter/352336326 (last access on 03.02.2023).

search.[84] However, in 2007 the Federal Court of Justice decided that this was not true and that an explicit provision allowing this investigative measure was necessary.[85] The general rule allowing any investigative measure (§§ 161(1), 163(1) StPO) can only apply to slight impairments of fundamental rights and does not cover highly intrusive measures such as a covert remote search of a computer.[86] This led to the adoption of § 100b StPO in 2017.[87] There are similar developments in the area of biological evidence.

5 Inviolable Boundaries in the Acquisition of Evidence by Law Enforcement Authorities

a) *Please indicate violations in the acquisition of evidence that make the evidence definitely invalid (i.e. indicate prohibited methods of proving facts);*

The most important provision concerning the method of acquiring evidence is § 136a StPO. It forbids ill-treatment, induced fatigue, physical intervention on the body, the administration of drugs, torture, deception or hypnosis. Threats and compulsion must be based on the measures provided for in criminal procedure law. Measures which impair the suspect's memory or his capacity to understand the wrongfulness of an act are also forbidden, § 136a StPO also applies to the interrogation of witnesses (§ 69(3) StPO). The evidence is excluded by law (§ 136a(3)2 StPO).

Evidence by a polygraph is also excluded for lack of evidentiary value.[88] In some cases, evidence is excluded if the person concerned was not properly informed of their rights. This is true for the testimony of witnesses who are related to the suspect (§ 52 StPO) and for the suspect who was not informed of their right to remain silent (§ 136(1), 163a(3)2, (4)2 StPO), but not for witnesses who were not informed of their right to remain silent (§ 55 StPO). There are

84 E.g. M. Hofmann, 'Die Online-Durchsuchung – staatliches „Hacken" oder zulässige Ermittlungsmaßnahme?' [2005] *Neue Zeitschrift für Strafrecht* 121, 121 ff.

85 BGHSt 51, 211.

86 BGHSt 51, 211 margin no. 22.

87 Gesetz zur effektiveren und praxistauglicheren Ausgestaltung des Strafverfahrens vom 17.8.2017, Federal Law Gazette (*Bundesgesetzblatt*) 2017 I, 3202, available at https://www.bgbl.de/xaver/bgbl/start.xav?startbk=Bundesanzeiger_BGBl&start=//*%5B@attr_id=%27bgbl117s3202.pdf%27%5D#__bgbl__%2F%2F*%5B%40attr_id%3D%27bgbl117s3202.pdf%27%5D__1675535401415 (28.03.2023).

88 BGHSt 44, 308, 319; BGH *Neue Zeitschrift für Strafrecht* 2011, 474, 475.

also exceptions when people did know their rights without being informed. These rules come from case-law.[89]

b) *Please indicate evidence the acquisition of which is definitely prohibited;*
If a witness refuses to testify (§§ 52, 53 StPO), they cannot be coerced to testify. It is also forbidden to read out an earlier testimony at trial or ask the interviewing person to give evidence from hearsay (§ 252 StPO).[90] The exclusion of this evidence is based on case-law.[91]

Similarly, according to § 160a(1) StPO, "[a]n investigation measure directed at a person designated in section 53 (1) sentence 1 no. 1, 2 or 4, a lawyer or a non-lawyer provider of legal services who has been admitted to a bar association shall be inadmissible if it is expected to produce information in respect of which such person would have the right to refuse to testify." This means that all investigative measures directed against clergymen, defence counsels, lawyers or members of a parliament are prohibited if they are expected to produce information that falls within the scope of the individual's right to refuse to testify. The same is true for measures that are not aimed at the witness (§ 160a(1)5 StPO).

Another important provision in this context is § 100d(1) StPO: "If there are factual indications to assume that a measure under sections 100a to 100c will only lead to findings in the core area of the private conduct of life, the measure shall be inadmissible." This prohibition is flanked by an explicit exclusionary rule in § 100d(2)2 StPO: "Findings in the core area of the private conduct of life which are made on the basis of a measure under sections 100a to 100c may not be used." Although these rules only apply to §§ 100a–100c StPO, the general principle behind it is accepted in German law. This means that any evidence that leads to findings in the core area of the private conduct of life is prohibited and excluded from trial.[92]

Another example is the prohibition of seizure (§ 97 StPO). Although there is considerable discussion about what falls within the scope of this prohibition, people agree that the consequence of a violation of this rule is that the evidence will be inadmissible.[93] However, it should be noted that the applicability of § 97 StPO sometimes depends on a balancing test (see §§ 97(5), 53(1) sentences 1 no. 5, 2, 3 StPO).

---

89 M. Heger and E. Pohlreich *Strafprozessrecht*, 2nd ed., Kohlhammer 2018, margin no. 398.

90 See M. Heger and E. Pohlreich *Strafprozessrecht*, 2nd ed., Kohlhammer 2018, margin no. 400 ff.

91 BGH *Neue Zeitschrift für Strafrecht* 2015, 710, 711.

92 BVerfGE 129, 208, 245.

93 M. Heger and E. Pohlreich *Strafprozessrecht*, 2nd ed., Kohlhammer 2018, margin no. 398.

Expunged previous convictions may not be utilized (§ 51 Federal Central Register Law = *Bundeszentralregistergesetz* – BZRG). Nor is it allowed to take evidence on the judges' deliberations (§§ 43, 45 DRiG).

c) *Please indicate a category of interests and values that are decisive for excluding evidence or restricting its examination.*

The theoretical background of exclusionary rules has already been explained above (supra 1 and 3 c). The main concern with independent exclusionary rules is the balance between a violation of fundamental rights and the public interest in effective prosecution. The more individual rights are impaired, the higher ranking has the public interest to be in order to prevent the exclusion of the evidence. There are some explicit independent exclusionary rules. For example, if a medical doctor's practice is searched and objects are seized that point at an illegal abortion by a patient, § 108(2) StPO states that these objects cannot be used as evidence against the patient. Other rules limiting the use of or excluding evidence that has been found by chance are §§ 161(3), 479(2), 100e(6) no 1 and 81a(3) StPO.

Dependent exclusionary rules require a violation of the law when collecting evidence. However, not all violations lead to the exclusion of the evidence. When evidence is to be excluded is much under debate and has been the subject of different theoretical approaches (supra 3 c). Generally, an intentional and purposeful violation of the law will lead to the exclusion of the evidence, e.g. a refusal to ask for judicial authorization.[94] Another factor that may be taken into account is the hypothetical possibility to acquire the evidence legally: if it had been possible to collect the evidence legally at the time, its exclusion is considered too formal.[95]

6 Conclusion

The area of criminal procedure law is strongly regulated in Germany. There are detailed provisions for the most common investigative measures. Although there is a catch-all competence for the prosecuting authorities to apply any investigative measure (§§ 161, 163 StPO), it effectively only applies to minor impairments. Investigative measures based on new technologies such as source telecommunication surveillance (*Quellen-*

94 U. Kindhäuser and K. Schumann *Strafprozessrecht*, 6th ed., Nomos 2021, § 23 margin no. 10, 30.

95 U. Kindhäuser and K. Schumann *Strafprozessrecht*, 6th ed., Nomos 2021, § 23 margin no. 31 ff.

Telekommunikationsüberwachung) or covert remote searches of information technology systems (*Online-Durchsuchung*) are usually so serious and bear such risks to the fundamental rights of the persons concerned that they require a special provision and higher procedural safeguards.

The reason for this is that German criminal procedure law is very much influenced by the Constitution (supra 3 d). Criminal investigations and certainly coercive measures impair the fundamental rights of the suspect and the addressee of the coercive measure, which might also be a witness. The Code of Criminal Procedure justifies these impairments, but, in turn, must comply with the principle of proportionality. This legal set-up is the key that opens the door to arguments based on the Constitution and to the jurisdiction of the Federal Constitutional Court, which has influenced criminal procedure law considerably. The experience of taking constitutional law into account also serves as a basis for including other sources of law such as the European Convention on Human Rights.

The impact of constitutional law is also obvious in the balancing approach that is predominantly used in order to decide on the exclusion of evidence. Confronting and balancing the public interest in prosecution and the individual's fundamental rights is a classic part of German constitutional law doctrine. This approach to exclusionary rules is very flexible. On a positive side, the flexibility makes it easy to dismiss evidence that has been collected legally if its use would violate fundamental rights gravely. On a negative side, the flexibility leads to intransparency, particularly when dealing with evidence that was collected illegally and that is not automatically excluded in German law. It has been pointed out that the reason for this flexible approach is that the German criminal procedure tries to establish the truth which is hampered by excluding evidence and that exclusionary rules are therefore "anomalies".[96] Whatever the reason, the current law on exclusionary rules is complicated and intransparent and, therefore, in need of reform. It is also odd that the law on the one hand sets strict boundaries for the investigation and limits the investigating authorities' freedom considerably, but on the other hand does not provide for clear consequences when these boundaries are violated.

Another aspect that is noteworthy is that the roles of the suspect and the public prosecution office seem to be particularly ill-balanced in the investigative phase. Although the investigating authorities are limited by the Code of Criminal Procedure and the Basic Law, they still can avail themselves of

96 T. Weigend, *The Potential to Secure a Fair Trial Through Evidence Exclusion: A German Perspective. Do exclusionary rules ensure a fair trial? A comparative analysis of evidentiary rules*, S. Gleß and T. Richter (eds), Springer 2019, pp. 87 f.

substantive investigative powers. In contrast, the suspect has limited influence on the investigation. They are less well informed and, despite having such a right, cannot force the prosecuting authorities to take evidence. The idea in German criminal procedure law is that the public prosecution service objectively tries to establish what really happened (the truth) and, therefore, takes incriminating and exonerating evidence (§ 160(2) StPO). Control-mechanisms are the intermediate procedure and especially the fact that the court must directly have access to the evidence. It happens often that the defendant tells a different narrative than the bill of indictment. However, if criminal proceedings are terminated without main proceedings, these checks do not come into effect. It is therefore necessary to have a closer look at the investigative phase and to try to establish more equality.

CHAPTER 3

On Limits of Freedom of Public Authorities with Respect to Obtaining Evidence at the Stage of Investigation under Turkish Criminal Procedure and Evidence Law

Haluk Toroslu, Uğur Orhan,** and Bedirhan Erdem****

1 Introduction

The law of evidence in criminal procedure, which regulates the admissibility of evidence, must give clear answers for two fundamental problems, how the crime-related-facts ought to be obtained as evidence by the state and to be admitted before the courts and to what extent the evidence is able to prove the criminal matter of facts. In Turkey (hereinafter referred to as "Türkiye"), where the criminal law and criminal procedure are still under the influence of Italian and German law, the scope and the content of Turkish national law of evidence in criminal procedure can be regarded as a part of continental European legal system. However, Turkish national law of evidence in criminal procedure shows its peculiar national characteristics, such as detailed written constitutional rules about obtaining evidence in criminal matters. Moreover, the strict and absolute prohibition on obtaining and evaluating unlawful evidence is applied under national law.

The study aims to present Turkish evidence law in criminal matters and its national peculiarities. Therefore, its focus is narrowed to the limits of state competence to obtain evidence at the investigation stage. Within this scope, the present study is structured into three parts: actors (2), rules (3), and the application of rules by these actors (4). In the first part, the public prosecutor

---

* Dr. iur., Associate Professor, İ.D. Bilkent University Faculty of Law, Department of criminal law and procedure.

** Dr. iur.

*** LL.M., Research Assistant, Leuphana Law School, Leuphana University Lüneburg, Chair of German and International Criminal Law, and PhD Candidate, Humboldt University of Berlin Faculty of Law.

 | DOI:10.1163/9789004710320_005

and judicial police unit as public authorities at the stage of investigation (2.1) and the courts as the provider of judicial control over procedural acts in the stage of investigation are examined (2.2). In the second part, on normative framework of rules (3.1) and selected principle (3.2), which govern predominantly the law of evidence, are reflected. The last and largest part is dedicated to articulating the concept of "unlawful" evidence under Turkish criminal procedure (4.1) and evaluating its effect on criminal procedure comprehensively (4.2).

2 Actors: Public and Judicial Authorities at the Stage of Investigation Regarding Evidence Collection and Examination

2.1 *Public Prosecutor and Judicial Police Units*

The collection and examination of evidence, particularly the investigation phase in criminal procedure, begins once the report of the alleged crime reaches the public prosecutor by means of the complaint or the notification. The legal framework for the notification and the complaint is regulated under articles (Art.) 158 and 159 of the Turkish Criminal Procedure Code ("*Ceza Muhakemesi Kanunu*", hereinafter "CPC"). According to Art. 160/2 of the CPC, the burden of collecting and presenting the evidence before the criminal court to prove the criminal charge is placed on the public prosecutor. According to Art. 170/2 "At the end of the investigation phase, if the collected evidence creates sufficient suspicion that the crime has been committed, the public prosecutor draws up an indictment." Pursuant to this provision, the public prosecutor is authorized by law to evaluate the evidence and draw a conclusion on the existence of sufficient suspicion. If sufficient grounds for the suspicion can be established, it is deemed necessary to initiate a public lawsuit before the competent court by filling and submitting the charging document (indictment) by the public prosecutor. However, the public prosecutor's evaluation of evidence can differ from the court's evaluation in the adjudication phase. As stated by the Court of Cassation of the Republic of Türkiye (*Yargıtay*, hereinafter "CC"):[1] 'The evaluation of evidence by the public prosecutor during an investigation, and the evaluation of the evidence by the court during adjudication have different characteristics. While the evidence collected during the investigation phase is examined by the public prosecutor within the framework of whether sufficient suspicion is created to file a lawsuit, on the other hand, the evaluation by the

1 Court of Cassation 18th Penal Chamber, no. 2019/7005, 2019/13389, (30.09.2019).

court in the adjudication phase concerns mainly on whether the evidence is sufficient for a conviction regarding whether the alleged crime has been committed, and whether the evidence can constitute a complete conscientious/ doubtless conviction.'

The public prosecutor is mainly responsible for the legitimate functioning of the investigation and for the collection of all the evidence related to the crime under the legal instruments, however, there are no special police forces in the judicial organization of the Republic of Türkiye, which serves exclusively under the public prosecutor to execute their investigation. Nevertheless, the public prosecutor is assisted by judicial police units (*Adli Polis* or *Kolluk*), when executing their judicial duties in carrying out the investigation.[2] The legal framework regarding the duties of the judicial police units within the general law enforcement organization has been drawn with the Judicial Law Enforcement Regulation (*Adli Kolluk Yönetmeliği*). Under Art. 5 of this Regulation (*Yönetmelik*), orders and instructions regarding the ongoing investigation cannot be given to judicial law enforcement officers by their superiors, as they lack judicial duty. However, judicial law enforcement officers are under the command and control of their hierarchical superiors in terms of their administrative duties other than their judicial duties. Since judicial law enforcement officers are included in their staff and units in the administration of general enforcement agencies, they are obliged to perform their duties and services, which are outside of their judicial duties, assigned by administrative superiors. On the other hand, special committees, such as *ad-hoc* inspection committees of the parliament or commissions for criminal matters relating to public officers' duties, take part in the prosecution of criminal offenses committed by those bearing certain characteristics, such as having the status of deputy or public officers. These so-called special investigation procedures, which are regulated in the special acts, originate from the non-criminal law objectives (such as parliamentary immunity or the protection of public officers from political intervention) so that they serve, normatively, as procedural impediments, or as objective conditions for criminal responsibility.

Pursuant to the current CPC Art. 161/2 application, judicial police units 'are obliged to promptly notify the public prosecutor under whose command they are functioning, about the events in which they have intervened, the arrested persons, and the measures that were taken' and they do not have the authority to act spontaneously or to conduct investigations without the instruction and order of the prosecutor.

2 V.Ö. Özbek, K. Doğan and P. Bacaksız, *Ceza Muhakemesi Hukuku*, Seçkin pub., 14th ed., Ankara 2021, p. 171 ff.

The aim here is to ensure that the control over the investigation is held only by the prosecutor,[3] who is also entitled to administrative competencies in the organizational structure of the judiciary. With the CPC and the Regulation, the legislator aimed to provide for a more active prosecutor, who has more authority in the investigation process, as well as more initiative and collaborative duties. With these granted competencies and assigned duties by the CPC, the public prosecutor is normatively designed to carry out the investigation, not only in the office but also by going out on the field (such as crime scenes, houses-to-be-searched) with the judicial police units.[4] However, this normative model of a highly active prosecutor has not been successfully implemented. This model still proves ineffective for crimes that take place away from the city center, where the courthouse is located. Another contributor to this inefficiency is the lack of prosecutors, especially in metropolitan cities, despite the significant increase over the past few years. In cases where the number of prosecutors is insufficient or the prosecutor cannot go out on the field, the law enforcement agencies further the investigation alone. According to CPC (Art. 160 *et seq.*), public law enforcement authorities enjoy a monopoly of investigation rights in criminal cases owing to the state monopoly on the use of force. They do not share their exclusive authority with any other private entity. As an exception, the investigatory authority of the judge for strictly limited cases is regulated under the CPC. According to Art. 163, 'If the public prosecutor cannot be reached in case of flagrante delicto and in case of peril in delay, or if the scope of the case exceeds the workforce of the public prosecutor, the judge (magister) can also carry out all procedures at the phase of investigation'.

2.2 *Courts*

The court (*magister*) is authorized to decide on coercive measures in order to collect relevant evidence during the investigation stage, only if the public prosecutor raises such a claim before the court. In those cases, the judge is authorized to examine evidence in the scope of the public prosecutor's claim for taking coercive measures. But for these procedures, the court lacks jurisdiction to admit evidence *ex officio*. As well under Art. 174/2 and Art. 174/1-b CPC regulating "Return of Indictment" reads as follows: '(1) After examining all the documents related to the investigation phase, within fifteen days from the date of submission of the indictment and the investigation documents, by pointing

3 C. Şahin and N. Göktürk, *Ceza Muhakemesi Hukuku-I*, Seçkin pub., 12th ed., Ankara 2021, p. 80.

4 S. Selçuk, *Suç Yargılama Süreci Hukuku Dogmatigi ve/ya Grameri*, İmge pub., Ankara 2022, p. 463 ff.

out incomplete or erroneous issues, the court shall decide on the return of the indictment to the office of the chief public prosecutor ... (b) due to it being drawn without collection of existing evidence that directly affects the conviction of the crime ...' In this narrow scope provided by this provision, at the end of the investigation phase, the court is entitled to evaluate the evidence with regard to the indictment.

The fourth section of the CPC governs coercive measures such as search and seizure, monitoring by technical means and pre-trial detention. The coercive measures regulated in this section, as a rule, are considered valid in all cases as they are included in the "General Provisions" of the Code. However, the coercive measures included in the CPC are not limited to those listed in the article. Physical examination and taking a sample from the body (Art. 75 *et al.*), molecular genetic examination (Art. 78 *et al.*), physical identity determination (Art. 81), and observation (Art. 74) are also considered protective measures. Coercive measures must depend on a judge's decision or an order of the authority determined by law. This authority is, as a rule, exclusively vested in the judge, while in some measures, directly to the public prosecutor. However, in case of peril in delay, this authority can be exercised by the public prosecutor or chief of the police units. Hence, for the sake of the validity of evidence, which was collected as a result of a coercive measure, such measure must be based on a decision of the authority, which is expressly authorized by law, and executed in accordance with the law.[5] Otherwise, the evidence has to be regarded as unlawful.

Considering the subject of the event they represent, the use of certain findings as evidence in criminal proceedings is prohibited. They cannot form the basis of judgment. Some findings are considered unsuitable as evidence in terms of their subject. For instance, as a rule, some protection measures can only be implemented by the decision of a judge, but in cases where there is peril in delay, the implementation of the measures can be ordered by the public prosecutor or the law enforcement superior. However, the decision taken in such cases must be submitted to the approval of the judge within the period stipulated in the law. It is not possible to use the findings obtained as a result of the proceedings based on the decisions not approved by the judge in due time as evidence.

CPC has adopted the "reconciliation procedure" for the resolution of disputes related to certain crimes without litigating them in court. In this context, in order to encourage reconciliation, it provides for the prohibition to use of

5 B. Öztürk, B.E. Kazancı and S. Soyer Güleç, *Ceza Muhakemesi Hukukunda Koruma Tedbirleri*, Seçkin pub., 4th ed., Ankara 2021, p. 29 ff.

certain findings discovered during mediation. Indeed, pursuant to CPC Art. 253/20, it is not possible to use the statements made during the mediation negotiations as evidence in any investigation, prosecution, or lawsuit.[6]

CPC further establishes an "accelerated trial procedure" where certain circumstances call for it, as a special reasoning method. According to Art. 250 CPC, it is possible to apply the accelerated trial procedure in cases where it is consented to by the suspect. Under an accelerated procedure, the prosecutor requests from the competent court the application of a certain sanction in return for the crime committed; the court decides on the request after hearing the suspect in the presence of a defense attorney. In cases where the accelerated procedure of trial is applied, the penalty is reduced by half.

According to Art. 250/10 CPC, in cases where the accelerated procedure of trial cannot be completed for any reason, the file is sent to the Chief Public Prosecutor's Office in order to conclude the investigation according to the general provisions. It is not possible to use the suspect's confession or consent for the accelerated procedure and accompanying documentation for application to accelerated the procedure as evidence in subsequent prosecution and adjudication.

3 Rules and Principles of Acquiring Evidence at the Stage of Investigation and Adjudication

3.1 *Normative Regulations in Turkish Law*

The regulations concerning the collection of evidence are provided under the Constitution and the CPC. Additionally, there are also relevant rules, for instance in the regulations on protection measures. These regulations are compatible with each other, thereby achieving normative homogeneity.

3.1.1 The Constitution

The Constitution contains detailed provisions regarding the collection of evidence. According to Art. 36, everyone has the right of claim and defense, and the right to a fair trial. While Article 37 regulates the guarantee of a legal judge (ordinary judge predetermined by law), the principles regarding crimes and punishments are regulated in detail under Art. 38. Especially the fifth and sixth paragraphs are essential for the study. These read respectively as follows: no

6 O. Değirmenci, *Onarıcı Adalet Uygulaması Olarak Ceza Muhakemesinde Uzlaştırma*, Seçkin pub., 1st ed., Ankara 2020, p. 154; B. Akbulut and M. Aksan, *Ceza Muhakemesi Hukukunda Uzlaştırma*, Seçkin pub., 2nd ed., Ankara 2019, p. 54.

one can be compelled to make a statement incriminating herself or her relatives shown in the law or to submit evidence in this way (Art. 38/5), and findings obtained illegally cannot be accepted as evidence (Art. 38/6).[7]

3.1.2 Criminal Procedure Code (CPC)

In parallel with the Constitution, under Art. 217 CPC, a judge shall only decide based on the evidence presented to the hearing and discussed before the court. The judge freely evaluates the evidence with their personal outlook and thinking, the imputed offence can be proved with any kind of evidence obtained in accordance with the law. According to Art. 206/2-a CPC, evidence obtained illegally must be rejected. In addition, it is necessary to evaluate and discuss evidence in the hearing, then to state both the evidence in the reason for the decision, which one was taken as a basis for the judgement, and which one was rejected because of inadmissibility. Also, the court is obliged to indicate separately and clearly inadmissible evidence in the reason of the sentence (Art. 230/1-b CPC).

As a result, it is possible to say that the Constitution and the CPC are compatible and homogeneous in terms of obtaining evidence and illegal evidence.

3.1.3 Other Legislations

Finally, although the principles of acquiring evidence are governed by the Constitution and the CPC, there are also some other legislations such as the Law on the Duties and Powers of the Police (*Polis Vazife ve Salahiyet Kanunu,* hereinafter "LDPP") as well as legislations on protection measures.

For instance, according to LDPP Art. 13, arrested persons shall be informed immediately about the grounds for their arrest in written form, if this is not possible, orally, and in the case of collective crimes until they are brought before a judge at the latest. A confession taken without such notification to the person, violates the right to learn allegation, and therefore is against the law[8] and cannot be used as evidence.

Although the general framework of the protection measures is drawn in the CPC, other regulations also contain important provisions on these, such as regarding the search process, the Regulation on Judicial and Prevention Searches (*Adlî ve* Önleme *Aramaları Yönetmeliği*) or regarding arrest,

---

7 For the view that this provision should not be included in the Constitution, see *also* D. Soyaslan, 'Hukuka Aykırı Deliller' (2003) VII/34 *Atatürk University Erzincan Faculty of Law Journal*, p. 9 ff.

8 F. Yenisey and A. Nuhoğlu, *Ceza Muhakemesi Hukuku*, Seçkin pub., 9th ed., Ankara 2021, p. 560.

detention and statement-taking; the Regulation on Arrest, Detention and Statement-Taking (*Yakalama, Gözaltına Alma ve* İfade *Alma Yönetmeliği*).

Examples of relevant rules on these regulations will be given below as appropriate.

3.2 *Selected Principles*

Protection measures for evidence collection (such as search and seizure or monitoring by technical devices) are provided under the CPC and other relevant regulations. Again, the relevant legal sources provide in detail how the statements of the suspect or the accused or the witness must be obtained. Evidence acquired in violation of these regulations cannot be taken as the basis for the judgment, as it will be deemed to have been acquired illegally.

During the prosecution stage, the court conducts the hearings orally and publicly. Evidence must be discussed by the parties and *the principle of adversarial trial* must be implemented. The principle of adversarial trial[9] means that the subjects participating in the proceedings, occupying the prosecution, defense and adjudicatory offices, all provide their opinion on the subject of the proceedings before the other parties for reconsideration.[10] The decision can only be based on the evidence discussed before the court and obtained in accordance with the law. It is widely accepted by practice that a decision cannot be made based on unlawful evidence.[11]

The criminal procedure seeks material facts. The judge is not bound by the evidence introduced by the parties. Therefore, anything can consist evidence in criminal proceedings. However, this inquisitorial evidence system shall not lead to complete arbitrariness of the court. Acquiring and selecting the evidence by the court must be based on reason and logic; and the judge must justify obtaining and using such evidence.

Under the principle of free evaluation of evidence, the evidence must have certain characteristics. Indeed, it must be realistic, rational, representative, obtainable, important in terms of proof (Art. 206/2-b of the CPC) and must not be against the law. The CC,[12] emphasized that the evidence should be real-

9 *'The right to an adversarial trial means, in a criminal case, that both prosecution and defense must be given the opportunity to have knowledge of and comment on the observations filed and the evidence adduced by the other party.' Brandstetter v. Austria*, no. 11170/85, 12876/87, 13468/87, § 67, ECHR 1991.

10 F.G. Taner, *Ceza Muhakemesi Hukukunda Adil Yargılanma Hakkı Bağlamında* Çelişme *ve Silahların Eşitliği*, Seçkin pub., 1st ed., Ankara 2019, p. 69 ff.

11 Court of Cassation CGA, no. 2013/610, 2014/512 (25.11.2014); *and* no. 2013/841, 2014/513 (25.11.2014).

12 Court of Cassation CGA, no. 2012/10–294, 2012/253, (26.04.2012).

istic, rational, reflecting the event in all details, suitable for proof and acquired in accordance with the law. In addition to these, the CC clearly stated that information that is not related to the event at trial cannot be evidence. Indeed, unrelated evidence is not "representative".[13]

Another consequence of the principle of free evaluation of evidence is that there are no specific procedural rules dictating certain points must be proved with certain evidence.[14] This being said, there are some exceptions limiting the evidence to a certain form. For example, a "trial record" is the only means applicable to prove the compliance of trial procedure (Art. 222 of CPC); or it is not possible to prove that a signed blank paper was filled out in contradiction to the oral agreement, with a witness unless expressly permitted under the Code of Civil Procedure.[15] It is necessary to note once again that the principle of free evaluation does not endorse the use of unlawful evidence, and unlawful evidence is considered *a limine* inadmissible.

Under the communality of evidence principle, evidence must be shared with all parties. In other words, it is not enough for the judge to know the content of the evidence alone, the parties must also be informed and have access to the evidence. This is achieved by presenting and discussing the evidence in the adjudication phase. According to the principle of the communality of evidence, the judge cannot render a judgement based on his personal knowledge. Since the judge's reliance on personal knowledge does not allow discussion of this information, so the right to defense is also impaired.

It is clearly regulated in CPC that the evidence must be presented, and the opinion must be obtained from the trial (Art. 217/1). Therefore, the competent judge who has personal knowledge about the alleged crime before the criminal procedure should abstain from the judgeship and become a witness.[16]

Whether the judge believes or partially believes in the evidence submitted is related to the evaluation of the evidence. The judge freely determines the value of evidence in relation to the matter, in the criminal procedure. This being said, the law does not provide for "superior" evidence. Indeed, confessions, which were once described as the "queen of evidence", no longer carry the same weight. The criminal judges rule on the fact that the alleged matter of the crime is fixed with full belief and in her conviction (Art. 217 CPC). For instance, the judge may favor the statement of a witness who was heard without taking

---

13 See *also* F. Birtek, *Ceza Muhakemesinde Delil ve* İspat, Adalet pub., 2nd ed., Ankara 2017, p. 47 ff.

14 N. Centel and H. Zafer, *Ceza Muhakemesi Hukuku*, Beta pub., 15th ed., İstanbul 2018, p. 236.

15 Court of Cassation Decision of Joint Chambers, no. 1988/1, 1989/2, (24.03.1989).

16 M. Feyzioğlu, *Ceza Muhakemesi Hukukunda Tanıklık*, US-A pub., 1st ed., Ankara 1996, p. 64.

an oath, over the statement of a sworn witness; or, despite the witness statements against the accused, he can rely on the statement of the accused. Likewise, evidence of documents or expert reports do not bind the judge. However, as stated earlier, free evaluation of evidence does not mean "arbitrary evaluation of evidence".

The "conscientious evidence system", which emerged as the opposite of the legal evidence system and is accepted in Turkish law, expresses both the freedom of evidence and the freedom to evaluate the evidence.[17]

As a result, there is no hierarchy among different forms of evidence in Turkish law.[18] All evidence has equal value in terms of its power of proof. Whether or not information or statements can constitute evidence depends on the conscientious conviction of the judge in terms of proof.

4 On Admissibility of Evidence and Unlawful Evidence

As in all legal systems, the main purpose to be achieved with "the admissibility of evidence", more precisely the ban on the evaluation of unlawful (inadmissible) evidence is to prevent the state from arbitrarily violating the fundamental rights and freedoms. In the Republic of Türkiye, the prohibitions on the use of unlawful evidence have not emerged primarily with the jurisprudence of the courts, but with the Constitution and the CPC. However, there is no uniformity on the term concerning on inadmissibility: The subject matter is differently mentioned within the CPC (in Art. 206 CPC, "against the Code (illegal)", in Art. 217 CPC "lawful", and in Art. 289 CPC "unlawful"), while Art. 38/6 of the Constitution clearly states that findings obtained illegally cannot be accepted as evidence. Nevertheless, it is clear that the phrase "unlawful" and "against the code" refers to the same legal quality with regard to criminal procedural law. Turkish criminal procedure law does not contain specific proceedings concerning the examination of the validity, or the legality of evidence collected. However, in accordance with Art. 170/4 CPC, the public prosecutor cannot issue an indictment based on unlawful evidence, and a judge/court cannot hold a decision about coercive measures or make a conviction based on unlawful evidence as per Art. 217/2 CPC and Art. 289/1-i CPC. This being said, under Art. 230/1-b CPC, unlawful evidence is kept in the case file. In line with the provisions of

17 M. Feyzioğlu, *Ceza Muhakemesinde* İspatın Ölçütü *Olarak Vicdani Kanaat*, Islık pub., 1st ed., Ankara 2015, p. 49; See *also* S. Selçuk, pp. 686–90 and 777.

18 N. Centel and H. Zafer, p. 237.

the Constitution and the CPC, an indictment must not be drawn up based on unlawful evidence; and if such a public lawsuit has been filed, the judge must refrain from relying on such unlawful evidence to convict the accused. In the event the judge decides on a conviction based on unlawful evidence, such verdict must be reversed at the appeal procedure (Art. 289 CPC).

In this context, the prohibition of illegally obtained evidence (in line with the Constitution of the Republic of Türkiye, "findings" is the more accurate term instead of "evidence") is regarded as one of the aspects of the rule of law in the field of criminal procedure in Türkiye. Evidence prohibitions determine the limits of the inquisitorial evidence system. In criminal procedure, "investigation of material fact" is not accepted at all costs; this purpose is limited by prohibitions of evidence.

These prohibitions are not only for the judiciary but also for the prosecution and defense authorities.[19] Art. 254 of the abrogated CPC (*No. 1412*) states that 'evidence obtained unlawfully by the investigation and prosecution organs cannot be taken as a basis for the judgment'; and the expression "investigation and prosecution organs" was clearly in place. Even though no such restriction has been introduced in terms of the current CPC and the Constitution, pursuant to the applicable law, unlawful evidence will be rejected regardless of who submits the evidence. The important point here is not who submits the evidence, but the way the evidence was introduced in the criminal proceedings.[20] It is possible to say that these prohibitions are applicable in terms of unlawful evidence collected by individuals. CC accepts that the evidence obtained unlawfully by private individuals cannot be used in criminal proceedings.[21] Evidence prohibitions aim to protect fundamental rights and freedoms. The current CPC further expands the prohibition of evidence. For example, failure to notify the fundamental and procedural rights (Art. 147) or various prohibited statements and interrogation methods such as ill-treatment, torture are included in the prohibition of evidence (Art. 148/3–4, Art. 75/1, Art. 76/1).

---

19 For the opposite view see *also* E. Yurtcan, *Ceza Yargılaması Hukuku*, Seçkin pub., 16th ed., Ankara 2019, pp. 314–15.

20 A. Gökcen and K. Çakır, 'Ceza Muhakemesinde Delil, Delillerin Muhafazası, Toplanması, Değerlendirilmesi ve Delil Yasakları' (2019) 21/Special ed. *Dokuz Eylül University Faculty of Law Journal*, p. 2937.

21 Court of Cassation 8th Penal Chamber, no. 2009/9930, 2009/13934, (09.11.2009); for the same direction see *also* Court of Cassation CGA, no. 2012/4–1283, 2014/430, (21.10.2014); Court of Cassation 13th Penal Chamber, no. 2012/7180, 2012/8523, (26.03.2012).

4.1 *Prohibited Procedures in Acquiring Evidence, Related Cases, and Examples*

Turkish law prohibits anyone from being compelled to make a statement that would incriminate themselves or their legal next of kin, and from presenting such incriminating evidence (the freedom from self-incrimination). This rule originates from the Constitution (Art. 38/5) and forms the basis of prohibitions on obtaining evidence.

The suspect's or accused's statement must be based on their free will; forbidden methods that impair the free will must not be used. Statements obtained through prohibited methods shall not be considered as evidence even if they are given with consent (Art. 148/3 CPC). These statements cannot be read during the prosecution phase, even for the purpose of clearing up the contradiction.

The grounds that harm free will can be divided into physical or moral interventions, and the promise of an unlawful benefit. It has been demonstrated by analogy which interventions in the law are physical or moral interventions that harm free will.[22] According to Art. 148/1 CPC, physical or moral interventions such as ill-treatment, torture, giving drugs, deceiving, exhausting, using force or threatening, using certain tools cannot be made.

Some examples of torture or inhuman or degrading treatment[23] are beating, making startling or loud noises, spitting, dragging, gagging, and negligent acts such as not allowing medical treatment, or not giving food. According to the Turkish Penal Code (*Türk Ceza Kanunu*, hereinafter "TPC") Art. 94/1, acts that cause physical or mental suffering to a person, incompatible with human dignity, affecting perception or willpower, and humiliation are considered torture. Any statement or evidence obtained by these methods are against the law.[24]

Additionally, cases in which a non-authorized person conducts an interrogation also fall into the scope of "prohibited method of taking statements". According to Art. 148/5 CPC, when the suspect's statement is needed to be retaken due to such an incident, if this statement is not taken by the law enforcement authorities instead of the public prosecutor, such statement will also be regarded as obtained in a prohibited manner.

---

22 N. Centel and H. Zafer, p. 256; Ö. Sırma Gezer, 'Hukuka Aykırı Delillerin Türk Ceza Muhakemesi Kanunu Kapsamında Değerlendirilmesi' (2017) 16/1 İstanbul *Kültür University Faculty of Law Journal*, p. 193.

23 For "torture", "ill-treatment", see *also Cezmi Demir and Others* App., no. 2013/293, §84, Turkish Constitutional Court (17.07.2014).

24 For detailed information and examples of "misbehavior" see *also* N. Centel and H. Zafer, p. 261.

CPC provides that some protective measures can only be applied in investigations and prosecutions of certain crimes. For instance, pursuant to Art. 135 CPC, collection of evidence by means of listening to or recording to correspondence can only be applied in relation to the crimes listed in the relevant article (catalog crimes).[25] In cases where the law goes to such a limitation, the evidence obtained through the application of the measure can only form a basis for a conviction to be given in relation to the catalog crimes.[26] Accepting the contrary would render these crime catalogs completely useless.[27]

If, during the implementation of search or seizure protection measures, evidence unrelated to the ongoing investigation or prosecution which creates suspicion that another crime has been committed, is obtained; this evidence is kept, and the situation is immediately reported to the Public Prosecutor's Office (Art. 138 CPC). If, during the interception of correspondence through telecommunication, evidence unrelated to the ongoing investigation or prosecution, but which may raise the suspicion that one of the crimes listed in the sixth paragraph of Art. 135 has been committed; this evidence is taken under protection and the situation is immediately reported to the Public Prosecutor's Office. If, during the interception of the communication, evidence is obtained that raises the suspicion that a crime other than the subject of the investigation or prosecution has been committed, if the other crime, the evidence of which was obtained by chance, is a crime that allows the implementation of the said measure, the evidence will be kept; however, if it is not one of the crimes in the catalog in the article, it will not be possible to use it as evidence.[28]

In cases where evidence is discovered by chance during a wiretap, without the existence of a valid order authorizing such recording and without a valid notification to the prosecutor, demonstrating that the person has committed a crime, the CC finds the evidence collected to be unlawful and does not be

25 V.Ö. Özbek, İnsan *Hakları Avrupa Mahkemesi Anayasa Mahkemesi ve Yargıtay Kararları Işığında Polis Hukuku ve Ceza Muhakemesi Hukukunda Temel Haklara Müdahaleler* (Önleyici *Tedbirler – Açık ve Gizli Koruma Tedbirleri*), Seçkin pub., 1st ed., Ankara 2021, p. 955.

26 Court of Cassation CGA, no. 2006/122, 2006/162, (13.06.2006); Court of Cassation CGA, No. 2014/98, 2016/83, (23.02.2016); Court of Cassation 4th Penal Chamber, no. 2011/13208, 2012/1504999, (19.06.2012); Court of Cassation 4th Penal Chamber, no. 2011/23270, 2012/16014, (04.07.2012).

27 Y. Ünver and H. Hakeri, *Ceza Muhakemesi Hukuku*, Adalet pub., 15th ed., Ankara 2019 p. 448.

28 N. Toroslu and M. Feyzioğlu, *Ceza Muhakemesi Hukuku*, Savaş pub., 21st ed., Ankara 2021 p. 300; Y. Ünver and H. Hakeri, p. 450; in the same direction see *also* Court of Cassation CGA, no. 2006/122, 2006/162 (13.06.2006).

accept them as evidence.[29] CPC regulates that the activities of the suspect or the accused in public places and the workplace can be monitored by technical means, and audio or video recordings can be taken for this purpose (Art. 140 CPC). This article also stipulates that the said measure cannot be applied in the residence of the person. According to this regulation, it is not possible to use the findings obtained as a result of monitoring the suspect or the accused's residence with technical means as evidence.[30]

Following the principle of "prohibited methods of statement and interrogation", the law prohibits not only the legal enforcement authorities, but also public prosecutors and interrogating judges from using these methods.

During a statement or an interrogation, suspects or defendants are entitled to be fully reminded of their rights. Omitting information, or notification by way of a summary constitutes restriction of the right of defense.[31] Pursuant to Art. 13 of LDDP, the person arrested must be informed of their reason for arrest in writing, and where not possible, immediately orally. In case of collective crimes, the arrested persons must be informed of the reason for arrest by the time they are brought before a judge. Any confession received without such notification is in violation of the right the be informed of allegations and rights.[32] The CC further considers the failure to remind the suspect or accused of their rights as an "absolute grounds for annulment".[33] The CC views the failure to remind the accused or suspect during questioning, as well as incomplete explanations, as a violation of the inquisitorial evidence system, in which the court is obliged for active involvement in investigating the facts in accordance with the law and the indictment.

For example, if the law enforcement officers create a climate of violence while recording the interrogation, the statement the suspect provides is considered obtained by unlawful methods. A CC decision[34] provides that a video recording of a conversation in a seeming climate of violence created by law enforcement during an interrogation negates the free will of the accused. Accordingly, the information shall not be considered as given by free will, and therefore is inadmissible.

Some cases may also give rise to prohibited procedures due to their specific elements. For instance, medical doctors are not allowed to disclose any

29 Court of Cassation CGA, no. 2007/5–23, 2007/167, (03.02.2007).
30 Court of Cassation CGA, no. 144/150, (29.11.2005).
31 N. Centel and H. Zafer, p. 255.
32 F. Yenisey and A. Nuhoğlu, p. 560.
33 Court of Cassation 8th Penal Chamber, no. 1995/11200, 1995/11900, (18.09.1995).
34 Court of Cassation 1st Penal Chamber, no. 2014/3819, 2014/209, (16.02.2004).

information which they have learned about their patients or about their relatives without the permission of the owner of the secret (Art. 46 CPC). Evidence obtained in this way is inadmissible.

There are some exceptions provided in the law which make it mandatory for the accused to retain a defense attorney while giving a statement or while being questioned. In cases where the presence of a defense attorney is required, the statement taken without a defense attorney is against the law and should not be considered as evidence (Art. 150 CPC). Law enforcement officers are entitled to take the statement of the suspect in criminal proceedings. In cases where the suspect does not benefit from the assistance of a defense attorney, such a statement cannot form the basis of the verdict, unless the suspect or accused confirms their statements before the judge or in court (Art. 148/4 CPC). Where it is required to re-take the suspect's statement on the same incident, following an initial round conducted by the law enforcement officers, such repetition must be conducted by the public prosecutor. In this case, the statement taken by the law enforcement officer is not considered as evidence (Art. 148/5 CPC).

CPC provisions allow compelling testimony, where testimony is considered mandatory. It is, therefore, possible to apply various coercive measures to obtain testimony in cases where the person fails to attend, hesitates to take an oath, or fails to make statements despite attending the testimony hearing (Art. 43 *et al.* CPC). This being said, the law provides various exceptions allowing a person the right to refrain from testifying (Art. 45). Any qualifying person may exercise their right to withdraw during both the investigation and prosecution phases. In accordance with the Art. 210/2, the testimony obtained in the investigation phase of a witness who has exercised her right to withdraw at the hearing cannot be used as evidence. The purpose of this provision is to prevent individuals from being compelled to make statements against their relatives.

As a rule, evidence obtained in accordance with the law can only be used for that case. Indeed, the witness testimony of a person cannot be used against him in another case where she is tried as a defendant, as a rule providing the contrary would not only impede the discovery process, but also violate the right to remain silent.[35]

Evidence may also be deemed prohibited by virtue of its subject. Indeed, some findings cannot constitute evidence due to their subject, such as information consisting of personal data.[36] The findings obtained during the physical examination carried out because of the decision of the public prosecutor cannot be used unless this process is approved by the judge or the court within

35 F. Yenisey and A. Nuhoğlu, p. 556.
36 F. Yenisey and A. Nuhoğlu, p. 568.

24 hours (Art. 75/1 CPC). Similarly, the findings obtained through a physical examination performed on other persons by the order of the public prosecutor cannot be used, unless approved by the judge (Art. 76/1 CPC).

Finally, some evidence may be evaluated as inadmissible owing to its impact on the fundamental rights and freedoms of the defendant. For example, if a person who has the right to withdraw from testifying uses this right later, his previous statements cannot be considered as evidence (Art. 210/2 CPC). Failing to remind those who have a right to withdraw from testifying makes the statement of a witness unlawful, a view that is also supported and acknowledged by the CC. In this case, statements provided by witnesses whose rights were not reminded, have not been considered as evidence.[37] Again, prohibited methods of statement shall not be applied when the witness is heard by the public prosecutor while the witness is being questioned at the trial. In case these prohibited methods are employed, the witness statements cannot be taken into consideration while sentencing.

4.2 *Unlawful Evidence and Its Results in Procedure*

The prohibition of evaluation of unlawful evidence constitutes an absolute prohibition without any legal exceptions in the Turkish legal system. The CPC provides that evidence obtained in violation of the prohibitions on collection of evidence cannot be evaluated. Statements obtained through prohibited procedures, even if given with consent, cannot be considered as evidence (Art. 148/3 CPC). Subsequent consent, provided after the fact, is also considered invalid.[38] As mentioned above, the imputed crime can only be proven with the evidence obtained in accordance with the law (Art. 217/2 CPC). Nevertheless, according to the CC and some scholars, the prohibition can be narrowed by weighing the legal interests (public interest in the inadmissible evidence, which proves the crime beyond a reasonable doubt, and personal interest of the person, whose rights were violated because of obtaining inadmissible evidence).[39]

For instance, the CC has founded that 'the evidence cannot be considered as "unlawfully obtained" such that it cannot be the basis of any conviction, since only the persons, who, following the Code, should be present during the search, were not present there'.[40] In another example, the Court articulated

37 Court of Cassation CGA, no. 213–19, (08.09.1999).

38 N. Toroslu and M. Feyzioğlu, p. 202.

39 See *also* Y. Ünver and H. Hakeri, p. 1612 ff.; D. Aydın, *Ceza Muhakemesinde Deliller*, Yetkin pub., 1st ed., Ankara 2014, p. 197 ff.

40 Court of Cassation CGA, no. 2011/8–278, 2012/96, (13.03.2012).

the following arguments: 'It is necessary to accept that it is lawful for the person to record her conversations with the other in a sudden situation, where there is no opportunity to obtain evidence against the perpetrator and there is no opportunity to reach the competent authorities regarding a crime being committed against her'.[41] Some scholars are claiming that a strict prohibition of unlawfully obtained evidence may lead to extremely severe consequences with regard to criminal justice and therefore according to them some criteria (i.e. weighing up legal interests) can be taken into consideration by the court. According to these scholars, who support the relative evaluation of illegally obtained evidence (relative unlawfulness theory or the theory of relativization), the right violated due to unlawful collection of evidence against the benefit that will arise as a result of its evaluation can be measured and weighted. If the latter interest is deemed more important, then unlawful evidence can be used in the trial.[42] In each case, the judge decides whether unlawful evidence can be used as a means of proof in the trial by making a comparison between the interest in revealing the crime and the violated right of the accused, based on the facts and circumstances of each case.[43]

Some scholars in the doctrine argue that if evidence has been collected illegally, it should be left to the discretion of the court whether or not to use this evidence when sentencing.[44] If the final decision does not violate the defendant's "right to a fair trial", evidence obtained unlawfully can be used in the judgment. However, according to this view, confessions obtained through prohibited interrogation methods, and personal data records ordered by law to be destroyed cannot be regarded as admissible under any circumstances.[45]

The Constitutional Court also agrees with the latter mentioned view in terms of the right to a fair trial in some of its individual application decisions. As a matter of fact, the Constitutional Court examines whether the fairness of the trial as a whole is violated as a result of the use of evidence obtained through unlawful methods. For instance, if unlawfully obtained evidence is the only decisive evidence in terms of the verdict, deciding solely based on this evidence violates the right to a fair trial in terms of the whole of the proceedings.[46] On the other hand, the Constitutional Court accepts that if the

41 Court of Cassation CGA, no. 2010/5187, 2011/131, (21.06.2011).

42 See *also* G. Akyürek, 'Ceza Yargılamasında Hukuka Aykırı Delillerin Değerlendirilmesi Sorunu' (2012) 101 *Türkiye Bars Association Journal* p. 68.

43 See *also* M.E. Alşahin, A. Gökcen, M. Balcı and K. Çakır, *Ceza Muhakemesi Hukuku*, Adalet pub., 5th ed., Ankara 2021, p. 337.

44 F. Yenisey and A. Nuhoğlu, p. 567.

45 F. Yenisey and A. Nuhoğlu, p. 579.

46 *Yaşar Yılmaz* App., no. 2013/6183, § 59 Turkish Constitutional Court (19.11.2014).

confession obtained in violation of the prohibition of torture and ill-treatment during the investigation phase is later confirmed in the court with free will and sentence depending on such confession will not violate the fairness of the trial as a whole. The court further states that it must be determined whether the trial was carried out in accordance with the fairness principle by evaluating the other evidence used within the scope of the trial.[47]

There are also some precedents where CC accepts the theory of relative unlawfulness. For instance, in some of its decisions, CC does not consider the evidence to be obtained unlawfully, despite the absence of some of the conditions sought in the law regarding search and seizure.[48]

However, the normative structure of the Turkish legal system, explicitly the Constitution and CPC, does strictly prohibit such criteria to *bypass* the absolute prohibition of unlawfully obtained evidence.[49] Hence, under the Criminal Code of Türkiye, criminal defenses, which eliminate the illegality of the act, such as consent, self-defense, and necessity cannot be reasons to accept illegally obtained finding as "lawful" evidence.[50]

Both the legal doctrine,[51] as well as the CC make a dual distinction between "prohibitions to obtain evidence" and "prohibitions to evaluate evidence". The Criminal General Assembly of the Court of Cassation (*Yargıtay Ceza Genel Kurulu*, hereinafter "CGA")[52] make the following explanations on the subject: '... it is imperative to protect personal or social values at the stage of searching for material fact. In order to protect these values, the legislator imposed some restrictions on the principle of freedom of evidence, called "evidence prohibitions". Evidence prohibitions are divided into two groups as "obtaining evidence" and "evaluation of evidence". Prohibitions regarding the way in which evidence is obtained are called "prohibitions of obtaining evidence", and prohibitions regarding the presentation and evaluation of that evidence in the trial, even if it has been obtained in accordance with the law, are called "evidence evaluation prohibitions".'

47 *Güllüzar Erman* App., no. 2012/542, § 65 Turkish Constitutional Court (04.11.2014).

48 Court of Cassation 7th Penal Chamber, no. 2013/5127, 2013/17549, (03.07.2013); Court of Cassation CGA, no. 2005/10–15, 2005/29, (15.03.2005), Court of Cassation CGA, no. 2007/7–147, 2007/159, (26.06.2007), Court of Cassation CGA, no. 2011/8–278, 2012/96, (13.03.2012).

49 N. Toroslu and M. Feyzioğlu, p. 202; Y. Ünver and H. Hakeri, p. 1614.

50 See *infra section 3 E.*

51 M.E. Alşahin, A. Gökcen, M. Balcı and K. Çakır, p. 325 ff.; Ö. Sırma Gezer, 'Hukuka Aykırı Delillerin Türk Ceza Muhakemesi Kanunu Kapsamında Değerlendirilmesi' (2017) 16/1 İstanbul *Kültür University Faculty of Law Journal*, p. 191.

52 Court of Cassation CGA, no. 483/599, (10.12.2013).

A dual analysis of Art. 217/2 CPC and Art. 38/6 Constitution in the context of unlawful evidence, although scholars are coming to a contrary conclusion, demonstrates that there can be no such "simple or formal illegality" as an "incidental unlawfulness".[53] In this context, the irregularities during collection of evidence, whether they may be a "formal illegality", "non-formal illegality", or "slight illegality", "severe illegality", "significant illegality", "insignificant illegality", "illegality affecting the whole of the trial", "illegality not affecting the whole of the trial", are not significant. Under the strict prohibition of evaluation, it is clearly prohibited to use the evidence obtained by unlawful methods in the proceedings.[54]

In this regard, it is also necessary to mention the "remote effect of unlawful evidence".[55] The dominant view in Turkish law is that other evidence obtained as a result of using illegal evidence is not admissible and therefore it is forbidden to be taken into account.[56] According to the applicable principle of "fruits of the poisonous tree",[57] any evidence obtained through illegally obtained evidence is also considered unlawful, even when they have been obtained through lawful means. CC decisions are also determinedly in this direction.[58]

The legal doctrine contains different views on the remote effect of illegal evidence. While some authors accept that the evidence collected from the unlawfully obtained evidence cannot be used in the proceedings; some authors accept this effect in a limited way. It must be noted that especially after the amendment in Art. 38 of the Constitution, the remote effect of the prohibition of evidence is more widely accepted by the doctrine and practice. Therefore, it is not possible for any other piece of evidence acquired by making

53 B. Öztürk and Others, *Nazari ve Uygulamalı Ceza Muhakemesi Hukuku*, Seçkin pub., 15th ed., Ankara 2021, p. 400; H. Karakehya, *Ceza Muhakemesi Hukuku*, Savaş pub., Ankara 2015, p. 263; M.V. Dülger, *Ceza Muhakemesi Hukukunda Dışlama Kuralı ve Hukuka Aykırı Delillerin Uzak Etkisi* (*Zehirli Ağacın Meyvesi* Öğretisi), Seçkin pub., 1st ed., Ankara 2014, p. 89; U. Orhan, *Ceza Muhakemesi Hukukunda Arama ve Elkoyma*, Yetkin pub., 1st ed., Ankara 2019, p. 91 ff., fn. 218.

54 See *also* M. Koca, 'Ceza Muhakemesinde Hukuka Aykırı Delilleri Değerlendirme Yasağı', *Atatürk University Erzincan Faculty of Law Journal* (2000) IV/1–2, p. 111 ff.; For detailed information see *also* M.E. Alşahin, A. Gökcen, M. Balcı and K. Çakır, p. 332.

55 M.V. Dülger, p. 106 ff.

56 Y. Ünver and H. Hakeri, p. 640; D. Aydın, p. 219; M.E. Alşahin, A. Gökcen, M. Balcı and K. Çakır, p. 332; B. Öztürk and Others, p. 416 ff.; For the opposite view see *also* H. Karakehya, p. 265.

57 *Silverthorne Lumber Co. v. United States* 251 US 385 (1920).

58 Court of Cassation CGA, no. 2005/144, 2005/150, (29.11.2005); Court of Cassation 11th Penal Chamber, no. 2011/6505, 2011/1134, (22.02.2011); See *also* Court of Cassation 10th Penal Chamber, no. 2020/21403, 2021/2205, (16.022021); Court of Cassation 10th Penal Chamber, no. 2020/6217, 2020/5213, (08.10.2020).

use of the suspect's statement obtained through prohibited methods, to constitute a basis for the conviction.[59]

The doctrine also provides for a distinction between "unlawful evidence due to the method of obtaining" and "unlawful evidence due to its subject matter". Where the law provides specific methods for collecting certain evidence, it is not possible to evaluate the findings obtained out of compliance with the provided methods. Additionally, the law also provides that certain findings cannot constitute evidence, regardless of the method they were collected.[60]

There is a consensus regarding evidence obtained by unlawful methods and the inability to use the evidence obtained by this method that a conviction cannot be based on the statement of the suspect or accused, which is obtained through the use of prohibited interrogation methods. The basis of this view is Art. 148 of CPC, which provides that the statement of the suspect and the accused must be based on their free will. Accordingly, any bodily or mental intervention such as ill-treatment, torture, exhaustion, deception, force or threats, use of certain tools, etc., are strictly prohibited to prevent tampering with free will. This provision further prohibits making an unlawful promise to the suspect in order to obtain information.

A statement obtained in this way cannot be considered as evidence. Even if the suspect has given consent to the prohibited method used, the statement taken in this way has no legal validity. As stated before, the consent given after the fact does not restore the legality of a declaration.[61]

Similarly, it is not possible for the suspect's consent to render the search carried out unlawfully, legal. Although the CC has decisions to the contrary, the findings obtained as a result of such a search cannot be used as evidence.[62]

Whether unlawful evidence can be used in favor of the defendant is another controversial issue. One view argues that the defendant may benefit from unlawful evidence in his favor to prove his innocence.[63] The dominant opinion, on the other hand, accepts that unlawful evidence cannot be used even in favor of the accused in the face of positive law.[64] Indeed, as a natural consequence of the strict prohibition, unlawful evidence should not be used in criminal proceedings, regardless of whose favor it is.

59 B. Öztürk and Others, p. 416 ff.; Court of Cassation 19th Penal Chamber, no. 2015/4649, 2015/3584, (02.07.2015).

60 N. Toroslu and M. Feyzioğlu, p. 201 ff.

61 N. Toroslu and M. Feyzioğlu, p. 202.

62 Y. Ünver and H. Hakeri, p. 412.

63 E. Şen, *Türk Hukukunda Telefon Dinleme, Gizli Soruşturmacı, X Muhbir*, Seçkin pub., 1st ed., Ankara 2008, p. 93.

64 M.E. Alşahin, A. Gökcen, M. Balcı and K. Çakır, p. 327; G. Akyürek, p. 78.

Despite the current regulations, CGA considers the violation due to the absence of a search witness in a search as "simple form of violation". Since no rights were considered to be violated as a result of this simple form violation, CGA has rejected the argument that the evidence collected was unlawful and could not constitute a basis for conviction.[65] On the other hand, in another decision, CGA had decided that the weapons, which were means of crime, were seized during the search that was performed unlawfully, (i.e., without a judge or a public prosecutor and in the absence of search witnesses) and therefore the evidence obtained unlawfully could not be taken as the basis of the verdict.[66]

Similarly, the Constitutional Court accepted, in an individual application, that the absence of search witnesses constituted a violation of the law. However, considering the method of execution of the search in the case, the Constitutional Court stated that the overall legality of acquiring the evidence wasn't suspicious except for the absence of such witnesses and decided that the right to a fair trial was not violated.[67] However, the Constitutional Court also ruled to the contrary. For example, the Court stated that the absence of one of the search witnesses was against the law, and continued that the use of such evidence obtained as a result of the illegal search as the sole and decisive evidence undermines the fairness of the trial as a whole and therefore the right to a fair trial is violated.[68]

Finally, it is also controversial whether unlawful evidence can be removed from the case file or not. Indeed, some scholars argue that unlawful evidence may impact on the evaluation by the judge and that it must therefore be removed.[69] However, Art. 230/1-b CPC provides for a clear bifurcation between evidence used in the case and evidence collected by unlawful means, in the tenor of the verdict delivered. The CC also supports this view.[70] Therefore, pursuant to the legal resources, unlawful evidence must remain in the file,

---

65 Court of Cassation CGA, no. 2007/147, 2007/159, (26.06.2007); in the same direction see *also* Court of Cassation CGA, no. 2011/278, 2012/96, (13.03.2012).

66 Court of Cassation 8th Penal Chamber, no. 2008/334, 2009/15739, (14.12.2009); in the same direction see *also* Court of Cassation CGA, no. 2009/7–160, 2009/264, (17.11.2009).

67 *Jakop Gabriel* App., no. 2013/2392, Turkish Constitutional Court (15.04.2015).

68 *Yaşar Yılmaz* App., no. 2013/6183, Turkish Constitutional Court (19.11.2014).

69 E. Şen, *Türk Ceza Yargılaması Hukukunda Hukuka Aykırı Deliller Sorunu*, Beta pub., 1st ed., İstanbul 1998, p. 209 ff.

70 Court of Cassation CGA, no. 7/160, 264, (17.11.2009).

regardless of the risk of harming the judgement of the judge, as the law requires separation and analysis on whether the evidence is unlawful or not.[71]

It should be emphasized once again that in the face of positive regulations, Turkish law accepts the understanding of strict prohibition of evidence. Although there are non-conforming decisions, it is obvious that both the CC and the Constitutional Court mostly accept the strict prohibition of evidence in terms of unlawful evidence. This being said, there are also some decisions where it appears that the courts have also accepted the unlawfully obtained evidence, taking into account the whole of the proceedings.

5 Conclusion

Turkish criminal procedure law is mostly homogenous in its approach toward illegal evidence. A collective evaluation of the above-mentioned provisions of the Constitution and the CPC demonstrates very clearly that a verdict cannot be made based on evidence obtained illegally.

While the judge may exercise freedom in the evaluation of evidence, the provisions and precedent regarding unlawful evidence create a framework that forms the limits of such free evaluation. Turkish law has adopted the strict prohibition of unlawful evidence. While there are dissenting opinions in both the doctrine and certain court cases, it is difficult to support these dissenting views considering the positive regulations.

Such prohibitions of evidence can be viewed as achievements of modern criminal procedure, as in essence, they aim to protect fundamental rights and freedoms. Failure to abide by these rules, even by way of a liberal interpretation or a flexible view, would constitute a violation of both the Constitution and the CPC, thereby damaging the gains obtained through the criminal procedure.

Bibliography

A. Gökcen and K. Çakır, 'Ceza Muhakemesinde Delil, Delillerin Muhafazası, Toplanması, Değerlendirilmesi ve Delil Yasakları' (2019) 21/Special ed. *Dokuz Eylül University Faculty of Law Journal*, p. 2911–951.

B. Akbulut, M. Aksan, *Ceza Muhakemesi Hukukunda Uzlaştırma*, Seçkin pub., 2nd ed., Ankara 2019.

71 F. Yenisey and A. Nuhoğlu, pp. 577–78; A. Gökcen and K. Çakır, p. 2944; B. Öztürk and Others, p. 405.

B. Öztürk and Others, *Nazari ve Uygulamalı Ceza Muhakemesi Hukuku*, Seçkin pub., 15th ed., Ankara 2021.

B. Öztürk, B.E. Kazancı, S. Soyer Güleç, *Ceza Muhakemesi Hukukunda Koruma Tedbirleri*, Seçkin pub., 4th ed., Ankara 2021.

C. Şahin and N. Göktürk, *Ceza Muhakemesi Hukuku-I*, Seçkin pub., 12th ed., Ankara 2021.

D. Aydın, *Ceza Muhakemesinde Deliller*, Yetkin pub., 1st ed., Ankara 2014.

D. Soyaslan, 'Hukuka Aykırı Deliller' (2003) VII/34 *Atatürk University Erzincan Faculty of Law Journal*, pp. 9–26.

E. Şen, *Türk Ceza Yargılaması Hukukunda Hukuka Aykırı Deliller Sorunu*, Beta pub., 1st ed., İstanbul 1998.

E. Şen, *Türk Hukukunda Telefon Dinleme, Gizli Soruşturmacı, X Muhbir*, Seçkin pub., 1st ed., Ankara 2008.

E. Yurtcan, *Ceza Yargılaması Hukuku*, Seçkin pub., 16th ed., Ankara 2019.

F. Birtek, *Ceza Muhakemesinde Delil ve İspat*, Adalet pub., 2nd ed., Ankara 2017.

F. Yenisey and A. Nuhoğlu, *Ceza Muhakemesi Hukuku*, Seçkin pub., 9th ed., Ankara 2021.

F.G. Taner, *Ceza Muhakemesi Hukukunda Adil Yargılanma Hakkı Bağlamında Çelişme ve Silahların Eşitliği*, Seçkin pub., 1st ed., Ankara 2019.

G. Akyürek, 'Ceza Yargılamasında Hukuka Aykırı Delillerin Değerlendirilmesi Sorunu' (2012) 101 *Türkiye Bars Association Journal*, pp. 61–82.

H. Karakehya, *Ceza Muhakemesi Hukuku*, Savaş pub., Ankara 2015.

M. Feyzioğlu, *Ceza Muhakemesi Hukukunda Tanıklık*, US-A pub., 1st ed., Ankara 1996.

M. Feyzioğlu, *Ceza Muhakemesinde İspatın Ölçütü Olarak Vicdani Kanaat*, Islık pub., 1st ed., Ankara 2015.

M. Koca, 'Ceza Muhakemesinde Hukuka Aykırı Delilleri Değerlendirme Yasağı' (2000) IV/1–2 *Atatürk University Erzincan Faculty of Law Journal*, pp. 105–46.

M.E. Alşahin, A. Gökcen, M. Balcı, K. Çakır, *Ceza Muhakemesi Hukuku*, Adalet pub., 5th ed., Ankara 2021.

M.V. Dülger, *Ceza Muhakemesi Hukukunda Dışlama Kuralı ve Hukuka Aykırı Delillerin Uzak Etkisi* (*Zehirli Ağacın Meyvesi Öğretisi*), Seçkin pub., 1st ed., Ankara 2014.

N. Centel and H. Zafer, *Ceza Muhakemesi Hukuku*, Beta pub., 15th ed., İstanbul 2018.

N. Toroslu and M. Feyzioğlu, *Ceza Muhakemesi Hukuku*, Savaş pub., 21st ed., Ankara 2021.

O. Değirmenci, *Onarıcı Adalet Uygulaması Olarak Ceza Muhakemesinde Uzlaştırma*, Seçkin pub., 1st ed., Ankara 2020.

Ö. Sırma Gezer, 'Hukuka Aykırı Delillerin Türk Ceza Muhakemesi Kanunu Kapsamında Değerlendirilmesi' (2017) 16/1, İstanbul *Kültür University Faculty of Law Journal*, pp. 189–201.

S. Selçuk, *Suç Yargılama Süreci Hukuku Dogmatigi ve/ya Grameri*, İmge pub., Ankara 2022.

U. Orhan, *Ceza Muhakemesi Hukukunda Arama ve Elkoyma*, Yetkin pub., 1st ed., Ankara 2019.

V.Ö. Özbek, İnsan *Hakları Avrupa Mahkemesi Anayasa Mahkemesi ve Yargıtay Kararları Işığında Polis Hukuku ve Ceza Muhakemesi Hukukunda Temel Haklara Müdahaleler* (Önleyici *Tedbirler – Açık ve Gizli Koruma Tedbirleri*), Seçkin pub., 1st ed., Ankara 2021.

V.Ö. Özbek, K. Doğan, P. Bacaksız, *Ceza Muhakemesi Hukuku*, Seçkin pub., 14th ed., Ankara 2021.

Y. Ünver and H. Hakeri, *Ceza Muhakemesi Hukuku*, Adalet pub., 15th ed., vol. 3, Ankara 2019.

CHAPTER 4

Limits of Freedom of Public Authorities with Respect to Obtaining Evidence at the Stage of Investigation

Hungarian Report

Herke Csongor and Szabó Barbara

1 A Presentation of the Main and Most Distinctive Features of Evidence System in the Light of the Applicable Model of Criminal Procedure and Major Procedural Principles of Examining and Evaluating Evidence

To summarise the data of the historical and comparative retrospectives of the law, depending on the legal norms of the legislator's desire to regulate the means and methods of proof, different systems of proof can be distinguished. Throughout history, the legislator has tried many times and, in many ways, to determine the scope of the evidence, i.e., to exhaustively list the evidence that can be used in criminal matters, and, on the other hand, to define the probative value and the value of the evidence in question through the legislation. This dual ambition should be distinguished by four stages:
(a) the positive bound and
(b) the negative bound or the
(c) completely free and
(d) systems of proof that are not entirely free.
The tied system of proof is also called a formal or legal system of proof.

ad (a) In the case of a positively bound system of evidence, the law exhaustively lists the evidence and also specifies their evidentiary power. According to this, there is evidence of whole, half, quarter, eighth, etc. value, depending on specific criteria. If the amount and quality of evidence specified by law are maintained, the defendant must be convicted. Such was the system .ad of proof in the inquisitive criminal proceedings that have been operating for centuries in the Middle Ages.

ad (b) In contrast, in the case of a system of evidence bound in the negative, the scope and the value of evidence are also defined by law, but the legislator emphasizes the minimum of evidence. It only includes at least what amount

 | DOI:10.1163/9789004710320_006

and quality of evidence are needed to convict the defendant at all. However, if this minimum of evidence is already available, the sentence of the accused is not mandatory.

ad (c) In the case of a free system of evidence, only "intimate conviction" shall be followed when the judgment has sentenced. The completely free system of proof cannot be verified, it opens up a certain space for imaginative or prejudice-based convictions, and not infrequently for judgment based on emotions, passions, i.e. kinship and dislikes.

ad (d) The system of evidence, which is not entirely free of charge, therefore prioritised the reasoned conviction, i.e. a duly 'justified conviction', rather than 'intimate conviction': the ad-decision authority gives an account in its judgment of what is accepted or did not accept as evidence. Thus, the evidence on which the judgment was based became known and largely verifiable to both the hearing audience, the participants in the case and the high court.

In addition, the scope of evidence permitted by law or excluded by law has been continuously expanded.

The system of proof of Hungarian criminal procedure law belongs to the fourth model, the not entirely free system of proof: in criminal proceedings, all means of proof laid down by law can be freely used, and all acts of proof can be freely applied.

2 Public Authorities Are Entitled to Acquire Evidence in a Criminal Action at the Stage of Investigation

2.1 *Notion: Public Authorities Are Entitled to Carry Out Investigations*

a) Please indicate legal grounds or other sources giving rise to the competence of appropriate authorities to carry out investigations, within which to examine evidence. In addition to the traditional law enforcement authorities of the prosecutor and the police, are any other entities admissible, such as special forces or specialized administrative authorities? What is the scope of their procedural competence and how can their procedural position be defined vis-à-vis the traditional enforcement authorities? Can a growing significance be found in the participation in criminal investigations of specialized law enforcement authorities, other than the traditional group of investigation bodies? Can the phenomenon of normative disintegration be observed, paving the way for numerous public authorities to conduct investigations in criminal cases?

The progression of the Hungarian criminal procedure can be viewed as follows:

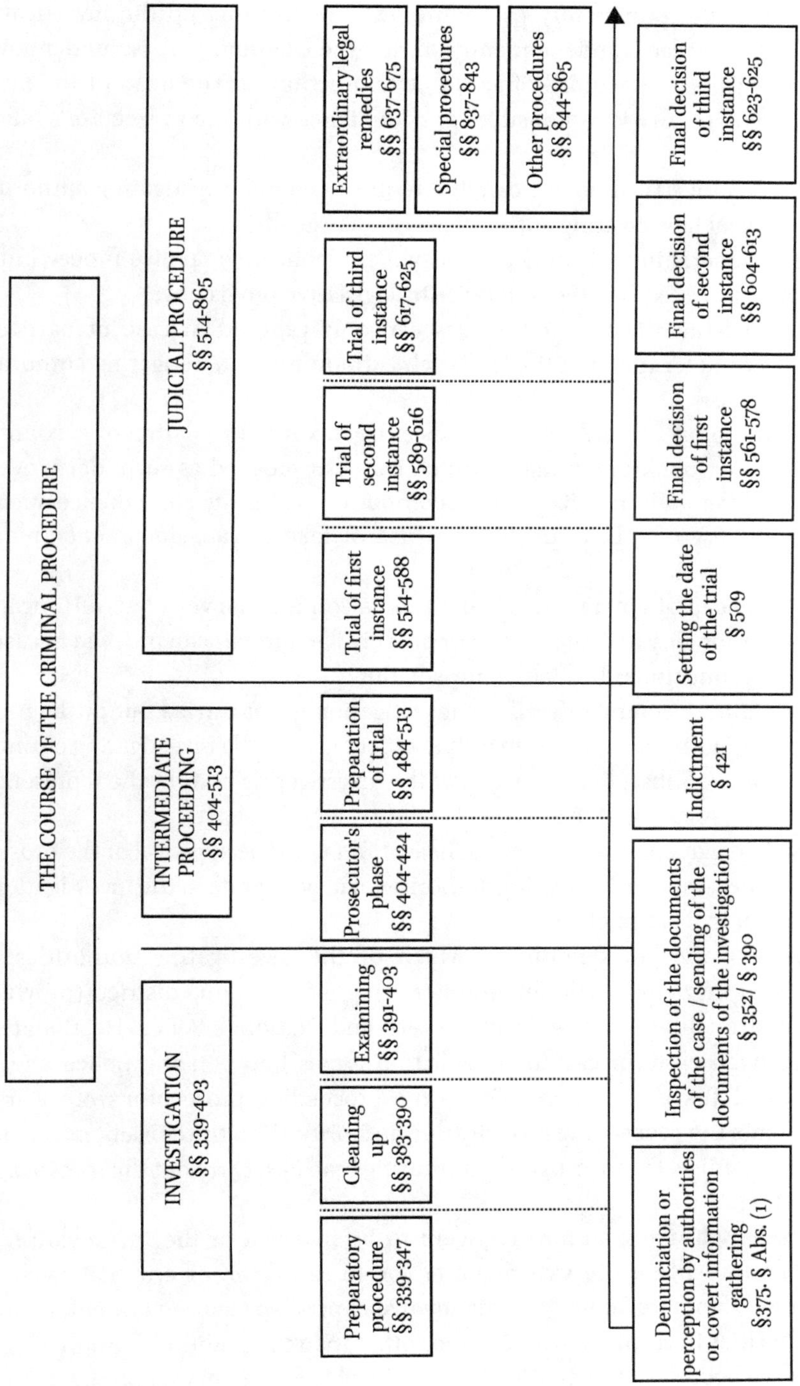
THE COURSE OF THE CRIMINAL PROCEDURE
INVESTIGATION §§ 339-403
INTERMEDIATE PROCEEDING §§ 404-513
JUDICIAL PROCEDURE §§ 514-865
Preparatory procedure §§ 339-347
Cleaning up §§ 383-390
Examining §§ 391-403
Prosecutor's phase §§ 404-424
Preparation of trial §§ 484-513
Trial of first instance §§ 514-588
Trial of second instance §§ 589-616
Trial of third instance §§ 617-625
Extraordinary legal remedies §§ 637-675
Special procedures §§ 837-843
Other procedures §§ 844-865
Denunciation or perception by authorities or covert information gathering §375. § Abs. (1)
Inspection of the documents of the case / sending of the documents of the investigation § 352/ § 390
Indictment § 421
Setting the date of the trial § 509
Final decision of first instance §§ 561-578
Final decision of second instance §§ 604-613
Final decision of third instance §§ 623-625

During the preparatory procedure and the cleaning up the investigating authority proceeds independently, during the examining phase under governance of the prosecutor's office (§ 31. Subsection 2). The head of the investigating authority is responsible for compliance with the prosecutor's office's instructions.

During investigation, we can differentiate general investigating authorities and special investigating authorities:
- The general investigating authority is the police. The police proceed in all cases unless stipulated otherwise by legislative provisions.
- Special investigating authorities can only proceed in case of particular crimes determined in the law. Such extraordinary investigating authorities are:
  - National Tax and Customs Office (e.g. tax fraud, violation of accounting order, bankruptcy fraud) which can also proceed as secondary investigating authority (i.e. crimes committed within its competence such as forgery of official documents, use of fake private documents, money laundering);
  - the captain of a vessel (aircraft) on a commercial vessel with Hungarian nationality insignia abroad or on a civilian aircraft can proceed in case of a crime under Hungarian jurisdiction;
  - military commander: if the investigation is not carried out by the prosecutor's office, the commanding officer can be the investigating authority (§ 701. Subsection 1), by way of the investigating body or the representing investigating officer.

Based on agreement between the heads, and with the approval of the prosecutor's office, more investigating authorities can cooperate in the investigation in a case or in a group of cases.

A separate law determines which of the investigating authorities can proceed (e.g. local (urban or district) police station, district (provincial or metropolitan) police headquarters and National Police Headquarters) in a given case. In case of jurisdiction issues between the police and the National Tax and Customs Office the proceeding prosecutor's office freely appoints the proceeding investigating authority. With the consent of the prosecutor's office, the investigating authorities can also carry out the investigation together.

Although many authorities seem to be involved in the investigation the police investigate the vast majority (or, to say, 99%) of criminal cases. We cannot, therefore, argue that the involvement of specialised law enforcement authorities in criminal investigations other than the traditional group of investigative bodies is of increasing importance, but rather an exception.

b) *Do public law enforcement authorities enjoy a monopoly (exclusivity) of investigation rights in criminal cases, or do they share this competence with private entities (e.g. as part of private investigations or in the case of less serious actions being brought by private prosecution)? Where a given legal system envisages separate proceedings in actions brought by private prosecution, can public law enforcement authorities participate in them and if yes, what is the extent of that participation? Does it cover the right to examine evidence?*

In essence, private prosecutions are almost never investigated. The private prosecution (or his legal representative) does not have investigative powers, nor is there any common practice of private investigation in Hungary. In two cases, an investigation may be ordered in a private prosecution. One case is when the court considers that an investigation is necessary (e.g. the complaint indicates who the perpetrator may have been, but the private prosecutor cannot indicate his personal details, e.g. the license plate number of his vehicle). The other is for the public prosecutor to take over the prosecution's representation when the prosecutor himself can order an investigation (e.g. the prosecutor sees that the case may not be an end to an easy assault, but an attempted grievous bodily harm where there is no longer room for a private prosecution).

2.2 Court's Right to Acquire Evidence at the Investigation Stage or Its Controlling Activities in Relation to Evidence Examined by Other Entities

a) *Is the court entitled to examine evidence at the stage of investigation and if yes, can it admit evidence ex officio or only at the parties' request, or are both those solutions possible simultaneously? Does the format of court investigation apply?*

The court in Hungary does not examine evidence during the investigative section, it does not cooperate in the investigative activities.

b) *At the investigation stage, does the court or another body hold the controlling rights in relation to evidentiary activities taken by law enforcement authorities and if yes, what controlling measures are afforded (e.g. does the examination of a specific piece of evidence require the court to give its prior consent)? What are the consequences of a failure to satisfy the condition of the court's or another entity's consent and other conditions from the perspective of the validity and effectiveness of the evidence examined? Can the specification of such pieces of evidence and the conditions of their admissibility established by the law be viewed as sufficient?*

At the investigative stage, the court does not have control rights concerning the evidentiary activities carried out by law enforcement authorities.

In certain investigative phases, the prosecutor's supervision-direction -instruction scope of activities are governed differently in the CPC:

- during cleaning up the prosecutor overviews the legitimacy (§ 25. § Subsection 2); within this framework it controls the legitimacy of the proceedings of the investigating authority; it can reverse unlawful decrees; it can call upon the investigating authority to amend the breach of the law and adjudge legal remedy requests, etc. (§ 26. Subsection 2); and the superior prosecutor's office supervises the exercise of the supervisory and direction powers of the prosecutor's office (§ 25. Subsection 4)
- during the examining the prosecutor does not only supervise anymore, but directs too (§ 25 Subsection 2): it can carry out all the supervision measures. In addition, it can specifically instruct or forbid the investigating authority to carry out procedural measures; it can change the investigating authority's decision and oblige the investigating authority to come to a decision, or to give report, etc. (§ 26. Subsection 3);
- apart from the above mentioned the prosecutor also has the right to instruct, if the prosecutor carries out the investigation himself: in this case the prosecutor can instruct whichever investigating authority to carry out procedural measures within its field of jurisdiction, the crime prevention and counter terrorism units (CTU) can be requested to carry out procedural measures (§ 349. Subsection 2).

The investigative jurisdiction and competence of the prosecutor is determined in separate legislation and highest prosecutor's normative instructions.

c) *Is there a procedure at the investigation stage that enables the parties and their counsels to challenge the evidence examined in violation of the applicable principles? If yes, please present it briefly, taking into account the procedural consequences of its usage (the application of the principle of automatic exclusion of evidence; the recognition of invalidity of evidence; the judge's right to assess the consequences of a method adopted to acquire evidence and evidence content) as well as the legal consequences for those who violated the law; please indicate the level of imperativeness of responses to a violation concerning the acquisition and examination of evidence, based on the applicable law and standpoints of doctrine and judicature.*

At the investigative stage, no procedure allows the defendant (victim) and the defender (legal representative) to discuss whether the evidence met the legal conditions. In the event of an infringement by the investigating authority, a complaint may be lodged, but this complaint shall be examined by the Public Prosecutor's Office. The court has the right to assess the method of obtaining evidence and the legality of the evidence only at the court stage.

3 Principles of Acquiring Evidence at the Stage of Investigation

a) *Normative grounds for evidentiary activities in a criminal action (the Constitution, procedural criminal law, police law, administrative law, regulations, instructions, guidelines, common law, others). Can a multitude of sources of regulations in this area be referred to or is there normative homogeneity in place?*

The evidentiary activity in Hungary is regulated only and exclusively by the Criminal Procedure Act, there is no other normative basis for it.

b) *Does the applicable law regulate the principles of evidentiary activities taken by law enforcement authorities restrictively (on a tight-rein basis) and, similarly – determine the consequences of violations committed by the investigators, or does it leave to them a broad discretion in the search for evidence followed by the court's right to discretionarily assess the collected evidentiary material and by the confrontation of evidence during a verbal and contradictory trial at court?*

In Hungarian law, there are no tight limits on the obtaining of evidence by the investigating authorities. The main consequence of the violations committed by investigators will be that the prosecutor will not press charges based on unlawfully obtained evidence, because they will not be evaluated in the court department. Of course, there are also consequences for violations committed by the investigating authority in violation of the Hungarian Criminal Code (for example: abuse of office, abuse in official proceedings, forced declaration, etc.). In the court stage, the court has the right to a discretionary assessment of the evidence gathered and to collide the evidence at oral and adversary hearings.

c) *Are there any criteria of the legality of evidence and criteria that disqualify the same established by the law? What role does the judicature play in establishing such criteria?*

In Hungary, there are two basic ways to exclude illegal evidence:
- in a general manner (general clause) within the scope of the general rules of evidence and principles;
- in a specific way (specifically) relating to each means of proof.

According to the general clause of evidence excluded by law, data obtained by the authority by criminal offence, other prohibited means or by substantially restricting the procedural rights of participants cannot be assessed as evidence.

However, the general prohibitions on proof are unfortunate because they are very difficult to interpret and even less applicable. The specific exclusion methods are not only clearer, but also much more effective. On the one hand, they not only draw attention to the prohibitions of evidence (e.g. barriers to testimony), but also immediately inform us that, in the event of a breach of those prohibitions, no usable evidence is produced (i.e. such a procedural act is not only irregular but also unnecessary), because, for example, the testimony of a witness questioned without warning of the right to freedom of witness cannot be taken into account as evidence.

The prohibitions of proof leading to the nullity of evidence in Hungary may cover three areas:

(a) the subject matter of the evidence;
(b) the means of a proof;
(c) how it is proved.

ad (a) The prohibitions on proof relating to the subject matter of the evidence arise mainly from certain provisions of the Criminal Code of Hungary, namely as regards the facts within the scope of the case and about the so-called ('exception veritatis'). It is clear from these rules that until the obligation of confidentiality is lifted or the evidence of reality is ordered by the court seised for legal reasons, the evidence obtained concerning the facts and circumstances covered by such a category cannot be taken into account.

ad (b) There are several prohibitions on proof concerning means of proof:

- cases of prohibitions and exemptions in the context of testimony;
- a reference to the barriers to witnessing concerning the expert opinion;
- declaration by the defendant in front of the expert (exploration);
- failure to issue a Miranda warning in connection with the defendant's testimony;
- the results of certain research not subsequently authorised by the court;
- the content of the unseen confiscated document;
- some of the evidence generated as a result of the secret acquisition, etc.

ad (c) As regards the method of proof, it would be particularly important for the Hungarian Criminal Procedure Act to declare the evidence obtained through certain unlawful coercive measures null and void (e.g. in the case of an unlawful search, search, seizure).

d) *Does the principle of freedom, meaning that any evidentiary measure and any evidentiary method are admissible (except those that a limine are unacceptable in civilized world), apply to the acquisition of evidence at the investigation stage? Or is it restricted by the applicability of general principles of the law, e.g. legalism, reliability, proportionality, necessity, and values such as human dignity, bodily inviolability, or the right to privacy? Where references are explicite missing in the law to the aforesaid standards, on what basis are those standards applied? How do doctrine and case law understand the notion of "fair evidentiary procedure"? Is this notion autonomous or does it constitute a part of the notion of "fair trial"?*

The Hungarian system of proof (as already mentioned) belongs to the not entirely free system of proof: all means of proof laid down by law can be used freely in criminal proceedings, and all acts of proof can be freely applied. However, the law may provide for the use of certain means of proof. The legislator, therefore, did not wish to define the scope of the evidence, but on the other hand, it imposes a constraint by requiring individual and joint consideration of the evidence. This regulation does not recognise any absolute or perfect evidence that does not require discretion (which would necessarily bind the authority).

In addition, several other provisions of the Law support this classification:

- the means of proof and the evidence do not have predetermined probative power. Accordingly, there is, therefore, no 'perfect evidence', i.e. evidence that would necessarily bind the determining authority or require special consideration or investigation.
- if the defendant admits to it, other evidence must also be obtained (unless otherwise specified by Hungarian Criminal Prosecution Act, see e.g. settlement). So there's no perfect evidence even for the "queen of evidence."
- the reasons for the edification decision shall include an assessment and assessment of the evidence. So, there is no room for imaginative, intuitive, prejudiced, etc. findings. Only by evaluating evidence(s) can the adhesive authority, etc. obtain a finding of fact, etc ...

From all this it can be clearly stated that the Hungarian Criminal Prosecution Act is 'reasoned conviction', i.e. it is on the ground of a system of not entirely free evidence. An integral part of a system of not entirely free evidence is the institution of evidence excluded by law: a fact derived from a means of proof obtained by the court, the public prosecutor or the investigating authority by criminal offence, by other prohibited means or by substantially restricting the procedural rights of participants cannot be regarded as evidence.

The Hungarian Criminal Prosecution Act however, does not include the concept of 'fair proof procedure'. The concept of 'fair trial' is also included only in the preamble to the Law, according to which the Criminal Prosecution Act was enacted (inter alia) 'to bring to account the perpetrators of criminal offences punishable by the Hungarian Criminal Code or international law in an effective and reasonable procedure ensuring that the fundamental right to a fair trial is exercised'. Of course, the principle of due process recognised by international law has also been incorporated into Hungarian law, since the Rome Convention for the Protection of Human Rights and Fundamental Freedoms (Council of Europe Convention ETS-005 of 4 November 1950) was promulgated by Act XXI of 1993 in Hungary, making it binding.

e) *Is the acquisition of evidence at the investigation stage restricted by concrete prohibitions, e.g. the prohibition to use specific sources of evidence or evidentiary methods (please indicate the level of subordination of evidentiary activities to strict law; or maybe this situation depends on the nature of evidence, e.g. its interference in human rights and freedoms, or on the type of crime)? Please indicate examples of evidentiary activities that are subject to the strictest legal restrictions.*

As already indicated, the prohibitions on obtaining certain evidence also apply during the investigation. For example, a witness questioned in breach of the provisions on impediments to giving evidence or a defendant interviewed for Miranda's failure to give a warning are generally not considered as a means of proof, but there are significant limits to the burden of testimony made before the expert, covert means and requests for data subject to authorisation, violations of the rules of research and seizure, and subsequent discounts, the usability of confessions. These are detailed in section 5b).

f) *Does the applicable law sufficiently define the boundaries of evidence acquisition admissibility, or maybe too categorically? What is the potential extent of the non-normative sphere in shaping such boundaries (general rules, pragmatism, habits)? Are the proportions between the two spheres (normative and non-normative) appropriate?*

Hungarian law basically defines the limits of admissibility of the collection of evidence. They are neither narrowed nor broadened by jurisprudence in general.

g) *As regards the acquisition of evidence during investigation, how at this stage is the deficit of the inapplicability of principles of equality of parties, equality of arms, and the contradictory principle compensated for, also taking into account the fact of general primacy of law enforcement authorities, in order to ensure a fair evidentiary procedure? Can the suspect and other entities share in this?*

In the course of the investigation, the defence is fundamentally excluded from the evidence-gathering process. There are only a few exceptions.

During the examining, the CPC governs the right to be present at procedural actions in a broader sense. Because reasonable suspicion has been conveyed and the suspect has been questioned, the presence rights of the defence become activated:

- the suspect and his defence counsel can be present at the hearing of experts, the inspection, reconstruction and presentation for recognition;
- the defence counsel can be present at the questioning of a witness that was motioned by him (through the suspect defended by him) and during evidentiary action with participation of such a witness.

Even in these cases, the defence does not need to be informed if urgency or other important interests (such as e.g. the protection of the witness) warrants this. However, the defence shall be informed on the procedural action within 8 days.

The presence of defence counsel is mandatory before indictment as well if a juvenile

- is being questioned as a suspect,
- is at a confrontation,
- is at presentation for identification,
- is being questioned on the scene,
- is at a reconstruction, and
- at the session in the subject of coercive measures bound to judicial consent and touching upon personal freedom.

h) *Is there a balance between the freedom of law enforcement authorities' actions, on which the crime combating efficiency depends, and limitations of that freedom arising from the need to ensure appropriate standards of evidentiary procedure? Does a comparison of those antagonistic to some extent perspectives show that the purpose of repression dominates at the expense of the procedural guarantees and the rights of individuals, or rather the purpose of the reliability of evidence at the expense of its effectiveness in the detection of the truth?*

There is no real balance in the investigation between the freedom of action of law enforcement authorities within the limits of that freedom. Investigative authorities enjoy a high degree of freedom in obtaining evidence, and this is limited by the fact that unlawful evidence cannot be used in criminal proceedings (or the acquisition of evidence contrary to the Hungarian Criminal Code may have further consequences).

i) *How can the fairness of evidentiary procedure be ensured in view of the conditions imposed by the commonly used consensual procedures, methods directed towards accelerating or shortening criminal proceedings, and the usage of alternative methods for criminal prosecution? Those measures not only fail to eliminate the issue of the boundaries of legal acquisition of evidence, but bring this issue into focus in connection with the conclusiveness of evidence being examined at the investigation stage. In these circumstances, are procedural guarantees ensured during the evidentiary procedure, together with due control over its legality at the investigation stage, bearing in mind the pressure for attaining the goal and swiftly end the proceedings?*

Procedural guarantees are guaranteed in Hungary during the evidentiary procedure. The legality of the evidence is regularly verified by the public prosecutor's office at the investigative stage. Although one of the main objectives of the new Hungarian Criminal Prosecution Act was to speed up proceedings, this is not very typical of the investigative department, but rather the judicial section was shortened as a result of measures to speed up the proceedings (settlement, admission of guilt by accepting the sentence offered by the prosecution, etc.).

4 Identifications of Risks of Violating Freedom in the Acquisition of Evidence by Law Enforcement Authorities

a) *Narrow focus of enforcement authorities to acquire evidence of being guilty; oppressive investigative methods; violation of human dignity; use of measures compelling individuals to meet certain evidentiary obligations, or use of a passive tactic consisting in provoking the suspect or other entities into providing evidence. What measures are taken to counteract such practices?*

In addition to the fact that the fact derived from a means of the proof obtained by the authority through a criminal offence, by other prohibited means or by a material violation of the criminal rights of the participants cannot be regarded as evidence, an additional limitation is that Article 303 of the Hungarian Criminal Code regulates forced declarations a criminal offence:

1. Any public official who attempts by force or threat of force, or by other similar means, to coerce another person into giving information or making a statement, or to withhold information, is guilty of a felony punishable by imprisonment between one to five years.
2. The penalty shall be imprisonment between two to eight years if the criminal offense defined in Subsection (1) is committed in a gang.
3. Any person who engages in preparations for the interrogation of a person for the coercion of information by force is guilty of misdemeanor punishable by imprisonment not exceeding two years.
4. The penalty may be reduced without limitation if the perpetrator unveils the circumstances of the criminal offense defined in Subsection (2) to the authorities before the indictment.

b) *A tendency to hierarchize evidence in favour of scientific evidence and at the expense of other pieces of evidence. Can an a priori privileged treatment of such evidence be seen as a threat to the legality and fairness of evidentiary procedure in connection with unsatisfactory motivation of enforcement authorities to verify and critically evaluate the same, and with the limited opportunities for private parties to challenge the same?*

In principle, it is not typical for new scientific evidence to lead to the investigating authorities not carrying out their activities in sufficient depth. Rather, such evidence is obtained (mainly under pressure from the Public Prosecutor's Office) even when it is not necessary, thereby significantly increasing the criminal cost. For example, in anti-life cases, the public prosecutor's office almost always requires DNA testing (if there is material for comparison), even if the defendant has admitted to committing the crime and there is a lot of direct and indirect evidence available anyway.

c) *Different boundaries for the freedom of law enforcement authorities to acquire evidence depending on the crime type; a failure by legal regulations to keep up with new technologies to be used in cases for most serious crimes gives rise to a threat of abuse and potentially easier excuse of such practices. How can the present legal regulation be assessed from this perspective (e.g. as to cyber or biological evidence) in the context of threats to the fairness of evidentiary procedure? Are other regulatory standards in place or are any such standards tolerated, being different from those as in the case of traditional evidence?*

There are no specific standards in Hungary, e.g. for cyber or biological evidence. As I mentioned, it is not typical that the use of modern methods would lead to the withering of traditional law enforcement techniques.

5 Inviolable Boundaries in the Acquisition of Evidence by Law Enforcement Authorities

a) *Please indicate violations in the acquisition of evidence that make the evidence definitely invalid (i.e. indicate prohibited methods of proving facts);*

In general, a fact derived from a means of the proof obtained by the authority through a criminal offence, by other prohibited means or by a material violation of the criminal rights of participants cannot be assessed as evidence (§ 167 (5)).

b) *Please indicate evidence the acquisition of which is definitely prohibited;*

For each piece of evidence, the Hungarian Criminal Prosecution Act lists the following prohibitions of proof:

- the testimony of a witness questioned in breach of the provisions on impediments to giving evidence cannot be taken into account as a means of proof (Section 169 (3));
- in the event of failure to record a witness warning or a response to a warning, the witness's testimony shall not be taken into account as a means of proof, unless the witness maintains his or her previous communication after the witness warning (§ 177 (3));

- in the event of failure to record the defendant's (Miranda) warning and the response to the warning, the defendant's testimony shall not be taken into account as a means of proof, unless the defendant has already received a warning previously charged during the proceedings and his defence counsel was present during his continued questioning, or he maintains his previous communication after the defendant's warning (§ 185 (3));
- the communication of the accused, witness and victim to the expert concerning the subject matter of the investigation, the investigation procedures and instruments, or the changes in the subject matter of the investigation or the act on which the proceedings are based shall not be used as evidence (196 (3));
- if the court or the public prosecutor's office rejects the motion for retrospective authorisation of the disguised device, the result of the use of the disguised instrument subject to authorisation shall not be used as evidence and the data thus obtained shall be deleted without delay (§ 223 (3)); § 229 (5); § 238 (5);
- the result of the use of a disguised instrument subject to judicial authorisation shall not be used as evidence if the person concerned is a person acting as a defender or a relative or a person subject to a witness barrier against whom a disguised instrument subject to judicial authority would not have been applicable (§ 254 (1));
- the result of the use of the undercover investigator cannot be used as evidence if the public prosecutor's office does not intend to use the result of the use of the undercover investigator as evidence, and becoming known for the fact of employing an undercover detective would directly endanger the life, physical integrity and personal freedom of the undercover detective (§ 255 (7));
- if the request for data subject to authorisation is not authorised by the public prosecutor's office, the data thus obtained cannot be used as evidence and must be deleted immediately (§ 262 (3));
- if the research is to be ordered by a court (research to be carried out in a notarial or law firm) and is not ordered by the court, the result thereof cannot be used as evidence (§ 303 (3));
- if the public prosecutor's office or the court does not order the seizure of the sealed document, the document may not be used as a means of proof in the ongoing case or in other criminal proceedings (§ 314 (2));
- in the event of termination of the preparatory proceedings, the data obtained in the course thereof may not be used as evidence in criminal proceedings (§ 346 (2));

- if the suspect accepts and fulfils the measure or decision envisaged by the public prosecutor's office and its conditions, or if the prospect of action or decision of the public prosecutor's office was unlawful, his testimony to that effect cannot be taken into account as evidence (§ 406 (2));
- if the public prosecutor's office and the defendant have not reached an agreement, the initiative and the related case-file may not be used as evidence or as a means of proof (§ 409 (4));
- the statement made by the suspect and the victim during the mediation procedure cannot be used as evidence in the case (§ 414 (3)).

c) *Please indicate a category of interests and values that are decisive for excluding evidence or restricting its examination.*

There are different degrees of the illegality of evidence:

(a) Breach of formal regulations and detailed provisions of a technical nature (irregular summons, failure to notify);
(b) Abandonment of certain procedural supplies and safeguards (e.g. only one official witness instead of two, no record of the search, etc.);
(c) Deficiencies or irregular steps related to the content (e.g. the interrogated could not give evidence in a coherent way, or no questions or confrontations were taken);
(d) Violation of the prohibitions of proof expressly or implicitly formulated in the Hungarian Criminal Prosecution Act (e.g. ignoring witness barriers, failure to warn the accused Miranda);
(e) The evidence was obtained in violation of the Constitution or in violation of the Hungarian Criminal Code. The most common case scenario is the question of evidence obtained in connection with unlawful coercive measures.

6 Conclusion

(An evaluation of the existing legal environment within the scope at hand; a reference to practice, case law, controversies in doctrine, a tendency of changes, and future perspectives; finally, this is a place for free comments if these framework matters seem insufficient to present the specifics of the topic of: Limits of freedom of public authorities with respect to obtaining evidence at the stage of investigation).

In the case of the first three degrees of illegality listed in the preceding point (points (a) to (b) to (c)), the means and methods relating to procedural acts with disabilities shall apply in particular: correction, addition, regular repetition of the procedural act, replacement, etc. Thus, judicial practice does not exclude evidence simply because the interpreter did not sign all pages of the minutes Hungarian Court Order: 432 of 1997, or the interpreter was not warned of the consequences of false interpretation Hungarian Court Order: 117.1996. But he also does not exclude the testimony of the suspect because, at the first interrogation, the defender was not present Hungarian Court Order 117 of 1998 (even if the defence is mandatory in the particular criminal case.)

In the event of a breach of the prohibitions of proof expressly or implicitly formulated in the Hungarian Criminal Prosecution Act, or in the case of obtaining evidence in violation of the Constitution or violation of the Hungarian Criminal Code, the evidence shall be completely excluded, there is no possible remedial rectifying here (e.g. in the event of failure to warn the witness or the accused). At the same time, it should be noted that very few occasions, e.g. forced declarations (at least, for this reason, impeachment) take place. While forced declarations were very common in socialism, after the change of regime in 1990, this is indeed a rarity. While research shows that psychological pressure still occurs today (e.g. a defendant interrogated without a defender is told to admit to committing a crime, otherwise he will be arrested for months or even years), physical abuse is very rare. We do not currently have the 2020 crime statistics, but between 2015 and 2019 a total of 26 cases were prosecuted for forced declarations in Hungary (2015: 4 cases; 4, 2016; 2017: 10 cases; 2018: 6 cases; 2019: 2 cases). This represents a very small percentage of crimes (in Hungary, the number of crimes during this period was as follows: (2015: 280,113 crimes; 2016: 290,779 crimes; 2017: 226,452 crimes; 2018: 199,830 crimes; 2019: 165,648 crimes). As a result of the forced declaration proceedings, no severe penalties were imposed either, e.g. in 2018 only one person was imprisoned (not in 2019), and in 2018 there were 1 public interest work and 1 waiting period, in 2019 there were only 1 fine and 1 recession (the other defendants were either acquitted or measures were applied only to him).

In the future, it would help to facilitate the legality of the evidence taken during the investigation if it is possible to request that the judgment at first instance be established in the case of unlawfully recorded evidence in the course of the investigation, and even if it is not inconceivable that the unlawful acquisition of evidence in the course of the investigation would be an explicit ground for retrial.

CHAPTER 5

Italian Evidence Law System: Limits to the Investigative Power

*Thomas Di Candia**

1 Overview of the Italian Evidence Law System

The recent «*riforma Cartabia*» (Cartabia's Reform)[1] changed several aspects of Italian criminal procedure, including some rules related to the investigative phase. However, the evidence law system – which limits the public authorities power while collecting evidence for the investigative stage – was only minimally affected.

The cornerstones of the Italian evidentiary system are the Constitution[2] and the Code of Criminal Procedure.[3]

The Constitution indicates the fundamental and insuperable principles of the evidentiary procedure. Firstly, the 111th Article of the Constitution,[4] in paragraph 1, provides that the evidence must be formed before the judge, thus configuring the principle of immediacy. Furthermore, Article 111 also provides that the evidence must be formed with the cross-examination technique between the parties, who must be in an equal position, allowing derogation only in the cases of objective impossibility of taking evidence in the cross-examination or in the case of consent-approval by the parties. Paragraph 3 establishes the principle of «orality» in the assumption of evidence (orality which means that

* PhD student at Department of Law, Economics and Cultures – University of Insubria, Italy.

1 The reform is named after Marta Cartabia, Minister of Justice from February 2021 to October 2022 in the Draghi government (67th of the Italian Republic). The most significant changes in criminal matters occurred with Law No. 134/2021 and Legislative Decree No. 150/2022. The reform aims to make the Italian criminal justice quick and efficient, thus meeting European standards on reasonable length of the trial.

2 The Constitution of the Italian Republic was enacted by the Constituent Assembly on 22nd December 1947 and entered into force on 1st January 1948.

3 From a formal point of view, the Code of Criminal Procedure was issued with the Decree of the President of the Republic n. 447 of 1988 and entered into force on 24th October 1989.

4 Article 111 of the Constitution governs the principles related to due process and was amended by the constitutional law n. 2/1999, which introduced five new paragraphs.

 | DOI:10.1163/9789004710320_007

evidence against the defendant must be presented by live witnesses in Court, subject to cross-examination).

The Code of Criminal Procedure provides additional principles on evidence and all detail rules.

The 1989 Code revolutionized the Italian criminal trial which, until then, embodied the «mixed» model of Napoleonic tradition. That former model was characterized by an investigative stage, secret and written, conducted by a «*giudice istruttore*» (judge of instruction). The evidence collected in the investigative phase was widely usable in the subsequent trial phase.

Whereas, the new Code of Criminal Procedure introduced a trial system based on the opposite accusatory (or adversarial) model, as it is clear from the delegation law which expressly provided that the new criminal trial should be based on the characteristics of that model.[5] In this sense, the Code provides for a general principle of separation between the pre-trial investigation phase, which serves the public prosecutor to understand whether he or she has sufficient ground to prosecute (i.e., to start a criminal trial)[6] or he or she must drop the case, and the trial phase, where the evidence for or against the defendant is formed before the judge.

5 See art. 2, paragraph 1 of Law 81/1987, which states that the new Code of Criminal Procedure must implement the principles of the Constitution, the rules of international conventions ratified by Italy and the characteristics of the accusatory system.

6 The Cartabia's Reform introduced a new criteria to decide on the prosecution. Previously, Article 408 C.C.P. provided that the prosecutor had to drop the case if the *notitia criminis* was groundless ('*se la notizia di reato è infondata*'). Article 22, para. 1, letter e) of the legislative decree n. 150/2022 brought a paradigm shift; the current text of Article 408, paragraph 1 provides that the prosecutor drops the case if the evidence gathered during the preliminary investigation does not allow for a reasonable prediction of conviction ('*una ragionevole previsione di condanna*'). There is a shift from a subsequent assessment on the crime report and whether the prosecution can be sustained at trial on the basis of the evidence gathered to a prognostic assessment on the outcome of the trial. The reason behind this choice (and others) is to reduce the high rate of acquittals that characterizes the Italian criminal trial (the conviction rate – which indicates the ratio between the number of cases for which the prosecutor has prosecuted and the number of convictions – was 51% over the period 2013–2018, while in other countries such as England and the U.S. it averaged around 90%. See M. Gialuz, J. Della Torre, *Giustizia per nessuno. L'inefficienza del sistema penale italiano tra crisi cronica e riforma Cartabia*, Giappichelli, Torino 2022, pp. 141–157). This normative change could involve a radical cultural shift, but the success of this innovation will depend greatly on the willingness of prosecutors to change their *forma mentis*, otherwise it risks being merely a lexical change. For more information see C. Santoriello, 'Le nuove regole di giudizio della Riforma Cartabia, tra una positiva sinergia e una possibile eterogenesi dei fini', (2022) *Archivio penale*, n. 2, pp. 2–6.

The Italian evidence system expresses the typical characteristics of the accusatory system.[7] In order to enhance the trial stage, based on the principles of publicity of the hearings, fairness and «orality», the evidence[8] collected during the investigation is used – with some exceptions – by the public prosecutor only to decide whether there are grounds for a criminal trial or not. The general principle is that the evidence on the criminal liability of the accused must be formed, during the trial phase with the cross-examination technique between the parties, before the judge who will decide on the guiltiness of the defendant.

Therefore, in the Italian procedural system there are three so-called dossiers, which may have different contents. The public prosecutor's dossier contains all of the acts this public authority carried out during the investigative stage. On the basis of the content of this dossier, the public prosecutor's office decides whether there is sufficient evidence to prosecute or not. Usually this dossier will not become available to the judge who will decide the trial. In parallel, a dossier of «*investigazioni difensive*» (defensive investigation) can be created, which contains all of the activities carried out by the lawyer – who represents the person accused of committing a criminal offence or the victim – during the investigation. Lastly, there is the trial dossier, which contains all of the evidence formed during the trial and, exceptionally, the evidence collected during the pre-trial phase which is no longer available or the evidence collected during the pre-trial phase which all of the parties have approved to include in the trial dossier.[9] The trial dossier contains exclusively the evidence which can be used by the judge at the end of the trial to decide whether the defendant is guilty or not.

It is clear the particular role of the evidence gathered at the stage of the pre-trial investigation. These elements generally serve only the public prosecutor to assess whether there are sufficient elements to carry out the criminal prosecution and only exceptionally (because their assumption cannot be repeated

7 For an analysis of the basic characteristics of the Italian accusatorial system see G. Illuminati, 'The Accusatorial Process from the Italian Point of View', (2005)35 *N.C. J. Int'l L. & Com. Reg.*, pp. 309–313. On the peculiarities and malfunctions of the Italian-style accusatory system see M. Panzavolta, 'Reforms and Counter-Reforms in the Italian Struggle for an Accusatorial Criminal Law System', (2004)*30 N.C. J. INT'L L.*, pp. 583–623, and G. Illuminati, 'The Frustrated Turn to Adversarial Procedure in Italy (Italian Criminal Procedure Code of 1988)', (2005)4 *Wash. U. Glob. Stud. L. Rev.*, pp. 570–581.

8 The term «evidence» should be specified. We should more specifically talk of «evidentiary elements» because this term refers to all those elements capable of providing useful indications for the decision of the judgment, thus including both evidence and clues.

9 The content of the trial dossier is detailed in art. 431 C.C.P., which regulates its formation. According to paragraph 1, letters b) and c) the trial dossier shall contain the records of unrepeatable actions conducted by the public prosecutor, the police and the lawyer.

at the trial, because they are obtained with the approval of the parties or due to the defendant's choice to access certain summary trials) they can be used by the trial judge in his/her decision on the defendant's criminal liability.

Because of the principle of separation between investigative and trial phase, the Code of Criminal Procedureformally distinguishes between the so-called *mezzi di ricerca della prova* (pre-trial activities aimed to collect evidence at the investigation stage, which cannot be repeated at the trial) and *mezzi di prova* (activities carried out in the trial, before the judge, in order to prove the guiltiness or the innocence of the defendant).[10] On one hand, the *mezzi di ricerca della prova* consist of the typical activities carried out in investigation, that may lead to the identification of evidence during this investigative stage (inspections, searches, seizures and interceptions). On the other hand, the *mezzi di prova* consist of various activities that can be carried out during the trial, in order to decide on the guiltiness or the innocence of the defendant (witness examination, parties examination, reconnaissance, comparisons, expertise and documentary evidence). A peculiar characteristic of the *mezzi di ricerca della prova* (and thus of their discipline) is the fact that these are acts originally aimed at seeking and fixing states or qualities: therefore, these activities cannot be repeated at the trial, with the consequence that they must be included in the trial dossier and can be used by the trial judge.[11]

Once introduced what can be done during the investigation stage, it is necessary to understand who can collect evidence during the investigative phase.

2 Investigative Stage: Subjects Involved in the Acquisition of Evidence

During the pre-trial phase evidence can be collected by several subjects: public authorities (public prosecutor and police), lawyer (both of the defendant and the victim) and the «*giudice per le indagini preliminari*» (judge for pre-trial investigation or judge of freedom).

In order to examine the issue of the limits of the public authorities power while collecting evidence during the investigative stage, a brief introduction to these subjects is required.

10 In particular, Title II of the Third Book of the Code of Criminal Procedure, on Evidence, sets out the legislation for *mezzi di prova*, while Title III regulates the *mezzi di ricerca della prova*.

11 The possibility of using these materials will be discussed in more detail see § 4.2.

2.1 *Public Authority*

A plurality of sources governs the competence of public authorities in the conduction of the investigation and, thus, in the collection of evidence at the investigative stage.

Firstly, Article 112 of the Constitution states the principle of mandatory prosecution by the public prosecutor, who must necessarily prosecute if there is sufficient evidence to go to trial, thus excluding any discretion of his or her Office.[12]

Furthermore, Article 109 of the Constitution provides, as a general rule, that the «judicial authority» (expression which in Italy covers both the public prosecutor and the judge) has at its direct dispose the «*polizia giudiziaria*».[13] Therefore, the public prosecutor may use (and always uses) the police in the collection of evidence during pre-trial investigation.[14]

The discipline of the investigative activity of the public authorities is further detailed by the Code of Criminal Procedure, which identifies, among others, a series of general rules on subjects and investigative activities.

The rules laid down in 'Book I', 'Title II', Articles from 50 to 54-*quarter* of the Code of Criminal Procedure, allow the identification of the public prosecutor's office[15] responsible for investigative functions. In the Italian legal system, the public prosecutor does not have his or her own and autonomous

---

12 Art. 112 of the Italian Constitution states that the public prosecutor has a duty to prosecute; this does not mean that every report of a criminal offence must end in a trial, but that the public prosecutor must prosecute whenever there is a probable cause that the person being investigated will be convicted at the end of the trial. In the event that this condition occurs, then the public prosecutor must prosecute without any discretion. For an in-depth discussion of this issue and, more generally, on the figure of the Italian public prosecutor see M. Caianiello, 'The Italian Public Prosecutor: An Inquisitorial Figure in Adversarial Proceedings?' in E. Luna, M. Wade (eds), *Transnational Perspectives On Prosecutorial Power*, Oxford University Press, Oxford 2011, pp. 256–267.

13 See Art. 109 of the Constitution, according to which the judicial authority, in particular the public prosecutor, directly disposes of the police. Members of the law enforcement are members of the *polizia giudiziaria* when they exercise public functions related to the exercise of judicial power. The police deals in particular with the search for the offender and the evidence.

14 On the topic of the relation between police and prosecutor see R. Montana, 'Paradigms of Judicial Supervision and Coordination between Police and Prosecutors: the Italian Case in a Comparative Perspective', (2009)17 *Eur. J. Crim. Criminal L. and Crim. Just.*, pp. 309–318.

15 Article 51 of the C.C.P. indicates the structure and organization of the public prosecutor's office. The prosecutors' offices are divided into Public Prosecutor's Offices at the court of first instance, General Prosecutor's Offices at the *corte d'appello* (second instance court) and Prosecutor General at *Corte di Cassazione* (the Supreme Court).

«competence» for offences, but is referred to as an «assignment of functions». The investigation are coordinated by the office of the public prosecutor which exercises the functions before the competent judge, with some exceptions for Mafia and terrorism offences, which will be illustrated shortly. It follows that, the public prosecutor who directs the investigation and decides on the prosecution is generally the one who exercises the functions before the competent judge, which will be identified on the basis of the specific rules that the Code and the other statutory law dedicate to the judge's competence.[16]

Another very important player in the collection of evidence is the police. Indeed, the public prosecutor may have at his or her disposal the police, to whom he or she may commit the execution of a series of investigative activities. Moreover, the police may also carry out several activities on their own initiative, especially in urgent cases or when the public prosecutor has not yet taken over control and direction of the investigation.[17]

Unlike other countries, the Italian criminal procedural system does not provide for intervention in the pre-trial phase of public authorities other than the public prosecutor and the police, such as special forces or specialized administrative authorities. Although, a special mention must be done for the authorities specialized in juvenile offences and those specialized in the fight against organized crime and terrorism.

Regarding the juvenile criminal proceedings,[18] there is a specialized public prosecutor «*Procura della Repubblica presso il Tribunale per i Minorenni*» before the specialized juvenile court «*Tribunale per i Minorenni*». This public prosecutor conducts preliminary investigation related to offences committed by juvenile subjects.

In order to fight Mafia and terrorism phenomena, a special system of organisation of the prosecutor offices was created. The *Procure Distrettuali Antimafia*

---

16 Article 4 and ff C.C.P. indicate a series of rules to identify in the specific case the judge competent for the proceeding. The Code distinguishes between different competences: functional, by type of criminal offence, by territory, by connection.

17 Articles 55–59 C.C.P. provide for the organisation of the *polizia giudiziaria*. The Code also indicates the investigative activities that the police may or may not carry out. In particular, the police can act on behalf of the public prosecutor (see article 370 C.C.P.) or on their own initiative (articles from 347 to 357 C.C.P. indicate the activities that the police can carry out on their own initiative and the relative limits). With reference to the limits on the powers of police in collecting evidence see § 4.2.

18 The Presidential Decree 448/1988 regulates the criminal proceedings against minors; in particular, Article 2 provides for the assignment of functions to a specialized public prosecutor at the juvenile court.

or *Direzioni Distrettuali Antimafia* (Anti-Mafia District Prosecutors)[19] have been set up territorially within every District of Court of Appeal.[20] The Anti-Mafia District Prosecutors conduct investigation for particularly serious criminal offences and criminal networks.[21]

There is also a coordinator of all the District Prosecutors, the National Anti-Mafia and Counter-Terrorism Central Prosecutor established at the General Prosecutor's Office in the *Corte di Cassazione* (Italian Supreme Court) in Rome.[22]

The reason behind this organisation is that Mafia and terrorism investigations are often complex, so it was decided not to fragment the investigative activities and to entrust them to a body with specific experience and knowledge.[23]

In their activities, the Anti-Mafia and Counter-Terrorism Prosecutors are supported by members of the police framed in the Anti-Mafia Investigation

---

19 The Anti-Mafia and Counter-Terrorism District Prosecutors are delegated prosecutors exclusively to the direction of investigations with respect to particular categories of criminal offences. The District Prosecutor's Office is an internal articulation of the Public Prosecutor's Office. Usually the Chief Prosecutor of the Public Prosecutor's Office appoints the Anti-Mafia and Counter-Terrorism District Prosecutor. A new office is not created, but the subjects responsible for all these investigations (District Anti-Mafia and Anti-Terrorism Prosecutor and substitutes) are appointed within the office. These are not rules establishing a new public prosecutor's office but give the Public Prosecutor's Office an additional task. The District Anti-Mafia Directorate (DDA) is the name of the pool of magistrates that make up the Anti-Mafia District Prosecutor's Office (PDAA), which in the Italian Republic's legal system is the body of the Public Prosecutor's Office at the courts of the capitals of the 26 districts of the Court of Appeal, to which jurisdiction over proceedings related to mafia-related crime is delegated. Informally it is called anti-mafia prosecutor's office.

20 The Italian judicial system distinguishes between *circondario* and *distretto*. The *circondario* is the territorial area of competence of the individual court, while the set of *circondario* that depend on a «*corte d'appello*» constitutes the district, i.e. the area over which the court of appeal has jurisdiction. In Italy there are 165 *circondario* of court and 26 appeal court districts.

21 The criminal offences with respect to which the Anti-Mafia and Counter-Terrorism Prosecutors exercise their functions are indicated in great detail by Article 51, paragraphs 3 *bis*, 3 *quarter* and 3 *quinquies* C.C.P. In particular, paragraph 3 *bis* lists a series of associative crimes, paragraph 3 *quarter* indicates criminal offences for terrorist purposes and paragraph 3 *quinques* lists a series of criminal offences in the field of child prostitution, sex tourism and child pornography, as well as criminal offences in computer field.

22 Article 371-*bis* C.C.P. provides that the National Anti-Mafia and Counter-Terrorism Central Prosecutor coordinates all the District Prosecutors.

23 For a more detailed discussion on the subject of Anti-Mafia Prosecutors system see S. Lorusso, '"Superprocura" e coordinamento delle indagini in materia di criminalità organizzata tra presente, passato e futuro', (2014)2 *Diritto Penale Contemporaneo*, pp. 24–37.

Directorate, who are agents specialized in the investigation of organized crime and terrorism.[24]

In carrying out investigations, the public prosecutors can rely on other police departments specialised in particular investigative activities. Just to mention a few, *Guardia di Finanza* is a law enforcement agency specialized in tax and fiscal investigation; the Postal Police is a Department of Italian Police, specialized in computer investigation; the RIS (*Reparto Investigazioni Scientifiche*) is a Department of the *Carabinieri* specialized in scientific investigation.

Lastly, in order to avoid waste of resources or unacceptable omissions in investigation, the Code of Criminal Procedure allows coordinating the investigations between the subjects involved: special mechanisms are provided for this purpose, such as the rules on «*contrasti positivi e negativi*» (positive and negative contrasts) between public prosecutor's offices.[25]

2.2 *Lawyer and Investigation*

Originally, only public authorities conducted investigation during the pre-trial phase. Indeed, our procedural system does not provide for the possibility of a private prosecutor. However, public authorities have (and always had) a duty to carry out investigation even in favour of the suspect.[26]

In the year 2000 an important innovation in terms of equality of «arms» between prosecution and defense occurred with the introduction, by Law 397/2000, of the discipline of «*investigazioni difensive*» (defensive investigation).[27] In this way the legislator tried to guarantee the right of defence and the equality of «arms» as fully as possible by allowing a private subject – the lawyer of the accused or of the victim – to collect evidence during the investigation stage. The provision stated at legislative level the powers of the lawyer in carrying out investigative activities.

---

24 For more information on the history, structure and functions of the Anti-Mafia Investigative Directorate see A. La Spina, 'The Paradox of Effectiveness: Growth, Institutionalisation and Evaluation of Anti-Mafia Policies in Italy' in C. Fijnaut, L. Paoli (eds), *Organised Crime in Europe Concepts, Patterns and Control Policies in the European Union and Beyond*, Springer, Dordrecht 2004, pp. 641–676.

25 Cases in which no public prosecutor considers that he or she has authority over a proceeding or where several prosecutors believe they are entitled are regulated by Articles 54, 54-*bis* and 54-*ter* C.C.P. In these cases, it is the Prosecutor General at the Court of Appeal or the Prosecutor General at the *Corte di Cassazione* who decides.

26 Art. 358 of the C.C.P. provides that the public prosecutor also carries out investigation both for and against the defendant.

27 The discipline of *investigazioni difensive* has its normative references in Article 327-*bis* and Articles 391-*bis* and ff C.C.P.

The Code of Criminal Procedure allows the defendant's, the injured party's or the victim's lawyer to carry out an investigation in order to collect evidence in favour of his or her client, even in advance (before the start of a criminal proceeding).[28]

The Code also regulates the activities that the lawyer can carry out during an investigation. In particular, the lawyer may take information from witnesses during the stage of investigation,[29] may request access to documents available to the public administration,[30] may make «technical findings».[31] The lawyer may also enter private or closed places with the prior authorization of the judge.[32]

However the lawyer's investigative freedom is limited by the need to exercise a coercive power, which is the exclusive prerogative of public authorities. Indeed, in the case that the witness refuses to be heard, the lawyer can only ask the public prosecutor to summon him within 7 days.[33] Similarly, in the event that the public administration refuses to provide the requested documentation, the lawyer may apply first to the public prosecutor and then to the judge to request his or her permission.[34]

This shows that there is a non-perfect equality of faculties between the public prosecutor and the lawyer. In addition, the Code configures a power of secrecy for the public prosecutor: it may prohibit, if necessary, the heard witnesses from communicating to the lawyer facts or circumstances of which they

---

28 In particular, the lawyer may carry out investigation from the moment of his or her appointment as provided for in articles 327-*bis* and Article 391-*nonies* C.C.P.

29 See Articles 391-*bis* and 391-*ter*, which regulate the ways in which the lawyer may collect information from witness at the investigation stage. In particular, Article 391-*ter* regulates the procedures for documenting the declarations of the witness.

30 The right of the lawyer to request the public administration for access to documents in its possession is provided for by Art. 391-*quater* C.C.P.

31 The lawyer can make observations on places and things, describing their state or carrying out technical measurements, documenting them in the manner provided for by art. 391-*sexies* C.C.P.

32 If there is no consent of the owner, the lawyer can access closed or private places with the motivated authorization of the judge, who also indicates the modalities (art. 391-*septies* C.C.P.).

33 See art. 391-*ter*, paragraph 10 of the Italian Criminal Procedure Code. This term is not peremptory, so in the event that too much time passes between the request of the lawyer and the provision of the prosecutor there is a real risk of injury to the defensive faculties, as in this period the witness could be influenced.

34 Paragraph 3 of Article 391-*quater* C.C.P. provides that in the if the public administration refuses to delivery the document requested by the lawyer, then the same may ask the public prosecutor to intervene. If the public prosecutor does not allow the lawyer access to the documents, the lawyer may apply to the court.

are aware for a maximum of two months, in order to protect the effectiveness of public authority investigations.[35] Obviously, a similar power is not granted to the lawyer.

In conclusion, it is clear that the investigative powers of lawyers are overall more limited than those of public authorities.[36]

2.3 *The Judge's Role*

Under the new Code of Criminal Procedure of 1989 the figure of the «judge of instruction» was eliminated.[37] The role of the judge in the pre-trial phase has changed. The judge who can intervene at this stage is called *giudice per le indagini preliminari*[38] and he or she has no investigative power because in the current system the public prosecutor is the *dominus* of the investigation.

The pre-trial investigation judge has a function of guaranteeing the rights of the accused.[39] The judge for pre-trial investigation has «*ad acta*» competence, for specific acts requested to him or her by the public prosecutor or the defendant's lawyer.

Firstly, the *giudice per le indagini preliminari* intervenes during *mezzi di ricerca della prova* activities that are particularly invasive and detrimental to the rights of the person, such as interceptions and data retention. In these cases, the judge for pre-trial investigations has preventive control, authorizing the activity requested by the public prosecutor, or subsequently, validating what has been done in cases of particular urgency.[40] In the event that the public authority acts despite the lack of authorization of the judge for pre-trial investigations or the judge for pre-trial investigations does not validate the investigative activity carried out, then the law expressly provides that the results cannot be used in court, which is a clear example of exclusionary rule.[41]

Moreover, the judge for pre-trial investigation has no power to collect evidence and cannot examine it at the stage of the investigation. However, there

---

35 See Art. 391-*quinquies* C.C.P.

36 For a more in-depth discussion of the topic of «*investigazioni defensive*» see L. Suraci, *Le indagini defensive penali*, Pacini, Pisa 2021, pp. 9–36.

37 See G. Illuminati, 'The Accusatorial Process from the Italian Point of View', (2005)35 *N.C. J. Int'l L. & Com. Reg.*, 2005, p. 308.

38 The Article 328 C.C.P. indicates the *giudice per le indagini preliminari* functions and the methods for identification.

39 For more detailed information on the guarantee function of the pre-trial investigation judge see M. Ferraioli, *Il ruolo di "garante" del giudice per le indagini preliminari*, CEDAM, Padova 2013, pp. 39–47.

40 See § 4.2.

41 The references are the Articles 257 C.C.P. for interceptions and 132 of the Privacy Code for data retention. See § 4.2.

is one exception to the admission of evidence at the investigation stage by the *giudice per le indagini preliminari*, namely *incidente probatorio*.[42]

Lastly, the judge for pre-trial investigation also has jurisdiction over the application of pre-trial custody and other temporary measures (*misure cautelari*), such as house arrest, obligation to appear before the criminal police, injunction to stay away from the family home, injunction to stay away from the places attended by the victim, prohibition to leave the country, and so on.[43]

3 General Principles concerning Obtaining Evidence during Investigation

The rules governing the evidentiary activities in the pre-trial phase are contained in different levels of the source system.

With specific reference to the general principles regarding the collection of evidence, the legal sources are the Constitution, the Code of Criminal Procedure and, to a lesser extent, special laws. In addition, a very important role in the application of these principles is played by case law. The role of supranational sources in collecting evidence in investigations will be discussed below.[44]

The Constitution sets a series of limits in order to protect certain fundamental rights (as liberty, property and privacy) from serial violation by the public authorities committed during the collection of evidence.

---

42 The *incidente probatorio* is a mechanism of early assumption (in pre-trial stage) of the evidence, it takes place through a closed hearing with the guarantees of cross-examination and equality between the prosecution and the defense. It is possible to resort to the *incidente probatorio* only in urgent situations where it is not possible to take evidence later in trial. It is a parenthesis of debate during the stage of investigation. Given the presence of the procedural guarantees (adversarial, equality, taking of evidence before a judge) the *incidente probatorio* report can be used in the trial against all the parties who participated in the *incidente probatorio*. In any case, this institute applies only at the request of the parties; the judge for pre-trial investigations cannot act on his or her own initiative. The reference framework is contained in the articles from 392 to 404 C.C.P. For more detailed information see M. Panzavolta, 'Reforms and Counter-Reforms in the Italian Struggle for an Accusatorial Criminal Law System', (2004)30 *N.C.J. INT'L L.*, 2004, p. 588.

43 The role and powers of the judge for pre-trial investigations in the field of *misure cautelari* are governed by 'Book IV' of the Code of Criminal Procedure, in particular Articles 272 and ff. *Misure cautelari* are measures that make it possible to temporarily limit the rights of the suspect during investigation when there are particular needs, such as the danger of flee, repetition of the criminal offence and contamination/suppression of evidence.

44 See § 4.2, 4.3 and 6.

The fundamental law provides for the mechanism of the so-called double protection by law and jurisdiction. The mechanism of the protection by law means that Parliament must predetermine in a general and abstract manner the cases and ways in which a fundamental freedom can be restricted during the investigation. With the protection by jurisdiction, a specific, individual and reasoned act of the judicial authority is also required to assess whether the conditions set out by law are met or not. Therefore, the Constitution provides that the fundamental right may be restricted through investigative activity only in the cases and manner prescribed by law and in presence of a reasoned judicial act verifying their recurrence in the specific case.

This dual mechanism is provided for in the area of the protection of liberty, in relation to inspections and personal search (Article 13 of the Constitution). The same is also configured to protect the principle of property, in the event of inspections, searches of premises and seizures (Art. 14 Const.). Finally, this double protection is provided for in matters of freedom and secrecy of correspondence (Art. 15 Const.).[45]

With reference to another general principle concerning the collection of evidence, the Constitution stipulates that it must be formed in the cross-examination between the parties. However, the fundamental law provides that evidence gathered during the investigative stage may be used in the trial in exceptional cases, derogating from the general adversarial principle of due process.[46]

The Code of Criminal Procedure provides some general rules on evidence collection that implement the aforementioned principles laid down in the Constitution.

In this regard, the Code implements the mechanism of the protection by indicating at the legislative level the cases and ways in which certain specific investigative activities may affect the rights protected by Articles 13, 14 and 15 of the Constitution. It indicates the methods and procedures by which these

45 On the mechanism of the double protection by law and jurisdiction in Articles 13, 14 and 15 of the Italian Constitution see A. Pisaneschi, *Diritto costituzionale*, Giappichelli, Torino 2022, pp. 106–108, pp. 505–514. See also P. Caretti, G. Tarli Barbieri, *Diritti fondamentali: Libertà e diritti sociali*, Giappichelli, Torino 2022, pp. 205–207 on double protection and personal freedom; pp. 259–273 on double protection and property; pp. 287–288 on double protection and privacy.

46 Article 111 of the Constitution provides that every trial must be held in the adversarial proceedings between the parties, on equal terms, before a third-party and impartial judge (paragraph 2). The evidence must be formed in the cross-examination between the parties (paragraph 4), unless otherwise agreed with the accused or due to objective impossibility (paragraph 5).

investigative activities, aimed at collecting evidence, must be carried out. In particular, the Code identifies the concrete conditions and characteristics of the authorisation act necessary to carry out inspections, searches, seizures and interceptions.[47]

Therefore this mechanism of the protection by law is implemented only in relation to typical investigative activities (so, an investigative activity is typical when it is described by the law).

In order to protect rights that may be infringed through atypical investigative activities, the Code provides for the exclusion of the evidential material obtained through the violation of the general prohibitions indicated in the area of trial evidence (articles 188, 189 and 191, paragraph 2 *bis* C.C.P.). These rules are also applicable to evidence collected in investigations in the terms that we will see later.[48]

With reference to the general principle laid down in Article 111, paragraph 5 of the Constitution, the Code indicates the exceptionally conditions under which it is possible to derogate from the general adversarial principle of due process and to use evidence gathered in the investigative phase by the judge to decide whether the defendant is guilty or not. In particular, the Code allows this exemption in case of summary trials such as summary judgment and plea-bargaining,[49] in the case of consent of the parties[50] and in the case of evidence collected in the investigation whose repetition in the trial has become impossible for unexpected and unforeseeable reasons.[51]

---

47 See § 4.2, concerning specific prohibitions on the use of *mezzi di ricerca della prova* and other typified investigative activity.

48 See § 4.1.

49 Summary trials are procedures other than ordinary, which make it possible to reduce or eliminate certain stages of criminal proceedings. A distinction is made between accelerating trials, which contract the investigative stage, and deflating proceedings, which reduce or eliminate the trial phase. The «*giudizio abbreviato*» (summary judgment) is a deflationary proceeding that allows the judge to decide on the basis of the acts collected in the investigation, avoiding the trial, and that allows the accused to benefit from reductions in sentence in case of conviction. The «*patteggiamento*» (plea bargaining) takes the form of the agreement between the prosecution and the defense regarding the penalty that the judge will have to apply to the specific case. The normative reference for the summary judgment are Articles 438 et seq. For the rules on the plea bargaining see articles 444 and ff C.C.P.

50 With the consent of the parties it is possible to enter into the dossier of the trial any investigative act (Article 431, paragraph 2 C.C.P.).

51 The trial dossier includes the evidence whose assumption in the trial is impossible because it is originally unrepeatable (Article 431, paragraph 1 letters b) and c) C.C.P.). The trial dossier also includes evidence that has become impossible to repeat in the trial,

Another legal source that implements constitutional principles on evidence are special laws (outside the Code of Criminal Procedure). Some special laws regulate the cases and ways in which specific investigative activities aimed at gathering evidence may be carried out. In particular, Article 132 of the so-called Privacy Code (Legislative Decree 196/2003) sets out the conditions under which it is possible to access external data of electronic communications (data retention) and the procedure to follow in order to obtain these data.[52] Another special rule is Article 13 of Legislative Decree 152/1991, which allows longer timeframes and less stringent conditions for carrying out interceptions when organized crime is considered.

Finally, although it does not formally constitute a normative source in the Italian system, the case-law, especially of the Supreme Court, plays a fundamental role in the application of the general principles and rules on the collection of evidence during the investigation stage. Indeed, the Court has a so-called «nomophylactic role», i.e. to ensure the exact observance and uniform interpretation of the law.[53]

On some occasions, the role of the Court has gone beyond the mere interpretation of the law, coming to create supplementary principles of regulatory gaps, such as the principle of «atypicality» of the investigation acts in the pretrial proceeding.[54]

From what has been said so far, it is clear that in the Italian procedure there is a tendency for homogeneity in the system of sources regarding the regulation of investigative activity: the general principles are provided for by the Constitution, the rules are contained in the Code of Criminal Procedure, with only a few provisions contained in special laws. The case law of the *Corte di Cassazione* intervenes, where necessary, in order to adapt the rules to the multiple peculiarities of the concrete case.

---

e.g. the witness heard on the facts under investigation who dies, making it impossible to examine him as a witness in the trial (see Article 512 Code of Criminal Procedure).

52 See § 4.2.

53 This function is expressly attributed to the *Corte di Cassazione* by the Article 65 of the Royal Decree N. 12/1941. For an in-depth analysis on the role of case law in criminal material and, in particular, on the Supreme Court's function of upholding and protecting the law in the Code of Criminal Procedure see L. Baccaglini, G. Di Paolo, F. Cortese, 'The value of judicial precedent in the Italian legal system', (2016) *Civil Procedure Review*, v.7, n.1, pp. 24–47.

54 See § 4.3.

4 Objective Limits to the Use of the Evidence Collected during Pre-trial Investigation

So far we have framed the Italian evidence system (chapter 1), identified the public authority in the pre-trial phase (chapter 2) and indicated the main legal references on the subjects of collection of evidence in investigation (chapter 3). We now have all the necessary knowledge to deal with the central issue of the limits of the power of public authorities in collecting evidence during the investigative phase.

In the Italian system, the public prosecutor and the police have a certain freedom to carry out investigative activities and to collect evidence in the investigation. This power, however, is not absolute and arbitrary: the system provides for a series of prescriptions and prohibitions, general or specific, whose violation leads to sanctions. A distinction can be made between substantive sanctions and procedural sanctions.

Substantial consequences affect the person of the public prosecutor or police officer who commits serious violations. Their conducts could have disciplinary relevance[55] but, in the most extreme cases and where the conditions are met, these subjects could also be liable under criminal law for violating the rules on the *mezzi di ricerca della prova*. Public authorities may be punished in case of abusive interceptions (art. 617 et seq. of the Criminal Code), arbitrary personal search and inspection (under Article 609 of the Criminal Code), acts of torture (the perpetration of which constitutes a criminal offence referred to in Article 613-*bis* of the Criminal Code, punished more severely if coming from an Officer), illegal arrest (Article 606 Criminal Code, punishable

55 In particular, the disciplinary responsibility of the public prosecutor and the judge is regulated by the Legislative Decree 109/2006, which indicates the rules of conduct to be followed by these subjects, the disciplinary sanctions and the enforcement procedure. An interesting example is the case dealt with in the judgment of *Cassazione civile*, United Sections, 1st February 2008, n. 2444. The Court has established that it constitutes a disciplinary offence the behaviour of the prosecutor which, in the course of those investigations, has subordinate at a hypnotic session a witness in order to recover the removed memories. This constitutes a violation of Article 188 of the Code of Criminal Procedure, which prohibits the use of methods or techniques capable of affecting the freedom of self-determination or altering the ability to remember and evaluate the facts. For a more in-depth discussion on the disciplinary liability of the public prosecutor see M. Fantacchiotti, M. Fresa, V. Tenore, S. Vitello, *La responsabilità disciplinare nelle carriere magistratuali: magistrati ordinari, amministrativi, contabili, militari, onorari, Avvocati dello Stato*, Giuffrè, Milano 2010, pp. 110–345. Police disciplinary liability is governed by Article 59 C.C.P. and by Articles 16 and 17 Legislative Decree No. 271 of 1989.

by imprisonment of up to three years), undue limitation of personal liberty (Article 607 Criminal Code, punishable by up to three years' imprisonment), abuse of authority against arrested or detained suspects (Article 608 Criminal Code, punished with imprisonment of up to two and a half years) or arbitrary search and personal inspection (Article 609 Criminal Code, punishable by up to one year imprisonment).[56]

Nevertheless, the most effective sanction that indirectly limits the power of public authority in the collection of evidence is the procedural one. The Code of Criminal Procedure provides for exclusionary rules[57] as a typical and general tool in the case of evidence acquired in violation of the law. This rule prohibits the use of evidence gathered by the prosecutor and police during the investigation – collected in violation of the general principle on evidence or the specific prohibitions on investigative activities – for the purpose of establishing the criminal liability of the accused in the trial. Thus exclusionary rule is a procedural sanction which forbids the judge to use some relevant evidence in his or her judgment on the case. Evidence acquired in violation of a prohibition imposed by law cannot be evaluated by him/her in order to decide. This sanction entails the judge inability to assess and use such evidence in his or her decision and renders invalid the decision that makes significant reference to unusable evidence.[58]

Therefore, compliance with the prohibitions established by law is the main limitation on the power of the public authority in collecting evidence at the stage of investigation.

There are different categories of prohibitions, some of which are general prohibitions on evidence (and also apply to evidence collected in investigation), others are specific prohibitions established in relation to the collection

56 On the criminal liability of the public prosecutor see. G. Fiandaca, 'Sulla Responsabilità Penale Del Giudice', (2009)11 *Il Foro Italiano*, vol. 132, pp. 409–421.

57 Exclusionary rule is part of the invalidities family. Not all violations of the procedural rules entail invalidity, some are mere irregularities that may have disciplinary relevance but do not affect the validity of the procedural act. Invalidities, on the other hand, have procedural consequences. There are four invalidities provided for by the Code: nullity, exclusionary rule, inadmissibility and forfeiture. Exclusionary is the type of invalidity that applies to breaches of the rules of evidence. For further information on exclusionary rules see F. Caprioli, 'Report on Italy' in S. Ruggeri (ed), *Transnational Inquiries and the Protection of Fundamental Rights in Criminal Proceedings*, Springer Berlin, Heidelberg 2013, pp. 439–456, see also G. Illuminati, 'Italy: Statutory Nullities and Non-usability' in Thaman S.C. (ed), *Exclusionary Rules in Comparative Law*, Springer, Dordrecht 2013, pp. 235–259.

58 Evidence that makes the act invalid whose reasoning makes significant reference to it is definable as unusable, see A. Nappi, *Guida al Codice di Procedura Penale*, Giuffré, Milano 2007, pp. 189–198.

of evidence with typified investigative activities (as in the case of the *mezzi di ricerca della prova*: inspections, searches, evidentiary seizure, interceptions, data retention).

4.1 *General Prohibitions of Using Evidence*

The 'Book III' of the Code of Criminal Procedure, named «*Prove*» (Evidence), identifies some general rules on evidence (Articles 187 and ff.) – including certain prohibitions whose violation is punished by the exclusionary rule – that indirectly delimit the power of public authorities in collecting evidence during the investigative phase.

The first absolute limitation, set forth in Article 188 Code of Criminal Procedure, is the prohibition on the use of evidence collected (during investigation or trial) by methods and techniques capable of affecting the person's freedom of self-determination or altering his or her ability to remember and evaluate facts.[59] Therefore, the public authority will not be able to use violent methods, threats and illicit pressures or other inquisitorial systems. The use of such techniques is not permitted, even with the person's consent, since the prohibition protects human dignity, a right that cannot be at disposal. Similarly, hypnosis techniques or other instruments capable of affecting the defendant's mental abilities are not permitted.[60] The Code specifies that evidence collected through the crime of torture may not be used, except in proceedings against the person accused of committing torture.[61]

The exclusionary rule on the use of evidence collected by methods and techniques capable of affecting the freedom of self-determination or capable of altering the ability to remember and evaluate the facts of the person also applies to evidence collected in investigative phase.[62]

---

59 For an interesting study on the relationship between the use of neuroscience and Article 188 C.C.P. see P. Ferrua, 'Neuroscientific Evidence and Criminal Trial' in A. D'Aloia, M.C. Errigo (eds), *Neuroscience and Law: Complicated Crossings and New Perspectives*, Springer Nature, Cham 2020, pp. 403–414.

60 The judgment *Cassazione civile*, United Sections, 1st February 2008, n. 2444 has expressly provided that hypnosis is a tool capable of influencing the freedom of self-determination or altering the ability to remember and evaluate facts and therefore renders the evidence collected in pre-trial investigations unusable.

61 The reference is to Article 191, para. 2 *bis* C.C.P. For an in-depth study of torture and exclusionary rule in the Italian criminal procedure see P. Bronzo, G. Colaiacovo, 'Inutilizzabilità delle prove e delitto di tortura nel sistema processuale italiano', (2021)1 *Revista Brasileira De Direito Processual Penal*, Volume 7, pp. 321–328.

62 The aforementioned *Cassazione civile*, United Sections, 1st February 2008, n. 2444 has expressly provided for it: 'Even in the phase of pre-trial investigation Article 188 C.C.P. indicates that methods or techniques capable of influencing the freedom of

A second limitation is related to atypical evidence, where «atypical» means «not described by the law». Article 189 of the Code of Criminal Procedure expressly provides for the possibility of recourse to atypical evidence by the judge at the trial stage, to decide whether the defendant is guilty or not. The limit is that this atypical evidence must be helpful in order to ascertain the truth and must not violate people's fundamental rights.·It is evident that these provisions aim to protect fundamental values such as human dignity and body inviolability.

Another general limit to the power of the public authorities in collecting evidence during the investigative stage, provided for in Article 191 Code of Criminal Procedure, is the general provision of the exclusionary rule for all evidence collected in violation of prohibitions established by law. This rule connects these general principles to specific prohibitions provided for by the Code in relation to typified investigative activities. Indeed, Article 191 of the Criminal Code states that evidence unlawfully collected in violation of law, including those provided for in relation to specific investigative activities, cannot be used.

Lastly, the power of public authorities to collect evidence during the investigative phase has a time limit, *id est* the maximum duration of preliminary investigation. The discipline was recently amended by the Cartabia's reform (specifically by Article 22 of Legislative Decree No. 150 of 2022).[63]

The Code of Criminal Procedure provides that investigation can last six months, one year or one year and six months, depending on the type of offence being investigated.[64] Prior to the expiry of the time limit, the prosecutor may ask, only once, the *giudice per le indagini preliminari* to extend the investigation

---

self-determination or altering the ability to remember and evaluate the facts may cannot be used, even with the consent of the person concerned'.

63 For one of the first reflections on Legislative Decree 150 of 2022, trial efficiency, and the new length of investigation see G. Garuti, 'L'efficienza del processo tra riduzione dei tempi di indagine, rimedi giurisdizionali e "nuova" regola di giudizio', (2022)3 *Archivio Penale*, pp. 3–16.

64 The general rule under Art. 406, para. 2 C.C.P. provides that the prosecutor concludes the preliminary investigation within a period of one year from the date the suspect's name is entered in the register of criminal offenses. This deadline is six months for less serious offenses, so-called *contravvenzioni*. While for more serious crimes (listed in Article 407 paragraph 2; e.g. Mafia-type unlawful association, murder, robbery, extortion, terrorism, etc.) the investigation can take up to one year and six months. Before the reform, Article 405, para. 2 indicated the time limit for investigation as 6 months or 1 year. For transitional rules, see Article 88-*bis* of the Legislative Decree No. 150 of 2022.

limit by an additional six months.[65] The maximum time limit for investigation, including extension, is eighteen months in general, one year for *contravvenzioni* or two years for most serious crimes.[66]

In the event that public authorities gather evidence by violating this time limit, the Code of Criminal Procedure provides an exclusionary rule. Article 407, Paragraph 3 C.C.P. provides that investigative activities carried out after the expiry of the time limit for the conclusion of the preliminary investigation – limit established by law or extended by the judge – may not be used.

An other special exclusionary rule is provided in Article 406, Paragraph 8 Code of Criminal Procedure for evidence collected while awaiting the judge's decision on the extension of the investigation period. If the judge does not allow the extension of the investigation then only evidence collected before the expiration of the original time limit (provided for in Article 405 C.C.P.) will be usable; what is gathered afterwards will not be usable.

In this chapter we looked at the general prohibitions on evidence; in the next chapter we will examine the specific prohibitions established in relation to the collection of evidence with typified investigative activities.

4.2 *Specific Prohibitions on the Use of Mezzi di Ricerca della Prova and Other Typified Investigative Activities*

The Code of Criminal Procedure provides for different treatments regarding investigative activities aimed at the collection of evidence.

The Code regulates in a strict and complete way the *mezzi di ricerca della prova* (inspections, searches, evidentiary seizures,[67] interceptions, data retention) and in a less rigid way other investigative activities that may be adopted by the public authorities, such as technical investigations, identification of persons or property, taking of summary information from witnesses at the investigation stage and questioning of the suspect.

---

65 See Article 405 para. 1 and 2 C.C.P. In the past, further extensions could be requested by the prosecutor if the investigation was particularly complex or if it was impossible to conclude the investigation within the deadline.

66 The reference is Article 407 para. 1 e 2. Paragraph 2 provides a very extensive list of crimes for which a longer investigation duration of 1 year and six months, extendable to 2, is possible.

67 The evidence seizure is that aimed at gathering evidence. It is distinguished from preventive and conservative seizures which are *misure cautelari.* Preventive seizure serves to avoid the commission of a new criminal offence or the consequences of the crime. Conservative seizure serves to ensure that in the event of conviction the defendant will be able to pay the costs of justice and any compensation for damages.

Regarding to the *mezzi di ricerca della prova*, there are specific prohibitions, protected by exclusionary rule.

Some types of *mezzi di ricerca della prova* involve stringent regulations, such as those provided for interceptions (including with the aid of malware)[68] and data retention.[69] These activities are subject to a similar discipline: they can only be carried out in the course of investigation for highly serious criminal offences.[70] In addition, they may only be carried out upon request by the public prosecutor and reasoned authorization by the judge;[71] in cases of urgency, the prosecutor may start the activity, but it must be validated within two days by the judge.[72] In the event of a breach of these rules, the evidence collected cannot be used for the purposes of the case decision.[73]

With specific reference to interceptions (including with the aid of malware), the Code provides numerous prohibitions that constitute limits to the power of the public authorities in collecting evidence during the investigative stage.[74]

---

68 The rules on interception are laid down in the Articles 266 and ff. C.C.P.

69 The Article 132 of Privacy Code (Legislative Decree 196/2003) is instead the reference standard for data retention.

70 Regarding the criminal offences which these investigative activities can be carried out, art. 266 C.C.P. provides that the interception of conversations or communications can be carried out only if certain types of criminal offences are investigated or, more generally, for criminal offences punished with imprisonment exceeding a maximum of five years. Similarly, Article 132, para. 3 of the Privacy Code provides that the activities of data retention can only be carried out in investigation related to criminal offences punishable by imprisonment of not less than three years or for specific types of criminal offence. These limitations are justified by the fact that these investigative activities, based on very invasive technologies, can be very detrimental to the right to privacy and because of the high costs involved in a system where resources, economic and human, are limited.

71 See Article 267, para. 1 C.C.P. on interceptions and Article 132, para. 3 of Privacy Code on data retention.

72 In relation to interceptions, Article 267, para. 2 C.C.P. provides that in cases of urgency and if there are justified reasons to believe that any delay can seriously hamper the investigation, the prosecutor may start the interception by reasoned decree. The judge must be informed within 24 hours of the measure and he/she decides on its validation by reasoned decree within 24 hours. If the decree of the public prosecutor is not validated within such time limit, the interception shall not be continued and its results shall not be used. With regard to data retention, Article 132, para. 3 *bis* of the Privacy Code provides that in case of urgency and if there are well-founded reasons to believe that the delay could seriously prejudice the investigation, the prosecutor order the acquisition of the data by means of a motivated decree. The judge, within the following 24 hours, decides on the validation by reasoned decree.

73 Exclusionary rule is expressly provided for by Articles 271 C.C.P. and 132, para. 3 *quater* of the Privacy Code.

74 For a general introduction to interceptions in the Italian system see A. Diddi, L. Filippi, A. Marandola, *La nuova disciplina delle intercettazioni. Legge 20 febbraio 2020, n. 7*, Pacini, Pisa 2020, pp. 11–39. With specific reference to the national discipline of interceptions

One of these prohibitions concerns the duration of interceptions. Such duration shall not exceed fifteen days, but the judge may extend it for further periods of fifteen days if the necessary conditions are still met.[75] There is no maximum term for the duration of interceptions, which may be extended several times until the conclusion of the investigation.

Another important rule states that interceptions must be carried out with the systems used by the public prosecutor's office. However, if such systems are insufficient or unsuitable and there are exceptional reasons of urgency, the prosecutor may order that such activities be performed using public service systems or systems employed by the criminal police. In exceptional cases interceptions may also be carried out with privately owned equipment.[76]

Other legislative provisions protected by an exclusionary rule are those related to the documentation of the content of interceptions. Indeed, intercepted communications shall be recorded and a record of related activities shall be drafted. The content of the intercepted communications shall be transcribed, even summarily, in the record.[77]

Article 271 of the Code of Criminal Procedure lists other prohibitions, the violation of which entails an exclusionary rule and also the destruction of the material collected. More specifically, the results of interceptions shall not be used if the activity has been performed in cases other than those provided for by Article 266 or in violation of the provisions of articles 267 (on preconditions and types of decisions) or 268, paragraphs 1 and 3 (on procedure for interceptions). Also, interceptions related to conversations or communications covered by professional secret shall not be used. Lastly, anything intercepted during the installation of a malware on portable electronic device and all data acquired outside the time and place limits specified in the authorisation decree, is subject to an exclusionary rule.[78]

---

with the aid of malware see W. Nocerino, 'I sistemi di controllo da remoto nella legislazione interna e sovranazionale', (2022)1 *DPCE Online*, v. 51, pp. 64–68, see also Brighi R., 'Funzionamento e potenzialità investigative del malware' in G. Giostra, R. Orlandi (eds), *Nuove norme in tema di intercettazioni. Tutela della riservatezza, garanzie difensive e nuove tecnologie informatiche*, Giappichelli, Torino 2018, pp. 211–234.

75 The reference is to Article 267, para. 3 C.C.P.

76 This rule is laid down in the Articles 268, para. 3 C.C.P.

77 See Article 268, para. 1 and 2 C.C.P. The exclusionary rule is provided for by Article 271 C.C.P.

78 On the specific topic of Article 271 C.C.P., interceptions and exclusionary rule, see W. Nocerino, A. Zampini, 'Vecchi e nuovi limiti di utilizzabilità delle intercettazioni nel sistema italiano', (2021)2 *Revista Brasileira de Direito Processual Penal*, Vol. 7, pp. 1418–1432, see also A. Diddi, L. Filippi, A. Marandola, *La nuova disciplina delle intercettazioni. Legge 20 febbraio 2020, n. 7*, Pacini, Pisa 2020, pp. 119–138.

Regarding data retention, the Article 132, paragraph 1 and 3 of the Privacy Code provides that the telephone service provider must retain, for investigation purposes, telephone traffic data for 24 months and call traffic data for 12 months. During this period, the judge, at the request of the public prosecutor or lawyer, may order the supplier to provide the data or to protect them by special measures. Article 132, paragraph 3 *quater* prohibits the use of data acquired by means other than those provided for in paragraph 3 and 3 *bis*.[79]

The other typified *mezzi di ricerca della prova* (inspections, searches, evidentiary seizures) are subject to a less stringent regulation: a decree of the public prosecutor, that justifies the reasons for the activity, is sufficient to carry it out.[80] In cases of urgency, the police can act on their own initiative, but within 48 hours the public prosecutor must validate such operations.[81] There are no limitations due to the type or gravity of criminal offences being investigated. Only procedural rules are provided for to guarantee the right to information of the suspect and to avoid arbitrary violations of the values of human dignity and property.[82] The violation of these prohibitions ends into an exclusionary rule.[83]

---

79 For an in-depth study of the new Italian data retention regulation, see R. Flor, S. Marcolini, *Dalla data retention alle indagini ad alto contenuto tecnologico. La tutela dei diritti fondamentali quale limite al potere coercitivo dello Stato. Aspetti di diritto penale processuale e sostanziale*, Giappichelli, Torino 2022, pp. 35–66. Of great interest is the analysis of the compatibility of the Italian data retention legislation with the requirements set forth in Article 15 of Directive 2002/58/EC, as interpreted by the recent rulings of the Court of Justice of the EU 'Quadrature' (C-511/18, C-512/18 and C-520/18, *Quadrature*, Grand Chamber, October 6th, 2020, ECLI:EU:C:2020:791) and 'Commissioner' (C-140/20, *Commissioner*, Grand Chamber, April 5th, 2022, ECLI:EU:C:2022:258). The Italian regulation appears to be critical in three aspects that are incompatible with the principle of proportionality; in particular, the Italian regulation provides for (1) generalized and undifferentiated data retention, (2) for a very long retention time, and (3) provides for a limitation of the offenses for which data retention can be used that is so generic as to come across as unopposed. On this issue see § 6.

80 The reference is to Articles 244, para. 1, 247, para. 2 and 253, paragraph 1.

81 This provision is contained in the Articles 352, para. 4 and 355, para. 1 and 2 C.C.P.

82 See Articles 245, para. 1 and 2, Article 249, para. 1 and 2, Article 251 C.C.P. In particular, Articles 245, para. 1 and 249, para. 1 provide that before the start of a body inspection or a body search, the person concerned shall be informed about his/her right to be assisted by a trusted person. Pursuant to Articles 245, para. 2 and 249, para. 2, inspections and body searches shall be performed respecting the dignity and, as far as possible, the modesty of the person being inspected or searched. Lastly, Article 251 provides that searches at domicile shall not commence before seven a.m. and after eight p.m., except in urgent cases.

83 This provision is due to the application of Article 191 Code of Criminal Procedure, which prohibits the use of evidence collected in violation of the prohibitions established by law. This is also the opinion of the case-law, see *Cassazione penale*, sec. IV, 22nd October 2019,

Other specific prohibitions protected by exclusionary rule are provided for some activities that are only partially regulated, such as technical investigation.

Technical investigations are very important especially because of their close relationship with scientific evidence. Indeed, the concept of judge *peritus peritorum* is fading, especially when the scientific evidence is complex and very sophisticated techniques are used (e.g. epidemiology or genetics). In these situations, it becomes difficult for the judge to evaluate the evidence, so the role of the experts and technical advisors becomes increasingly important. One consequence is the risk that in more complex situations the judge tends to flatten his or her reasoning to the conclusions of the expert witness. This situation could pose a danger to the legality and fairness of the evidentiary procedure. Therefore, in order to protect the accused person and guarantee an adversarial process even in the taking of scientific evidence, the Code of Criminal Procedure generally provides that the accused person may be assisted by a technical advisor during the operations at both the investigation and trial stages.[84]

Regarding specific prohibitions in the collection of evidence through technical investigation, the Code provides that in case of non-repeatable technical investigation[85] the suspect must be informed of the possibility of participating. He or she may request the judge to make an *incidente probatorio*[86] and the public prosecutor is prohibited from carrying out the unrepeatable investigation while awaiting for the judge's decision, except in cases of exceptional urgency. If the prosecutor orders that non-repeatable activities to be carried out, in spite of the explicit reservation made by the suspect and even if the

n. 31869. On the different and interesting issue of «*inutilizzabilità derivata*» (a sort of «rule of the fruit of the poisonous trees»), the Italian Constitutional Court has expressed itself several times ruling out the applicability of this rule. The Court stated that was usable the evidence that was obtained by a seizure following an invalid search. On this topic see N. Galatini, 'Alla ricerca della 'inutilizzabilità derivata'. Note a margine di Corte cost., sent. 3 ottobre 2019, n. 219, e a Corte cost., sent. 26 novembre 2020 n. 252', (2021)3 *Sistema Penale*, pp. 151–163.

84 Article 360, para. 3 C.C.P. establishes the suspect's right to appoint a technical advisor for the non-repeatable technical investigation and to make observations. During the trial, the accused may submit his own consultant for cross-examination, see Article 501 C.C.P. In cases where the judge orders a «*perizia*» (expert opinion), entrusting the technical evaluation to a third-impartial expert, the accused may appoint his own technical adviser; the reference is Article 225, para. 1 C.C.P.

85 Non-repeatable technical investigations are very important because they allow for the collection of evidence that cannot be repeated at trial and thus form part of the trial record, being used by the judge to decide. See § 1.

86 See footnote 42.

conditions of exceptional urgency are not met, the results of the technical investigation shall not be used during the trial.[87]

Specific rules are provided also for a very invasive technical investigation such as DNA analysis. If forced DNA sampling from a non-consenting person is necessary, the judge must authorize or validate it.[88] The prosecutor must request authorisation from the judge, who will authorise it if the conditions of seriousness laid down in Article 224-*bis* of the Code of Criminal Procedure are met. In cases of urgency, if there are reasonable grounds to believe that the delay would seriously or irrecoverably jeopardise the investigation, the public prosecutor shall authorise the activity or order the accused person to appear in order to undergo it. Within 24 hours the judge decides on the confirmation.

Article 359-*bis*, paragraph 3 C.C.P. provides that the activities are invalid and the information gathered through such activities may not be used if the decree doesn't contain the elements and notices required by Article 224, paragraph 2 Code of Criminal Procedure. Another exclusionary rule is provided in case of the activities are in contrast with the prohibitions expressly set by law, or endanger the life, physical integrity or health of the person or may cause serious sufferings, according to medical science. Expert activities shall, in any case, be performed respecting the dignity and modesty of the person under examination. In any case, the least invasive techniques that produce identical results shall be preferred.[89]

Another very important and not thoroughly regulated investigative activity is questioning.[90] Indeed, this is the most delicate moment for the suspect and can lead to abuses by the public authorities (such as the use of threats or other methods that do not respect human dignity). For these reasons, domestic legislation provides for a series of rules to guarantee the questioned,

---

87 The reference framework for technical investigation is Article 360 C.C.P. In particular the paragraphs 4 and 5 regulate the request by the suspect to carry out an *incidente probatorio* and the exclusionary rule.

88 See the Article 359-*bis* C.C.P. which regulates the compulsory biological sampling on living people. Paragraph 1 regulates the ordinary mode, paragraph 2 the procedure in urgent cases.

89 For an in-depth discussion of DNA-based investigation and critical aspects see G. Di Cesare, L. Parlato, 'The role of DNA as scientific evidence', (2017)1, *Medicina nei secoli. Journal of History of Medicine and Medical Humanities*, vol. 29, pp. 19–31.

90 For an interesting analysis of some of the critical issues in the Italian questioning discipline compared to European Union law see G.L. Candito, *The Influence of the Directive 2012/13/EU on the Italian System of Protection of the Right to Information in Criminal Procedures* in S. Ruggeri (ed), *Human Rights in European Criminal Law*, Springer, Cham 2015, pp. 229–260.

compliance with some of which is provided for under exclusionary rule of the statements made.

Article 376 of the Code of Criminal Procedure rules compulsory appearance of the accused person and provides that the prosecutor may summon the suspect for questioning after receiving an authorisation by the judge.

Before the activity begins, the Code provides that the questioned person is previously warned of his or her rights, including not answering the questions that will be asked.[91] This right to silence includes the possibility of lying, without committing any criminal offence, except in relation to his or her own identity and in relation to the responsibility of other persons (otherwise, he/she commits the criminal offences of false information to the prosecutor, provided for by art. 371-*bis* Italian Criminal Code, and slander, provided for by art. 368 Criminal Code).

To protect the dignity of the questioned person, the discipline also provides that during the questioning the suspect is not handcuffed.[92] In addition, the use of methods or techniques which are likely to affect the freedom of self-determination or to alter the capacity to remember and evaluate facts, which are detrimental to human dignity, are prohibited.

Another important protection for the suspect is that the questioning must take place in the presence of the suspect's lawyer (if he/she does not have one, it will be nominated *ex officio*). The lawyer has a role of control over the correct work of the public authority in carrying out the questioning.[93] To guarantee the suspect and to limit possible abuses by the public authority, the Code of Criminal Procedure provides that the police can also collect information from the suspect only in the presence of his or her lawyer; any information collected in the absence of the lawyer should not only not be used, but not even documented.[94]

---

91 The reference is Article 64, para. 3 C.C.P.

92 See Article 64 C.C.P., which is intended to protect the dignity of the person, who must be free when questioned, subject to the necessary precautions to avoid escape or the use of violence.

93 In particular, the reference is the Article 364 C.C.P., by virtue of which the defendant's lawyer must participate at the questioning, being notified at least 24 hours in advance. In the event that the suspect is without a trusted lawyer, this is appointed *ex officio*.

94 The reference standard is Article 350 C.C.P. The police can take information from the suspect only in the presence of his or her lawyer. However, the police can collect information useful for investigation in the immediacy and on the place of the fact and without the presence of the lawyer. Such information and indications obtained in the absence of the lawyer cannot be recorded or documented.

The power of the public authority at the investigative stage is also limited by the prohibition on the use in criminal proceedings of documents containing information illegally obtained.[95]

Regarding the limits of power of a specific subject, the Code provides that the police may act either by delegation from the prosecutor or on their own initiative. In the latter case, the police are subject to specific prohibitions. Indeed, police officers, on their own initiative, may collect summary information useful for investigation purposes from the suspect only if he/she has not been placed under arrest, otherwise he/she can only be questioned by the prosecutor.[96] In addition, police officers may also, on their own initiative, carry out personal or local searches if they have reasonable grounds to believe that the person hides objects or traces related to the offence on his/her body that can be deleted or lost or that such objects or traces are in a certain place or that the suspected person or the escapee is in such place. Within 24 hours the officer must inform the prosecutor, who will confirm the search within the following 24 hours.[97]

These specific prohibitions – which constitute limits to the power of public authorities in gathering evidence through typical investigative activities – are the result of the legislator's balancing of investigative needs and the protection of fundamental freedoms (personal liberty, property and privacy) and are inspired by the principles of proportionality and necessity.

4.3 *Limits to the Use of Evidence Collected through Atypical Investigative Activity*

The Code of Criminal Procedure regulates the general prohibitions on evidence and the specific prohibitions on the typified investigative activities just examined, but it does not determine whether it is possible to carry out atypical investigative activities (not mentioned in the Code) and, above all, whether the evidence collected through these atypical activities can be used in the trial by the judge.

The Code does not say anything about activities other than those specifically provided for and regulated, such as, for instance, surveillance (including satellite surveillance via GPS or IMSI catchers),[98] audio-video recordings made by

95 See Article 240 C.C.P.

96 The reference is Article 350, para. 1 C.C.P.

97 See Article 352, para. 1 e 4 C.C.P.

98 On the topic of IMSI catchers (or cell-site simulators) and the possible uses of this technology for surveillance purposes see A. Camon, 'Il cacciatore di IMSI', (2020)1 *Archivio penale*, pp. 177–195.

a private, investigative video footage (including with the use of drones), digital investigation via social networks[99] and the use of Trojan malware for purposes other than «*intercettazione ambientale*» (acoustic surveillance). On this point, the *Corte di Cassazione* has created the principle of « *atipicità*» (atypicality) of the *mezzi di ricerca della prova*, admitting the possibility of resorting to investigative activities other than those provided for by the Code of Criminal Procedure.[100] In this sense, even the Report to the Preliminary Draft of the Code of Criminal Procedure would allow the use of unregulated investigative activities because everything collected at the investigation stage, only serves the prosecutor to decide as fully as possible whether to prosecute or not; indeed, what was collected would not be used to decide on the criminal liability of the accused, except in exceptional cases.

In particular, the *Corte di Cassazione* has held possible to perform atypical investigative activities because these methods still lead to the collection of both typical and atypical evidence, the use of which is limited by the general rules of evidence. Therefore, since the Supreme Court stated that it is possible to carry out these atypical activities, the question arises as to what limits and prohibitions are imposed on the public authority in the execution of non-regulated activities.

On this point, the case-law of the *Corte di Cassazione* has clarified that these activities are in any case subject to the prohibitions laid down in the general provisions on evidence (articles 188 and ff. C.C.P.);[101] hence, atypical investigative activity must not consist of methods or techniques capable of affecting

99 For a study of the activities of audio-video recordings made by a private, investigative video footage and digital investigation via social networks see N. Triggiani, 'Le videoriprese investigative e l'uso dei droni' in A. Scalfati (ed), *Le indagini atipiche*, Giappichelli, Torino 2019, pp. 161–187, G. Padua, 'Installazione privata di telecamere e impiego dei contenuti' in A. Scalfati (ed), *Le indagini atipiche*, Giappichelli, Torino 2019, pp. 191–207 and C. Conti, M. Torre, 'Spionaggio digitale nell'ambito dei social network' in A. Scalfati (ed), *Le indagini atipiche*, Giappichelli, Torino 2019, pp. 535–565.

100 See the recent judgment *Cassazione penale*, sec. II, 25th November 2020, n. 34211, also *ex plurimus Cassazione penale*, sec. V, 19th February 2014, n. 18997 and *Cassazione penale*, sec. II, 27th March 2008, n. 16818.

101 See judgment *Cassazione penale*, United Sections, 26th June 2014, n. 32697: 'Non-communicative contents of legitimately authorized interceptions are usable as atypical evidence under Article 189 C.C.P., since the rules on interceptions under Articles 266 ff. of the Code of Criminal Procedure do not apply in such cases'. See also *Cassazione civile*, United Sections, 1st February 2008, n. 2444 has expressly provided for it: 'Even in the phase of pre-trial investigation art. 188 C.C.P. indicates that methods or techniques capable of influencing the freedom of self-determination or altering the ability to remember and evaluate the facts may cannot be used, even with the consent of the person concerned'.

freedom of self-determination or altering the ability to remember and evaluate facts (art. 188 C.C.P.). If the evidence collected is atypical this must not compromise the moral freedom of the person (Art. 189 C.C.P.). In general, evidence collected through atypical investigative activity must not be acquired in violation of prohibitions established by law (Art. 191 C.C.P.).

These prohibitions are mitigated, however, by the fact that the Supreme Court has limited in a significant way the application of the theory of the fruit of the poisonous tree,[102] therefore, lawful and usable evidence could well be derived from unlawful atypical investigative activities.

This approach has only partially filled the regulatory gaps and has led to a whole series of problems with regard to the protection of fundamental rights of the individuals. Indeed, in some cases, this principle of «atypicality» creates serious risks of violations, such as for the use of satellite surveillance via GPS, for the use of Trojan malware for purposes other than acoustic surveillance between physically present people or, generally, for the use of high-tech investigation. In these cases the absence of a specific discipline cannot be overcome with the sole use of this principle without entailing a strong risk of violation of fundamental rights, first among all the right to privacy.[103]

With reference to satellite surveillance via GPS, the Supreme Court has ruled that these techniques are atypical investigative activities (or atypical *mezzi di ricerca dalla prova*) and they can be used without the need for prior authorization because they do not interfere with the constitutional rights to secrecy of correspondence and the inviolability of the domicile;[104] however, in these

---

102 The case-law has excluded the application of the common law theory of the fruits of the poisoned tree. In particular, the *Corte di Cassazione* has highlighted that in the Italian trial the principle of *male captum bene retentum* applies in the case of unlawful searches; the subsequent seizure and, consequently, its probative value, is valid. See *Cassazione penale*, sec. II, 25th June 2014, n. 31225: 'On the subject of seizure, in the hypothesis of things subject to mandatory confiscation, the irregularity of the seizure report operated by the police does not invalidate the provision of validation of the public prosecutor in application of the principle "*male captum bene retentum*"'.

103 For some considerations on the use of the Trojan malware for purposes other than acoustic surveillance see Flor. R., Marcolini S., *Dalla data retention alle indagini ad alto contenuto tecnologico. La tutela dei diritti fondamentali quale limite al potere coercitivo dello Stato. Aspetti di diritto penale processuale e sostanziale*, Giappichelli, Torino 2022, pp. 68–69, see also W. Nocerino, A. Zampini, 'Vecchi e nuovi limiti di utilizzabilità delle intercettazioni nel sistema italiano', (2021)2 *Revista Brasileira de Direito Processual Penal*, Vol. 7, pp. 1444–1445, and F. Caprioli, 'Il "captatore informatico" come strumento di ricerca della prova in Italia', (2017)2 *Revista brasileira de direito processual penal*, Vol. 3, pp. 484–485.

104 See *Cassazione penale*, sec. IV, 21st April 2022, n. 21856: 'The "remote" tracking, by means of satellite tracking system (GPS), of a subject's movements, falling within the atypical

cases the Court did not consider international obligations on respect for the right to privacy (Article 8 European Convention on Human Rights and Articles 8 Charter of Fundamental Rights of the European Union).

Regarding Trojan malwares, their use to carry out acoustic surveillance is allowed and specifically regulated by the Code,[105] with the application of the very stringent discipline provided for interceptions, and based on the double protection by law and jurisdiction. However, the Trojan malware could also be used for other purposes, such as remotely activating the device's camera, copying data on the device, taking screenshots, stealing passwords and so on.[106] Since the use of the Trojan for these different purposes is not regulated, it could fall under atypical investigative activities.

The *Corte di Cassazione* tolerates the use of these practices, merely deeming these atypical investigative activities not capable of affecting freedom of self-determination (or, more generally, they do not violate any of the rules set forth in Articles 188, 189 and 191 C.C.P.), but without considering its capacity to undermine the fundamental rights of secrecy of correspondence (Article 14 Constitution), inviolability of the domicile (Article 15 Constitution) and privacy (Article 8 of the ECHR and Articles 8 CFREU). In this way, case-law allows incoherently to use without any limitation investigative techniques that are highly detrimental to the rights of the individual – for which there is a mechanism of protection by law[107] – by exploiting new technologies, such as the use of satellite surveillance via GPS and the use of Trojan malware devices to record video remotely, copy the data on the device, monitor the screen, etc.

Based on these observations, it can be stated more generally that an insurmountable limitation on the atypical investigative activity power of the public authorities is respect for fundamental rights, which are protected by the Constitution and supranational sources through the provision of the mechanism

mezzi di rircerca della prova, can be used in criminal proceedings without the need for prior authorization by the judicial authority, as it does not result in an interference with the right to confidentiality of communications, nor in an infringement of the inviolability of the home'. In this sense see also *Cassazione penale*, Sec. II, 13th February 2013, n. 21644 and *Cassazione penale*, Sec. IV, 27th November 2012, n. 48279. For further considerations see § 6.

105 The use of Trojan malware by infecting portable electronic devices for the purpose of carrying out acoustic surveillance is provided for in the article 266, paragraphs 2 and 2 *bis* C.C.P.

106 A list of possible uses of the computer capture device for different uses of the Trojan malware for purposes other than acoustic surveillance between physically present people is made by Judgment of *Cassazione Penale*, United Sections, 28th April 2016, n. 26889, Scurato.

107 See § 3.

of protection by law. Specifically these rights are personal liberty, inviolability of the domicile, freedom and secrecy of correspondence, for the limitation of which the Constitution (Articles 13, 14 and 15) provides a mechanism of double protection by law and jurisdiction. Another limit is the right to privacy, enshrined in Article 8 of the European Convention on Human Rights, which says that the right to respect for private and family life, home and correspondence may be restricted only in cases provided by law.[108] A similar limit is placed by the Charter of Fundamental Rights of the European Union; in particular, Article 7 provides for the right to respect private and family life, home and communications, while Article 8 enshrines the right to the protection of personal data and provides for its limitation only in cases laid down by law. Therefore, public authorities may not carry out atypical investigative activities detrimental to these fundamental rights in absence of a law establishing the cases and manner of their execution.

The sanction provided for this type of violation is the exclusionary rule set forth in Article 191 of the Code of Criminal Procedure, which stipulates that evidence acquired in violation of prohibitions established by law – and a *fortiori ratione* established by the Constitution or by supra-national norms superordinate to the law – may not be used in the trial to decide on the liability of the defendant.[109]

---

108 This right constitutes a direct limitation for the Italian public authority through Article 117 of the Constitution. Indeed, in decisions 348 and 349 of 2017 the Italian Constitutional Court clarified that the articles provided for in the European Convention on Human Rights have direct effect in the domestic legal system as international obligations and the Court further said that the provisions contained in these international obligations constitute an interposed standard of review for assessing the compatibility of domestic laws to constitutional principles.

109 For similar considerations – in relation to the atypical technological investigative activity carried out in violation of the protection mechanisms provided by Articles 13–15 Const. and Article 8 ECHR – see S. Marcolini, *Le indagini atipiche a contenuto tecnologico nel processo penale: una proposta*, (2015)2 *Cassazione Penale*, p. 775. In particular, according to the author, until the legislature provides the cases and ways to affect the fundamental right there is a general prohibition of intervention by public authorities under Article 191 of the Code of Criminal Procedure. The case-law of the Constitutional Court and the Corte di Cassazione also extends the exclusionary rule provided for in Article 191 C.C.P. to atypical investigative activities carried out in violation of fundamental rights protected by the Constitution. In particular see *Cassazione Penale*, United Sections, 23rd February 2000, No. 6: 'The judicial control over the acquisitive measure which pertains to a *mezzo di ricerca della prova* is implemented through the detectability, also *ex officio* at every state and level of the proceedings, of the exclusionary rule under Article 191 of the Code of Criminal Procedure, which is also applicable to so-called "unconstitutional" evidence

Finally, these limits also apply to the lawyer who performs atypical investigative activities during the *investigazioni difensive*.[110] The lawyer must act in accordance with the general principles established in Article 188 and ff. of the Code of Criminal Procedure and without violating the fundamental rights safeguarded by the mechanism of protection by law. However, it should be highlighted that in practice the possibilities for the lawyer to carry out atypical investigative activities are very limited due to the absence of coercive power.

5 Subjective Limits to the Use of Evidence Gathered during the Investigative Stage

The power of public authorities in collecting evidence during the investigative stage also has subjective limits. Indeed, some evidence gathered during the investigative phase in compliance with all procedural rules may still not be usable against certain subjects, since there is a kind of subjective exclusionary rule.

Firstly, evidence gathered through specific investigative activities may not be used against a defendant whose lawyer was not notified of the activity or was not allowed to participate.

In the event of searches, seizures, opening of packages and urgent investigation of places, things or persons, the suspect's lawyer is entitled to attend without the right to be notified in advance.[111] If the lawyer is prevented from participating, evidence gathered during the activity cannot be used against the defendant.

In the event of questioning, inspection, identification of persons or confrontation, the suspect's lawyer must be notified at least 24 hours before the activity, with certain exceptions.[112] The same as above, if the lawyer is not notified or prevented from participating, the evidence gathered shall not be used against the defendant during the trial.

---

because it is taken in a way that violates fundamental rights'. On this point, see also *Corte Costituzionale* judgment No. 229/1998.

110 For the definition and regulation of *investigazioni difensive* see § 2.2.

111 The reference are Articles 356 and 365 C.C.P.

112 See Article 364, para. 3 C.C.P. Paragraph 5 provides, exceptionally, that in cases of absolute urgency if there are reasonable grounds to believe that the delay may compromise the search for or the securing of the sources of evidence, the prosecutor may anticipate the time limit. The notice may be omitted if the prosecutor performs an inspection and there are reasonable grounds to believe that the traces or other material items of the offence may be altered.

A further subjective exclusionary rule is provided regarding the questioning of the suspect, who must be warned before questioning that if he or she makes statements about facts concerning the liability of others he or she will become a witness in relation to those facts. In the absence of this notice any statements made about facts concerning the liability of others may not be used against them and the person being interrogated will not become a witness in relation to those specific facts.[113]

Another subjective limitation concerns the use of evidence gathered during the investigation related to other proceedings. The general rule is that records of evidence collected in the investigation of another proceeding may not be acquired, only evidence gathered in the trial or in *incidente probatorio*[114] may be used. However, the acquisition of records of unrepeatable actions that cannot be repeated, or that have become impossible to acquire due to unforeseeable circumstances, is permitted.[115] Moreover, there is a subjective limitation linked to the records of statements, as they can only be used against the accused whose lawyer has participated in evidence gathering in the other proceeding, otherwise the evidence cannot be used against him.[116]

A kind of exclusionary rule also applies to the *responsabile civile*, the person with civil liability for damages caused by the offender (e.g. the insurer of a vehicle). The *responsabile civile* may intervene in criminal proceedings on its own initiative or at the summons of the civil party or the public prosecutor.[117] In the event that the *responsabile civile* has not voluntarily intervened, he may even request to be excluded from the criminal proceeding if the evidence gathered during the investigation, without he or she having been informed of the possibility of participation, is prejudicial to his or her defence. The case-law of the *Corte di Cassazione* has held this exclusion applicable in cases where non-repeatable technical investigation[118] or *incidente probatorio* were carried out before the *responsabile civile* was sued.[119]

113 See Article 64, paragraph 3 *bis*, second period C.C.P. on general rules for questioning.

114 For a definition of *incidente probatorio* see n. 42.

115 The reference is Article 238, para. 1 and 3 C.C.P.

116 See Article 238, para. 2 *bis* C.C.P.

117 Articles 83–88 C.C.P. regulate the summoning, intervention, constitution and exclusion of the *responsabile civile*.

118 The reference is *Cassazione penale*, sec. IV, 26 September 2018, n. 58243: 'The civil responsible party has the right to be excluded from the criminal trial if it has not been timely subpoenaed to participate in a non-repeatable technical assessment aimed at consecrating, in the adversarial process between the parties, evidence potentially prejudicial to it'.

119 *Cassazione penale*, sec. IV, 14 December 2018, n. 12870 interprets Article 86, para. 2 C.C.P. by stating that it is applicable at the *incidente probatorio*. See also *Cassazione penale*, sec. IV, 28 April 2016, n. 39028.

In all these cases, the power of the public authority in collecting evidence during the investigative stage finds an indirect limitation in the impossibility of using it against a specific subject.

6 Open Issues and Future Perspectives

In conclusion, summarizing what has been said so far, the power of the public authorities in the collection of evidence during investigative stage is wide, but not unlimited.

In general terms, the Italian criminal law system is based on the principle of separation between the investigation and trial phases; the evidence collected during the stage of investigation by the public prosecutor and the police should only serve to enable the public prosecutor to determine whether to prosecute or not, as it cannot be examined and used by the judge for the purpose of the decision. Indeed, in purity, the only evidence the judge can use to decide on the criminal liability of the accused should be that admitted during the hearing, in the cross-examination between the parties.

However, the Code tempers the principle of separation between investigation and trial, providing for a series of exceptions – which in reality do not occur so infrequently – that allow the trial judge to know and use evidence collected during investigation for the purpose of decision. In particular, the evidence collected in investigation can be used in the trial with the consent of the parties, in the case of unrepeatable evidence (such as inspections, searches, seizures, interceptions, data retention, non-repeatable technical investigations) or as a consequence of the choice to resort to some summary trials.[120]

Because of the high frequency of these important exceptions in practice – which in fact often make evidence gathered in the investigative phase largely usable in the trial –, it is very relevant to place limits on the power of public authorities to collect evidence at the investigative stage; this is the only way to effectively protect the defendant and the general Italian due process principles of cross-examination, orality and immediacy.

From a general point of view, the domestic legal order limits the public power to collect evidence at the investigative stage providing a complex system of prohibitions and sanctions.

First of all, the Criminal Code and special laws provide for a number of disciplinary sanctions and offenses that can be imposed on the prosecutor or police

120 See § 1.

officer who violates certain criminal or disciplinary rules provided for the collection of evidence during investigation (substantive and direct sanctions).[121]

The system then provides for indirect sanctions that prevent the judge from using evidence collected during the investigation stage to decide on the criminal liability of the defendant. Violation of a procedural rule on evidence collection (procedural prohibition) is followed by the application of the exclusionary rule.

This exclusionary rule applies in cases provided for among the general principles on evidence (Article 188 and ff. Code of Criminal Procedure). Specifically, evidence must be gathered (including in investigation) by methods or techniques that are not capable of affecting the moral freedom, the freedom of self-determination or the freedom of altering the ability to remember and evaluate the facts; moreover, evidence must be collected in compliance with the prohibitions provided by law (and, as seen above, with the constitutional and supranational norms set up to protect the fundamental freedoms of the person).[122] The law may provide for objective or subjective prohibitions in connection with the collection of evidence, making the exclusionary rule applicable against all or only some of the defendants.[123]

From a theoretical point of view, the concept of 'prohibitions provided by law' contained in Article 191 of the Code of Criminal Procedure is declined as follows.

For typical investigative activities, the law (or rather the Code) provides – more or less comprehensively depending on whether they are *mezzi di ricerca della prova* or other typical investigative activities that are only partially regulated – the cases and ways in which they can be carried out by public authorities. This in accordance with the constitutional and supranational provision of the reservation of law on fundamental freedoms. It is the law that must clearly determine the cases and ways in which a fundamental right may be restricted, balancing the opposing requirements on the basis of the principle of proportionality.[124]

In relation to unregulated investigative activities there is a general rule of tempered atypicality. For case law, atypical investigative activities are permissible at the investigative stage (including for the purpose of gathering evidence) as long as they do not violate the main rules of evidence (Articles 188 and 189

121 See § 4.

122 See § 3, 4.1 and 4.3.

123 See § 5.

124 For the detailed explanation of this system and a list of the main prohibitions on specific investigative activities, see § 4.2.

C.C.P.) and do not affect fundamental freedoms for which there is mechanism of protection by law (for personal liberty is provided for in Article 14 of the Constitution, for inviolability of the domicile the reference is Article 14 Const., for freedom and secrecy of correspondence see Article 15 Const., for privacy the references are Article 8 of the ECHR and Articles 7 and 8 of the CFREU). No investigative activities of public authorities are possible in absence of a law that predetermines cases and ways of intrusion into these fundamental rights.[125]

Despite such a well-defined theoretical framework, it is observed that in practice the actual situation is more complex; the legislature and case law do not always follow this system of limits and sanctions.

Indeed, there are typical investigative activities whose methods of execution – although governed by the Code of Criminal Procedure and thus formally complying with the mechanism of protection by law – either conflict with supranational norms or do not identify with sufficient clarity the cases and ways to limit the fundamental right. An interesting case of this kind of problem is the recent national regulation of data retention.

As noted above, Article 132, paragraph 1 and 3 of the Privacy Code provides that the telephone service provider must retain, for investigative purposes, telephone traffic data for 24 months and call traffic data for 12 months. In addition, activities of data retention can only be carried out in investigation related to criminal offences punishable by imprisonment of not less than three years or to offences of threatening, harassing or disturbance of people by means of the telephone (Article 132, paragraph 3 Privacy Code). However, this discipline contrasts with the rules of the European Union and, in particular, with Article 15 of Directive 2002/58/EC,[126] as interpreted by the recent rulings of the Court of Justice of the European Union 'Quadrature' and 'Commissioner'. First of all, the Italian legislation provides for a generalized and undifferentiated data retention, in fact all types of data referring to all subjects are retained indiscriminately, there is a mass memorisation without any selection. Secondly, the retention period provided is very long, this in violation of the principle of proportionality. Lastly, Article 132, paragraph 3 Privacy Code provides for the possibility of data retention by crime with a very low penalty limit (and thus in relation to a very large number of crimes) so that it appears as if there is no

---

125 See § 4.3.

126 Directive 2002/58/EC of the European Parliament and of the Council of 12 July 2002 concerning the processing of personal data and the protection of privacy in the electronic communications sector (Directive on privacy and electronic communications) [2002] OJ L 201, pp. 37–47.

limit.[127] This allows for a systematic, discretionary and disproportionate violation of the fundamental right to privacy provided for by the Constitution, the ECHR and the CFREU.

Regarding atypical investigative activities, the case-law of the *Corte di Cassazione* sometimes admits the use of investigative techniques that are highly detrimental to the privacy protection even in the absence of a specific law regulating cases and ways to perform that activity. Two examples of this criticality are satellite surveillance via GPS and the use of Trojan malware for purposes other than acoustic surveillance.[128]

Specifically, the Supreme Court ruled that satellite surveillance via GPS is an atypical investigative activity and can be carried out without the need to follow special rules (such as prior authorization from a judge) because it is an activity that does not interfere with the constitutional rights to secrecy of correspondence and inviolability of the home (protected by Article 15 and 14 Constitution). However, in this case the Court did not consider the international obligations on respect for the right to privacy under Article 8 ECHR and Articles 7–8 CFREU, which expressly provide a mechanism of protection by law to preserve this freedom.

Another example of the case-law's tolerance for investigative practices that violate the mechanism of protection by law provided for in Article 8 ECHR is the use of Trojan malware for purposes other than acoustic surveillance. The Supreme Court also admits the use of Trojan malware for activities such as acquiring the content of a mobile device, remotely activating the camera, recording the screen or stealing passwords. However, the use of Trojan malware for these kind of purposes is not regulated by the Code of Criminal Procedure (unlike the use of Trojan malware for the purpose of acoustic surveillance, Art. 266, paragraphs 2 and 2 bis C.C.P.) and case-law does not require that particular rules be followed in the execution of this highly privacy-damaging activity. Thus, this situation creates unreasonable disparities: in the event that the Trojan malware is used to carry out acoustic surveillance, it is necessary to follow the procedure provided for by the Code (only most serious criminal offences, motivated authorization of the judge or validation, and so on), while

127 For an in-depth analysis of the critical issues of the data retention discipline regarding European Union law see R. Flor, S. Marcolini, *Dalla data retention alle indagini ad alto contenuto tecnologico. La tutela dei diritti fondamentali quale limite al potere coercitivo dello Stato. Aspetti di diritto penale processuale e sostanziale*, Giappichelli, Torino 2022, pp. 53–66.

128 See § 4.3.

in the event that the same tool is used to acquire the passwords of a device or remotely activating its camera the same guarantees are not provided.

In conclusion, although the Italian legal system provides an overall efficient system of limits to the power of public authorities in collecting evidence at the investigative stage, it is clear that there are some critical aspects regarding investigative activities based on advanced and invasive technologies. The most reasonable solution to this problem is legislative intervention to regulate (fully or in more detail) these activities, so as to comply with the mechanism of protection by law provided by the constitution and supranational sources.

More generally, it would be desirable a legislative regulation to adapt the legal framework to the evolution of investigative practices used by public authorities. In this sense, the legislature has only recently introduced the discipline for the use of Trojan malware for the sole purpose of conducting acoustic surveillance and regulated data retention activities: both provisions are far from satisfactory in terms of truly protecting the right to privacy for the reasons mentioned above.

Today and in the near future, attention in the field of criminal justice is focused on the Cartabia's reform, the provisions of which are aimed at reducing the length of trials. However, this does not exclude that in the near future, hopefully not too far away, the legislature will pay more attention to the new technologies used by public authorities in their investigative activities by improving the discipline of data retention and by regulating, in compliance with the mechanism of the protection of law, the atypical investigative activities that are detrimental to fundamental rights.

CHAPTER 6

Power to Search and Its Limits in Polish Criminal Investigations

*Karolina Kremens**

1 Introduction[1]

The interference with the rights and freedoms of the individual is an inevitable part of a criminal investigation. In order to resolve a criminal case, identify the perpetrator and gather evidence against him or her, criminal justice authorities frequently must resort to measures conducted against certain rights of individuals, such as right to privacy, property or liberty. This is because some information might be concealed, whether intentionally or not, and some individuals might be eager to hinder or obstruct the proceedings, which can only be overcome through coercion. As a result, the law provides for coercive measures[2] that the authorities are allowed to employ to fulfil their duties in the investigation of crimes. Yet the power to apply such measures can never be absolute. Efforts are constantly being made to limit the power of criminal justice authorities to impose coercive measures, in particular during criminal investigations. Thus, the question shall be asked what sets the limits of such measures, that is who should be responsible for making such decisions as

---

* LLM, PhD, habil., Digital Justice Center, Faculty of Law, Administration and Economics, University of Wrocław.

1 This work is a result of the research project financed by the Polish National Science Center 2018/30/E/HS5/00338 entitled "Reasonable Search. Between Effectiveness of Investigation and Rights of Individual". It also came about within the framework of the Academic Excellence Hub – Digital Justice Center carried out under the Initiative of Excellence – Research University at the University of Wrocław. The earlier version of this article was presented during the General Congress of International Academy of Comparative Law on 23–28 October 2022. I am grateful to all participants for their helpful comments. I am also thankful to Kamil Sobański, Research Assistant at the Digital Justice Center, for his remarkable help in editing this paper.

2 See on the definition of coercive measures in Karolina Kremens, *Powers of the Prosecutor in Criminal Investigation. A Comparative Perspective*, Routledge, New York 2021, pp. 262–66.

 | DOI:10.1163/9789004710320_008

well as when, how and according to what procedure these measures should be applied. And, probably most importantly, if such limits are breached what should be the remedies in order to rectify the situation and exclude the evidence obtained by such means.

This chapter aspires to answer the question of the limits of power that criminal justice agencies have during Polish criminal investigations when coercive measures are imposed. The analysis is conducted using the search as an example of such a coercive measure. Searches are key investigative measures frequently used in all criminal justice systems. This is because they are also among the most powerful tools to discover evidence and are usually easy and quick to carry out. However, failure to conduct them lawfully and reasonably has a direct impact on the admissibility of evidence during trial. Also, they significantly interfere with the rights of the individual, which makes them a coercive tool that very easily may deprive a person of privacy and take away his or her dignity. For that reason, provisions concerning search must be shaped in a way that will reconcile the effectiveness of the investigation and adequate protection against unlawful searches. This makes them the ideal object of this analysis.

This chapter commences with a short presentation of the scope of criminal investigation. It discusses the main and most distinctive features of the evidence system in the light of the applicable model of criminal procedure and fundamental principles governing that stage of criminal process. Setting the scene is key to understanding the context in which searches are performed in Poland and limitations to their imposition. The next part (subchapter 3) is devoted to the threshold that enables criminal justice authorities to conduct searches, whether with a search warrant or carried out in exigent circumstances without such pre-authorization. It also focuses on the rules regulating the conduct of search. In particular, the obligation to carry out this coercive measure in accordance with the proportionality principle will be analysed. Subchapter 4 discusses the authorities responsible for ordering and carrying out searches. This is analyzed in the light of arguments made in the literature criticizing the prosecutor as the authority to issue search warrants. Finally, subchapter 5 outlines the remedies for illegally obtaining evidence through search and while breaking the procedural rules upon which searches are regulated. In this part the work will attempt to evaluate the exclusion of evidence under such circumstances as available in Polish law against the rules adopted in other countries. The chapter ends with conclusions containing a critical evaluation of the Polish regulation of search practices.

2 The Scope of Polish Criminal Investigations[3]

Polish law operates under the Continental model of criminal procedure. As a classic inquisitorial system,[4] Polish criminal proceedings are divided into long and formal criminal investigation and short court proceedings focused on the reproduction of evidence collected at the earlier stage of the criminal process.[5] The court proceedings are always initiated by the prosecutor and may take the form of a formal trial or may be concluded in one of the deformalized procedures including the negotiated justice mechanisms.

Like all Continental systems, the Polish criminal procedure relies heavily on written sources of law. Some general grounds relating to this area are provided in the Polish Constitution,[6] for example in Art. 40 on the prohibition of the use of torture, Art. 42(3) on the presumption of evidence and Art. 49 on the freedom of communication. Yet the main source of law concerning rules of evidence in criminal proceedings is the Polish Code of Criminal Procedure.[7] Some additional rules concerning evidence-taking may however also be found in other laws regulating the system and organization of authorities participating in criminal proceedings, e.g. the Police Act[8] and Prosecution Service Act.[9] Despite the numerous sources of law, the system is generally following the rules set in the Code, which makes the system relatively homogenous.

The most important feature of the Polish criminal investigation is that the pretrial findings are considered as evidence. The purpose of both criminal

3 For the comprehensive analysis of Polish criminal proceedings in English, including at the stage of criminal investigation, see Wojciech Jasiński and Karolina Kremens, *Criminal Law in Poland*, Kluwer Law International, Alphen aan den Rijn 2019.

4 Note that the traditional classification of models of criminal procedure has been broadly criticized in literature including by Mirjan Damaška, 'Evidentiary Barriers to Conviction and Two Models of Criminal Procedure: a Comparative Study' (1973) 121 *University of Pennsylvania Law Review* 506, 556 and more recently by Maximo Langer, 'The Long Shadow of the Adversarial and Inquisitorial Categories' in Markus D. Dubber and Tatjana Hörnle (eds) *The Oxford Handbook of Criminal Law*, Oxford University Press, Oxford 2014, pp. 887–912.

5 Note that between 1 July 2015 and 16 March 2016 Poland experimented with an idea of enhanced adversariality in criminal proceedings. See Wojciech Jasiński and Karolina Kremens, *Criminal Law in Poland*, Kluwer Law International, Alphen aan den Rijn 2019, pp. 48–49.

6 *Konstytucja Rzeczypospolitej Polskiej* of 2 April 1997 (Dz. U. z 1997 r., Nr 78, poz. 483) [hereinafter: Constitution of Poland].

7 *Kodeks postępowania karnego* of 6 June 1997 (Dz.U. 2017, poz. 1904) [hereinafter: CCP].

8 *Ustawa o Policji* of 6 April 1990 (Dz.U. 2023 poz. 171) [Police Act].

9 This also concerns acts regulating the functioning of other criminal justice authorities engaged in criminal investigation mentioned above.

investigation and trial is to collect, preserve and conduct evidence to determine the facts on a certain case. Therefore, the aim of the criminal investigation is not only focused on gathering enough material to establish whether the formal accusation against a suspect should be filed with the court but also to preserve evidence for the purpose of future court proceedings (Article 297 § 1 (5) CCP). As a result, the collection of evidence at the early stages of the criminal process is performed under formal rules and recorded carefully in the case file (dossier).[10] During the trial the court, fully acquainted with the contents of that file, heavily relies on the pretrial findings, which discourages direct presentation and examination of evidence in an open court. Since at the closure of an investigation the defence has a right to a full disclosure of the case file (Article 321 CCP), this does not raise too many objections. And while pretrial findings are considered as evidence, the rules of evidence are applicable during both stages of the criminal process and not only during the trial. Hence, criminal justice authorities responsible for the conduct of criminal investigation observe the rules on admissibility of evidence and their exclusion on the same basis as the court does during the trial. Even though the summary of pretrial findings and their overall assessment is made by the court during the trial, the prosecutor or police when admitting evidence to the dossier must also consider the same rules (Article 170 CCP) that the court would analyse while considering the judgment.

Such an approach affects the role of the accused and the victim in the examination of evidence during the criminal investigation. As a rule, the criminal investigation is conducted *ex officio*, which means that the investigative measures are conducted regardless of the will of other participants to the criminal process (Article 9 § 1 CCP). However, the law also provides for taking the evidence upon the request of the victim and accused (Article 167 CCP), which applies both to investigation and court proceedings. Thus, the victim and accused are allowed to actively participate in the criminal investigation by taking part in witness interrogations and are permitted to demand additional investigative measures to be undertaken by the police (Article 315 CCP). Private investigations conducted by suspect or victims, like those that exist for example in the Italian system,[11] are not allowed. Even in rare cases of so-called

10 Note that the Polish criminal process is not following the Italian double-dossier (*doppio fascicolo*) system. See more in Michele Panzavolta, 'Reforms and Counter-Reforms in the Italian Struggle for an Accusatorial Criminal Law System' (2004) 30 *North Carolina Journal of International Law & Commercial Regulation* 577, pp. 586–587.

11 Cf. Article 327bis of the Italian Code of Criminal Procedure. Doris De Vocht, 'Poland' in Ed Cape, Zaza Namoradze, Roger Smith, Taru Spronken (eds) *Effective Criminal Defence in Europe*, Intersentia, Antwerp 2010, p. 465.

private offences where the victim has the option to directly accuse the suspect in a form of private accusation (*oskarżenie prywatne*),[12] the law does not provide for the conduct of any form of private criminal investigation – in fact there is not even an investigation. It is provided that the police are obliged just to record an accusation made by the victim orally or in written form and must secure evidence if there is a need to do so (Article 488 § 1 CCP). Afterwards, the recorded accusation is transferred by the police to a court, which initiates court proceedings. All other evidentiary actions are undertaken by the police upon the court's request if the court decides that it is necessary (Article 488 § 2 CCP). This is however not considered an investigation but just a sort of investigatory action conducted during the court's proceedings.[13]

Polish law recognizes a system of principles that the criminal process is driven upon which specifically affects the examination and evaluation of evidence. The exact number of such principles and criteria that distinguish them from other principles of the criminal process are unclear and developed by different scholars in various ways.[14] Most commonly as the most important the principle of material truth is invoked. This principle implies that all evidence that may contribute to establishing the truth about the crime in question should be collected and assessed (Article 2 § 2 CCP). Yet even this principle is not absolute and superior to others. It is limited by the right to defence, the right to remain silent, the *in dubio pro reo* principle as well as existing exclusionary rules, which makes it difficult or sometimes impossible to establish the "real truth" during criminal proceedings.[15] This also plays a role in the case of negotiated agreements accepted under Polish law in various forms (Article 335 and 387 CCP), which affects the degree of certainty when it comes to establishing the facts of the case. Although the efficiency of criminal proceedings is an important factor and certainly not all cases deserve a careful examination, the lowering of the standard should be complemented by

12 Offences falling under this category are very limited in number, specifically: causing minor bodily harm or a minor impairment to health, slander, insult and breach of personal inviolability and are considered not to involve the public interest. See Articles 59–61 and 485–499 CCP.

13 Katarzyna Dudka, 'Wybrane problemy dochodzenia w sprawach o przestępstwa prywatnoskargowe' (2005) 6 *Prokuratura i Prawo*, pp. 32–37.

14 Cf. Marek Cieślak, *Zagadnienia dowodowe w procesie karnym*, Wydawnictwo Prawnicze, Warszawa 1955, p. 100; Romuald Kmiecik (ed), *Prawo dowodowe. Zarys wykładu*, Wolters Kluwer, Warszawa 2008, p. 69 and Andrzej Gaberle, *Dowody w sądowym procesie karnym*, Wolters Kluwer, Warszawa 2010, p. 22.

15 See Zbigniew Sobolewski and Grażyna Artymiak (eds), *Zasada prawdy materialnej. Materiały z konferencji*, Wolters Kluwer, Warszawa 2006.

providing guarantees, especially those concerning the accused. However, in the Polish system there are no additional safeguards aimed at the conduct of evidence in that regard. Worse, there is no mechanism that forces the court in each case to verify whether the guilty plea has been delivered by the accused knowingly and willingly.

The importance of the material truth principle is strongly observed in the Polish law of criminal process, which is best seen by its impact on the examination of evidence during trial. As a result, the principle of adversariality is observed in Poland only to a limited extent as the court, by law and its interpretation, is responsible for calling and examining evidence during trial regardless of the activity of the parties (Article 167 § 1 CCP). This makes the prosecutor and the accused passive, as their role is shaped by the court's proactive approach and is complementary to it. Since the court is also bound by the principle of material truth and is exclusively responsible for establishing the truth during a trial, by habit the parties step aside and frequently wait for the court's mistakes in order to appeal against them.[16]

The strong position of the principle of material truth in Polish criminal proceedings is visible by the complementary character of other principles.[17] For one, the criminal investigation is conducted pursuant to the principle of legality (Article 10 CCP),[18] which should be understood as an obligation to conduct an investigation and prosecute a case without almost any discretion in that regard. Also the principle of direct examination of evidence is most usually understood as committing the court to base its judgment solely on facts disclosed during the trial (Article 410 CCP), having direct access to evidence and basing its judgment mainly on primary and not secondary evidence.[19] Among this group is also the principle of objectivity (Article 4 CCP), which binds authorities to examine and to consider all circumstances, both for and against the accused.[20] Finally, the principle of free assessment of evidence (Article 7

---

16 Cf. Paweł Wiliński (ed), *Kontradyktoryjność w polskim procesie karnym*, Wolters Kluwer, Warszawa 2013 and Piotr Hofmański, 'Zasada kontradyktoryjności' in Paweł Wiliński (ed), *Zasady procesu karnego. System prawa karnego procesowego*, vol. III, part 1, Wolters Kluwer, Warszawa 2014, pp. 635–90.

17 Jerzy Skorupka, *Proces karny*, 3rd ed., Wolters Kluwer, Warszawa 2020, p. 188.

18 See broadly on the understanding of principle of legality in Polish literature by Maria Rogacka-Rzewnicka, *Oportunizm i legalizm ścigania przestępstw w świetle współczesnych przeobrażeń procesu karnego*, Wolters Kluwer, Warszawa 2007.

19 Hanna Paluszkiewicz, 'Zasada bezpośredniości' in Paweł Wiliński (ed), *Zasady procesu karnego. System prawa karnego procesowego*, vol. III, part 2, Wolters Kluwer, Warszawa 2014, pp. 1005–119.

20 Cf. discussion on interrelation between principle of objectivity and impartiality in Wojciech Jasiński, 'Zasada bezstronności sądu. Zasada niezawisłości i niezależności sądu'

CCP) plays an important role during the examination and evaluation of evidence. According to this principle, authorities responsible for the proceedings make decisions based on their own conviction, which should be founded upon all the proof and appraised at their own discretion, with due consideration of the principles of sound reasoning and personal experience.[21] An important role is also played by the right to public trial,[22] including the rules concerning taking evidence in oral and written form[23] and the attribution of the burden of proof during trial.[24]

3 Search and Circumstances under which It Is Conducted

Under Polish law the search is perceived as conflicting primarily with a right to protection of privacy as expressed in Article 47 of the Polish Constitution but is also seen as interference with the inviolability of a person or his or her home, protected under Article 41(1) and Article 50 of the Polish Constitution. The Polish Constitution remains silent when it comes to the determination of the circumstances under which the search can be conducted, how it should be done and who is empowered to decide on the imposition of search. All these issues are left up to the Code of Criminal Procedure. The Code provides for search (*przeszukanie*) of premises and other places as well as persons and objects (Article 219 § 1 and 2 CCP). Based on this vague regulation, searching of all imaginable places, vehicles, personal apparel and objects belonging to the searched person, as well as computers and clouds etc., are permitted. Thus, the law does not limit the scope of persons who can be searched or places in which it can be conducted and allows for the applicability of that measure to all types of offences.

---

in Paweł Wiliński (ed), *Zasady procesu karnego. System prawa karnego procesowego*, vol. III, part 2, Wolters Kluwer, Warszawa 2014, pp. 1204–07.

21 Jerzy Skorupka, 'Zasada swobodnej oceny dowodów' in Paweł Wiliński (ed), *Zasady procesu karnego. System prawa karnego procesowego*, vol. III, part 2, Wolters Kluwer, Warszawa 2014, pp. 1120–200.

22 Kazimierz Zgryzek, 'Zasada jawności' in Paweł Wiliński (ed), *Zasady procesu karnego. System prawa karnego procesowego*, part 1, Wolters Kluwer, Warszawa 2014, pp. 768–840.

23 Anna Gerecka-Żołyńska, 'Zasada ustności i pisemności' in: Paweł Wiliński (ed), *Zasady procesu karnego. System prawa karnego procesowego*, vol. III, part 1, Wolters Kluwer, Warszawa 2014, pp. 841–98.

24 See Wojciech Jasiński and Jerzy Skorupka (eds), *Ciężar dowodu i obowiązek dowodzenia w procesie karnym*, Wolters Kluwer, Warszawa 2017; Małgorzata Żbikowska, *Ciężar dowodu w polskim procesie karnym*, Wolters Kluwer, Warszawa 2019.

The threshold that must be met to undertake search, regardless of whether with a warrant or not, is described as reasonable grounds to believe (*uzasadnione podstawy do przypuszczenia*) that a suspect or a sought object are located in the place where the search will be conducted or are in possession of a person who is about to be searched (Article 219 § 1 CCP). Unfortunately, case law provides little or no guidance on how to interpret that requirement[25] and it is unclear whether this requirement sets a standard of prima facie obviousness.[26] Instead of specifying the prerequisite of ordering or conducting searches, the law exposes the aim of the search, being the need to find, arrest and (forcibly) bring the suspected person into custody as well as discover objects which might constitute evidence in a case, or which are subject to seizure in criminal proceedings.

In the literature one can find the position that it is not possible to decree the prerequisite for conducting a search in any way other than in very general terms.[27] Indeed, it is difficult to imagine formulating any prerequisite in more detail. At the same time, the high degree of generality of the rule, giving wide room for manoeuvre in the actions taken by criminal justice agencies, weakens the right to privacy and gives it somewhat bogus protection.[28] Scholars emphasize that it contains both an objectified element ("reasonable grounds"), referring to real information that the object in question is located in a given place, and a subjective element ("assumption").[29] It seems that the only possible answer to these doubts is to leave the premise built in a general way, while encasing it in case law based on practice in such a way that the meaningful scope of the premise can be clearly reconstructed. There is no doubt that, for the time being, such jurisprudence is disappointingly poor and does not provide a basis for determining what facts allow one to consider that the premise has in fact occurred.

---

25 See generally on threshold to conduct criminal investigation in Poland in Karolina Kremens, *Powers of the Prosecutor in Criminal Investigation. A Comparative Approach*, Routledge, New York 2021, p. 122.

26 Radosław Koper 'Przeszukanie w wypadkach niecierpiących zwłoki' (2014) 11–12 *Prokuratura i Prawo* 14, p. 19.

27 Piotr Hofmański, 'Prawo do poszanowania prywatności (art. 17 Paktu i art. 8 Europejskiej Konwencji Praw Człowieka) a rozwiązania polskiego prawa karnego materialnego i procesowego' in Jan Skupiński and Jolanta Jakubowska-Hara (eds) *Standardy praw człowieka a polskie prawo karne*, Scholar, Warszawa 1995, p. 266.

28 Jacek Grochowski, 'Przeszukanie w procesie karnym jako instytucja wyznaczająca granice konstytucyjnych praw osobistych' (1991) 17 *PPK*, p. 133.

29 Jacek Grochowski, 'Podstawy dowodowe przeszukania w kodeksie postępowania karnego' (1992) 18 *PPK*, p. 45.

The way in which the search is conducted should be understood in the light of the proportionality principle. In the prism of Article 227 CCP, the search should be carried out moderately, according to its purpose, with due diligence, with respect for the privacy and dignity of the persons concerned, and without causing unnecessary harm or distress. This provision is an interpretative guideline and, at the same time, a guarantee of standard for the application of this institution. As rightly noted in the literature, "the gravity of the violation of constitutional freedoms and personal rights manifested by the institution of search and seizure of property and search of a person dictates the obligation to limit their use to the necessary minimum, and to avoid causing unnecessary harm and distress".[30] Yet, despite the provision being so paramount, the prevailing view is that conducting search in violation of Article 227 CCP does not impair its legality.[31] Instead of being a firm method to prevent and deter obtaining evidence by illegal means this remains rather a benevolent rule. The absence of any actual procedural consequences of a breach of Article 227 CCP which result in the compulsory removal of an item in violation of the proportionality principle leads to the conclusion that no effective safeguards of individuals' rights have been established.

The regulation of searches in the Polish criminal justice system should be considered far from complete. This is not only due to the lack of addressing the threshold to conduct search properly but also to improperly responding to the modern challenges posed to criminal proceedings by new technologies. This is because rules for searching places and people and their belongings were formed long before the era of the digital revolution and did not anticipate the existence and complexity of electronic devices storing gigabytes of data such as computers, smartphones and clouds. Moreover, the somewhat more detailed rules that have been created over time[32] do not always provide a sufficient legal regime with regard to when digital evidence can be accessed, who should be responsible for doing so and by what means this can be done.[33] Whether such information can be accessed simply by browsing through a phone or in a more complicated way that requires an expert to break through a security system, the amount of data available and its nature is incomparable to

30 Sławomir Steinborn, 'Komentarz do art. 227 k.p.k.' in Sławomir Steinborn (ed), *Kodeks postępowania karnego. Komentarz do wybranych przepisów*, LEX/el. 2016, thesis 1.

31 Tomasz Grzegorczyk, *Kodeks postępowania karnego. Komentarz*, wyd. 6, tom I, Wolters Kluwer, Warszawa 2014, p. 799.

32 This includes wiretapping (Article 237 CCP) and data retention (Article 236a CCP).

33 See Karolina Kremens, 'Granice ingerencji w prawo do prywatności i prawo własności w postępowaniu karnym' in Jerzy Skorupka (ed), *Model dopuszczalnej ingerencji w prawa i wolności jednostki w procesie karnym*, C.H. Beck, Warszawa 2019, pp. 288–93. Cf. Maciej Rogalski, *Podsłuch procesowy i pozaprocesowy*, Wolters Kluwer, Warszawa 2019.

a search of a place or a person and therefore, it seems, requires separate rules for obtaining such highly sensitive information.

One of the key issues that the Polish search laws omit, and which needs to be quickly regulated, is the problem of searches of smartphones found during the arrest of a person. The problem of allowing judicial authorities to conduct searches of a smartphone in the same way as all other searches stems from the nature of the phone as an object. It is clearly different from any other object that can be discovered through a routine search of a person. Being portable, a smartphone can be used for many purposes giving free space for social and emotional communication. The key question, then, remains whether law enforcement agencies should have similar powers to search smartphones as they have when searching a person and his or her belongings during an arrest.

Although Polish criminal procedure regulations do not explicitly regulate this issue, the reasons justifying such incidental searches will arise from the need to ensure the safety of the arresting officers and the need to prevent the detainee from destroying evidence. The issue to be considered here remains not whether a search of a person and his or her carried items can be undertaken in the course of an arrest, although this issue would undoubtedly require a more detailed analysis, but whether a smartphone should be treated like any other item discovered at the time of arrest with the detainee and whether it should be subject to the same rules that apply to searches of other items discovered with the detainee such as a bag or wallet. The answer to the question posed in this way significantly impinges on whether a separate prior decision to search is required to review the contents of an object of such a specific type as a phone, or whether such a decision need not be made at all using the available rules. And even though this question is of fundamental importance referring directly to how the right to privacy is protected, this issue has not been addressed in the Polish case law, nor in the national academic debate.[34] While in other countries the debate on the power of the police to search mobile phones without a warrant is the subject of lively discussion and has already generated strong reactions in the highest courts as well as among legislators,[35] there are no signs of any attempt to regulate this very important area of interference with privacy in Poland.

34 See however Karolina Kremens, 'O znaczeniu prawa porównawczego dla nauki polskiego procesu karnego na przykładzie przeszukań telefonów komórkowych' in Dobrosława Szumiło-Kulczycka (ed.) *W pogoni za rzetelnym procesem karnym. Księga Jubileuszowa Profesora Stanisława Waltosia*, Wolters Kluwer, Kraków 2022.

35 See broadly on US, Canadian and Dutch law by Bryce C. Newell and Bert-Jaap Koops, 'From horseback to the moon and back: comparative limits on police searches of smartphones upon arrest' (2020) 72 (1) *Hastings Law Journal* 229.

Instead, the Polish debate on evidence-gathering focuses more on the natural tendency of law enforcement agencies to search only for incriminating evidence, especially in the context of insufficient access to a lawyer at an early stage of a criminal process.[36] The oppressive investigative methods that add to the violation of human dignity are continuously criticized in yearly reports of the National Preventive Mechanism Against Torture.[37] The situation could be remedied to some extent by proper implementation of the six EU directives and focused on the rights of suspected and accused persons during criminal processes.[38] Among the recommendations, the obligation to record the interrogation and other procedural steps concerning the suspect can be found. This, together with recordings made by body-worn cameras, especially during warrantless searches including searches incident to arrest, seem specifically easy to be employed immediately.

4 Authority to Order and Conduct Searches

According to Polish law, searches may be conducted during criminal investigation by the prosecutor as well as police and other criminal justice agencies when so ordered by the prosecutor (Article 220 § 1 CCP). This extensive power of the prosecutor to personally conduct the search is rooted in very broad

36 See articles in Piotr Kardas 'Gwarancje praw jednostki na wstępnym etapie postępowania karnego w prawie europejskim i polskim' (2019) 1 *Europejski Przegląd Sądowy* 4. See also Helsinki Foundation on Human Rights – *Wzmacnianie praw osób podejrzanych i oskarżonych. Rola krajowych instytucji ochrony praw człowieka*, Warszawa 2019, p. 54 https://www.hfhr.pl/wp-content/uploads/2020/04/Wzmacnianie-praw-os%C3%B3b-podejrzanych-i-oskar%C5%BConych-NHRI-krajowy-web.pdf (accessed 24.03.2023); Barbara Grabowska-Moroz (ed) *Prawo dostępu do obrońcy w świetle prawa europejskiego*, Helsinki Foundation for Human Rights, Warszawa 2018, https://www.hfhr.pl/wp-content/uploads/2018/05/Prawo-dostępu-do-obroncy-w-swietle-prawa-UE-20180410.pdf (accessed 24.03.2023).

37 See Report for 2021 at https://bip.brpo.gov.pl/sites/default/files/Raport_KMPT_2020_interaktywny.pdf (accessed 24.03.2023).

38 Directive 2010/64/EU of 20 October 2010; Directive 2012/13/EU of 22 May 2012; Directive 2013/48/EU of 22 October 2013; Directive (EU) 2016/343 of 9 March 2016; Directive (EU) 2016/800 of 11 May 2016; Directive (EU) 2016/1919 of 26 October 2016. See the analysis of the process of implementation of Directives in Poland in Karolina Kremens *et al.*, 'Poland. There and Back Again. A Struggle with Transposition of EU Directives' in G. Contissa et al. (eds) *Effective Protection of the Rights of the Accused in the EU Directives. A Computable Approach to Criminal Procedure Law*, Brill, Leiden 2022, pp. 154–169.

powers granted to the prosecutor over the whole criminal investigation.[39] By law the prosecutor bears full responsibility for every criminal investigation conducted in Poland (Article 298 § 1 CCP and Article 326 § 1 CCP). The prosecutors are expected to either conduct it in person or supervise the investigation if conducted by another criminal justice authority. This distinction of the form of prosecutorial engagement in criminal investigation is strongly determined by the form in which the investigation is conducted, namely inspection (śledztwo) or inquiry (*dochodzenie*).[40] This distinction mainly determines the length of proceedings and the degree of its formality. In the case of inspections that are carried out for more serious crimes (Article 309 CCP), the role of the prosecutor is more exposed, as some investigative actions, such as interrogation of the suspect (Article 313 § 3 CCP), must be taken only by the prosecutor. In the case of inquiries, the investigation is primarily vested in the hands of the police or another investigating agency and the prosecutor maintains a supervisory role (Article 325a § 1 CCP), which gives them more freedom in shaping the course of actions. As data shows, only 11% of investigations are conducted in the form of inspections,[41] making it a visible minority. Of this number almost 90% of inspections are fully entrusted to the police.[42] Therefore, most of the criminal investigations in Poland are conducted by a criminal justice agency other than the prosecutor, while the prosecutor usually provides only a supervisory role over them.[43] Nevertheless, this approach translates to the dominating position of the prosecutor when many important decisions during criminal investigation are undertaken, including search warrants.

Despite the rule allowing the prosecutor to conduct searches personally (Article 220 § 1 CCP), almost all searches are carried out by the police or other criminal justice agencies prescribed by law. This corresponds with general

39 See Karolina Kremens, *Powers of the Prosecutor in Criminal Investigation. A Comparative Approach*, Routledge, New York 2021.

40 See more on this distinction in Doris De Vocht, 'Poland' in Ed Cape, Zaza Namoradze, Robert Smith, Taru Spronken (eds) *Effective Criminal Defence in Europe*, Intersentia, Antwerpen-Oxford 2010, p. 429.

41 *Sprawozdanie z działalności powszechnych jednostek organizacyjnych prokuratury za rok 2019* [Report on the activities of prosecution service of Poland in 2019], https://pk.gov.pl/wp-content/uploads/2020/03/PK-P1K.pdf (accessed: 29.11.2021), p. 1.

42 Among 79,918 inspections initiated in 2019 as many as 71,329 were fully transferred to the police upon prosecutorial decision – *Sprawozdanie z działalności powszechnych jednostek organizacyjnych prokuratury za rok 2019* [Report on the activities of prosecution service of Poland in 2019], https://pk.gov.pl/wp-content/uploads/2020/03/PK-P1K.pdf (accessed: 29.11. 2021), p. 1.

43 Cf. Karolina Kremens, *Powers of the Prosecutor in Criminal Investigation. A Comparative Approach*, Routledge New York 2021, pp. 160–63.

competencies granted to various agencies to carry out criminal investigations. As a rule, the police (*Policja*)[44] are set as the primary agency empowered to conduct criminal investigations in Poland (Article 298 § 1 CCP). The police are structurally independent from the prosecution service and do not take a form of judicial police at the prosecutor's disposal as known from other criminal justice systems.[45] It is described as a uniformed and armed agency serving the public, intended to protect the security of people as well as to maintain public safety and order (Article 1 (1) of the Police Act).

Even though the majority of criminal investigations in Poland are carried out by the police, a large number of agencies may also be involved. Their position cannot be considered as subordinated to the police, as they work independently of each other. All are working under the supervision of the prosecutor, who maintains the power to receive information regarding the investigation, to review the case file, to indicate the direction that the proceedings should take, and to issue orders relevant in this regard.[46] According to Article 312 CCP the power to conduct criminal investigation is attached to the Border Guard (*Straż Graniczna*), Internal Security Agency (*Agencja Bezpieczeństwa Wewnętrznego*), National Revenue Administration (*Krajowa Administracja Skarbowa*), Central Anticorruption Bureau (*Centralne Biuro Antykorupcyjne*) and Military Gendarmerie (Żandarmeria *Wojskowa*). Moreover, in the case of inquiries (but not inspections), the array of agencies is even broader. These are in the first place the agencies listed in a separate act adopted by the Minister of Justice,[47] that is: the Trade Inspection Authority (*Inspekcja Handlowa*), the

---

44 See on the police structure in Teodor Bulenda, Beata Gruszczyńska, Andrzej Kremplewski, Piotr Sobota, 'The Prosecution Service Function within the Polish Criminal Justice System' in Jörg-Martin Jehle and Marianne Wade (eds), *Coping with Overloaded Criminal Justice Systems. The Rise of Prosecutorial Power Across Europe*, Springer Berlin, Heidelberg 2010, p. 273.

45 See for example judicial police (polizia giudiziaria) in Italy – Astolfo Di Amato, *Criminal Law in Italy*, Kluwer Law International, Alphen aan den Rijn 2013, p. 158 and Michele Caianiello, *Increasing Discretionary Prosecutor's Powers: The Pivotal Role of the Italian Prosecutor in the Pretrial Investigation Phase.* Oxford Handbooks Online, Oxford 2016, p. 9.

46 Karolina Kremens, 'Limits of powers of public authorities with respect to obtaining evidence at the stage of investigation', in Biruta Lewaszkiewicz-Petrykowska (ed), *Rapports polonais – XXIe Congrès international de droit compare*, Wydawnictwo Uniwersytetu Łódzkiego, Łódź 2022, p. 317.

47 *Rozporządzenie Ministra Sprawiedliwości w sprawie organów uprawnionych obok Policji do prowadzenia dochodzeń oraz organów uprawnionych do wnoszenia i popierania oskarżenia przed sądem pierwszej instancji w sprawach, w których prowadzono dochodzenie, jak również zakresu spraw zleconych tym organom* [Regulation of the Minister of Justice on criminal justice agencies authorized, apart from the police, to conduct investigations and agencies authorized to bring and support charges before the court of first instance in

State Sanitary Inspection Authority (*Państwowa Inspekcja Sanitarna*) and the President of the Office of Electronic Communications (*Prezes Urzędu Komunikacji Elektronicznej*). Moreover, additional state agencies are provided with similar powers in other parliamentary acts, that is the Forest Guard (*Straż Leśna*) if the investigation concerns trees or wood from forests owned by the state[48] or the National Hunting Guard (*Państwowa Straż* Łowiecka) regarding offences concerning hunting.[49] The police maintain the presumption of competence to carry out investigations in the case of all criminal offences, while the competence of other agencies is limited to certain specifically prescribed types of offences only.[50] Due to their limited jurisdiction the number of criminal investigations conducted by other agencies is very limited;[51] however, they are all authorized to conduct searches both with a search warrant and in exigent circumstances.

The power to order search during an investigation by issuing a search warrant rests with the prosecutor, and the law does not consider a court or a judge or any other authority as competent to do so at this stage of criminal proceedings (Article 220 § 1 and 2 CCP).[52] The prosecutor is also empowered to provide the mandatory post factum authorization of search conducted in exigent circumstances in a form of confirmation (Article 220 § 3 CCP). The law provides straightforwardly for a preference of searches with a warrant by stating that if a search is not conducted by the prosecutor in person, the agency willing to search a place or a person should obtain a prosecutorial search warrant prior

cases where inquiries have been conducted, as well as the scope of cases commissioned to these bodies] of 22 September 2015, Dz.U. 2015 poz. 1725.

48 Article 47(2) *ustawy o lasach* [Forest Act] of 28 September 1991, Dz. U. 2021, poz. 1275 with amendments.

49 Article 37(1)(3) *ustawy – Prawo* łowieckie [Hunting Law] of 13 October 1995, Dz. U. 2022 poz. 1173.

50 For example, the Border Guard may conduct the investigation only in matters of recognition, prevention and detection of offences related to the crossing of the state border or those concerning foreigners working in Poland (Article 1(2)(4)(a) of the *Ustawa o Straży Granicznej* of 2 October 1990 [Border Guard Act], Dz.U. 2022 poz. 1061). See also Wojciech Jasiński and Karolina Kremens, *Criminal Law in* Poland, Kluwer Law International, Alphen aan den Rijn 2019, pp. 29–36.

51 For example, the Central Anticorruption Bureau opened only 256 investigations in 2017 – *Informacja o wynikach działalności Centralnego Biura Antykorupcyjnego w 2017 r.* [Information on the activities of the Central Anticorruption Bureau in 2017], https://cba.gov.pl/ftp/filmy/Informacja_o_wynikach_dzialalnosci_Centralnego_Biura_Antykorupcyjnego_w_2017_r..pdf (accessed: 29.11. 2021), p. 7.

52 Note that the law provides that during court proceedings, that is after filing indictment with the court, the sole power to order search rests with the court (Article 220 § 1 CCP).

to exercising the measure.[53] The obvious need to conduct searches urgently forced lawmakers to allow the police to conduct a search without a warrant, although the term "exigent circumstances" (*wypadki niecierpiące zwłoki*) justifying such searches is continuously criticized for being too unclear and imprecise.[54] In view of the lack of specification of this term by case law it has been accepted in the literature that exigent circumstances occur whenever "commencing an investigative action with a delay resulting from time lost while obtaining prosecutorial warrant or lack of action, would result in the loss, distortion or destruction of evidence".[55] The existence of these circumstances must be evaluated in the light of the setting that occurred when the search was conducted and not from the perspective of the time when the evaluation of the need to undertake the measure is being made post factum.

Every search conducted without a warrant must be immediately confirmed by the prosecutor, which forces the police to request such post-authorization in every single case (Article 220 § 3 CCP). The lack of such application or the decision not to authorize the conducted warrantless search have potentially grave consequences. If the search is not confirmed by the prosecutor within seven days from the day it took place, the objects seized during the search must immediately be returned to the owner (Article 230 § 1 CCP). This happens regardless of the request of the owner to receive such confirmation. The only exception to this rule is when the items are seized from the owner who voluntarily hands them over, which means that the search was not in fact necessary (Article 217 § 2 CCP). In such case the subsequent confirmation is dependent only upon the request of the owner of voluntarily provided things.

At this point the question shall be asked whether vesting power to issue search warrants with the prosecutor appropriately protects the rights of persons that have been searched. This applies to the same extent to prosecutorial power to issue a post factum decision confirming warrantless searches in exigent circumstances. The general rule provides that to sufficiently protect the individual during criminal investigation, the interference with rights and freedoms may be made only by an independent and impartial authority. Under Polish law falling under such a regime are the pretrial detention of a suspect (Article 250 § 2 CCP) as well as examination of the mental health of a suspect combined with his or her observation in a medical institution (Article 203 § 1 CCP),

53 Nowak and Steinborn (2013), p. 519.

54 Andrzej Sakowicz, 'Poszanowanie życia prywatnego w postępowaniu karnym' (2000) 6 *Jurysta* 21, p. 21.

55 Radosław Koper 'Przeszukanie w wypadkach niecierpiących zwłoki' (2014) 11–12 *Prokuratura i Prawo* 14, p. 20–21 and the literature cited in footnote 14.

both interfering with the right to liberty. Also wiretapping (Article 237 § 1 CCP) and the seizure of documents possessed by the defence counsel covered by the lawyer–client privilege (Article 225 § 1 CCP) are considered as a grave interference with privacy and therefore subjected to judicial authorization. On the other hand, searches, as well as arrests (Article 247 CCP) interfering with the right to liberty, do not enjoy the same level of protection, despite their obvious ability to infringe the right to privacy and property.

As the Polish Constitution does not regulate the question of authority eligible to order searches, the answer to it may be looked for in the case law of the European Court of Human Rights (ECtHR), which provides for a minimum standard for protection of the rights of an individual among European countries gathered within the Council of Europe.[56] Unfortunately, when dealing with searches, considered as interference with the right to privacy as protected by Article 8 (2) of the European Convention on Human Rights and Freedoms (ECHR), the ECtHR focuses mainly on the conduct of such a measure in "accordance with law",[57] whether the interference furthers a legitimate aim[58] and if it is "necessary in a democratic society".[59] Generally, the ECtHR concluded that the independent judicial supervision of searches is necessary.[60] However, in the Court's opinion the judicial warrant issued prior to a search is not mandatory if counterbalanced by the availability of an *ex post factum* judicial review.[61]

Despite unrigid views of the ECtHR, the broad powers of the prosecutor towards the imposition of search have been criticized in Polish literature. Scholars have argued that the level of engagement of the prosecutor in criminal investigation makes him or her too prejudiced to make an independent evaluation of the need to conduct a search.[62] Moreover, since the recent changes in Polish law aimed at the full subordination of the prosecution service to the Minister of Justice, the Polish prosecution service cannot be presumed

56 See Karolina Kremens, 'The Authority to Order Search in Comparative Perspective: The Call for the Judicial Oversight' (2020) 6 (3) *Revista Brasileira di Direito Processual Penal* 1585, pp. 1610–11.

57 *Halford v. The United Kingdom*, no. 20605/92, 25 June 1997.

58 *Mozer v. The Republic of Moldova and Russia*, no. 11138/10, 23 February 2016, §194.

59 See among others *Buck v. Germany*, no. 41604/98, 28 April 2005 and *Ratushna v. Ukraine*, no. 17318/06, 2 December 2010.

60 *Sallinen and Others v. Finland*, no. 50882/99, 27 September 2005, § 89.

61 *Smirnov v. Russia*, no. 71362/01, 7 June 2007, §45 and *Heino v. Finland*, no. 56720/09, 15 February 2011, §46.

62 Sławomir Steinborn, 'Problem organu uprawnionego do stosowania przeszukania w toku procesu karnego w świetle unormowań konstytucyjnych i prawnomiędzynarodowych' (2008) 19 *Gdańskie Studia Prawnicze*, p. 375; Jerzy Skorupka, 'Konstytucyjne i konwencyjne granice przeszukania w postępowaniu karnym (cz. II)' (2007) 11–12 *Palestra* 52, p. 52.

as anything other than fully subordinated to the executive[63] and thus incompetent to undertake decisions detrimental to the individual's rights and freedoms.[64] From this perspective, the subsequent judicial review of prosecutorial decisions is considered as insufficiently protecting searched individuals, which will be discussed below.

5 Remedies and Exclusion of Evidence Obtained through Illegal Search

Under Polish law all searches are subjected to judicial review (Article 236 § 1 CCP). The standing to file such complaint[65] extends not only to the parties to the proceedings (victim and suspect) but, more generally, to all persons whose rights, resulting from the search, have been violated. A complaint can be filed regardless of whether the search has been conducted based on a warrant or without it. The judicial review is made by the judge (the court). According to the ECHR, the mere fact of the availability of such a remedy will not in itself necessarily amount to a sufficient safeguard against abuse, as such a remedy must be considered as effective and this is assessed in the light of the specific circumstances of every case.[66] Thus, it is key who is responsible for reviewing the complaint that is leading to judicial review. As a rule, in Polish criminal proceedings, the prosecutor who receives the complaint against the search, before transferring it to the court, may decide to agree with the complainant. This ceases the procedure and only in the case of disagreement with the complainant is the procedure of judicial review triggered. Although it must be admitted that positive prosecutorial review of a complaint is quite rare.

As a result, filing the complaint leads to the full judicial review made during criminal investigation by the judicial authority. It is crucial to address who is reviewing the complaint in such capacity. Polish criminal procedure does not recognize the traditional feature of the inquisitorial system – the investigative

63 European Commission for Democracy Through Law (Venice Commission), Opinion on the Act on the Public Prosecutor's Office as Amended, No.892/2017, Strasbourg, 11 December 2017, https://www.venice.coe.int/webforms/documents/default.aspx?pdffile=CDL-AD(2017)028-e, para. 115.

64 Karolina Kremens, 'The Authority to Order Search in Comparative Perspective: The Call for the Judicial Oversight' (2020) 6 (3) *Revista Brasileira di Direito Processual Penal* 1585, p. 1616.

65 Frequently in literature the term "complaint" is used interchangeably with the term "interlocutory appeal".

66 *Geraschenko v. Ukraine*, no. 20602/05, 7 November 2013, § 130.

judge. The system also lacks a separate judicial figure such as the German *Ermittlungsrichter* or Italian *giudice per le indagini preliminari* devoted to judicial activities during criminal investigation. Instead, the Polish law provides for certain general powers for the court during criminal investigation that are exercised by judges who also regularly sit on trials (Article 298 § 2 CCP). Importantly, the law does not provide for assigning one judge to one criminal investigation, which would increase the efficiency especially of complex cases. Instead, decisions concerning the same investigation may be undertaken by different random judges learning each time about the circumstances of the case, which seems a significant waste of time and resources. This also extends to judicial engagement during investigation in questioning of a witness if there is a risk that it will be impossible to examine him or her during the trial, e.g. due to the likely death of a witness (Article 316 § 3 CCP) or when special procedures for interrogations of vulnerable victims and witnesses are involved (Article 185a-c CCP). It recently led to a discussion on the pros and cons of introducing the investigative judge or judge for preliminary investigation back into the Polish system.[67]

The most important issue in this context is, nevertheless, the issue of exclusion of evidence resulting from illegal searches. Generally, the Polish system diversely regulates consequences of violation of the conditions of legality of evidence and evidentiary actions conducted during criminal investigation.[68] There are no rules that would comprehensively address the legality of evidence. However, some criteria that disqualify the evidence may be considered as exclusionary rules (*zakazy dowodowe*) that should be understood as instruments resolving conflicts between legally protected social and individual interests.[69] They can be systematized as the rules that prohibit the proving of certain facts,[70]

---

67 Cezary Kulesza, *Sędzia śledczy w modelu postępowania przygotowawczego na tle prawnoporównawczym*, Dział Wydawnictw Filii UW w Białymstoku, Białystok 1991 and Tomasz Grzegorczyk, 'Kilka refleksji na temat sugestii wprowadzenia instytucji sędziego śledczego' in Piotr Hofmański (ed), *Węzłowe problemy procesu karnego*, Wolters Kluwer, Warszawa 2010, pp. 105–14.

68 Wojciech Jasiński, *Nielegalnie uzyskane dowody w procesie karnym*, Wolters Kluwer, Warszawa 2019, p. 495.

69 Cf. Zbigniew Kwiatkowski, *Zakazy dowodowe w procesie karnym*, Zakamycze, Kraków 2005, p. 63–91.

70 This category consists of: prohibition of the use of force or illicit threats during interrogation or hypnosis, chemical substances or technical means in order to influence physical processes in the body of the testifying person or to allow monitoring of the unconscious reactions of the body; prohibition of obtaining testimonial evidence from the suspect/accused and witnesses as well as other statements in conditions precluding freedom of

rules that prohibit using certain sources of evidence[71] and rules that prohibit certain methods of acquiring evidence.[72] As the determination of criminal responsibility is stated as the most general aim of Polish criminal process (Article 2 § 2 (1) CCP), achieving this goal demands carefully establishing the facts of the case, which in some situations may collide with individual interests that must also be protected. Therefore, exclusionary rules are designed to balance many interests including human dignity, body integrity, inviolability of the home, family relations or certain privileges. These values are categorized as relating to the rule of law principle, protection of the rights and freedoms of individuals, integrity of the criminal justice system and the deterrent effect of such a rule. Some provisions even directly prohibit the use of such evidence. This concerns, for example, the consequences of taking evidence despite the direct prohibition to do so, which happens in the case of testimonies received under threat or violence (Article 171 § 7 CCP).

Despite the adoption of various rules that can be considered as exclusionary rules, the law does not provide directly for straightforward procedural consequences of a violation of provisions concerning search. The only direct restriction concerns not obtaining on time (within seven days) the confirmation of such a search conducted in exigent circumstances – in such a case the evidence must be returned to the owner (Article 230 § 1 CCP). As discussed above, there are also no legal consequences leading to the exclusion of evidence obtained disregarding the principle of proportionality (Article 227 CCP) as there are no consequences of breaking the set-out rules. As the Code is silent on implications of conducting a search against procedural requirements in this way, it is

---

expression and prohibition of supplementing testimonial evidence by documents and notes.

71 This category consists of: prohibition of interrogating a priest as to facts of which he learned during confession; prohibition of interrogating a defence counsel or a lawyer providing arrestee with legal advice on issues covered by lawyer–client privilege; prohibition of interrogating a mediator as to facts that he learned about from the accused or the victim during mediation; prohibition of obtaining an opinion from an expert witness who is incompetent to deliver such an opinion in that case due to his or her relation to the case or its participants; prohibition of the use of a statement of the accused made to a medical expert witness or to a physician providing medical assistance concerning the act that he or she is accused of; prohibition of a physical examination of a victim who has refused to testify executing his or her privilege.

72 This category consists of: prohibition of proving the committing of a crime for which the reoffending defendant has already been convicted; prohibition of proving a right contrary to a constitutive decision of another court; prohibition of proving the conduct of judges' deliberations and voting; prohibition of proving the content of testimony given by a witness who has exercised his or her right to refuse to testify; prohibition of proving facts and circumstances concerning the crown witness.

a matter of interpretation of existing rules in particular in the light of Constitution and ECHR standards.

The system became even more complicated after amending in 2016 the Code with a peculiar exclusionary rule emerging from Article 168a k.p.k.[73] Generally, this rule governs the admissibility of evidence obtained in violation of the rules of procedure or by means of an offence. Since 2016 the courts have engaged in the reinterpretation of Article 168 k.p.k. Numerous judgments provided some guidelines and for the most part argued for the clarification of this rule in the light of the Polish Constitution and international norms.[74] Although the direct reading of the provision leads to accepting all evidence into a criminal process, even those resulting from a crime, the proper analysis of this norm based on systemic interpretation allows for the identification of such evidence that should generally be considered as illegal and in consequence excluded.[75] This concerns evidence obtained through an offence or obtained by violating procedural rules if the person engaged in that process was a public official acting in his or her official capacity or in connection with behaviour of any person that constitutes murder, intentional injury to health or deprivation of liberty. However, the lack of direct rules leading to the exclusion of results of illegal searches and the need to find the ways of such inclusion through complicated interpretation of Code provisions and Constitutional rules makes the system very hard to accept. Unfortunately it also translates into practice that following the lack of direct exclusionary rules broadly admits illegally obtained evidence. Thus, the Polish system generally allows in practice more evidence to get into the system by not adopting strict regulations on the gathering of evidence during investigation, vesting in the hands of the court responsibility to evaluate it at the outcome of the trial.

6 Conclusions

Regardless of the need to conduct investigations to fight crime efficiently, the use of coercive measures must be performed only when certain grounds are

73 For a complex analysis of the reasons behind the adoption of this rule and its interpretations see Wojciech Jasiński, *Nielegalnie uzyskane dowody w procesie karnym*, Wolters Kluwer, Warszawa 2019, p. 502–524. See also Konrad Lipiński, 'Klauzula uadekwatniająca przesłanki niedopuszczalności dowodu w postępowaniu karnym (art. 168a k.p.k.)' (2016) 11 *Prokuratura i Prawo* 44, pp. 44–59.

74 Judgment of the Court of Appeal in Wrocław of 15 July 2016, II Aka 168/16 and Judgment of the Court of Appeal in Wrocław of 27 April 2017, II AKa 213/16.

75 Wojciech Jasiński, *Nielegalnie uzyskane dowody w procesie karnym*, Wolters Kluwer, Warszawa 2019, pp. 540–542.

met and may be conducted only according to procedural rules. Thus, the laws regulating when and how searches may be carried out must be clearly and coherently designed. But even the best laws might not be enough. As observed by the US Supreme Court – which remains also true for other criminal justice systems – "[u]ncontrolled search and seizure are the first and most effective weapons in the arsenal of every arbitrary government"[76]. Accordingly, establishing of who orders, performs and controls searches is as crucial as the rules designed to regulate their conduct.

In this context provisions concerning imposition, conduct and control over searches in the Polish criminal procedure must be considered as at least insufficient. First, the critique relates to the inadequate definition of the circumstances which would justify a search. The lack of a clearly prescribed threshold under which searches may be conducted, paired with the absence of relevant case law, give a very broad leeway for criminal justice authorities to carry out searches. This is particularly problematic in the case of searches conducted in exigent circumstances.

Second, serious reservations must be raised by the lack of regulation in Polish law of searches conducted with the use of modern technology. Shockingly, the power of the police to access smartphones and make immediate use of information found on various portable devices is not seriously questioned or generally perceived as demanding any legislative intervention. This example shows how carelessly Polish law treats the right to privacy, which is particularly easy to interfere with by electronic means. Therefore, it may be argued that the evidentiary standards are not differentiated enough depending on their level of interference with the rights and freedoms of an individual, which also relates to the digital evidence and evidence obtained by electronic means.

Third, the power given to the prosecutor to issue search warrants must also be criticized. Searches must be subjected to the scrutiny of an independent organ that would be entitled to authorize these measures prior to their execution and assess them when they have already taken place. The prosecutor cannot be regarded as such an authority as he or she does not have the same level of impartiality and independence as the judge. The close relation of the Polish Prosecution Service with the executive as well as the close cooperation built upon the individual cases investigated together with criminal justice agencies raise the chances that the prosecutor will become prejudiced towards the investigative actions planned and conducted by these agencies. The fact that searches with warrant are the vast minority of all searches does not seem

---

76 *Brinegar v US* 338 US 160 (1949) 180.

to change that perception. Admittedly, moving the power to order searches to the judiciary, in terms of deciding on interference in the sphere of civil rights, may not be the ultimate mechanism effectively preventing unnecessary interference with privacy but, undoubtedly, minimizes the possibility of such errors. Certainly, the judicial oversight of the searches does not ensure lawful and reasonable behaviour in all cases but undoubtedly increases the likelihood of protection of an individual's rights.

At the same time, providing in Polish law for the possibility of judicial review of all searches, regardless of whether conducted with warrant or not, must be evaluated positively. Despite being triggered by complaint of an individual who believes that his or her rights were affected by a search, the mere existence of a verification mechanism, at least in theory, allows judicial oversight over search practices. When compared to some other systems, where admittedly rigid exclusionary rules exist but only if the case reaches the trial stage, the motion for judicial review seems a remarkable tool allowing for early evaluation of the legality of searches. Nevertheless, the appreciation of this solution is lowered by the lack of adequate reasons for exclusion of evidence at this stage of proceedings. As there are no legal consequences leading to the exclusion of evidence obtained illegally or improperly while the principle of proportionality seems to apply only artificially, this may violate individual rights and freedoms.

7 Summary

It can happen that the rights and freedoms of the individual in the criminal process clash with certain measures used during the proceedings. Coercive instruments are used which can create issues related to the right to privacy, property and individual liberty. The use of such measures should not be absolute and limits are imposed on their implementation. This chapter deals with the limits of power in the Polish criminal proceedings in the context of coercive measures. Firstly, it presents the scope of Polish criminal investigations. It also describes the search and the circumstances under which it occurs. In addition, it presents the authority responsible for ordering and conducting the search. This part also presents remedies and the exclusion of evidence obtained through illegal search. The conclusion of this chapter is that coercive measures can only be used under the designated conditions and carried out according to procedures. However, Polish criminal procedure in this regard is not sufficiently responsive to the challenges of new technologies. There is also too broad a leeway for criminal justice authorities in this area. Furthermore, the role of the prosecutor in issuing search warrants is criticized.

Bibliography

Bulenda Teodor, Gruszczyńska Beata, Kremplewski Andrzej, Sobota Piotr, 'The Prosecution Service Function within the Polish Criminal Justice System' in Jörg-Martin Jehle and Marianne Wade (eds), *Coping with Overloaded Criminal Justice Systems. The Rise of Prosecutorial Power Across Europe*, Springer Berlin, Heidelberg 2010.

Caianiello Michele, *Increasing Discretionary Prosecutor's Powers: The Pivotal Role of the Italian Prosecutor in the Pretrial Investigation Phase*. Oxford Handbooks Online, Oxford 2016.

Cieślak Marek, *Zagadnienia dowodowe w procesie karnym*, Wydawnictwo Prawnicze, Warszawa 1955.

Damaška Mirjan, 'Evidentiary Barriers to Conviction and Two Models of Criminal Procedure: a Comparative Study' (1973) 121 *University of Pennsylvania Law Review* 506.

De Vocht Doris, 'Poland' in Ed Cape, Zaza Namoradze, Roger Smith, Taru Spronken (eds) *Effective Criminal Defence in Europe*, Intersentia, Antwerp 2010.

Di Amato Astolfo, *Criminal Law in Italy*, Kluwer Law International, Alphen aan den Rijn 2013.

Dudka Katarzyna, 'Wybrane problemy dochodzenia w sprawach o przestępstwa prywatnoskargowe' (2005) 6 *Prokuratura i Prawo*.

European Commission for Democracy Through Law (Venice Commission), Opinion on the Act on the Public Prosecutor's Office as Amended, No.892/2017, Strasbourg, 11 December 2017, https://www.venice.coe.int/webforms/documents/default.aspx?pdffile=CDL-AD(2017)028-e.

Gaberle Andrzej, *Dowody w sądowym procesie karnym*, Wolters Kluwer, Warszawa 2010.

Gerecka-Żołyńska Anna, 'Zasada ustności i pisemności' in: Paweł Wiliński (ed), *Zasady procesu karnego. System prawa karnego procesowego*, vol. III, part 1, Wolters Kluwer, Warszawa 2014.

Grabowska-Moroz Barbara (ed), *Prawo dostępu do obrońcy w świetle prawa europejskiego*, Helsinki Foundation for Human Rights, Warszawa 2018, https://www.hfhr.pl/wp-content/uploads/2018/05/Prawo-dostępu-do-obroncy-w-swietle-prawa-UE-20180410.pdf.

Grochowski Jacek, 'Podstawy dowodowe przeszukania w kodeksie postępowania karnego' (1992) 18 *PPK*.

Grochowski Jacek, 'Przeszukanie w procesie karnym jako instytucja wyznaczająca granice konstytucyjnych praw osobistych' (1991) 17 *PPK*.

Grzegorczyk Tomasz, *Kodeks postępowania karnego. Komentarz*, wyd. 6, tom I, Wolters Kluwer, Warszawa 2014.

Grzegorczyk Tomasz, 'Kilka refleksji na temat sugestii wprowadzenia instytucji sędziego śledczego' in Piotr.

Hofmański Piotr, 'Prawo do poszanowania prywatności (art. 17 Paktu i art. 8 Europejskiej Konwencji Praw Człowieka) a rozwiązania polskiego prawa karnego materialnego i procesowego' in Jan Skupiński and Jolanta Jakubowska-Har (eds) *Standardy praw człowieka a polskie prawo karne*, Scholar, Warszawa 1995.

Helsinki Foundation on Human Rights – *Wzmacnianie praw osób podejrzanych i oskarżonych. Rola krajowych instytucji ochrony praw człowieka*, Warszawa 2019, https://www.hfhr.pl/wp-content/uploads/2020/04/Wzmacnianie-praw-os%C3%B3b-podejrzanych-i-oskar%C5%BConych-NHRI-krajowy-web.pdf.

Hofmański Piotr (ed), *Węzłowe problemy procesu karnego*, Wolters Kluwer, Warszawa 2010.

Hofmański Piotr 'Zasada kontradyktoryjności' in Paweł Wiliński (ed), *Zasady procesu karnego. System prawa karnego procesowego*, vol. III, part 1, Wolters Kluwer, Warszawa 2014.

Informacja o wynikach działalności Centralnego Biura Antykorupcyjnego w 2017 r. [Information on the activities of the Central Anticorruption Bureau in 2017], https://cba.gov.pl/ftp/filmy/Informacja_o_wynikach_dzialalnosci_Centralnego_Biura_Antykorupcyjnego_w_2017_r..pdf.

Jasiński Wojciech, *Nielegalnie uzyskane dowody w procesie karnym*, Wolters Kluwer, Warszawa 2019.

Jasiński Wojciech, 'Zasada bezstronności sądu. Zasada niezawisłości i niezależności sądu' in Paweł Wiliński (ed), *Zasady procesu karnego. System prawa karnego procesowego*, vol. III, part 2, Wolters Kluwer, Warszawa 2014.

Jasiński Wojciech and Kremens Karolina, *Criminal Law in Poland*, Kluwer Law International, Alphen aan den Rijn 2019.

Jasiński Wojciech and Skorupka Jerzy (eds), *Ciężar dowodu i obowiązek dowodzenia w procesie karnym*, Wolters Kluwer, Warszawa 2017.

Kardas Piotr, 'Gwarancje praw jednostki na wstępnym etapie postępowania karnego w prawie europejskim i polskim' (2019) 1 *Europejski Przegląd Sądowy* 4.

Kmiecik Romuald (ed), *Prawo dowodowe. Zarys wykładu*, Wolters Kluwer, Warszawa 2008.

Koper Radosław 'Przeszukanie w wypadkach niecierpiących zwłoki' (2014) 11–12 *Prokuratura i Prawo* 14.

Kremens Karolina, Wojciech Jasiński, Dorota Czerwińska, Dominika Czerniak 'Poland. There and Back Again. A Struggle with Transposition of EU Directives' in G. Contissa et al. (eds) *Effective Protection of the Rights of the Accused in the EU Directives. A Computable Approach to Criminal Procedure Law*, Brill, Leiden 2022.

Kremens Karolina, 'Granice ingerencji w prawo do prywatności i prawo własności w postępowaniu karnym' in Jerzy Skorupka (ed), *Model dopuszczalnej ingerencji w prawa i wolności jednostki w procesie karnym*, C.H. Beck, Warszawa 2019.

Kremens Karolina, 'Limits of powers of public authorities with respect to obtaining evidence at the stage of investigation', in Biruta Lewaszkiewicz-Petrykowska (ed), *Rapports polonais – XXIe Congrès international de droit compare*, Wydawnictwo Uniwersytetu Łódzkiego, Łódź 2022.

Kremens Karolina, 'O znaczeniu prawa porównawczego dla nauki polskiego procesu karnego na przykładzie przeszukań telefonów komórkowych' in Paweł Wiliński, Dobrosława Szumiło-Kulczycka (eds) *W pogoni za rzetelnym procesem karnym. Księga Jubileuszowa Profesora Stanisława Waltosia*, Wolters Kluwer, Kraków 2022.

Kremens Karolina, *Powers of the Prosecutor in Criminal Investigation. A Comparative Perspective*, Routledge, New York 2021.

Kremens Karolina, 'The Authority to Order Search in Comparative Perspective: The Call for the Judicial Oversight' (2020) 6 (3) *Revista Brasileira di Direito Processual Penal* 1585.

Kulesza Cezary, *Sędzia śledczy w modelu postępowania przygotowawczego na tle prawnoporównawczym*, Dział Wydawnictw Filii UW w Białymstoku, Białystok 1991.

Kwiatkowski Zbigniew, *Zakazy dowodowe w procesie karnym*, Zakamycze, Kraków 2005.

Langer Maximo, 'The Long Shadow of the Adversarial and Inquisitorial Categories' in Markus D. Dubber and Tatjana Hörnle (eds) *The Oxford Handbook of Criminal Law*, Oxford University Press, Oxford 2014.

Lipiński Konrad, 'Klauzula uadekwatniająca przesłanki niedopuszczalności dowodu w postępowaniu karnym (art. 168a k.p.k.)' (2016) 11 *Prokuratura i Prawo* 44.

Newell Bryce C. and Koops Bert-Jaap, 'From horseback to the moon and back: comparative limits on police searches of smartphones upon arrest' (2020) 72 (1) *Hastings Law Journal* 229.

Paluszkiewicz Hanna, 'Zasada bezpośredniości' in Paweł Wiliński (ed), *Zasady procesu karnego. System prawa karnego procesowego*, vol. III, part 2, Wolters Kluwer, Warszawa 2014.

Panzavolta Michele, 'Reforms and Counter-Reforms in the Italian Struggle for an Accusatorial Criminal Law System' (2004) 30 *North Carolina Journal of International Law & Commercial Regulation* 577.

Raport Rzecznika Praw Obywatelskich z działalności Krajowego Mechanizmu Prewencji Tortur [Report of the Commissioner for Human Rights on the activities of the National Torture Prevention Mechanism], https://bip.brpo.gov.pl/sites/default/files/Raport_KMPT_2020_interaktywny.pdf.

Rogacka-Rzewnicka Maria, *Oportunizm i legalizm ścigania przestępstw w świetle współczesnych przeobrażeń procesu karnego,* Wolters Kluwer, Warszawa 2007.

Rogalski Maciej, *Podsłuch procesowy i pozaprocesowy*, Wolters Kluwer, Warszawa 2019.

Sakowicz Andrzej, 'Poszanowanie życia prywatnego w postępowaniu karnym' (2000) 6 *Jurysta* 21.

Skorupka Jerzy, 'Konstytucyjne i konwencyjne granice przeszukania w postępowaniu karnym (cz. II)' (2007) 11–12 *Palestra* 52.

Skorupka Jerzy, *Proces karny*, 3rd ed., Wolters Kluwer, Warszawa 2020.

Skorupka Jerzy, 'Zasada swobodnej oceny dowodów' in Paweł Wiliński (ed), *Zasady procesu karnego. System prawa karnego procesowego*, vol. III, part 2, Wolters Kluwer, Warszawa 2014.

Sobolewski Zbigniew and Artymiak Grażyna (eds), *Zasada prawdy materialnej. Materiały z konferencji*, Wolters Kluwer, Warszawa 2006.

Sprawozdanie z działalności powszechnych jednostek organizacyjnych prokuratury za rok 2019 [Report on the activities of prosecution service of Poland in 2019], https://pk.gov.pl/wp-content/uploads/2020/03/PK-P1K.pdf.

Steinborn Sławomir, 'Komentarz do art. 227 k.p.k.' in Sławomir Steinborn (ed), *Kodeks postępowania karnego. Komentarz do wybranych przepisów*, LEX/el. 2016.

Steinborn Sławomir, 'Problem organu uprawnionego do stosowania przeszukania w toku procesu karnego w świetle unormowań konstytucyjnych i prawnomiędzynarodowych' (2008) 19 *Gdańskie Studia Prawnicze.*

Wiliński Paweł (ed), *Kontradyktoryjność w polskim procesie karnym*, Wolters Kluwer, Warszawa 2013.

Zgryzek Kazimierz, 'Zasada jawności' in Paweł Wiliński (ed), *Zasady procesu karnego. System prawa karnego procesowego*, part 1, Wolters Kluwer, Warszawa 2014.

Żbikowska Małgorzata, *Ciężar dowodu w polskim procesie karnym*, Wolters Kluwer, Warszawa 2019.

Table of Legal Acts

Kodeks postępowania karnego, act of 6 June 1997 (Dz.U. 2017, poz. 1904).

Konstytucja Rzeczypospolitej Polskiej of 2nd April 1997 (Dz. U. z 1997 r., Nr 78, poz. 483).

Rozporządzenie Ministra Sprawiedliwości w sprawie organów uprawnionych obok Policji do prowadzenia dochodzeń oraz organów uprawnionych do wnoszenia i popierania oskarżenia przed sądem pierwszej instancji w sprawach, w których prowadzono dochodzenie, jak również zakresu spraw zleconych tym organom [Regulation of the Minister of Justice on criminal justice agencies authorized, apart from the police, to conduct investigations and agencies authorized to bring and support charges before the court of first instance in cases where inquiries have been conducted, as well as the scope of cases commissioned to these bodies] of 22 September 2015, Dz.U. 2015 poz. 1725.

Ustawa o lasach [Forest Act] of 28 September 1991, Dz. U. 2021, poz. 1275 with amendments.

Ustawa o Policji [Police Act] of 6 April 1990, Dz.U. 2023 poz. 171.
Ustawa – Prawo łowieckie [Hunting Law] of 13 October 1995, Dz. U. 2022 poz. 1173.
Ustawa o Straży Granicznej of 2 October 1990 [Border Guard Act], Dz.U. 2022 poz. 1061

Table of Cases

Brinegar v US 338 US 160 (1949) 180.
Buck v. Germany, no. 41604/98, 28 April 2005.
Geraschenko v. Ukraine, no. 20602/05, 7 November 2013.
Halford v. The United Kingdom, no. 20605/92, 25 June 1997.
Heino v. Finland, no. 56720/09, 15 February 2011.
Judgment of the Court of Appeal in Wrocław of 15 July 2016, II Aka 168/16.
Judgment of the Court of Appeal in Wrocław of 27 April 2017, II AKa 213/16.
Mozer v. The Republic of Moldova and Russia, no. 11138/10, 23 February 2016.
Ratushna v. Ukraine, no. 17318/06, 2 December 2010.
Sallinen and Others v. Finland, no. 50882/99, 27 September 2005.
Smirnov v. Russia, no. 71362/01, 7 June 2007.

CHAPTER 7

Limits of Freedom of Public Authorities with Respect to Obtaining Evidence at the Stage of Investigation

Canadian Report

Alexandre Stylios and Gustave Warby***

1 Most Distinctive Features of Evidence System and Major Procedural Principles of Examining and Evaluating Evidence in Canada

Canada's law of evidence is characterised by its adversarial nature, i.e. the judge plays a primarily neutral role, while each party adduces its own evidence. It is also a system of 'legal' evidence. In other words, the evidence that each party leads must conform to certain general and exclusionary rules, be they statutory or found at common law. While a judge may intervene *proprio motu* in relation to the admissibility of a particular piece of evidence,[1] it is generally incumbent

* Professor, Faculty of Law, Université Laval (Quebec, Canada).
** LL.B candidate (class of '22).

1 See for example the application of s. 276 of the *Criminal Code* in *R v Barton*, 2019 SCC 33 "Section 276 of the Criminal Code governs the admissibility of evidence about a complainant's prior sexual activities and the uses to which that evidence may be put. The animating purposes behind the s. 276 regime are to protect the integrity of the trial by excluding irrelevant and misleading evidence, protect the accused's right to a fair trial, and encourage the reporting of sexual offences by protecting the security and privacy of complainants. Section 276(1) provides that in proceedings in respect of certain listed offences, evidence of a complainant's prior sexual activity is not admissible to support an inference that, by reason of the sexual nature of that activity, the complainant is more likely to have consented to the sexual activity in question or is less worthy of belief. This section is categorical in nature and applies irrespective of which party led the evidence. Section 276(2) provides that evidence of the complainant's prior sexual activity adduced by or on behalf of the accused is presumptively inadmissible unless, after certain procedures have been followed, the trial judge rules to the contrary. The s. 276 regime applies to any proceeding in which an offence listed in s. 276(1) has some connection to the offence charged, even if no listed offence was particularized in the charging document. Crown-led prior sexual activity evidence is subject to the common law principles articulated in R. v. Seaboyer, [1991] 2 S.C.R. 577."

 | DOI:10.1163/9789004710320_009

upon a party to raise objections to said evidence at the moment at which it is led by the opposing party.

In order to be admissible, evidence must be relevant which is a fundamental principal in most law of evidence in common law jurisdiction.[2] This question of law is up to the trial judge. The principle that any evidence relevant to the litigation is admissible is accompanied by several exceptions. They are governed by rules excluding certain forms of evidence, such as hearsay or character evidence. The application of these rules is also the responsibility of the trial judge. The trier of fact (such as the jury) who will have to rule on the guilt or innocence of the accused will have to assess the credibility of the evidence, such as testimony. Outside of jury trials, the single judge serves as trial judge and trier of fact.

Contrary to some other commonwealth jurisdictions, Canada is yet to fully codify its law of evidence. Although the *Canada Evidence Act* provides a statutory framework for certain evidentiary rules, it is far from a full codification of the applicable rules, most of which still stem from the common law. Another salient feature of the law of evidence in Canadian criminal law is the principle of constitutionalism. As the *Constitution Act, 1982*[3] is the supreme law of the land, all rules governing the conditions of obtaining and adducing of evidence must conform with those rights that are constitutionally entrenched, notably but not exclusively: s. 7 (Life, liberty and security of persons);[4] s. 8 (protection against illegal search and seizure);[5] s. 9 (protection against unlawful detention and arrest)[6] and s. 10b) (right to instruct counsel).[7] The Canadian *Charter of Rights and Freedoms* provides for remedy in the event that these rights are violated, notably at ss. 24(1) (just and appropriate remedy)[8] and 24(2) (exclusion

2 As the Canadian Supreme court ruled in R v Corbett, [1988] SCC 385 : "The organizing principles of the law of evidence may be simple stated. All relevant evidence is admissible, subject to a discretion to exclude matters".

3 The Constitution Act, 1982, Schedule B to the Canada Act 1982 (UK), 1982, c 11 (the "*Charter of Rights and Freedoms*").

4 Section 7 : "Everyone has the right to life, liberty and security of the person and the right not to be deprived thereof except in accordance with the principles of fundamental justice."

5 Section 8 : "Everyone has the right to be secure against unreasonable search or seizure".

6 Section 9 : "Everyone has the right not to be arbitrarily detained or imprisoned".

7 Section 10b) : "Everyone has the right on arrest or detention : [...] to retain and instruct counsel without delay and to be informed of that right;".

8 Section 24(1) : "Anyone whose rights or freedoms, as guaranteed by this Charter, have been infringed or denied may apply to a court of competent jurisdiction to obtain such remedy as the court considers appropriate and just in the circumstances".

of evidence obtained via a violation of one's constitutional rights).[9] Furthermore, any law or regulation found to be in contradiction with the Constitution may be impugned pursuant to s. 52 of the *Constitution Act, 1982*. Finally, it is also to be noted that, pursuant to s. 91(27) the *Constitution Act, 1867*,[10] criminal law (including both evidentiary and procedural matter) falls within the purview of the federal parliament.

2 Public Authorities Are Entitled to Acquire Evidence in a Criminal Action at the Stage of Investigation

2.1 *Notion: Public Authorities Are Entitled to Carry Out Investigations*

a) *Please indicate legal grounds or other sources giving rise to the competence of appropriate authorities to carry out investigations, within which to examine evidence. In addition to the traditional law enforcement authorities of the prosecutor and the police, are any other entities admissible, such as special forces or specialised administrative authorities? What is the scope of their procedural competence and how can their procedural position be defined vis-à-vis the traditional enforcement authorities? Can a growing significance be found in the participation in criminal investigations of specialised law enforcement authorities, other than the traditional group of investigation bodies? Can the phenomenon of normative disintegration be observed, paving the way for numerous public authorities to conduct investigations in criminal cases?*

Powers to carry out investigations and to examine evidence are found both at common law and in statute, most notably the *Criminal Code* (hereafter, Cr.C.). While certain 'classic' powers are explicitly provided for in statute – notably the issuing of warrants, s. 487 et seq. Cr.C.–, there are nonetheless a wide range of investigatory powers that are still found at common law. For example, in 2004, the Supreme Court of Canada (SCC) held in *R v Mann*,[11] that the common law provides for the legal detention of a suspect for investigative purposes where the detaining officer has reasonable grounds to suspect their involvement in the commission of an offence and that the detention is objectively

9 Section 24(2) : "Where, in proceedings under subsection (1), a court concludes that evidence was obtained in a manner that infringed or denied any rights or freedoms guaranteed by this Charter, the evidence shall be excluded if it is established that, having regard to all the circumstances, the admission of it in the proceedings would bring the administration of justice into disrepute".

10 The Constitution Act, 1867, 30 & 31 Vict, c 3.

11 R v Mann, 2004 SCC 92.

warranted in light of the circumstances. These powers stem from the so-called ancillary powers doctrine was first used in *R v Dedman*,[12] reaffirmed in *Fleming v Ontario*.[13] The ancillary powers doctrine permits the police to infringe a citizen's individual liberty, provided that the infringement is 'ancillary to the fulfilment of recognized police duties'.[14] Common law of police have been described as the preservation of the peace, the prevention of crime and the protection of life and property.[15]

In Canada, the majority of investigations are undertaken by traditional law enforcement agencies, notably the Royal Canadian Mounted Police (RCMP), as well as provincial and local police forces. However, it should be noted that certain administrative agencies possessing delegated powers may also initiate investigations. For example, the Commissioner of Competition possesses broad investigative powers pursuant to Part II of the *Competition Act*.[16] These powers include *ex parte* applications for warrants (s. 15) and the ability to compel witnesses (s. 11–2). Furthermore, where the Commissioner believes that the commission of an offence has occurred pursuant to Part VI of the Act, they may remit the matter to the Attorney General of Canada (AG). Should the evidence be sufficiently compelling, criminal proceedings may, at the behest of the AG, be instituted by the Public Prosecution Service of Canada (PPSC) against the accused. The expansive powers accorded to the Commissioner of Competition are illustrative not only of the phenomenon of normative disintegration amongst public authorities charged with the application of the law, but also with the continuing expansion of the administrative state in Canada.

It should be noted that an audit conducted by an administrative body may be considered as a criminal investigation if the predominant purpose of the particular inquiry is the determination of penal liability. In order to determine whether such an audit has "crossed the Rubicon", "courts must assess the totality of the circumstances, and make a determination as to whether the inquiry or question in issue engages the adversarial relationship between the state and the individual".[17] Factors to be considered may vary depending the

12 R v Dedman, 1985 SCC 2.

13 Fleming v Ontario, 2019 SCC 45.

14 *Ibid*, para 45: "The basis of the doctrine is that police actions that interfere with individual liberty are permitted at common law if they are ancillary to the fulfillment of recognized police duties. Intrusions on liberty are accepted if they are reasonably necessary – in accordance with the test set out below – in order for the police to fulfill their duties".

15 R v Dedman, 1985 SCC 2 para 14.

16 Competition Act, RSC, 1985, c. C-34.

17 R v Jarvis, [2002] 3 SCR 757.

organizational settings of the provincial or federal governmental departments or agencies involved.

b) *Do public law enforcement authorities enjoy a monopoly (exclusivity) of investigation rights in criminal cases, or do they share this competence with private entities (e.g. as part of private investigations or in the case of less serious actions being brought by private prosecution)? Where a given legal system envisages separate proceedings in actions brought by private prosecution, can public law enforcement authorities participate in them and if yes, what is the extent of that participation? Does it cover the right to examine evidence?*

In practice, public law enforcement agencies enjoy a monopoly of investigative rights in relation to criminal litigation. Even in the case of private prosecutions, all information pertaining to the allegation of criminal conduct in question must first be submitted to a justice of the peace (s. 504 Cr.C.), who subsequently refers the matter to a provincial court judge for examination (s. 507.1 Cr.C.). The provisions relating to public prosecution at s. 507 Cr.C. continue to apply, and the presiding judge is required to provide reasonable notice to the Attorney General before summons or warrants are issued. Furthermore, the Supreme court of Canada has held that both the Attorney General and the Crown have the power to enter a stay of proceedings following the hearing.[18] Thus, the right of private citizens to instigate criminal proceedings are greatly curtailed and a fairly rare occurrence in Canadian criminal law where criminal prosecution is largely considered a prerogative of the state, even if private investigation have some history in common law.

2.2 *Court's Right to Acquire Evidence at the Investigation Stage or Its Controlling Activities in Relation to Evidence Examined by Other Entities*

a) *Is the court entitled to examine evidence at the stage of investigation and if yes, can it admit evidence ex officio or only at the parties' request, or are both those solutions possible simultaneously? Does the format of court investigation apply?*

Given the adversarial nature of courts in Canada, evidence is usually examined when it is adduced, be it by the Crown or by the defence. Usually, this examination takes place during trial through a "*voir dire*" (a separate hearing) in case a jury is present. The judge (trier of law) in charge of the trial will determine if the evidence is admissible. However, where charges have been laid against

18 R v Dowson, [1983] 2 SCR 144, and McHale v Ontario, 2010 ONCA 361 (leave to appeal refused, [2010] S.C.C.A. No. 290).

the accused, and in the absence of a plea of guilty, the court must instigate s. 515 Cr.C proceedings for interim release if the accused has not been released by the police or if the judge ruled against such a release. The right to not be denied pre-trial bail without reasonable cause stems from the presumption of innocence enshrined at s. 11e) of the Canadian *Charter of Rights and Freedoms* (Charter).[19] Therefore, the presiding judge may make 'such inquiries [...] as he considers desirable', s. 518(1)(a) Cr.C. As this process is largely informal, the normal rules of evidence do not apply.[20] Likewise, a judge may examine evidence during a preliminary inquiry. Once more, the rules of evidence are less stringent than during the evidentiary phase of a trial and the judge may receive and examine evidence that would otherwise be inadmissible where it is deemed to be 'credible or trustworthy', pursuant to s. 540(7) Cr.C. As set out in Part XVIII of Cr.C., the role of discovery at the stage of the preliminary inquiry is to determine whether, in light of the *prima facie* reliability of the evidence, a jury duly instructed could return a verdict of guilty.[21] Accordingly, the inquiry does not take the form of a trial and the powers of the judge to compel the production of certain evidence are limited.[22]

b) *At the investigation stage, does the court or another body hold the controlling rights in relation to evidentiary activities taken by law enforcement authorities and if yes, what controlling measures are afforded (e.g. does the examination of a specific piece of evidence require the court to give its prior consent)? What are the consequences of a failure to satisfy the condition of the court's or another entity's consent and other conditions from the perspective of the validity and effectiveness of the evidence examined? Can the specification of such pieces of evidence and the conditions of their admissibility established by the law be viewed as sufficient?*

The answer to these questions is yes. The Canadian courts exercise significant oversight regarding certain evidentiary activities of law enforcement agencies at the investigative stage. The most notable of these is the power to issue warrants. Notwithstanding the reasonability test developed in *R v Collins*,[23] as unauthorised searches violate one's s. 8 Charter right to privacy, it is generally necessary for the police to procure a warrant before proceeding. In the case of a search warrant, the police must demonstrate that they have reasonable grounds to believe that they will uncover objects of evidentiary nature, or that

19 R v Antic, 2017 SCC 27.
20 Toronto Star Newspapers Ltd. v Canada, 2010 SCC 21.
21 R v Arcuri, 2001 SCC 54 and R v Ireland, 2005 ONCJ 218.
22 Patterson v The Queen, [1970] SCR 409.
23 R v Collins, [1987] 1 SCR 265.

have been used in the commission of a crime, or that the search will reveal the whereabouts of a suspect, s. 487(1) Cr.C. As the SCC held in *R v Buhay*,[24] the burden of proof in establishing reasonable grounds lies with the Crown. Should the search be undertaken without prior authorisation, evidence uncovered therein may be deemed inadmissible according to the standard articulated by the SCC in *R v Grant*,[25] and reaffirmed in *R v Le*.[26]

c) *Is there a procedure at the investigation stage that enables the parties and their counsels to challenge the evidence examined in violation of the applicable principles? If yes, please present it briefly, taking into account the procedural consequences of its usage (the application of the principle of automatic exclusion of evidence; the recognition of invalidity of evidence; the judge's right to assess the consequences of a method adopted to acquire evidence and evidence content) as well as the legal consequences for those who violated the law; please indicate the level of imperativeness of responses to a violation concerning the acquisition and examination of evidence, based on the applicable law and standpoints of doctrine and judicature.*

Given the adversarial nature of Canada's courts and the absence of an investigating judge, the accused is incapable of challenging evidence at the investigatory stage.

3 Principles of Acquiring Evidence at the Stage of Investigation

a) *Normative grounds for evidentiary activities in a criminal action (the Constitution, procedural criminal law, police law, administrative law, regulations, instructions, guidelines, common law, others). Can a multitude of sources of regulations in this area be referred to or is there normative homogeneity in place?*

There is no normative homogeneity concerning evidentiary matters in criminal litigation in Canada. A multitude of different rules flows from different sources: the Constitution, the common law, statute (both federal and provincial), as well as regulations and internal guidelines that govern the conduct of Crown prosecutors and the police.

b) *Does the applicable law regulate the principles of evidentiary activities taken by law enforcement authorities restrictively (on a tight-rein basis)*

24 R v Buhay, 2003 SCC 30.
25 R v Grant, 2009 SCC 32.
26 R v Le, 2019 SCC 34.

> *and, similarly – determine the consequences of violations committed by the investigators, or does it leave to them a broad discretion in the search for evidence followed by the court's right to discretionarily assess the collected evidentiary material and by the confrontation of evidence during a verbal and contradictory trial at court?*

The evidence collected by law enforcement agencies during their investigation is generally only assessed as it is led by the prosecution during the evidentiary phase of the trial or during a *voir dire*. While evidence that is otherwise admissible may be subject to exclusion by virtue of the judge's discretionary powers, *R v Seaboyer*,[27] the opposite cannot be said to be true; indeed, evidence that is inadmissible may not be deemed admissible through the sole exercise of judicial discretion, *R v Collins*.[28]

In fact, the use of judicial discretion allows the judge not to admit relevant and admissible evidence if he considers that its probative value is too low in relation to the prejudice it causes to the accused.[29] Canadian law allows the judge to exclude evidence that could affect the fairness of the proceedings when it does not have great probative value. It is up to the jury to assess the probative value of evidence. The application of the Charter and the principles of fairness it protects does not have the effect of setting aside the rules of evidence, and in particular the fundamental rule of relevance, in favor of judicial discretion based on the perception of the judge as to the probative value of evidence.[30]

In front of a jury, the judge should take care to hear the evidence without the presence of the jury, before excluding it in the exercise of his judicial discretion. In *R v Seaboyer*, the Supreme Court recognized that the exercise of judicial discretion even allowed the judge to exclude otherwise admissible evidence presented by the defence. The Court, however, sets out a rule of caution in such a case, "*because rare are the cases of exclusion of truly relevant and reliable evidence, particularly when this evidence is presented in support of a defence*".[31]

The exercise of judicial discretion is generally applied when the evidence tends to show the bad character of the accused or his propensity to commit crimes. This does not mean that relevant evidence which also tends to show the accused's bad character or propensity to commit crimes cannot be admitted.

27 R v Seaboyer, [1991] 2 SCR 577.
28 R v Collins, [1987] 1 SCR 265.
29 R v Seaboyer, [1991] 2 SCR 577.
30 R v Buric, (1996) 106 CCC (3d) 97 (CA Ont).
31 R v Seaboyer, [1991] 2 SCR 577.

As Supreme court, Judge Lamer J. stated in *R v Morris*,[32] such evidence will be admissible provided the judge first determines its admissibility by comparing its probative value with respect to the issue raised (for example, the identity) and the detrimental effect they are likely to have.

Moreover, pursuant to s. 24(2) of the Charter, the type of violation and the gravity of the conduct in question plays a major role in the determination of the admissibility or exclusion of evidence that is obtained in contravention of Charter rights, *R v Grant*.[33] Three groups of factors will need to be considered with respect to the exclusion of evidence under subsection 24(2) of the Charter:

1. the effect of the admission of the evidence on the fairness of the trial;
2. the seriousness of the violation;
3. the effect of the exclusion of evidence on the repute of the administration of justice.

Within these three groups, various other factors are set out, but do not constitute formal exclusionary factors to avoid transforming the exclusionary rule into an immutable rule, thus allowing the courts to consider the long-term consequences of exclusion or use of the evidence obtained.

c) *Are there any criteria of the legality of evidence and criteria that disqualify the same established by the law? What role does the judicature play in establishing such criteria?*

Given that the majority of rules governing the law of evidence in Canada are primarily found at common law, the judiciary plays a central role in clarifying the law, creating new rules and ensuring their evolution, as well as articulating standards. The courts must also ensure that those common law rules conform to the values that undergird the Charter.[34] Notwithstanding a specific exclusionary rule, the essential criterion by which evidence may be deemed admissible or inadmissible is relevance, either logical or legal.[35] Logical relevance can be defined as the relationship between the proven fact and the fact that we seek to establish. Often it is a question of logic and common sense. For example, the motive for the crime may be used to prove *mens rea*, even if the motive is not an essential element of the crime.[36] In principle, all relevant evidence will be admissible unless excluded by statute or common law. Conversely, the

32 R v Morris, [1983] 2 SCR 190.

33 R v Grant, 2009 SCC 32.

34 *Hill v Church of Scientology of Toronto*, [1995] 2 SCR 1130.

35 R v Lewis, [1979] 2 SCR 821, R v Morris, [1983] 2 S.C.R. 190, and reaffirmed recently in R v White, 2011 SCC 13.

36 R v Lewis, [1979] 2 SCR 821.

judge can refuse the administration of evidence that has no relevance to the dispute. Relevant evidence may be excluded by a rule of law or rule of evidence which renders it inadmissible. Thus, evidence of a propensity to commit crimes, or even evidence of a propensity to commit a crime such as the one charged, cannot be admitted into evidence.[37]

d) *Does the principle of freedom, meaning that any evidentiary measure and any evidentiary method are admissible (except those that a limine are unacceptable in civilized world), apply to the acquisition of evidence at the investigation stage? Or is it restricted by the applicability of general principles of the law, e.g. legalism, reliability, proportionality, necessity, and values such as human dignity, bodily inviolability, or the right to privacy? Where references are explicitly missing in the law to the aforesaid standards, on what basis are those standards applied? How do doctrine and case law understand the notion of 'fair evidentiary procedure'? Is this notion autonomous or does it constitute a part of the notion of 'fair trial'?*

As we have noted, the central governing principle upon which evidence is deemed to be admissible is that of its relevance. However, evidence, despite its ostensible relevance, may be subject to a series of exclusionary rules. The first of these could be described as a rule of proportionality. In *R v Wray*,[38] the SCC held that where the prejudicial nature of otherwise admissible evidence greatly outweighs its probative value, the presiding judge may declare it inadmissible as a means of ensuring procedural fairness. Where evidence is subject to an exclusionary rule, it may nonetheless be admissible in accordance with an exception to the exception. This is notably the case of necessity where evidence is deemed inadmissible pursuant to the hearsay rule. In *R v Khan*,[39] the SCC established a case-by-case exception to the hearsay rule known as the 'principled approach'. Where the hearsay evidence is both necessary and reliable, it may be deemed admissible.[40] Other rules, notably those pertaining to human dignity, bodily inviolability and the right to privacy are constitutionally enshrined in the Charter and raise the possibility of exclusion pursuant to s. 24(2). Procedural fairness is not an autonomous notion, but rather one that englobes the entire trial. In this regard, 'fair evidentiary procedure' falls within the scope of procedural fairness.[41] In Canada, procedural fairness and natural justice are derived from the common law and include the right to be heard

---

37 R v Morris, [1983] 2 SCR 190.
38 R v Wray, [1971] 1 SCR 272.
39 R v Kahn, [1990] 2 SCR 531.
40 R v Khelawon, 2006 SCC 57.
41 R v Harrer, [1995] 3 SCR 562.

(*audi alteram partem*) and the right to a hearing before an impartial adjudicative body (*nemo judex in sua causa*). Since 1982, these protections have been afforded to the accused in criminal matters by the Charter, notably ss. 7 and 11d). It should be noted that the scope of procedural fairness in contemporary Canadian criminal law goes far beyond that of the traditionally limited common law notions of natural justice. Furthermore, as the SCC held in *R v Rodgers*,[42] what is fair is highly context dependent and varies from case-to-case.

e) *Is the acquisition of evidence at the investigation stage restricted by concrete prohibitions, e.g. the prohibition to use specific sources of evidence or evidentiary methods (please indicate the level of subordination of evidentiary activities to strict law; or maybe this situation depends on the nature of evidence, e.g. its interference in human rights and freedoms, or on the type of crime)? Please indicate examples of evidentiary activities that are subject to the strictest legal restrictions.*

The prohibition of different investigatory methods is almost entirely dependent on the context and the gravity of the infringement upon one's rights. For example, although entry into a dwelling house without an entry warrant will normally be prohibited, there are exceptions to the rule: e.g. imminent danger to life, s. 529.3(1) Cr.C.,[43] and 'hot pursuit'.[44] Where the violation of one's rights is particularly flagrant and serious, there may be a quasi-automatic prohibition of the evidence obtained. This is often the case where DNA evidence is taken from the accused while detained, without prior consent and unlawfully.[45] Even so, an exception may still apply where the DNA sought is not that of the accused, although the sample is taken directly from their body.[46] Prohibitions are often most strictly enforced where they pertain to legal privileges. Nonetheless, privileges are also still subject to certain exceptions.

f) *Does the applicable law sufficiently define the boundaries of evidence acquisition admissibility, or maybe too categorically? What is the potential extent of the non-normative sphere in shaping such boundaries (general rules, pragmatism, habits)? Are the proportions between the two spheres (normative and non-normative) appropriate?*

Over the last 40 years, the SCC has largely elucidated and delineated the boundaries of evidence admissibility. While not all aspects of evidence acquisition constitute trite law, they are generally well known and not subject to a large

42 R v Rodgers, 2006 SCC 15

43 See also R v Patterson, 2017 SCC 15.

44 Tétard v R, 2010 QCCA 2235.

45 R v Stillman, [1997] 1 RCS 607, and R v Fearon, 2014 SCC 77.

46 R v Saeed, 2016 SCC 24.

amount of uncertainty. Where a degree of uncertainty may arise is in cases where the SCC has called for an explicitly contextual analysis. This is notably the case when analysing Charter violations. In 2009, in *R v Grant*,[47] the SCC overruled the quasi-automatic exclusionary rule that it had previously established in *R v Collins*.[48] In doing so, the Court sought to strike a balance between boundaries that were too categorical and those that were insufficiently defined. Additionally, the SCC has taken a largely pragmatic and teleological approach to evidentiary matters, particularly in regard to those who are vulnerable and whose testimony would normally be inadmissible – namely, minors and those who are developmentally disabled.[49]

g) *As regards the acquisition of evidence during investigation, how at this stage is the deficit of the inapplicability of principles of equality of parties, equality of arms, and the contradictory principle compensated for, also taking into account the fact of general primacy of law enforcement authorities, in order to ensure a fair evidentiary procedure? Can the suspect and other entities share in this?*

In order to mitigate the deleterious effects of the vast imbalance between the state and the accused, certain rights are afforded the accused by the Charter: for example, the protection from self-incrimination (ss. 11c) and 13), the presumption of innocence (s. 11d)) and the right to instruct counsel (s. 10b)). Moreover, s. 7 of the Charter provides for full answer and defence. Thus, the SCC held in *R v Stinchcombe*[50] and reaffirmed in *R v McNeil*,[51] that all relevant evidence – inculpatory and exculpatory – that is not subject to privilege must be disclosed to the defence by the Crown. This includes third party evidence where it is likely to be relevant.[52] In exceptional circumstances a stay of proceedings may be an appropriate remedy pursuant to s. 24(1) of the Charter where it can be demonstrated that the Crown has failed to disclose relevant evidence and that the absence of disclosure has been highly prejudicial to the accused's right to a full defence.[53]

h) *Is there a balance between the freedom of law enforcement authorities' actions, on which the crime combating efficiency depends, and limitations of that freedom arising from the need to ensure appropriate standards of evidentiary procedure? Does a comparison of those antagonistic to some*

47 R v Grant, 2009 SCC 32.
48 R v Collins, [1987] 1 SCR 265.
49 R v Khan, [1990] 2 SCR. 531, and R v D.A.I., 2012 SCC 5.
50 *R v Stinchcombe*, [1991] 3 SCR 326.
51 R v McNeil, 2009 SCC 3.
52 R v Gubbins, 2018 SCC 44.
53 R v O'Connor, [1995] 4 SCR 411.

extent perspectives show that the purpose of repression dominates at the expense of the procedural guarantees and the rights of individuals, or rather the purpose of the reliability of evidence at the expense of its effectiveness in the detection of the truth?

As we have noted above, the criminal justice system in Canada attempts to strike a balance between, on the one hand, the need for repression of criminal activity, which is injurious for society, and, on the other, the protection of the individual who finds themselves at the mercy of the state's vastly superior power. *Cf.*, all of the examples, *supra*.

i) *How can the fairness of evidentiary procedure be ensured in view of the conditions imposed by the commonly used consensual procedures, methods directed towards accelerating or shortening criminal proceedings, and the usage of alternative methods for criminal prosecution? Those measures not only fail to eliminate the issue of the boundaries of legal acquisition of evidence, but bring this issue into focus in connection with the conclusiveness of evidence being examined at the investigation stage. In these circumstances, are procedural guarantees ensured during the evidentiary procedure, together with due control over its legality at the investigation stage, bearing in mind the pressure for attaining the goal and swiftly end the proceedings?*

Privilege applies where the defence has entered into settlement discussions with the Crown, regardless of whether or not the negotiations are ultimately conclusive.[54] Furthermore, the SCC has established presumptive ceilings beyond which delays are unreasonable and which may lead to a stay of proceedings.[55]

4 Identifications of Risks of Violating Freedom in the Acquisition of Evidence by Law Enforcement Authorities

a) Narrow focus of enforcement authorities to acquire evidence of being guilty; oppressive investigative methods; violation of human dignity; use of measures compelling individuals to meet certain evidentiary obligations, or use of a passive tactic consisting in provoking the suspect or other entities into providing evidence. What measures are taken to counteract such practices?

Most measures relate to the exclusion of evidence (s. 24(2) of the Charter) or a stay of proceedings (s. 24(1) of the Charter), as noted above. Sometimes, they

54 R v Delchev, 2015 ONCA 381.

55 R v Jordan, 2016 SCC 27.

may result in damages being awarded, particularly where a court makes findings of bad faith or malice on the part of the Crown.[56]

b) *A tendency to hierarchize evidence in favour of scientific evidence and at the expense of other pieces of evidence. Can an a priori privileged treatment of such evidence be seen as a threat to the legality and fairness of evidentiary procedure in connection with unsatisfactory motivation of enforcement authorities to verify and critically evaluate the same, and with the limited opportunities for private parties to challenge the same?*

It may be a threat in certain circumstances. Nonetheless, scientific evidence remains subject to the standard articulated by the SCC in *R v Mohan.*[57] 9. It must be (1) logically relevant (2) necessary in assisting the trier of fact (3) it must not be subject to an exclusionary rule (4) the expert must be sufficiently qualified and (5) the court must undertake a cost-benefit analysis regarding the reliability of the evidence. It is incumbent upon the judge not to be obsequious and uncritical when scrutinising the scientific evidence that is adduced, i.e. the judge must not abdicate their role as the ultimate arbiter when evaluating the admissibility of evidence and –in the absence of a jury – its probative value.

More specifically, according to *Mohan*, the logical connection must be significant when the expertise uses a new scientific theory or technique. In that case, we evoke the idea of a decisive expertise: the judge will be more vigilant to check how far the evidence is logically related to the fact that it tends to establish. He should ask himself the following questions:

- What is the nature of the matter to which the evidence, (an important or incidental/crucial matter or accessory)?
- The deductions drawn from the new scientific theory are they really related to a substantive issue?
- What is the magnitude of the deductions presented (thin or considerable)? What is the part of subjective interpretation in the given scientific explanation?
- What is the degree of adequacy of the scientific evidence by relation to the fact that it proves in the dispute (relevance substantial)? Does abstract theory apply to facts? facts of the cause?

c) *Different boundaries for the freedom of law enforcement authorities to acquire evidence depending on the crime type; a failure by legal regulations to keep up with new technologies to be used in cases for most serious crimes gives rise to a threat of abuse and potentially easier excuse of such practices. How can the present legal regulation be assessed from this perspective*

56 Henry v British Columbia (Attorney General), 2015 SCC 24.

57 R v Mohan, [1994] 2 SCR 9.

(e.g. as to cyber or biological evidence) in the context of threats to the fairness of evidentiary procedure? Are other regulatory standards in place or are any such standards tolerated, being different from those as in the case of traditional evidence?

The law of evidence in Canada provides for the adducing of electronic or 'cyber' evidence. The *Canada Evidence Act*, as well as most, if not all, provincial Evidence Acts establish a framework that permits each party to lead electronic evidence and to prove the contents of the documents tendered. Apart from certain procedural differences, the nature of electronic evidence not substantially different from that of 'real', physical evidence. Thus, the law has been able to keep up with technological developments over the last 20 to 30 years. Furthermore, the federal government, as well as most provinces, have adopted legislation that seeks to protect the personal information of private citizens. Where risk of procedural unfairness arises is primarily in the realm of counter-terrorism legislation, notably Part II.1 Cr.C., and the *Anti-terrorism Act*.[58]

5 Inviolable Boundaries in the Acquisition of Evidence by Law Enforcement Authorities

a) *Please indicate violations in the acquisition of evidence that make the evidence definitely invalid (i.e. indicate prohibited methods of proving facts);*

It is difficult to speak of truly 'inviolable' boundaries in Canadian criminal law. Indeed, s. 1 of the Charter provides that rights may be subject to 'such reasonable limits prescribed by law as can be demonstrably justified in a free and democratic society'. The s. 1 test was first articulated by the SCC in *R v Oakes*.[59] There are, nonetheless, certain forms of conduct that will almost certainly be unlawful and that will not pass the '*Oakes* test'. Certain methods of proving facts during trial are, however, explicitly prohibited. For example, evidence of a complainant's past sexual activity that is adduced for the sole purpose of proving that they consented or were more likely consent to the alleged sexual activity or that they are less trustworthy is prohibited pursuant to s. 276 Cr.C. Likewise, where the accused has exercised their right to silence by not

58 Anti-terrorism Act (S.C. 2001, c. 41). For an in-depth study of some of these issues, see NESBITT, M., and HAGG, D., 'An Empirical Study of Terrorism Prosecutions in Canada: Elucidating the Elements of the Offences', (2020) 57–3 Alberta Law Review 595.

59 R v Oakes, [1986] 1 SCR 103.

testifying in the course of the proceedings, it is forbidden for the Crown to adduce character evidence.[60]

b) *Please indicate evidence the acquisition of which is definitely prohibited;*

The unlawful obtaining of bodily evidence that constitutes a gross violation – e.g. a cavity search – of one's right to bodily autonomy and privacy pursuant to s. 8 of the Charter.[61]

c) *Please indicate a category of interests and values that are decisive for excluding evidence or restricting its examination.*

The Charter provides for the exclusion of evidence where the use of said evidence is likely to bring the administration of justice into disrepute, s. 24(2).[62] The category of interests protected in this case are those of the entire legal system.

6 Conclusion

(An evaluation of the existing legal environment within the scope at hand; a reference to practice, case law, controversies in doctrine, a tendency of changes, and future perspectives; finally, this is a place for free comments if these framework matters seem insufficient to present the specifics of the topic of: Limits of freedom of public authorities with respect to obtaining evidence at the stage of investigation).

An interesting and ongoing controversy in the case law arose in the wake of the Supreme Court judgement *R v Nedelcu* in 2012.[63] The Charter protects the accused from being compelled to testify and from self-incrimination pursuant to ss. 11c) and 13, except in the case of perjury or the giving of contradictory testimony. Traditionally, where an accused has in prior cases been compelled to testify as an ordinary witness, their testimony may not be used in subsequent criminal proceedings against them.[64] However, the SCC substantially changed the scope of the protection afforded by s. 13 of the Charter in. Writing for the majority, Moldaver, J., held that s. 13 applies only to 'incriminating testimony'. Therefore, to invoke the protection afforded by s. 13, one must prove not only that they were compelled in the earlier proceedings but also, and most importantly, that the nature of the testimony is itself incriminating. For Moldaver, J.,

60 R v Farrant, [1983] 1 SCR 124.
61 R v Stillman, [1997] 1 SCR 607.
62 R v Le, 2019 SCC 34.
63 R v Nedelcu, 2012 SCC 59.
64 R v Henry, 2005 SCC 76.

the incriminating nature of statements made by the accused must be interpreted restrictively and is primarily limited to the constitutive elements of the offence (i.e. the *actus reus* and *mens rea*). Undoubtedly, where difficulties are likely to arise is in respect to testimony that falls into a liminal or intermediate category, not *strictly* incriminating, but very likely to incriminate or, at the very least, to be highly prejudicial to the accused's defence.

Another example of controversy concern confessions obtained during a Mister Big operation. Since 1990, Canadian courts have been confronted with a new police technique of Canadian invention, that resulting from what is known as a "Mister Big" operation. This technique is particularly applied in the case of serious unsolved crimes. The police bond with the accused by letting him believe that they are members of a criminal organization into which they want to integrate him. At the end of the exercise, the suspect must take stock of his criminal life with the big boss of the organization. The suspect therefore confides in Mr. Big during a tight interrogation where he is subjected to strong pressure, sometimes even to veiled threats. A Mr. Big confession is invariably accompanied by evidence that the accused voluntarily participated in a "simulated crime" and had a strong desire to be part of a criminal organization.

As the Supreme Court points out in *R v Hart*,[65] the existing rules of law do not allow the imposition of legal guarantees on the confessions resulting from this type of operation which does not engage the right of the accused to keep silence, because he is not detained, or the obligation for the public prosecutor to establish the voluntariness of the statement to a person in authority, since, when he confesses, the accused does not know that Mr. Big is actually a policeman. The Supreme Court in R. v. Hart also acknowledged that while unreliable confessions "provide compelling evidence of guilt and present a clear and straightforward path to conviction," they "have been responsible for wrongful convictions – a fact we cannot ignore."[66] In *Hart*, the Supreme Court came to the conclusion that the current law did not offer sufficient protection to the accused who confesses to a crime in the context of an operation of this kind. Faced with the risk of admitting unreliable confessions and showing proof of the accused's propensity to agree to commit crimes, and also faced with the risk of allowing the police to resort to reprehensible behaviour, the Court decides to establish new rules of evidence regarding the admissibility of statements obtained in such circumstances:

---

65 R v Hart, 2014 SCC 52.

66 *Ibid*, para 6.

> [80] In my view, the lack of an effective mechanism to control the behavior of officers who engage in such a clandestine operation is problematic. The law must allow the trial judge to meaningfully deal with police misconduct in this context.

The solution proposed by the Court has two parts. The first enshrines a new rule of evidence at common law to determine whether or not a confession is admissible. Thus, when the state tricks a person into joining a fictitious criminal organization and attempts to obtain a confession, that confession is presumed inadmissible. This presumption is rebutted if the Crown proves on a balance of probabilities that the probative value of the confession outweighs its prejudicial effect. In this context, the probative value of the confession lies in its reliability:

> [85] [...] Its prejudicial effect stems from the bad character evidence that must be admitted in order to place the operation and the confession obtained in context. If the Crown is unable to demonstrate that the accused's confession is admissible, the other evidence relating to the Mr. Big operation becomes irrelevant and therefore inadmissible. Like the confessions rule that applies to traditional police questioning, this rule places a specific limitation on the exception to the hearsay rule that applies to statements made by the person concerned.

The second branch is that of abuse of process to solve the problem of police misconduct. Moreover, the Court does not rule out that a confession obtained under such conditions may be excluded in exceptional cases, even if it respects the proposed two-pronged approach, if its admission affects the fairness of the trial. Applying these principles in this case, the Court came to the conclusion that *Hart*'s confessions arising directly from the operation were not admissible and that the circumstances in which they were made cast serious doubt on their reliability.

In a later decision, *R v Mack*,[67] the Supreme court came to admit the accused's confession. In this case, even if the Crown admitted that the wiretap had constituted an unlawful and unreasonable search, the Court maintained the admissibility of the confessions which were strongly corroborated, in particular because the charred remains of the victim had been able, thanks to the statements of the accused, to be found. The Court will specify that the

---

67 R v Mack, 2014 SCC 58.

approach established in *Hart* aims to alleviate the problems raised, in terms of evidence, by the confessions obtained in the context of a Mr. Big operation, but it does not eliminate them. Rather, it is incumbent on the trial judge to give the jury proper instructions on how to weigh these confessions. The nature and extent of the directives required vary from case to case. In the absence of a dedicated formula, some beacons can however be stopped. The judge must explain to the jurors that it is up to them to decide whether the accused's confession is reliable or not. He must then examine with them the factors that are relevant to the assessment of the confession and the related evidence. For example, he must draw their attention to the duration of the operation, the number of interactions between the police and the accused, the nature of the relationship that developed between the officers and the accused, the nature of the inducements and their importance, the use of threats, the conduct of the interrogation, as well as the personality of the accused. In addition, the trial judge must advise the jurors that the confession may contain indicia of its reliability (or unreliability). He must also invite them to take into account its more or less detailed nature, whether or not it led to the discovery of other evidence, the mention of terms of the crime not revealed to the public or the fact that he describes faithfully or not certain prosaic data which the accused would not have known if he had not committed the crime. With respect to proof of bad character, the proper approach is more familiar. The judge must explain to the jury that this evidence is admitted only to put the confession in context. He should make it clear to the jury that he cannot rely on this evidence alone to convict the accused. Moreover, he should remind him that the simulated criminal activity is a pure invention of state officials, who encouraged the accused to participate in it.

CHAPTER 8

Limits of Freedom of Public Authorities with Respect to Obtaining Evidence at the Stage of Investigation

Taiwan Report

*Kai-Ping Su**

1 A Presentation of the Main and Most Distinctive Features of Evidence System in the Light of the Applicable Model of Criminal Procedure and Major Procedural Principles of Examining and Evaluating Evidence[1]

The most distinctive feature of Taiwan's evidence law system is its interaction with and development under Taiwan's "reformed adversarial system". Taiwan substantially changed its criminal procedural model in 1999, when the National Judicial Reform Conference held by the Judicial Yuan (Taiwan's highest judicial organ) decided to transform the inquisitorial structure of criminal trials to a new structure that is billed as a "reformed adversarial system". This new system is actually a hybrid of an inquisitorial system and an adversarial system. It is billed as a "reformed adversarial system", because advocates for this hybrid system believe that it can work better in Taiwan than the typical common-law style court of the adversarial system. In 2002, an amendment to Taiwan's Code of Criminal Procedure (hereinafter, "Taiwan's CCP") was passed by Taiwan's legislature. This amendment implements the 1999 recommendation of the Judicial Yuan and details the "hybrid" nature of Taiwan's new criminal court structure.

The amended Article 163 of Taiwan's CCP provides,

> The court *may*, for the purpose of discovering the truth, *ex officio* investigate evidence; in case for the purpose of maintaining justice or

* J.S.D., University of California, Berkeley School of Law. Associate Professor, National Taiwan University, College of Law.

1 Submitted November 3rd, 2021. Updated February 17th, 2022. I extend my gratitude to Professor Maria Rogacka-Rzewnicka for her efforts in editing this volume, and to the reviewers for their valuable feedback. I also thank National Taiwan University and Taiwan's National Science and Technology Council for their support.

 | DOI:10.1163/9789004710320_010

discovering facts that are critical to the interest of the accused, the court *shall ex officio* investigate evidence.

That is, in Taiwan's reformed adversarial system, while prosecutors bear the burden of proof of the crime charged,[2] judges are still authorized to investigate evidence in court, instead of sitting back and taking a passive umpire role. Also, it is not an optional role. Judges are *required* to investigate evidence actively, if the evidence is related to "maintaining justice or discovering facts that are critical to the interest of the accused."[3] The lawmakers and advocates for the hybrid system, designed the system to prevent judges from slacking off, and retained an active role for judges in the administration of justice. The hope is this new court system will be better than either a purely inquisitorial or purely adversarial system. Therefore, the new system was referred to as the "reformed" adversarial system. Nonetheless, considering that the investigation of evidence is the core of criminal trials, some scholars are critical of Taiwan's "reformed" system. They say it is still an inquisitorial system, augmented with some adversarial characteristics.

No matter whether or not Taiwan's legal policymakers truly wanted to transform the criminal trial system into an adversarial one, a form of adversarial system has taken root in Taiwan's criminal court system. This transition from a typical inquisitorial system to a hybrid structure has subsequently allowed the introduction of more adversarial and common-law style legal policies into Taiwan's criminal courts, in particular, the rules of evidence.[4]

2 Public Authorities Are Entitled to Acquire Evidence in a Criminal Action at the Stage of Investigation

2.1 *Notion: Public Authorities Are Entitled to Carry Out Investigations*

a) *Please indicate legal grounds or other sources giving rise to the competence of appropriate authorities to carry out investigations, within which to examine evidence. In addition to the traditional law enforcement authorities of*

2 Article 161, Paragraph 1 of Taiwan's CCP: "The public prosecutor shall bear the burden of proof as to the facts of the crime charged against an accused, and shall indicate the method of proof."; Article 161–1 of Taiwan's CCP: "The accused may indicate methods of proof favorable to him against the facts charged."

3 *The Reformed Adversarial System*, http://www.judicial.gov.tw/work/work02/work02–01.asp.

4 For a more comprehensive analysis of the success and failure, theory and practice of Taiwan's reformed adversarial system, *see, e.g.* Kai-Ping Su, *Criminal Court Reform in Taiwan: A Case of Fragmented Reform in a Not-Fragmented Court System*, 27 WASHINGTON INTERNATIONAL LAW JOURNAL 203–240 (2017 December).

the prosecutor and the police, are any other entities admissible, such as special forces or specialized administrative authorities? What is the scope of their procedural competence and how can their procedural position be defined vis-à-vis the traditional enforcement authorities? Can a growing significance be found in the participation in criminal investigations of specialized law enforcement authorities, other than the traditional group of investigation bodies? Can the phenomenon of normative disintegration be observed, paving the way for numerous public authorities to conduct investigations in criminal cases?

In addition to the traditional law enforcement authorities of the prosecutor and the police, Taiwan's CCP also allows the military police and other people "authorized by law to exercise the duty and power of a judicial policeman in special matters." In Taiwan, all the people who are authorized to exercise the duty and power to investigate criminal cases are members of "the judicial police".

In an Act named "The Judicial Police Dispatching Act", the judicial police include:

1. Police sergeants, or police officers.
2. Military police.
3. Police sergeants, or police of the railway, forestry, fisheries, mining or other professional police agencies.
4. Patrol team police of customs or salterns.

The judicial police should follow the orders of a prosecutor or a judge within the limits of matters relating to their duties.

There are two major reasons for the prosecutor to order the judicial police, other than the ordinary police to investigate cases. First, the judicial police may have special knowledge or skills related to specific cases. For example, forestry police may be familiar with the geography of forests, where timber trespass cases happen, while ordinary police are not. Second, when a police force, itself, is being investigated, the prosecutor is motivated to order other judicial police to carry out the investigation so as to preserve confidentiality and to avoid conflicts of interest. For example, in a corruption case where the ordinary police are involved, the prosecutor is likely to order military police or the agents of Investigation Bureau to carry out the investigation.

There is no empirical evidence showing that specialized police force or law enforcement authorities are used more frequently than ordinary police by the prosecutor in criminal investigations. Nor is the phenomenon of normative disintegration observed in Taiwan. Nevertheless, a prosecutor will frequently order the agents of Investigation Bureau to carry out a criminal investigation. The Bureau of Investigation is affiliated to Taiwan's Ministry of Justice, so is the prosecutor. Although I don't have empirical evidence showing whether the Bureau is used more often by the prosecutor than the ordinary police, the

Bureau of Investigation seems to be the primary organization for investigating major crimes.

The tasks of the Bureau include the prevention of domestic insurrection, foreign aggression, corruption, narcotics, money laundering, major economic crime, computer crime, organized crime, and so on.

b) *Do public law enforcement authorities enjoy a monopoly (exclusivity) of investigation rights in criminal cases, or do they share this competence with private entities (e.g. as part of private investigations or in the case of less serious actions being brought by private prosecution)? Where a given legal system envisages separate proceedings in actions brought by private prosecution, can public law enforcement authorities participate in them and if yes, what is the extent of that participation? Does it cover the right to examine evidence?*

Taiwan has a two-track criminal prosecution system: public prosecution and private prosecution. As Article 319 of Taiwan's CCP provides, "The victim of a crime may file a private prosecution, or if he is without, or of limited, legal capacity, or is dead, such private prosecution may be filed by his statutory agent, lineal relative, or spouse." The same article also requires private prosecution to be filed with an attorney's assistance, in order to avoid the abuse of judicial system.

However, a private prosecutor, i.e., the person who files a private prosecution, does not have the same power to investigate that a public prosecutor has. Public prosecutors, with assistance of the police, can arrest suspects, interrogate them, petition to courts for warrants for search and seizure, and so on. Private prosecutors have none of the above powers. Private prosecutors may hire their own detectives to investigate, but these detectives do not have as much power as the police do. My impression is that private prosecutors also rarely hire their own investigation team. In a sense, private prosecutors only are, victims who have the standing to prosecute cases, that public prosecutors decline to pursue. Since private prosecutors are required to retain attorneys, it is more costly than public prosecution, if all other things are equal. Other than prosecution, private prosecutors do not have the powers of public prosecutors or police. Therefore, there is no power sharing between public and private prosecutors. Nor do private prosecutors have the right to examine evidence in the investigation period, while prosecutors and the police do.

2.2 *Court's Right to Acquire Evidence at the Investigation Stage or Its Controlling Activities in Relation to Evidence Examined by Other Entities*

a) *Is the court entitled to examine evidence at the stage of investigation and if yes, can it admit evidence ex officio or only at the parties' request, or are both those solutions possible simultaneously? Does the format of court investigation apply?*

No, at the stage of investigation, Taiwan's courts, in principle, do not participate in evidence examination. The exceptions, if there are any, are when courts review petitions for warrants for search and seizure, or petitions for pre-trial detention. That is, when the police or public prosecutors want to search or seize evidence, or have suspects detained, they provide supporting evidence for courts to review, to decide whether a warrant should be issued, or a pretrial detention is appropriate. These are the rare circumstances where courts are involved in evidence examination during the investigation stage.

b) *At the investigation stage, does the court or another body hold the controlling rights in relation to evidentiary activities taken by law enforcement authorities and if yes, what controlling measures are afforded (e.g. does the examination of a specific piece of evidence require the court to give its prior consent)? What are the consequences of a failure to satisfy the condition of the court's or another entity's consent and other conditions from the perspective of the validity and effectiveness of the evidence examined? Can the specification of such pieces of evidence and the conditions of their admissibility established by the law be viewed as sufficient?*

Yes, some evidence collection activities that the law enforcement officers undertake need the court's approval, at the investigation stage. That is, a warrant from the court is necessary for the law enforcement to take certain measures to collect evidence. For example, search and seizure require court approval. The prosecutor also had the right to issue warrants for search and writ until 2001. The court is currently the only agency which can approve a search or seizure in Taiwan. When there is an emergency, plus some other conditions are satisfied, the prosecutor and law enforcers may exceptionally search and seize without the court's *prior* approval. However, even under these exceptional circumstances, the prosecutor and law enforcers still need to get the court's approval in three days after the search and seizure. Otherwise, the evidence acquired by the search and seizure will be inadmissible at trial. (Article 131 of Taiwan's CCP)

Similarly, when a prosecutor or law enforcers need to access the communication records of citizens, they should, in principle, apply to the court for an access warrant. If there is an emergency, and the warrant cannot be obtained before the collection of communication records, the prosecutor and law enforcers still need to apply to the court for a warrant, when the emergency is over. However, for more severe offenses where the minimum punishment is imprisonment of ten years or longer, and some specified offenses such as robbery, human trafficking, drug crimes, etc., the prosecutor can issue an access warrant without the court's consent. (Article 11–1 of the Communication Security and Surveillance Act)

c) *Is there a procedure at the investigation stage that enables the parties and their counsels to challenge the evidence examined in violation of the applicable principles? If yes, please present it briefly, taking into account the procedural consequences of its usage (the application of the principle of automatic exclusion of evidence; the recognition of invalidity of evidence; the judge's right to assess the consequences of a method adopted to acquire evidence and evidence content) as well as the legal consequences for those who violated the law; please indicate the level of imperativeness of responses to a violation concerning the acquisition and examination of evidence, based on the applicable law and standpoints of doctrine and judicature.*

Since this question asks about the procedure at the investigation stage for the parties to "challenge the evidence examined" in violation of law or principles, my answer is "no". The examination of evidence, or more precisely speaking, its admissibility, is the duty and work of the court when the case proceeds to the trial stage. At the investigation stage, the law enforcement may not have that much concern about the admissibility at the trial stage. Therefore, the law enforcers may still attempt to acquire some evidence that may not necessarily be admissible at trial, to aid their investigation. Polygraph tests are an example of this. Most courts do not admit polygraph tests as evidence at trial, but the police officers still use them from time to time, because polygraph tests can provide clues that help direct their investigation. However, it does not mean law enforcers would use illegal means to acquire evidence. Illegal means, such as illegal search, seizure, and detention, will not only result in inadmissible evidence but also very likely constitute criminal offenses that law enforcers can be prosecuted for.

3 Principles of Acquiring Evidence at the Stage of Investigation

a) Normative grounds for evidentiary activities in a criminal action (the Constitution, procedural criminal law, police law, administrative law, regulations, instructions, guidelines, common law, others). Can a multitude of sources of regulations in this area be referred to or is there normative homogeneity in place?

I understand this two-part question as "what laws and regulations govern collection of evidence in Taiwan?", and "Do these norms may overlap with each other?" As to the overlap, my answer is "yes".

Taiwan's Code of Criminal Procedure provides the main principles for evidence collection, whereas other regulations are made to regulate specific evidentiary activities in certain situations. For example, Taiwan's CCP provides: "If necessary, the person, property, electronic record, dwelling, or other premises of an accused or a suspect may be searched." (Article 122, Paragraph 1) and "The person, property, electronic record, dwelling, or other premises of a third party may be searched only when there is probable cause to believe that the accused or the suspect, or property or electronic record subject to seizure is there." (Article 122, Paragraph 2).

However, Taiwan's CCP says nothing about communication surveillance, for example. Another law, The Communication Security and Surveillance Act, provides the procedures to acquire evidence by surveillance measures and the effect of the evidence acquired. For instance, in this Act, Article 5, Paragraph 1 provides, "An interception warrant may be issued, if there is sufficient evidence that the accused or the suspect is involved in one of the following crimes, which may severely endanger national security, economic order or social order, and that there is reasonable belief that the content of his/her communication is relevant to the case being investigated, and that other methods to collect or investigate the evidence are difficult, or don't exist. …" Therefore, laws applied to different types of evidence and their evidentiary acquiring processes can be different.

b) *Does the applicable law regulate the principles of evidentiary activities taken by law enforcement authorities restrictively (on a tight-rein basis) and, similarly – determine the consequences of violations committed by the investigators, or does it leave to them a broad discretion in the search for evidence followed by the court's right to discretionarily assess the collected evidentiary material and by the confrontation of evidence during a verbal and contradictory trial at court?*

The answer tends to be the latter. The evidence acquired in the investigation stage would not be legally excluded until the evidence is submitted to the court and subject to the court's exclusionary decisions. However, there are two differences from the way this situation is described in the question, that should be noted:

First, the court only has discretion to decide to exclude evidence for some evidence. For example, evidence acquired by a violation of the search and seizure rule, as provided in Article 122 of Taiwan's CCP and described in the previous answer, will be examined by the court to decide whether it should be excluded. The general rule for the court to decide the evidence exclusion issue is provided by Article 154 of Taiwan's CCP: "The admissibility of the evidence, obtained in violation of the procedure prescribed by the law by an official in execution of criminal procedure, shall be determined by balancing the protection of human rights and the preservation of public interests, unless otherwise provided by law." However, other evidence acquired by illegal means is subject to direct exclusion without the court's discretion. For example, confessions of the accused cannot serve as evidence if it is acquired by illegal means against the accused's will. Because Article 156 of Taiwan's CCP provides, "Confession of an accused not extracted by violence, threat, inducement, fraud, exhausting interrogation, unlawful detention or other improper means and consistent with facts may be admitted as evidence."

Second, the court's decisions about evidence exclusion sometimes affect the prosecutors' willingness to submit certain types of evidence to the court. For example, the police in Taiwan sometimes use polygraph tests in the early stages of an investigation, to direct the focus of their investigation. However, since the court rarely accepts the polygraph tests as evidence to make a decision, in particular in the past decade, prosecutors tend to refrain from using this kind of evidence in court.

c) *Are there any criteria of the legality of evidence and criteria that disqualify the same established by the law? What role does the judicature play in establishing such criteria?*

Taiwan's CCP, and other related laws such as the Communication Security and Surveillance Act, clearly indicate the legality or illegality of evidence, usually by identifying the means obtaining evidence. For example, Article 156 of the CCP provides, "Confession of an accused not extracted by violence, threat, inducement, fraud, exhausting interrogation, unlawful detention or other improper means and consistent with facts may be admitted as evidence."

The judicature in Taiwan plays an important role to establish the above criteria. It is usually the Judicial Yuan, Taiwan's highest judicial organ, which is responsible for making proposals to establish new rules and change existing rules in the CCP and related laws. Although these proposals may be changed, sometimes a lot, before they can be passed by Taiwan's Congress to become valid laws, the Judicial Yuan's opinions and proposals about legality standards are usually influential to lawmakers.

d) *Does the principle of freedom, meaning that any evidentiary measure and any evidentiary method are admissible (except those that a limine are unacceptable in civilized world), apply to the acquisition of evidence at the investigation stage? Or is it restricted by the applicability of general principles of the law, e.g. legalism, reliability, proportionality, necessity, and values such as human dignity, bodily inviolability, or the right to privacy? Where references are explicite missing in the law to the aforesaid standards, on what basis are those standards applied? How do doctrine and case law understand the notion of "fair evidentiary procedure"? Is this notion autonomous or does it constitute a part of the notion of "fair trial"?*

All the general principles, including proportionality and necessity, apply to Taiwan's acquisition of evidence at the investigation. To assure a "fair evidentiary procedure", it is the court which has the authority and is responsible to supervise whether these principles are applied correctly. In regard to search and seizure, for example, the court intervenes at the investigation stage, by granting a warrant. That is, legal enforcers have to apply to courts for warrants to search and seize evidence, unless there is an emergency as listed in Taiwan's CCP. For example, Paragraph 2 and Paragraph 3 of Article 131 provides,

"(Paragraph 2) During the investigation stage, a public prosecutor may conduct a search without a warrant or instruct the public prosecuting affairs official, judicial police officer, or judicial policeman to do so, and report to the public prosecutor general, if there really is probable cause to believe that circumstances are exigent and there are sufficient facts to justify an apprehension that the evidence will be destroyed, forged, altered, or concealed within the next twenty four hours, unless a search is conducted immediately."

"(Paragraph 3) If the search specified in the preceding two paragraphs is conducted by a public prosecutor, the search must be reported to the court concerned within three days. If it is conducted by a public prosecuting affairs official, judicial police officer, or judicial policeman, it must report to the public prosecutor of the public prosecutor office concerned and the court within three days. If the court decides that the search is not approved, the court will revoke it within five days."

As for "a fair trial", the methods of evidence acquisition in the investigation stage are examined through the lens of evidentiary exclusion during trials. As Article 158–4 of Taiwan's CCP provides, "The admissibility of the evidence, obtained in violation of the procedure prescribed by the law by an official in execution of criminal procedure, shall be determined by balancing the protection of human rights with the preservation of public interests, unless otherwise provided by law." More details about the court's determination of the "balance between the protection of human rights with the preservation of public interests" will be provided in the following questions and answers.

e) *Is the acquisition of evidence at the investigation stage restricted by concrete prohibitions, e.g. the prohibition to use specific sources of evidence or evidentiary methods (please indicate the level of subordination of evidentiary activities to strict law; or maybe this situation depends on the nature of evidence, e.g. its interference in human rights and freedoms, or on the type of crime)? Please indicate examples of evidentiary activities that are subject to the strictest legal restrictions.*

Yes, the acquisition of some kinds of evidence is strictly restricted by concrete prohibitions. For example, Article 158–2 of Taiwan's CCP provides,

"(Paragraph 1) Any confession, or other unfavourable statement obtained from the accused, or a suspect in violation of provisions of Paragraph 2 of

Article 93–1[4] or Paragraph 1 of Article 100–3[5] shall not be admitted as evidence. The preceding provision does not apply to a situation where it is proved that the said violation was not in bad faith and the confession or statement concerned was made voluntarily out of free will.

(Paragraph 2) The provision of the preceding paragraph shall apply mutatis mutandis to the situation where a public prosecutor investigator, judicial police officer, or judicial policeman violates the provisions of Paragraph 1, Subparagraphs 2 or 3 or Paragraph 2 of Article 95[6] in interrogating an accused or suspect arrested with or without a warrant.

---

4 The 24 hours, as described in the provisions of Article 91 and paragraph 2 of the preceding Article, shall exclude the elapsed time as described in the following conditions. But there must be no unnecessary delay:

1. The delay caused by traffic problems, or by other force majeure.
2. Time spent during escorted transfer.
3. When no questioning is allowed pursuant to the provisions of Article 100–3 Paragraph 1.
4. When, in fact, no interrogation is conducted due to sudden changes of health of the accused or suspect.
5. Where the accused or suspect expressed the desire to retain an attorney, the time spent waiting for the arrival of a defense attorney instead of conducting interrogation, shall not exceed 4 hours. Where the accused's income level is low or middle-to-low, and has submitted a request for an appointment of a public defender or attorney pursuant to the provisions of Article 31 Paragraph 5; or where the accused or suspect, who is unable to make a complete statement due to mental disorder or other mental deficiencies and the notification is sent to appoint an accompanying assistant pursuant to the provisions of Article 35 Paragraph 3, the time spent waiting for the arrival of a defense attorney or accompanying assistant, instead of conducting interrogation, shall not exceed 4 hours.
6. Where the accused or suspect requires the assistance of an interpreter, the time spent waiting for an interpreter instead of conducting the interrogation, shall not exceed 6 hours.
7. After the prosecutor has given the bail release, or the custody release order, the time spent waiting for the process of being released on bail, or to the custody of another shall not exceed 4 hours.
8. The duration when the criminal suspect is brought forward in front of a judge for arraignment.

No interrogation shall be conducted within the time described in all preceding paragraphs.

5 The interrogation of criminal suspects by judicial police officer or judicial policeman shall not proceed at night, except for the following circumstances:

(1) Express consent by the person being interrogated;
(2) Identity check of the person arrested with or without a warrant at night;
(3) Permission by a public prosecutor or judge;
(4) In case of emergency.

6 The accused shall be informed of the following items before an interrogation is conducted:

1. The right to remain silent, and that no statements should be made against his/her own will.

As to evidentiary activities that are subject to the strictest legal restrictions in Taiwan, it is the acquisition of evidence. Article 156, Paragraph 1 of Taiwan's CCP stipulates the acceptable means for obtaining a confession. It states, "Confession of an accused not extracted by violence, threat, inducement, fraud, exhausting interrogation, unlawful detention or other improper means and consistent with facts may be admitted as evidence."

f) *Does the applicable law sufficiently define the boundaries of evidence acquisition admissibility, or maybe too categorically? What is the potential extent of the non-normative sphere in shaping such boundaries (general rules, pragmatism, habits)? Are the proportions between the two spheres (normative and non-normative) appropriate?*

Generally speaking, there are two categories of evidence acquisition admissibility according to Taiwan's CCP. The first category is evidence acquisition methods in violation of procedural rules, which have admissibility outcomes specified in the CCP. For example, confession acquired by illegal means is inadmissible (Article 156). Another example, any unfavorable statement obtained from the accused in the night (from sunset to sunrise the other day) shall not be admitted as evidence, unless this violation was not in bad faith and the statement concerned was made voluntarily out of free will (part of Article 158–2).

The second category is evidence acquisition methods in violation of procedural rules, which do NOT have specific admissibility outcomes in the CCP. In this situation, the court will decide the admissibility of evidence by "balancing the protection of human rights with the preservation of public interests" (Article 158–4). As you can see, since this second category can cover all the situations where the CCP does not specify an admissibility outcome, there is no space for the "non-normative sphere" to exist in the context of Taiwan's CCP. Also, as far as I have observed, this general classification is not disputed by legal professionals.

g) *As regards the acquisition of evidence during investigation, how at this stage is the deficit of the inapplicability of principles of equality of parties, equality of arms, and the contradictory principle compensated for, also taking into account the fact of general primacy of law enforcement authorities,*

2. The right to retain an attorney. If the accused is qualified to request for legal aid, pursuant to the laws, due to his/her low-income, or middle-to-low-income, aborigine status, or other qualifications, he may request to have an attorney retained for him.

When an accused, without a counsel present, indicates that he/she has retained a defense attorney, the interrogation shall cease immediately. However, this rule does not apply where the accused consents to continue with the interrogation.

in order to ensure a fair evidentiary procedure? Can the suspect and other entities share in this?

This is a major issue in Taiwan's criminal justice system. The suspect/defendant, during police and prosecutorial investigation, does not have a legal or constitutional right to "actively" acquire favorable witnesses and evidence. At any stage of the criminal procedure, defendants can apply to the police, the prosecutor, or the court to summon witnesses and to collect evidence in their favor. However, few defendants and their defense counsels would "actively" approach witnesses on their own, unless they can be sure that the witnesses are friendly to them.

Even though there is no explicit rule which restricts defendants from approaching witnesses or seeking evidence, most defendants and their defense counsels do not do so, because actively approaching witnesses or collecting evidence may be suspected to be an attempt to threaten or bribe the witnesses, or hide or destroy the evidence. Such suspicions can result in defendants being detained. In my opinion, the lack of clear legal rules to provide an effective and legitimate way for defendants to actively seek witnesses and evidence in their favor results in the government having more power to prosecute than individuals have to defend themselves.

h) *Is there a balance between the freedom of law enforcement authorities' actions, on which the crime combating efficiency depends, and limitations of that freedom arising from the need to ensure appropriate standards of evidentiary procedure? Does a comparison of those antagonistic to some extent perspectives show that the purpose of repression dominates at the expense of the procedural guarantees and the rights of individuals, or rather the purpose of the reliability of evidence at the expense of its effectiveness in the detection of the truth?*

If I understand this question correctly, it asks an eternal question: how to balance combating crime and the protection of human rights, in regard to evidence acquisition. For Taiwan, my answer is that a general balance does exist in a way. It does not mean that a balance between the two values is delicately molded by Taiwan's lawmakers and law enforcement officers, but that a smooth procedural channel to challenge, and further change the imbalance, does exist. That is, as issues come up in individual cases, judges decide the balance based on general guidelines, precedence, and their own opinions. From granting warrants to legal enforcers in the investigation stage, to striking evidence illegally obtained during trial, Taiwan's courts seem to maintain a fair attitude to deal with the potential conflicts between the two values in individual cases. Particularly, when courts find that applicable laws may be combating crime too much at the expense of human rights, Taiwan's courts from time to time will pause their trial procedure and apply to the Taiwan Constitutional Court (TCC) for a constitutional interpretation of the laws at issue. This is also a way to reconfirm that the laws enabling the government to seek the truth and combat crime are still constitutional.

It is noteworthy that the TCC entered a new era on January 4th, 2022, when the amended Constitutional Court Procedure Act (CCPA) took effect. According to the TCC's website,[7] this amended CCPA expands the jurisdiction of the TCC, revises its organization and administration, and initiates a new designation and format for the decisions of the TCC, among other major changes. The CCPA of 2022 adds a new type of litigation: constitutional complaint against final court decisions, which enables the TCC to exercise a power of concrete review on top of its abstract review powers. This new amendment is expected to further protect fundamental rights of individuals in individual cases.

i) *How can the fairness of evidentiary procedure be ensured in view of the conditions imposed by the commonly used consensual procedures, methods directed towards accelerating or shortening criminal proceedings, and the usage of alternative methods for criminal prosecution? Those measures not only fail to eliminate the issue of the boundaries of legal acquisition of evidence, but bring this issue into focus in connection with the conclusiveness of evidence being examined at the investigation stage. In these circumstances, are procedural guarantees ensured during the evidentiary procedure, together with due control over its legality at the investigation stage, bearing in mind the pressure for attaining the goal and swiftly end the proceedings?*

Other than the normal procedure where all evidentiary rules apply, there are three types of simplified procedures provided by the CCP. They are summary trial procedure (Article 273–1), summary procedure without trial (Article 449), and bargaining process (Article 455–2). Evidential rules are relaxed in these simplified procedures, to achieve a faster conclusion. A prominent example of a relaxed rule is the admission of hearsay in summary trial procedure and summary procedure without trial (Article 159 II). The investigation of other evidence in court, such as confession, physical evidence, and witnesses' testimony, also follows a more relaxed standard than the normal procedure does.

There is no doubt that evidentiary procedure is omitted, more or less, in these simplified procedures, in exchange for a faster process or a preferable outcome for parties. However, it is rare to hear that legal professionals or ordinary people argue against this exchange in Taiwan. Therefore, my impression

7 https://www.judicial.gov.tw/en/cp-2083–358640–47e30–2.html.

is that most people seem to feel the current exchange between simpler procedures and the wholeness of evidentiary rules is acceptable.

4 Identifications of Risks of Violating Freedom in the Acquisition of Evidence by Law Enforcement Authorities

a) *Narrow focus of enforcement authorities to acquire evidence of being guilty; oppressive investigative methods; violation of human dignity; use of measures compelling individuals to meet certain evidentiary obligations, or use of a passive tactic consisting in provoking the suspect or other entities into providing evidence. What measures are taken to counteract such practices?*

Article 156, Paragraph 1 of Taiwan's CCP stipulates the acceptable means for obtaining a confession. It states, "Confession of an accused not extracted by *violence, threat, inducement, fraud, exhausting interrogation, unlawful detention or other improper means* and consistent with facts may be admitted as evidence."

This article intends to exclude confessions obtained by any problematic means. In addition to a catch-all rule for "other improper means", Taiwan's CCP also specifies six specific types of illegal means: violence, threat, inducement, fraud, exhausting interrogation, unlawful detention. This is the one and only regulation in Taiwan's CCP governing the concept of "illegal means" of extracting confessions. Even in the "Precautionary Matters on Courts' Handling Criminal Procedures," which provides more detailed explanations of the content of Taiwan's CCP for the court's reference, it still only provides the same six specified illegal measures (violence and five types of coercion) and one general rule.

The design of the burden of proof, that a confession was volunteered, is a key enforcement mechanism for the regulation. That is, who should be responsible for proving that the confession was made voluntarily or not. This mechanism can be better understood considering the legal structures of Taiwan's "reformed adversarial system".

The "adversarial" aspects of Taiwan's "reformed adversarial system" come into play when criminal courts decide the admissibility of a confession. Although it has been a longstanding law in Taiwan that involuntary confessions shall be inadmissible in trial, since 1935, Taiwan's CCP did not provide any rules regarding the burden of proof that a confession was voluntary until 2003. This was the year after Taiwan's CCP adopted the reformed adversarial system. the 2003 version of Taiwan's CCP, Article 156, Paragraph 2 states, "If the accused claims that his confession was extracted by improper means, his confession shall be investigated prior to investigating other evidence; if the said confession is presented by the public prosecutor, the court shall order the public prosecutor to prove the method used to obtain the confession." This is also the current good law. Article 156 of Taiwan's CCP has not been changed since the 2003 amendment.

The official elucidation regarding this revision of Taiwan's CCP explicitly states that this new law is "borrowed from the common law system and incorporated into the newly adopted legal structure of the reformed adversarial system". Therefore, the confession regulations in Taiwan's CCP shows prominent adversarial characteristics, which are intentionally designed to fit in the reformed adversarial system adopted in 2002.

b) *A tendency to hierarchize evidence in favour of scientific evidence and at the expense of other pieces of evidence. Can an a priori privileged treatment of such evidence be seen as a threat to the legality and fairness of evidentiary procedure in connection with unsatisfactory motivation of enforcement authorities to verify and critically evaluate the same, and with the limited opportunities for private parties to challenge the same?*

I am not sure I understand this question. If this question is about whether scientific evidence is overvalued and difficult to defend against in Taiwan, my answer would be "yes and no". It is true that scientific evidence, such as DNA evidence, is extremely powerful to prove a defendant's guilt or not. However, as far as I know, there is no apparent complaint about the power of scientific evidence as "a threat to the legality and fairness".

On the other hand, this question may also ask whether there are a kind or kinds of evidence that legal enforcers may overvalue, at the cost of human rights or other values. If so, this only thing I can think of is confession of defendants. Since confession, made by defendants in the investigation stage or in court, can serve as evidence in Taiwan's criminal courts, it is valued as powerful evidence. In particular, when the confession discloses some information which can only be known by the offender himself (such as where the dead body or stolen goods are secretly hidden), it is even stronger. This is why the confession has been considered as "King or Queen of Evidence" in Taiwan, as well as other places.

Nonetheless, as I described in other parts of my answers to this survey, Taiwan's CCP has adopted measures to prevent the over- reliance on confession evidence. For example, the confession of an accused, or a co-offender, shall not be used as the sole basis of conviction. Other necessary evidence shall still be investigated to see if the confession is consistent with facts (Article 156).

c) *Different boundaries for the freedom of law enforcement authorities to acquire evidence depending on the crime type; a failure by legal regulations to keep up with new technologies to be used in cases for most serious crimes gives rise to a threat of abuse and potentially easier excuse of such practices. How can the present legal regulation be assessed from this perspective (e.g. as to cyber or biological evidence) in the context of threats to the fairness of evidentiary procedure? Are other regulatory standards in place or are any such standards tolerated, being different from those as in the case of traditional evidence?*

I understand this question to be, "do Taiwan's law enforcement authorities have more discretion to collect evidence, using emergent technologies, when the crime is more serious?" In Taiwan's CCP, where the general rules about legally acquiring evidence are established, there is no explicit distinction between serious and minor offences in regard to what is allowed. That is, according to Taiwan's CCP, all offenses are generally subject to the same rules. For example, using illegal means such as torture to acquire a confession from a suspect is prohibited, no matter what kinds of crimes that suspect is accused of.

However, there are two other sets of rules that make Taiwan's situation more complicated:

First, there is a rule in Taiwan's CCP, itself, which governs how the court is to process illegally obtained evidence, that does factor in the seriousness of the crime. Article 158–4 of Taiwan's CCP provides, "The admissibility of the evidence, obtained in violation of the procedure prescribed by the law by an official in execution of criminal procedure, shall be determined by balancing the protection of human rights with the preservation of public interests, unless otherwise provided by law." When this article was made in 2003, its legislative rationale indicated the influential factors that criminal courts should consider, when they are "balancing the protection of human rights and the preservation of public interests" to decide to exclude evidence or not. These influential factors include "the risks or harms of the investigated criminal offenses."[8] That is, the seriousness of the offenses may affect the court's decision about evidence admissibility at trial.

Second, in other laws, there are evidential rules that govern the means of acquiring evidence by the seriousness of offenses charged. For example, according to Article 11–1 of the Communication Security and Surveillance Act states, when the offense under investigation can possibly punished by an imprisonment of three years or more, and there is evidence showing that communications records and information of the communicators are necessary and relevant to the investigation, the prosecutor should file a written application to the court for a warrant to access the records and information. (Paragraph 1 of

8 A complete list of these influential factors is quoted in my response to the following Question V. (c).

Article 11–1) That is to say, for a less serious offense of which the punishment may not exceed a three-year prison term, the access to communication records and communicators' information should be prohibited. This law makes yet another distinction, paragraph 3 of the same article provides, if the offense under investigation is punishable by a minimum imprisonment of ten years, or belongs to some specified crimes, the prosecutor may access the communication records and information of communicators *ex officio*, without the approval of the court. (Paragraph 3 of Article 11–1)

In addition, Taiwan's society is aware of the risks of new technology infringing human rights, when used by law enforcement. When the law enforcement uses drone or CCTV clips to collect evidence, they are subject to the general review standards, for example, to determine if the usage invades privacy, or not. My general impression is that Taiwan's law enforcement is not keen to apply new technology to investigate crimes and collect evidence, perhaps because they know using new technology may be controversial and may result in the suppression of evidence.

5 Inviolable Boundaries in the Acquisition of Evidence by Law Enforcement Authorities

a) *Please indicate violations in the acquisition of evidence that make the evidence definitely invalid (i.e. indicate prohibited methods of proving facts);*

I will answer this question with the next question in the following response.

b) *Please indicate evidence the acquisition of which is definitely prohibited;*

If I understand the above questions a) and b) correctly, the question a) is about the prohibited methods of acquiring evidence, whereas the question b) is about materials which are not accepted as evidence. That is, the question a) is about the means, and b) the evidence. However, generally speaking, Taiwan's CCP does not separate these two concepts. Rather, the CCP prohibits methods of acquiring evidence and the acquired evidence, together. To reflect this regulation pattern, I will also not separate the two concepts when I list related articles of Taiwan's CCP:

> **Article 100–1:**
> The whole proceeding of examining the accused shall be recorded without interruption in audio, or, if necessary, in video, provided that the situation is urgent, and audio recording is not possible, after clearly stating in the record, that an audio recording is not possible.

Except for the circumstances prescribed in the Proviso of the preceding paragraph of this article, if there is an inconsistency between the content of the written record and that of the audio or video recording regarding the statements made by the accused, the said portion of the statement shall not be used as evidence.

Article 158–2:

Any confession, or other unfavourable statement obtained from the accused, or a suspect in violation of provisions of Paragraph 2 of Article 93–1[9] or Paragraph 1 of Article 100–3[10] shall not be admitted as evidence.

---

9 The 24 hours, as described in the provisions of Article 91 and paragraph 2 of the preceding Article, shall exclude the elapsed time as described in the following conditions. But there must be no unnecessary delay:

1. The delay caused by traffic problems, or by other force majeure.
2. Time spent during escorted transfer.
3. When no questioning is allowed pursuant to the provisions of Article 100–3 Paragraph 1.
4. When, in fact, no interrogation is conducted due to sudden changes of health of the accused or suspect.
5. Where the accused or suspect expressed the desire to retain an attorney, the time spent waiting for the arrival of a defense attorney instead of conducting interrogation, shall not exceed 4 hours. Where the accused's income level is low or middle-to-low, and has submitted a request for an appointment of a public defender or attorney pursuant to the provisions of Article 31 Paragraph 5; or where the accused or suspect, who is unable to make a complete statement due to mental disorder or other mental deficiencies and the notification is sent to appoint an accompanying assistant pursuant to the provisions of Article 35 Paragraph 3, the time spent waiting for the arrival of a defense attorney or accompanying assistant, instead of conducting interrogation, shall not exceed 4 hours.
6. Where the accused or suspect requires the assistance of an interpreter, the time spent waiting for an interpreter instead of conducting the interrogation, shall not exceed 6 hours.
7. After the prosecutor has given the bail release, or the custody release order, the time spent waiting for the process of being released on bail, or to the custody of another shall not exceed 4 hours.
8. The duration when the criminal suspect is brought forward in front of a judge for arraignment.

No interrogation shall be conducted within the time described in all preceding paragraphs.

10 The interrogation of criminal suspects by judicial police officer or judicial policeman shall not proceed at night, except for the following circumstances:

1. Express consent by the person being interrogated;
2. Identity check of the person arrested with or without a warrant at night;

The preceding provision does not apply to a situation where it is proved that the said violation was not in bad faith and the confession or statement concerned was made voluntarily out of free will.

The provision of the preceding paragraph shall apply *mutatis mutandis* to the situation where a public prosecutor investigator, judicial police officer, or judicial policeman violates the provisions of Paragraph 1, Subparagraphs 2 or 3 or Paragraph 2 of Article 95[11] in interrogating an accused or suspect arrested with or without a warrant.

Article 158–3:

If a witness or expert witness fails to sign an affidavit that his statement is truthful, as required by law, his testimony or expert opinion shall not be admitted as evidence.

c) *Please indicate a category of interests and values that are decisive for excluding evidence or restricting its examination.*

According to Taiwan's CCP, the voluntariness of defendants' confession is the only inviolable boundary in the acquisition of evidence by law enforcement authorities. That is to say, if a confession is collected by means against the will of defendants, it cannot serve as evidence, without any exception. Therefore, the interests and values that are decisive for excluding confession should be defendants' will, or in other words, the respect for voluntariness of defendants.

Other restrictions are more subjective. Article 158–4 of Taiwan's CCP, for example, provides, "The admissibility of the evidence, obtained in violation of the procedure prescribed by the law by an official in execution of criminal procedure, shall be determined by balancing the protection of human rights with the preservation of public interests, unless otherwise provided by law." When this article was made in 2003, its legislative rationale indicated the influential

---

3. Permission by a public prosecutor or judge;
4. In case of emergency.

11 The accused shall be informed of the following items before an interrogation is conducted:

1. The right to remain silent, and that no statements should be made against his/her own will.
2. The right to retain an attorney. If the accused is qualified to request for legal aid, pursuant to the laws, due to his/her low-income, or middle-to-low-income, aborigine status, or other qualifications, he may request to have an attorney retained for him.

   When an accused, without a counsel present, indicates that he/she has retained a defense attorney, the interrogation shall cease immediately. However, this rule does not apply where the accused consents to continue with the interrogation.

factors that criminal courts should consider, when they are "balancing the protection of human rights and the preservation of public interests" to decide to exclude evidence or not. These influential factors considered by criminal courts reflect the values and interests decisive for excluding evidence. They include:

(i) the scenario where legal proceedings were violated in obtaining evidence;
(ii) the intention of the people who violated legal process, to obtain evidence;
(iii) the kinds and degrees of rights and interests of the suspects and defendants that were infringed;
(iv) the risks or harms of the investigated criminal offenses;
(v) the deterrence effect, towards future illegal evidence collection, if the evidence is suppressed;
(vi) the availability of legal means to obtain evidence;
(vii) the degree of damage to defendant's defence caused by the illegally obtained evidence.

6 Conclusion

(An evaluation of the existing legal environment within the scope at hand; a reference to practice, case law, controversies in doctrine, a tendency of changes, and future perspectives; finally, this is a place for free comments if these framework matters seem insufficient to present the specifics of the topic of: Limits of freedom of public authorities with respect to obtaining evidence at the stage of investigation).

To understand how justice (or injustice) has been done in Taiwan, a brief introduction to Taiwan's criminal court structure is necessary. The "Reformed Adversary System" is generally considered to be the guiding core framework that defines the relationship between courts and the parties in Taiwan's criminal trials. Taiwan's criminal courts adopted this "reformed adversary system" in 2002. Before that, Taiwan's criminal trials had a longstanding inquisitorial structure, where judges were actively involved in the investigation of facts and were responsible for "finding the truth" while conducting criminal trials. In contrast, in a typical adversarial system the parties are responsible for presenting evidence before an essentially passive and neutral adjudicator. Taiwan's system, billed as a "reformed" adversary system, is in fact a hybrid of the adversarial system and the inquisitorial system. The hybrid nature can be clearly perceived in the 2002 amendment of Article 163 of Taiwan's CCP, which provides:

"The court may, for the purpose of discovering the truth, ex officio investigate evidence; to maintain justice or discover facts that are critical to the interests of the defendant."

That is, in Taiwan's criminal trials, not only prosecutors bear the burden of proof as to the crime charged, but also judges are authorized to investigate evidence in court. Taiwan's judges do not simply sit back and take a passive role while the parties present their evidence. Judges are even required to actively investigate evidence, when the evidence is regarding "maintaining justice or discovering facts that are critical to the interest of the defendant." Those who advocate for the new system believe that the word "reformed" suggests an improvement over the typical adversarial system. Lawmakers were hesitant to embrace a system where judges are passive observers. Instead, the lawmakers expected judges to actively maintain justice, in case one of the parties slacks off and fails to present their case appropriately. In this sense, this new court system is believed by lawmakers and advocates to be better than a pure inquisitorial or adversarial system. Therefore, the new system was referred to as the "reformed" adversarial system.

While judges are trusted with maintaining justice and protecting defendants' rights, the judiciary is not the only institution required by the CCP to devote itself to these two objectives. In the reformed adversary system, the police, prosecutors, and even defence attorneys are also involved in the pursuit of justice and finding truth related to rights of defendants.

As Taiwan's CCP Article 2 provides:

(Paragraph 1) A public official who conducts proceedings in a criminal case shall give equal attention to circumstances both favourable and unfavourable to a defendant.

(Paragraph 2) An accused may request any public official specified in the preceding paragraph to take measures supporting their defence.

The "public official[s]" in the above text of the CCP mainly refers to judges, prosecutors, and the police. That is, the police and prosecutors are not only responsible for arresting suspects and prosecuting defendants, but also for assisting in their defence.

CHAPTER 9

Limits of Freedom of Public Authorities with Respect to Obtaining Evidence at the Stage of Investigation in Estonia

*Anneli Soo**

1 A Presentation of the Main and Most Distinctive Features of Evidence System in the Light of the Applicable Model of Criminal Procedure and Major Procedural Principles of Examining and Evaluating Evidence

1.1 *Responsibility for Investigation*

In Estonia it is the duty of the Prosecutor's Office to direct pre-trial proceedings (i.e. the investigation) and ensure the legality and efficiency of these proceedings. In court, the Prosecutor's Office represent public prosecution whereas the court chairs the court proceedings. It is important to note that usually the same prosecutor who conducted the criminal investigation, will be the accusing side in the court proceedings.

1.2 *General Description of Estonian Criminal Procedure*

In Estonia the criminal proceedings begin with by the first investigative activity or other procedural operation conducted by an investigative body (for clarification, please refer to Question 2.1a) or the Prosecutor's Office, if a reason and grounds for commencement are present and if the circumstances precluding criminal proceedings are absent. The reason for the commencement of criminal proceedings is a report of a criminal offence or other information indicating that a criminal offence has taken place. The grounds for criminal proceedings are constituted by ascertainment of criminal elements in the reason for the criminal proceedings.

After the criminal proceedings are commenced, bodies conducting proceedings, mainly investigative bodies (such as the police) conduct pre-trial

* PhD, Associate Professor in Criminal Law the University of Tartu, Estonia.

 | DOI:10.1163/9789004710320_011

investigation under supervision and guidance of the Prosecutor's Office. It depends on the concrete proceedings whether the investigation officials of an investigative body act in everyday basis more or less independently or the prosecutor supervising the case leads the proceedings vigorously and in a detailed manner.

In any case, when an official of an investigative body is convinced that all evidentiary materials necessary in a criminal matter have been collected, they immediately send the criminal file to the Prosecutor's Office. In the file materials are systematised and the pages numbered. The file is accompanied by the physical evidence, recordings and a sealed envelope containing the personal data of anonymous witnesses. The official of an investigative body also submits a summary of the pre-trial proceedings to the Prosecutor's Office. After receiving these materials the prosecutor either declares the pre-trial proceedings completed, requires the investigative body to perform additional acts or terminate criminal proceedings on the bases and pursuant to the procedure provided for in law.

In Estonia the pre-trial proceedings is in its nature inquisitorial, whereas the court proceedings is adversarial. At the initial stages of criminal proceedings it is not mandatory to notify the suspect that an investigation has been started towards them, and even if they are notified, the defence counsel only has limited access to the criminal file, which makes the counsel's role considerably passive in pre-trial proceedings. The Prosecutor's Office, who will later be the accuser in the court, is responsible for gathering all necessary evidence. However, it should be noted that according to the Code of Criminal Procedure (CCP)[1] § 211 (2), the Prosecutor's Office is obliged to gather all evidence both vindicating and accusing the suspect. As said, the court proceedings is adversarial. As declared by § 14 (1) of the CCP, "in judicial proceedings, the functions of prosecution, defence and adjudication of the criminal matter shall be performed by different persons subject to proceedings."

2 Public Authorities Are Entitled to Acquire Evidence in a Criminal Action at the Stage of Investigation

2.1 *Notion: Public Authorities Are Entitled to Carry Out Investigations*

a) *Please indicate legal grounds or other sources giving rise to the competence of appropriate authorities to carry out investigations, within which to examine evidence.*

1 Available in English at: https://www.riigiteataja.ee/en/eli/509072021004/consolide.

The main legal ground giving competence to appropriate authorities to carry out investigations is the Code of Criminal Procedure:

https://www.riigiteataja.ee/en/eli/509072021004/consolide

In addition to the traditional law enforcement authorities of the prosecutor and the police, are any other entities admissible, such as special forces or specialized administrative authorities? What is the scope of their procedural competence and how can their procedural position be defined vis-à-vis the traditional enforcement authorities?

The authorities entitled to perform procedural operations in criminal procedure, including acquire and examine evidence, are defined as investigative authorities or investigative bodies. These authorities can perform procedural operations independently unless the permission of court or order of the Prosecutor's Office is required.[2]

Code of Criminal Procedure states a list of investigative authorities:

- Police and Border Guard Board
- Internal Security Service: A broader function of the Estonian Internal Security Service as a government agency within the area of government of the Ministry of Internal Affairs is maintenance of national security through collection of information and implementation of preventive measures as well as investigation of offences to the extent established by the Government of the Republic Regulation.[3]
- Tax and Customs Board: The area of activity of the Board includes administration of state revenues, implementation of national taxation and customs policies and protection of the society and legal economic activities.[4]
- Competition Board: Estonian Competition Authority exercises supervision in the fields of competition, natural gas, district heating, postal services, public water supply and sewerage and railways. In addition, the Authority settles disputes regarding airport fees. The Authority is in the area of government of the Ministry of Justice.[5]
- Military Police: The key tasks of the Military Police of the Estonian Defence Forces include supervising the discipline, carrying out criminal proceedings in service-related crimes and proceeding disciplinary investigations. The Military Police of the Estonian Defence Forces also ensures the protection of the foreign ministers of defence, the management of

2 CCP, § 32 (1).
3 https://kapo.ee/en/content/general-information-0/.
4 https://www.emta.ee/eng/contacts-and-about-us.
5 https://www.konkurentsiamet.ee/en/about-us-contacts/organization/activities-and-structure.

the armed forces, and the management of the international organisations.[6]
- Environment Board: Their task is to implement state policies on environmental use, nature conservation and radiation safety and to monitor the fulfilment of the laws and norms established for the protection of the natural environment. The Board is also involved in the development and updating of legal acts and other official documents regulating the environmental field.[7]
- Department of Prisons of the Ministry of Justice and the prisons: They perform the functions of an investigative authority directly or through an institution administered by them or through a local office. The Department of Prisons of the Ministry of Justice is the central authority of the Estonian Prison Service, the task of which is to manage and develop the work of prisons. The Department is led by the Ministry of Justice Deputy Secretary-General for Prisons and consists of four divisions managed by the Chief Chaplain and Heads of Division that also act as Assistants to the Deputy Secretary-General. The Deputy Secretary General for Prisons issues orders to prisons in all relevant areas of activity.[8]

Can a growing significance be found in the participation in criminal investigations of specialized law enforcement authorities, other than the traditional group of investigation bodies? Can the phenomenon of normative disintegration be observed, paving the way for numerous public authorities to conduct investigations in criminal cases?

There is no information suggesting such tendency.

b) *Do public law enforcement authorities enjoy a monopoly (exclusivity) of investigation rights in criminal cases, or do they share this competence with private entities (e.g. as part of private investigations or in the case of less serious actions being brought by private prosecution)?*

Private entities do not have any specific investigation rights in criminal proceedings, the competence is exclusively held by investigative authorities listed above, and by the Prosecutor's Office, Estonian legislation does not state any special rights for private investigators or insurance companies.

If a private entity (private or legal person) is a suspect, accused, victim, civil defendant or a third party[9] in a criminal investigation, it has certain procedural

6 https://mil.ee/en/landforces/military-police/.

7 https://keskkonnaamet.ee/en/organization-contacts/organization/introduction.

8 https://www.vangla.ee/en/intitutions/prisons-department-ministry-justice.

9 Third party is a person who is not a party of a criminal investigation mentioned above, but its rights or obligations may be decided on when dealing with the criminal matter or applying a specific procedure.

(participation) rights. For example, such persons have the right to submit evidence, requests, and complaints, examine the minutes of procedural operations and give statements on them, etc.[10]

Where a given legal system envisages separate proceedings in actions brought by private prosecution, can public law enforcement authorities participate in them and if yes, what is the extent of that participation? Does it cover the right to examine evidence?

The institution of private prosecution is unknown to Estonian law; the right of collecting and examining evidence, charge and accuse are solely under the privilege of the investigation bodies and the Prosecutor's Office (see above).

2.2 *Court's Right to Acquire Evidence at the Investigation Stage or Its Controlling Activities in Relation to Evidence Examined by Other Entities*

a) *Is the court entitled to examine evidence at the stage of investigation and if yes, can it admit evidence ex officio or only at the parties' request, or are both those solutions possible simultaneously? Does the format of court investigation apply?*

The court does not examine evidence at the stage of investigation. However, the court is the authorised body for issuing permits for investigative bodies who wish to acquire certain types of evidence, please refer to the next questions for specification.

b) *At the investigation stage, does the court or another body hold the controlling rights in relation to evidentiary activities taken by law enforcement authorities and if yes, what controlling measures are afforded (e.g. does the examination of a specific piece of evidence require the court to give its prior consent)?*

The court needs to issue permits before investigative bodies are allowed to conduct any surveillance activities (e.g. covertly watching a person, thing or area, covertly taking comparative samples and performing initial examinations, covertly examining a thing and covertly replacing it).[11]

The Court's permit is also required for conducting searches of a notary's office or attorney's law office or at the persons processing information for journalistic purposes, if there is reason to believe that the suspect used or uses the site or vehicle to be searched at the time of commission of a criminal act or during the pre-court proceedings, and the person is suspected of committing a more serious crime specified in the Code of Criminal Procedure.

---

10 CCP, § 33 et seq.

11 CCP, § 126^3 (4) et seq.

In other cases, a search or other investigation procedures may be conducted with a permit from the Prosecutor's Office or independently (depending on the nature of an investigation activity).

What are the consequences of a failure to satisfy the condition of the court's or another entity's consent and other conditions from the perspective of the validity and effectiveness of the evidence examined?

2.3 *Surveillance Activities*

The Estonian Supreme Court has stated that if an investigative body has failed to acquire a permit for conducting surveillance activities, the evidence acquired is automatically inadmissible. Even if the permit has been issued by the Court, but without sufficient grounds or incorrectly in some other way, the evidence collected via surveillance activities is still automatically inadmissible.[12]

In general, surveillance activities are permitted on the bases provided for in Code of Criminal Procedure if collection of data by other activities or taking of evidence by other procedural operations is impossible, is impossible on time or is especially complicated or if this may prejudice criminal proceedings in the case. In addition, surveillance activities cannot endanger the life or health of persons, cause unjustified property and environment damage or unjustified infringement of other personality rights.[13]

2.4 *Other Evidence*

Evidence other than from surveillance activities can still be admissible, even when some breaches have occurred in the acquiring process. The Supreme Court has stated that evidence is deemed inadmissible only if there has been a material breach in the evidence gathering process.[14] As the courts are the bodies to examine and evaluate evidence in the court proceedings, it is also their task to evaluate the admissibility.[15]

The Supreme Court has elaborated on what the main criteria for evaluating the admissibility of evidence is:

- which provision of the law was breached, i.e., the defensive purpose of the provision
- how extensive the breach was
- whether the breach was intentional
- which crime was being investigated

12 Judgment of the Supreme Court 3-1-1-14-14, 30.06.2014, p 780.

13 CCP, § 126[1].

14 Ruling of the Supreme Court 1-16-6179, 18.06.2021, p 58.

15 CCP, § 61 (2).

- how extensive is the public interest or the interest of the victims in investigating the crime
- would it have been possible to acquire the same evidence without the breach by using a different method
- what is the relevance of the evidence in the case
- whether the right to defense of the accused is being considered when admitting the evidence.[16]

Can the specification of such pieces of evidence and the conditions of their admissibility established by the law be viewed as sufficient?

The criteria for evaluating evidence gathered via surveillance is rather accurate and could be considered sufficient. When it comes to any other piece of evidence, the evaluation is highly dependent on the circumstances of each separate case. It could be concluded from the Supreme Court's practice that in more serious cases which are under public attention for which punishments are more severe, more errors can be made while gathering evidence (as seen in the previous question, public interest is one of the aspects on assessing the breach). Therefore, it may be claimed that the bigger the crime, the less procedural guarantees apply.

c) *Is there a procedure at the investigation stage that enables the parties and their counsels to challenge the evidence examined in violation of the applicable principles?*

Before a statement of charges is prepared, a participant in proceedings or a person not subject to the proceedings has the right to file an appeal with the Prosecutor's Office against a procedural operation or order of the investigative body if they find that violation of the procedural requirements in the performance of the procedural operation or preparation of the order has resulted in the violation of his or her rights.[17] Therefore, there is no specific procedure for challenging the evidence, but a complaint can be filed about the procedural operation via which the evidence was acquired. To clarify, the content of evidence cannot be challenged in any way, but only the gathering process.

If yes, please present it briefly, taking into account the procedural consequences of its usage (the application of the principle of automatic exclusion of evidence; the recognition of invalidity of evidence; the judge's right to assess the consequences of a method adopted to acquire evidence and evidence content) as well as the legal consequences for those who violated the law;

All evidence is being evaluated by the court in the court procedure, not at the investigation stage.

16 Ruling of the Supreme Court 1-16-6179, 18.06.2021, p 59.
17 CCP, § 228 lg 1.

The Code of Criminal Procedure does not state any specific consequences for officials' violations in the evidentiary procedures. However, it is possible to impose a disciplinary punishment on police officers, but such decisions are not handled by the criminal court during the criminal proceedings.[18]

Please indicate the level of imperativeness of responses to a violation concerning the acquisition and examination of evidence, based on the applicable law and standpoints of doctrine and judicature.

As explained above in Question 2.2b, the regulation for collecting evidence via surveillance activities is more imperative, all other violations in the evidence acquiring procedure must be assessed separately by the court.

Code of Criminal Procedure states a single generally imperative provision: "Evidence shall be taken in a manner which is not prejudicial to the honour and dignity of the persons participating in the taking of the evidence, does not endanger their life or health or cause unjustified proprietary damage. Evidence shall not be taken by torturing a person or using violence against him or her in any other manner or by means affecting a person's memory capacity or degrading his or her human dignity."[19]

3 Principles of Acquiring Evidence at the Stage of Investigation

a) *Normative grounds for evidentiary activities in a criminal action (the Constitution, procedural criminal law, police law, administrative law, regulations, instructions, guidelines, common law, others). Can a multitude of sources of regulations in this area be referred to or is there normative homogeneity in place?*

As the Code of Criminal Procedure is crucial for regulating evidentiary activities and it can be viewed as central, no problems concerning multitude of laws can be identified.

All activities for acquiring evidence described in the Code of Criminal Procedure must be conducted considering fundamental rights stated in the Constitution, but this does not mean a multitude of sources in the procedure.

b) *Does the applicable law regulate the principles of evidentiary activities taken by law enforcement authorities restrictively (on a tight-rein basis) and, similarly – determine the consequences of violations committed by the investigators, or does it leave to them a broad discretion in the search for*

18 Police and Border Guard Act, § 86. Available in English at: https://www.riigiteataja.ee/en/eli/510082021002/consolide.

19 CCP, § 64 (1).

evidence followed by the court's right to discretionarily assess the collected evidentiary material and by the confrontation of evidence during a verbal and contradictory trial at court?

As explained above, it is the court's task to assess the evidence and their methods of acquisition. The criteria for evaluating the admissibility is rather broad and largely open for interpretation by the court (except for the evidence gathered via surveillance).

The main possible consequence of violations in the evidence acquisition process is inadmissibility of the evidence. Personal liability of the investigators may derive from the Police and Border Guard Act in a disciplinary form, but such matters are not evaluated within the criminal court proceedings.

Therefore, the discretion of investigative bodies is rather broad.

c) *Are there any criteria of the legality of evidence and criteria that disqualify the same established by the law? What role does the judicature play in establishing such criteria?*

Please refer to Question 2.2b.

d) *Does the principle of freedom, meaning that any evidentiary measure and any evidentiary method are admissible (except those that a limine are unacceptable in civilized world), apply to the acquisition of evidence at the investigation stage? Or is it restricted by the applicability of general principles of the law, e.g. legalism, reliability, proportionality, necessity, and values such as human dignity, bodily inviolability, or the right to privacy?*

Please refer to Question 2.2c.

Where references are *explicite* missing in the law to the aforesaid standards, on what basis are those standards applied? How do doctrine and case law understand the notion of "fair evidentiary procedure"? Is this notion autonomous or does it constitute a part of the notion of "fair trial"?

Please see the criteria provided by the Supreme Court in Question 2.2b.

e) *Is the acquisition of evidence at the investigation stage restricted by concrete prohibitions, e.g. the prohibition to use specific sources of evidence or evidentiary methods (please indicate the level of subordination of evidentiary activities to strict law; or maybe this situation depends on the nature of evidence, e.g. its interference in human rights and freedoms, or on the type of crime)? Please indicate examples of evidentiary activities that are subject to the strictest legal restrictions.*

Please refer to Question 2.2c and others above.

f) *Does the applicable law sufficiently define the boundaries of evidence acquisition admissibility, or maybe too categorically? What is the potential extent of the non-normative sphere in shaping such boundaries (general rules, pragmatism, habits)? Are the proportions between the two spheres (normative and non-normative) appropriate?*

As described above, the admissibility is evaluated by the court and there are very few imperative provisions and the courts have created certain principles in the practice which have been described above (please refer to Questions 2.2b and 2.2c).

g) *As regards the acquisition of evidence during investigation, how at this stage is the deficit of the inapplicability of principles of equality of parties, equality of arms, and the contradictory principle compensated for, also taking into account the fact of general primacy of law enforcement authorities, in order to ensure a fair evidentiary procedure? Can the suspect and other entities share in this?*

According to the Code of Criminal Procedure, the purpose of the pre-trial proceedings, i.e., the investigative stage is ascertaining the facts vindicating or accusing the suspect or accused by the investigative body and the Prosecutor's Office.

The prosecutor's office is independent in the performance of its functions arising from law, and it acts pursuant to Prosecutor's Office Act, other Acts, and legislation issued on the basis thereof.[20] Prosecutors have the obligation to remain unbiased when evaluating the evidence in pre-court proceedings according to Prosecutors' Code of Ethics.[21]

h) *Is there a balance between the freedom of law enforcement authorities' actions, on which the crime combating efficiency depends, and limitations of that freedom arising from the need to ensure appropriate standards of evidentiary procedure? Does a comparison of those antagonistic to some extent perspectives show that the purpose of repression dominates at the expense of the procedural guarantees and the rights of individuals, or rather the purpose of the reliability of evidence at the expense of its effectiveness in the detection of the truth?*

The main balancing force between the two principles is the court, as it is its task to assess the admissibility of evidence. However, as stated above, the assessment is closely connected to the public interest of the offender being punished (as described in 2.2b). Therefore, sometimes efficiency takes precedence over the rights of the defence (especially in the cases of close public scrutiny).

i) *How can the fairness of evidentiary procedure be ensured in view of the conditions imposed by the commonly used consensual procedures, methods directed towards accelerating or shortening criminal proceedings, and the*

20 Prosecutor's Office Act, § 1 (1^1). Available in English at: https://www.riigiteataja.ee/en/eli/515092021001/consolide.

21 Available at: https://www.prokuratuur.ee/et/organisatsioon/prokuroride-eetikakoodeks.

usage of alternative methods for criminal prosecution? Those measures not only fail to eliminate the issue of the boundaries of legal acquisition of evidence, but bring this issue into focus in connection with the conclusiveness of evidence being examined at the investigation stage.

In these circumstances, are procedural guarantees ensured during the evidentiary procedure, together with due control over its legality at the investigation stage, bearing in mind the pressure for attaining the goal and swiftly end the proceedings?

Settlement procedure and alternative procedure have both been created for more effective and time-efficient solving of criminal cases.

In the settlement procedure (one could call it also plea-bargaining) it is the judge's obligation to determine whether the accused has understood and agreed to the settlement, i.e., the prosecutor has not put pressure on the accused. The judge also has the right to return the criminal file to the Prosecutor's Office if the they do not consent to the legal assessment of the criminal offence or the type or the category or term of the punishment.

It is also possible to solve a case in alternative procedure meaning that a criminal matter is solved based on the materials of the criminal file without oral examination of witnesses or experts, as the benefit for agreeing with this written form of procedure is that the punishment is reduced by one third. In this type of procedure the court still has an obligation to evaluate the legality and the admissibility of the evidence in the criminal file (but without oral examination). Furthermore, it is required to have the suspect's consent for solving the matter, and if suspect does not agree, they have a right to demand that the matter in being solved in general court proceedings (via adversarial proceedings).

4 Identifications of Risks of Violating Freedom in the Acquisition of Evidence by Law Enforcement Authorities

a) *Narrow focus of enforcement authorities to acquire evidence of being guilty; oppressive investigative methods; violation of human dignity; use of measures compelling individuals to meet certain evidentiary obligations, or use of a passive tactic consisting in provoking the suspect or other entities into providing evidence. What measures are taken to counteract such practices?*

Before a statement of charges is prepared by the investigative authorities, a participant in proceedings or a person not subject to the proceedings has the right to file an appeal with the Prosecutor's Office against a procedural operation or order of the investigative body if they find that violation of the procedural requirements in the performance of the procedural operation or preparation of the order has resulted in the violation of their rights.[22]

The suspect also has the right to submit evidence in the criminal proceedings (for more detail, please refer to Question 2.1b).[23]

Also the suspect can turn to the Chancellor of Justice when they feel that their rights have been violated.[24]

As mentioned above, an investigative body and the Prosecutor's Office shall ascertain both, the facts vindicating or accusing the suspect or accused.[25]

b) *A tendency to hierarchize evidence in favour of scientific evidence and at the expense of other pieces of evidence. Can an a priori privileged treatment of such evidence be seen as a threat to the legality and fairness of evidentiary procedure in connection with unsatisfactory motivation of enforcement authorities to verify and critically evaluate the same, and with the limited opportunities for private parties to challenge the same?*

Code of Criminal Procedure states that no evidence has predetermined weight and the court shall evaluate all evidence in aggregate according to the conscience of the judges. This principle has also been repeatedly emphasized by the case law of Estonian Supreme Court.

Recent developments in relation to technological evidence should be stressed here. Until recently, location data of cellular phones acquired from communications companies was a widespread type of evidence, as such information is automatically recorded, rather accurate and reliable for determining persons' possible locations and easy to access for public authorities. However, ECJ and the Supreme Court of Estonia have ruled that such data can no longer be used in criminal proceedings (see more in the next answer).

c) *Different boundaries for the freedom of law enforcement authorities to acquire evidence depending on the crime type; a failure by legal regulations to keep up with new technologies to be used in cases for most serious crimes gives rise to a threat of abuse and potentially easier excuse of such practices.*

How can the present legal regulation be assessed from this perspective (e.g. as to cyber or biological evidence) in the context of threats to the fairness of evidentiary procedure? Are other regulatory standards in place or

22 CCP, § 228.

23 CCP, § 34.

24 Chancellor of Justice Act. Available in English at: https://www.riigiteataja.ee/en/eli/528052020006/consolide.

25 CCP, § 211 (2).

are any such standards tolerated, being different from those as in the case of traditional evidence?

Code of Criminal Procedure states that no evidence has predetermined weight and the court shall evaluate all evidence in aggregate according to the conscience of the judges. This principle has also been repeatedly emphasized by the case law of Estonian Supreme Court.

Preliminary ruling C-746/18 of the ECJ stated that by public authorities is not allowed as evidence unless for combating serious crime or preventing serious threats to public security. The ruling also stated that any national legislation providing public prosecution with the authority of issuing permits for the abovementioned activity must be considered invalid.[26] Before this ruling, however, location data of cellular phones acquired from communications companies was a widespread type of evidence, as such information is automatically recorded, rather accurate and reliable for determining persons' possible locations and easy to access for public authorities.

In the light of ECJ's preliminary ruling,the Supreme Court of Estonia also ruled that location data of cellular phones cannot be stored in such widespread amounts (as it was required from cellular companies thus far) for the purpose of criminal investigations and the prosecutor has no right to issue permits for acquiring such data from communications companies.[27]

5 Inviolable Boundaries in the Acquisition of Evidence by Law Enforcement Authorities

a) *Please indicate violations in the acquisition of evidence that make the evidence definitely invalid (i.e. indicate prohibited methods of proving facts);*

Please refer to Questions 2.2b and 2.2c.

b) *Please indicate evidence the acquisition of which is definitely prohibited;*

The law does not state any type of evidence which is prohibited, collecting evidence in the manners described above is prohibited rather than a specific type of evidence.

---

26 ECJ 02.03.2021, C-746/18, or a preliminary ruling under Article 267 TFEU from the Riigikohus (Supreme Court, Estonia), made by decision of 12 November 2018, received at the Court on 29 November 2018, in criminal proceedings against H. K., other party: Prokuratuur.

27 Ruling of the Supreme Court 1-16-6179, 18.06.2021.

d) *Please indicate a category of interests and values that are decisive for excluding evidence or restricting its examination.*

Please refer to Question 2.2b.

6 Conclusion

In Estonia the pre-trial proceedings are conducted by the investigative authorities under supervision of the Prosecutor's Office. The court does not intervene in the course of the criminal proceedings: it only issues the permits when law so requires and resolves the complaints made on the activities of the investigative authorities and of the Prosecutor's Office. Evidence is gathered, but not assessed during the pre-trial proceedings. It is the duty of the Prosecutor's Office to gather both vindicating and accusing information, i.e. the objectiveness of the Prosecutor's Office is the key element for successful and fair pre-trial proceedings.

Admissibility of evidence is decided in the court proceedings. When it comes to the procedural rules on gathering the evidence, the Estonian Supreme Court has stated that if an investigative body has failed to acquire a permit for conducting surveillance activities, the evidence acquired is automatically inadmissible. Even if the permit has been issued by the Court, but without sufficient grounds or incorrectly in some other way, the evidence collected via surveillance activities is still automatically inadmissible. Evidence other than from surveillance activities can still be admissible, even when some breaches have occurred in the acquiring process. The Supreme Court has stated that evidence is deemed inadmissible only if there has been a material breach in the evidence gathering process The Supreme Court has elaborated on what the main criteria for evaluating the admissibility of evidence is:

- which provision of the law was breached, i.e., the defensive purpose of the provision
- how extensive the breach was
- whether the breach was intentional
- which crime was being investigated
- how extensive is the public interest or the interest of the victims in investigating the crime
- would it have been possible to acquire the same evidence without the breach by using a different method
- what is the relevance of the evidence in the case
- whether the right to defense of the accused is being considered when admitting the evidence.

Therefore, it can be stated that the criteria for evaluating evidence gathered via surveillance is rather accurate and could be considered sufficient. When it comes to any other piece of evidence, the evaluation is highly dependent on the circumstances of each separate case. It could be even concluded from the Supreme Court's practice that in more serious cases which are under public attention for which punishments are more severe, more errors can be made while gathering evidence. As a result, it may be claimed that the bigger the crime, the less procedural guarantees apply.

CHAPTER 10

National Report of Japan

*Tatsuhiko Inatani**

1 Public Authorities Entitled to Conduct Investigation and the Private Prosecution System in Japan

Japanese criminal procedure law (JCPL) grants investigative authorities to judicial police (Art. 189II of JCPL) and public prosecutors (Art. 191I). Under the supervision of a public prosecutor, an assistant officer can conduct investigation. In addition, special units are established in National Police Agency, some prefectural police departments, and some prefectural public prosecutor's office for special cases that require expertise. For example, the Japanese National Police Agency has a special department for cybercrime and the Tokyo Prosecutor's Office has a special department for *economic crimes*, including white collar crime and corruption. Other statutes grant criminal investigative authorities to other public officials, such as drug enforcement officers, coast guard officers, and labor standards inspectors, for certain special offenses (Art. 54 of the Narcotics and Psychotropics Control Law; Art. 14 of the Japanese Coast Guard Agency Law, and Art. 102 of Labor Standards Law).

The relationship between traditional police and the drug enforcement office is collaborative in a sense that both offices conduct joint investigation and exchange officers between them. Japan lacks a formal coordination system; instead public authorities communicate with one another, especially via exchange of officers. However, the number of these officers is far smaller than that of the traditional police;[1] thus, only the police and prosecutor's office investigate the majority of cases.

In general, Japan lacks a private criminal prosecution system, and the public prosecutor monopolizes the power to prosecution (Art. 247 of JCPL). For this

* Kyoto University.

1 The number of Japanese police officer is about 300,000 in sum (national and local) https://www.npa.go.jp/hakusyo/h25/honbun/html/p6110000.html. The number of drug enforcement officer is only 296 https://www.ncd.mhlw.go.jp. The number of coast guard is 14328 https://www.kaiho.mlit.go.jp/info/books/report2021/html/ninmu/ninmu21_01.html. The number of labor standards inspector is 3018 https://www.mhlw.go.jp/bunya/roudoukijun/kantoku01/dl/r02.pdf.

 | DOI:10.1163/9789004710320_012

reason, public authority is monopolized by criminal investigation and prosecution authorities.

The only exception to this monopoly is arrest in the act. Essentially, JCPL allows anyone to arrest in the act (art. 213 of JCPL).

2 Right of the Court to Acquire Evidence at the Investigation Stage or Its Controlling Activities in Relation to Evidence Examined by Other Entities

The Court cannot conduct criminal investigation through its initiative due to the adversarial system adopted by JCPL. However, at the request of the public prosecutor, the Court conducts investigative interviews with witnesses when they evidently possess knowledge essential to prove a crime and refuse to be interviewed by the public prosecutor, the assistant to the public prosecutor, and a judicial police officer (Art. 226 of JCPL). Witnesses may change their statements at trial (Art. 227 of JCPL).

In JCPL, a warrant is essential for the Court to control investigative activities. According to Art. 33 of the Japanese Constitution (JC), except for arrest in the act, public authorities must acquire a judicial warrant, which specifies offenses, to arrest a suspect. On the basis of this article, JCPL requires probable cause for a normal arrest warrant (Art. 199 of JCPL) and sufficient doubt for emergency arrest for a limited number of felonies (Art. 210 of JCPL).

In addition, the JC requires a judicial warrant for search and seizure, which specifies the place and object of such activities and is based on probable cause (Art. 35 of JC). According to this article, JCPL requires a judicial warrant for the search, seizure, seizure with request for materializing, and inspection (Art. 218 of JCPL).

According to a case law, if public authorities intentionally fail to obey the warrant requirement, then evidence acquired by investigative activities that violate the requirement should be excluded from trial.[2] However, evidence acquired from the independent activities of illegal investigation is not necessarily excluded from trial.[3]

According to certain scholars, the specification of the object described in the warrant is insufficient, especially for digital evidence, due to the lack

---

2 *See* Judgement of Japanese Supreme Court 1978.9.7. *Keishuu* 32-6-1327, Judgement of Japanese Supreme Court 2003.2.14. *Keishuu* 57-2-121, Decision of Japanese Supreme Court 2009.9.28 *Keishuu* 63-7-868.

3 *See* Decision of Japanese Supreme Court 1988.9.16 *Keishuu* 42-7-1051.

of a procedure designed for digital data. Moreover, only information media, including personal computers and smartphones, are subject to seizure. In other words, once public authorities acquire a seizure warrant for information media, they can essentially read, analyze, and use all data contained within it without supervision.[4]

The Court's interpretation of the scope of warrant requirement is complicated and confusing; thus, determining that public authorities intentionally fail to obey warrant requirement in the case where new technologies, which may infringe privacy, are employed during investigation, is extremely difficult. A few scholars criticize this scenario of applying the exclusionary rule, because the rule is the major legal device for judicial control over investigative activities.[5]

In Japan, no procedural right exists to challenge the admissibility of evidence at the investigative stage for suspects and their legal counsels. Only after prosecution can defendants and their counsels file a motion to exclude at trial or at the pre-trial procedure.

3 Principles of Acquiring Evidence at the Stage of Investigation

As described in Section 2, the warrant requirement is a fundamental legal principle for controlling investigative activities, and JC and JCPL describe the principle.

In addition to the warrant requirement, restriction over compulsory disposition is essential in JCPL. According to Art. 197I of JCPL, compulsory disposition may not be applied unless special provisions were established in JCPL. According to the case law of the Japanese Supreme Court,[6] compulsory disposition is an investigative measure which infringes the fundamental rights protected by the JC, including the right to privacy.[7] Therefore, if the employed measure is classified as compulsory disposition, then such a measure is prohibited except in the case where it is established by a special provision in JCPL. Moreover, according to influential commentaries, compulsory disposition is under warrant requirement by interpretation of the JC.[8] If an unwritten

4 *See* Tatsuhiko Inatani, PRIVACY PROTECTION IN CRIMINAL PROCEDURE-TOWARD DUE PROCESS ON DELIBERATIVE DEMOCRACY (『刑事手続におけるプライバシー保護–熟議による適正手続の実現を目指して』) (Kohbundo 2017), 339–341.

5 *See id.* at 33–35.

6 *See* Decision of Japanese Supreme Court 1976.3.16. *Keishuu* 30-2-187.

7 *See* Judgement of Japanese Supreme Court 2017.3.15 *Keishuu* 71-3-13.

8 *See* Inatani *supra* note 4, at 65–69.

compulsory disposition is conducted, then the fruit of such an investigation should be excluded. This principle of restriction over compulsory disposition is derived from Art. 31 of JCPL, which generally protects due process for a person undergoing criminal procedure.[9]

However, the distinction between compulsory and non-compulsory disposition is ambiguous and confusing, especially in the area where emerging technologies which may infringe privacy. Previously, the special provision for inspection is used to conduct investigative steps, which utilizes emerging technologies, because the definition of inspection is very broad (recognizing objects through the action of the five senses). However, the Japanese Supreme Court does not allow cases where the police uses GPS to monitor the activities of suspects under a normal inspection warrant and requires the establishment of a special provision for such activities.[10] This direction is welcomed in a sense that the abusive application of inspection provisions is finally prohibited. Nevertheless, the criterion for the distinction remains very ambiguous and confusing. Therefore, a few scholars argue that rethinking the legal structure for regulating investigative activities, which is well designed for reducing the risk of abuse or misuse of investigative authorities, is timely.[11]

JCPL does not guarantee the right to access to evidence acquired by public authorities at the investigative stage due to its adversarial character. Defendants and their counsels can only access evidence through a disclosure process according to Arts. 316–14 and 316–27 of JCPL. Defendants and their counsels can file a motion for disclosure on the basis of the list of evidence possessed by the prosecutor (Art. 316–14II of JCPL). Therefore, defendants and their counsels can access the necessary evidence only after the prosecution. Thus, one can infer that the principle of equal arm is largely secured due to the limited duration of pre-trial detention (maximum of 23 days) in Japanese criminal procedure (Arts. 203, 204, 205, and 208 of JCPL).

Notably, investigators caused serious problems in interrogating suspects, however in certain pathological cases. However, the right against self-incrimination (Art. 38 of JC) and the right to remain silent (Art. 311 of JCPL) of suspects are seemingly appropriately protected in the majority of cases due to the introduction of mandatory recording during interrogation for serious offenses (Art. 301–2).

---

9 *See id.* at 280–300.

10 *See* Judgement of Japanese Supreme Court 2017.3.15 *Keishuu* 71-3-13.

11 *See* Inatani *supra* note 4 at 18–35, 85–94.

In addition to the recording, introducing the assistant of legal counsel during interrogation and investigation has been a hot topic; however, the opinions of specialists are still divided on this issue.

In general, except for the case where emerging technologies or digital evidence is important, as previously described, Japanese criminal procedure appropriately maintains the balance between probing for the truth and the protection of fundamental rights.

In Japanese law, a self-incriminating transaction between the defendant and the prosecutor is prohibited by the case law of the Japanese Supreme Court.[12] A simplified procedure is established on the basis of the confession of the defendant for a limited number of minor offenses (art. 291 of JCPL). If this provision is applied, then the prosecutor does not need to obey the strict rules of evidence, including hearsay rules (art. 320 II of JCPL), and many provisions are not applicable (Arts. 296, 297, 300–302, 304–307, and 307–2 of JCPL). In summary, according to the trial procedure for evident and petit offenses (from Arts. 350–16 to 350–29 of JCPL) and on the basis of the confession of the defendant, the Court should immediately decide a case after a simple examination of evidence.

However, the simplified process is uncommon in Japan, because the Court must examine nearly all evidence in the majority of cases, and many defendants have the impression that the treatment is unfair compared with normal proceedings.[13] Even in a summary trial proceeding, the defendant must be assisted by a legal counsel and always can file to motion, which requires the Court to refer the case to the normal procedure. In fact, given the character of the summary process, the Japanese Supreme Court observes that the process does not induce false confession and does not violate the right against self-incrimination.[14]

Generally, in Japan, the alternative procedure to a normal criminal trial proceeding is limited in terms of quantity as well as quality; therefore, procedural rights protected under the normal procedure and the regulation over investigation are not materially infringed.

12 *See* Judgement of Japanese Supreme Court 1995.2.22 *Keishuu* 49-2-1.

13 *See* Tadashi Sakamaki, Criminal Procedure (2nd ed.) (『刑事訴訟法【第2版】』) (Yuhikaku 2020), 451.

14 See judgement of Japanese Supreme Court 2009.7.14 *Keishuu* 63-6-623.

4 Identifications of Risks of Violating Freedom in the Acquisition of Evidence by Law Enforcement Authorities

In JPCL, the risk of abuse and misuse of investigative authorities, which may infringe free and open democracy, is regulated by the warrant requirement and the special regulation for compulsory disposition, as cited in Section 3. In addition, a sting operation is allowed in limited situation where these measures are indispensable and do not materially violate the will of the target.[15]

If public officials intentionally violate these regulations, then the evidence acquired by the illegal investigation is excluded, or the Court dismisses the charge against the defendant.

Regarding biological evidence, there is an important exception to the warrant requirement, which is collecting the suspect's waste disposed of in a public place.[16] In this case, law enforcement officers can use DNA samples contained in such a waste for DNA testing and can also registrate the result of the test in the national DNA database without meaningful regulation of the statute. These activities are regulated only by the inner rule and regulation of the police. Therefore, some argue that this unregulated situation violates the principle of restriction over the compulsory disposition and due process, because JCPL and JC obviously require the regulation of statute enacted by the legislator for compulsory disposition that risks free and open democracy.[17]

Thus far in Japan, scientific evidence is not privileged in the fact-finding process in the case where a suspicious scientific evidence leads to the conviction of the innocent.[18] Evidently, a reliable scientific evidence is introduced to trial, including DNA testing; however, Japanese judges are generally very cautious in reviewing its admissibility which requires the competence of an examiner, scientific accuracy and reliability of the method, and an appropriate procedure for scientific examination.[19]

In certain cases, the scientific experiment and examination conducted by experts appointed by defense counsel finally lead to proof of the innocence of the defendant. The majority of notable examples are found in child abuse

15 Decision of Japanese Supreme Court 2004. 7.12. *Keishu* 58-5-333.

16 *See* judgement of Japanese Supreme Court, 2008.4.15 *Keishuu* 62-5-1398.

17 *See* Inatani *supra* note 4, at 329–333.

18 *See* https://www.npa.go.jp/bureau/criminal/sousa/torishirabe/houkokushogaiyou.pdf.

19 *See* Sakamaki, *supra* note 13, at 504–506.

cases, where many Courts deny the scientific reliability of the so-called shaken baby syndrome.[20]

In Japan, certain compulsory dispositions are only applicable to serious offenses, including emergency arrest (Art. 210), wire-tapping (Art. 212–2 of JCPL and the Interception of Communication for Crime Investigation Act), and GPS tracking.[21] These investigative steps are seemingly well regulated, at least when law enforcement officials acquire evidence. However, as previously mentioned in Sections 2 and 3, the investigative steps for digital evidence and those that utilize emerging technologies continue to lack regulation.

5 Inviolable Boundaries in the Acquisition of Evidence by Law Enforcement Authorities

Article 36 of JC prohibits any torture conducted by public officials. This article is established due to worst experience of abuse of police power during WWII. Therefore, any investigative measures classified as torture are absolutely prohibited, and the fruits of such kind of activities are never allowed in trial with no exception.

According to an influential commentary, investigative steps that shock the conscious should be considered torture. Therefore, investigative steps that invade or risk the body or health of the suspect, such as stomach pumping,[22] should be classified under torture.[23]

6 Conclusion

Japanese criminal procedure law generally strikes a good balance between probing truth and protection of fundamental rights at the stage of evidence acquisition.

However, certain exceptions exist. Notably, investigative steps for digital evidence are problematic, because JCPL lacks a particular disposition for digital data, and information media remain the object for seizure. The Japanese

---

20 *See e.g.* judgement of Osaka High Court 2019.10.25, judgement of Osaka High Court 2020.1.28, and judgement of Osaka High Court 2020.2.6.

21 *See* Judgement of Japanese Supreme Court 2017.3.15 *Keishuu* 71-3-13.

22 *See* Rochin v. California, 342 U.S. 165 (1952).

23 *See* Masahito Inoue, Compulsory Disposition and Non-Compulsory Disposition (new ed.) (『強制捜査と任意捜査【新版】』) (Yuhikaku 2014), 12.

government currently aims to digitally transform its entire administrative structure, and criminal justice is not an exception. In fact, the legislation committee of specialists are currently reflecting on the digital transformation of criminal procedure law. However, the discussion is very primitive and still intends to retain the provisions that regulate search and seizure. These outdated provisions should be amended as soon as possible given the risk of a dragnet search of personal data. The reason is that smartphones can contain digital data, which are related to all aspects of daily activities and may reveal many sensitive information. If the purpose of the warrant requirement is to prohibit general search and seizure, then this practice should be regulated more appropriately.

Another problem is the regulation of investigative activities after the acquisition of personal information. No meaningful regulation is in place for the police and the prosecutor when they possess, analyze, and use personal data after acquisition. However, this unregulated situation, including the situation surrounding DNA testing and DNA database, may be a door to hyper-panopticon in the digital era and the serious risk of abuse and misuse of personal data.

As previously mentioned, rethinking the legal structure for regulating investigative activities, which is well designed for reducing the risk of abuse or misuse of investigative authorities, is at a critical timing. This process should apply not only to legal but also to technical devices, such as artificial intelligence (AI) and Internet of Things (IoT), which enable the monitoring of the activities of investigators and track the journey of evidence.

To make radical development of informational technologies, including AI, IoT and other emerging technologies, accompany the legal system, a more dynamic legal system is required. This initiative is possible through the fruitful collaboration between judicial bodies and legislators based on a more politically sensitive Constitution than the one currently in place.[24]

24 *See* Inatani, supra note 4, at 339–43.

Index

www.ingramcontent.com/pod-product-compliance
Lightning Source LLC
Chambersburg PA
CBHW071227230926
51849CB00001B/48
* 9 7 8 9 0 0 4 7 1 0 3 1 3 *